SUBJECTIVISM, INTELLIGIBILITY AND ECONOMIC UNDERSTANDING

Essays in Honor of Ludwig M. Lachmann on his Eightieth Birthday

Edited by
Israel M. Kirzner

NEW YORK UNIVERSITY PRESS
Washington Square, New York

Published in the U.S.A. in 1986 by
NEW YORK UNIVERSITY PRESS
Washington Square, New York, N.Y. 10003

Manufactured in Great Britain

Library of Congress Cataloging in Publication Data
Main entry under title:
Subjectivism, intelligibility and economic understanding.
Bibliography: p.
Includes index.
1. Austrian school of economists—Addresses, essays, lectures. 2. Economics—Addresses, essays, lectures.
3. Subjectivity—Addresses, essays, lectures.
4. Lachmann, Ludwig M.—Addresses, essays, lectures.
I. Kirzner, Israel M. II. Lachmann, Ludwig M.
HB98.S82 1986 330.15′7 85–20831
ISBN 0–8147–4589–X (alk. paper)

Contents

Preface

This volume consists of papers written by 24 scholars from around the world, who share a deep appreciation and admiration for the contributions to the social sciences made by Ludwig Lachmann over a long, fruitful—and, happily, still vigorous—scholarly career. Ludwig M. Lachmann, Emeritus Professor at the University of the Witwatersrand, Johannesburg, South Africa, and Visiting Research Professor at New York University, attains his eightieth birthday on February 1, 1986. It is with great pleasure indeed that this volume is presented to Professor Lachmann as a token of honor, respect and gratitude, at this most happy occasion.

No attempt is made in this volume to present an intellectual biography of Ludwig Lachmann. Such a portrait was written by Walter E. Grinder, under the title "In Pursuit of the Subjective Paradigm," as part of the Introduction to *Capital, Expectations, and the Market Process, Essays on the Theory of the Market Economy*, by Ludwig Lachmann, edited by Walter E. Grinder (Kansas City: Sheed Andrews & McMeel, 1977). That volume also contains an appendix listing the economic writings of Ludwig M. Lachmann (until 1977). For present purposes it is sufficient to state that for close to half a century Ludwig Lachmann has been a leading figure among the very small number of economists who have consistently appreciated and staunchly upheld the role of subjectivist insights in the explication of social phenomena. In England, in South Africa, and in the United States, he has, from the thirties through the eighties, succeeded by his gently persistent writing and teaching in spreading subjectivist ideas in the profession, undeterred by the powerful intellectual forces that have, during this time, steered economics onto a totally different course. Ludwig Lachmann's profound and sensitive explorations surrounding, in particular, the subjectivism of expectations, and the radical uncertainties introduced by the passage of time, have constituted a courageous, often-lonely voice, in the face of fashionably mechanistic—and so-often sterile—approaches to theoretical economics. That the 24 authors of the papers in this volume have contributed studies that probe into the role of subjectivism in achieving economic understanding is itself eloquent tribute to the far-reaching effect of Professor Lachmann's ideas and intellectual influence.

Quite apart from being a tribute to Professor Lachmann's lifelong scholarly output, the appearance of this volume constitutes an affectionate acknowledgement of Ludwig Lachmann's unique and inspiring personality, both as scholar and as gentleman. Blessed with an extraordinary memory and intellectual keenness, Ludwig Lachmann has never ceased to impress his colleagues and his students by the honesty and integrity of his utterances, by the gentleness and patience with which he has dealt with intellectual friend and foe alike, and by the unfailing kindness, friendliness, and modesty of his demeanor. The editor of this volume has for a quarter of a century learned to appreciate the benevolent and hard-headed good sense of Ludwig Lachmann's personal advice and counsel.

This editor will perhaps be pardoned for drawing attention to the altogether special contributions made by Professor Lachmann to the creation and growth of the Austrian Economics Program at New York University. Through the generosity of the Moorman Foundation, of Quincy, Illinois, Professor Lachmann has, ever since January 1975, been enabled to fulfil a pivotal and seminal role in this program. As a result, Ludwig Lachmann has played a crucially important part in the remarkable revival of interest in Austrian economics that has, definitely, even if only marginally, occurred in the economics profession. It is wholly appropriate that 11 of the contributors to this volume came under Ludwig Lachmann's intellectual influence, as colleagues or students, at New York University.

Despite Ludwig Lachmann's participation in this renaissance of Austrian economics in our time, the present volume is not a collection of Austrian papers. It is a reflection of the impartial integrity of Professor Lachmann's scholarly work that his contribution have, over the years, come to be appreciated by world-renowned scholars from a variety of intellectual camps. Moreover, there have often been important elements in the work of Professor Lachmann's Austrian colleagues, with which he has found himself unable to agree. This has not in the least obscured Ludwig Lachmann's enormously valuable contribution to the Austrian Economics Program. And this volume, extending as it does far beyond the confines of Austrian Economics, appropriately mirrors the breadth of the scope and character of Professor Lachmann's own work.

As editor it is my pleasant privilege gratefully to acknowledge the assistance of those without whom this volume would not be appearing. To the contributors to the volume I am grateful both for the enthusiasm with which the first tentative proposal for such a project was endorsed and for the promptness and high quality of their contributions. It is a particular pleasure to cite the contributions of two elder statesmen among economists, whose respective prolific works have for many decades decisively enriched the discipline, Sir John Hicks and Professor George L. S. Shackle. The enormously high regard with which Ludwig Lachmann has held Sir John's work, and his unbounded admiration for Professor Shackle's profoundly subjectivist writings, make their participation in this volume particularly appropriate and valuable.

Among those whose advice at specific stages in the planning and emergence of this volume was deeply appreciated, I gratefully record the following: Mark Addleson, Stephan Boehm, Richard Ebeling, Jan Kregel, Don Lavoie, and George Pearson. The director of New York University Press, Colin Jones, has been extremely supportive and helpful at every stage.

Finally I wish to thank Mrs. Margot Lachmann most deeply not only for her assistance in the emergence of the present volume honoring her husband, but also for the years of support that enabled Ludwig to spend so much time at New York University and to make such important scholarly contributions. This volume is presented to Ludwig with the hope that Margot and he will continue to enjoy many years of good health together and to witness and to participate in the expansion of the subjectivist revolution for which his own work is in so large a degree responsible.

ISRAEL M. KIRZNER

Notes on the Contributors

Mark Addleson is Lecturer in Economics at the Business School, University of the Witwatersrand, Johannesburg, South Africa.

Stephan Boehm is Lecturer in the Faculty of Social and Economic Sciences, University of Graz, Austria.

Lawrence A. Boland is Professor of Economics at Simon Fraser University, Burnaby, British Columbia, Canada.

Richard M. Ebeling is Assistant Professor of Economics at the University of Dallas, Irving, Texas.

John B. Egger is Research Associate at the Institute for Research on the Economics of Taxation, Washington, D.C.

Ulrich Fehl is Professor of Economics at the University of Oldenburg, Western Germany.

Roger W. Garrison is Assistant Professor of Economics at Auburn University, Auburn, Alabama.

Sir John Hicks, Fellow of All Souls College, Oxford, received the Nobel Memorial Prize for Economics in 1972.

Jack High is Assistant Professor of Economics at the Center for the Study of Market Processes, George Mason University, Fairfax, Virginia.

Terence W. Hutchison is Emeritus Professor of Economics, University of Birmingham, England.

Israel M. Kirzner is Professor of Economics at New York University.

J. A. Kregel is Professor of Economics, Bologna Center, Johns Hopkins University, Italy.

Richard N. Langlois is Assistant Professor of Economics at the University of Connecticut, Storrs, Connecticut.

Don Lavoie is Assistant Professor of Economics at the Center for the Study of Market Processes, George Mason University, Fairfax, Virginia.

Peter Lewin is Visiting Professor of Economics, University of Texas at Arlington.

Willi Meyer is Professor at the Department of Economics, Philipps=University of Marburg, Germany. He teaches economics and philosophy of science.

Karl Mittermaier is a Lecturer in the Department of Economics, University of the Witwatersrand, Johannesburg, South Africa.

Gerald P. O'Driscoll, Jr. is Senior Economist, Federal Reserve Bank of Dallas, Dallas, Texas.

Mario J. Rizzo is Associate Professor of Economics at New York University.

Mark Perlman is the University Professor of Economics at the University of Pittsburgh.

George L. S. Shackle is Professor Emeritus of Economics at the University of Liverpool, England.

P. D. F. Strydom is Senior Economist, Central Merchant Bank, Johannesburg, South Africa.

Christopher Torr is Lecturer in Economics at the University of the Witwatersrand, Johanesburg, South Africa.

Lawrence H. White is Assistant Professor of Economics at New York University.

1 "Radical Subjectivism" and the Language of Austrian Economics

MARK ADDLESON

I INTRODUCTION

This paper is offered to Professor Ludwig Lachmann in celebration of his eightieth birthday. It is singularly appropriate that his friends and colleagues should have chosen to honor the occasion with contributions on the theme of subjectivism in the social sciences. By doing so we testify to the richness of the legacy of his scholarly writings which already span half a century and, we hope, will continue to provide pleasure, insight and guidance for many years to come.

In the range and depth of Professor Lachmann's writings we find two intimately connected themes which serve to define his oeuvre. This paper is concerned with the place of radical subjectivism in economics, and its relationship to Austrian economics in particular.

Our honoree's staunch and eloquent espousal of Austrian economics is well known. His allegiance continued through the ascendancy of the "neoclassical synthesis," and he remains a protagonist in the revival of Austrian ideas that began in the mid seventies.[1] In no way, however, is this unshaken faith in the analytical superiority of the Austrian scheme attributable to a narrowness of vision or to the out-of-hand rejection of divergent views. As a Weberian, Lachmann accepts the fact that different individuals see the world from different perspectives. Indeed it is in the need for a scheme which enables economists to explore the implications of people's different and often incompatible perspectives that Austrian economics recommends itself.

A second and, perhaps, the predominant influence on his work, is Lachmann's commitment to subjectivism. In our view a subjectivist methodology is adapted and applied more conscientiously and Lachmann's subjectivism is more thoroughgoing than those of other economists, both contemporaries and predecessors. Austrian economics is the *means* for developing and expressing a "radically" subjectivist theory of economic phenomena; for explaining the phenomena by rendering them intelligible in terms of the nature of the plans and activities which give rise to them. Lachmann's respect for the Austrian tradition is founded on his association of this tradition with subjectivism and with the dogged attempt to extend the compass of a subjectivist theory. In continuing towards this goal he had drawn on, and thus forged, links with ideas which, while their origin might not be Austrian or even economics in a narrow sense, are nevertheless relevant to the development of subjectivism.

Radical subjectivism has its roots in many fertile soils. It incorporates the ideas of Max Weber and George Shackle, the phenomenology of Alfred Schutz, the economics of Mises and Hayek, to name some of the more obvious progenitors. The fruit, however, is unique. In the development of ideas as much as in other fields of human endeavor—and in contrast to Marshall's famous dictum—progress is seldom smoothly evolutionary. Instead, there are discontinuities. The Shackleian is no stranger to the notions of novelty and originative mental "acts" and, therefore, to a product which is more than the sum of its parts. This is not to say, however, that the development of a theoretical framework follows the same pattern. There are many factors which work to conserve, or preserve, the orthodox or the familiar.

New ideas have to be identified as such and, like any other information, be interpreted by those who wish to use them. What happens to those ideas evidently hinges, in large measure, on how they are viewed and on the perspectives that are brought to bear in the process of interpretation.

For a time it may be difficult to relate new ideas to an existing body of thought. *Ex ante*, it is generally not possible to say what form a "synthesis" will take. Will an assimilation suppress the really novel or original elements? Such apparently, was the initial fate of Keynes's *General Theory*. Alternatively, and possibly only gradually, the new, and the old may be found to be incompatible in many respects. In the process of making fuller use of the potential that is perceived in the new ideas an existing schema is increasingly subverted. It is submitted that the development of radical subjectivism within the Austrian tradition provides an example of this.

For a long time, even though the "marginally," or more aptly "catallactist,"[2] revolution was held to be a turning point for economic theory, differences amongst the contributions of the founders of that revolution were viewed as matters of emphasis rather than of substance.[3] As the work of Menger and his successors has come to be reevaluated from perspectives facilitated by more recent philosophical developments, however, the importance of the subjectivist element in Austrian theory is being identified and its implications articulated. It is in this context that we pose the question "How different is Austrian economics?" The answers are intended to serve mainly as counterpoint for the purpose of examining the relationship between radical subjectivism and Austrian theory.

II THE NEOCLASSICAL AND AUSTRIAN PARADIGMS

The Austrian's claim to a distinct paradigm typically is prefaced by the statement that "Austrian economists are subjectivists"[4] But are neoclassicists not also subjectivists? A neo-Ricardian, contrasting the neoclassical theory of value with his own, would surely argue that they are. That we find grounds for supporting the Austrian claim is in large measure the result of Professor Lachmann's efforts. Through his writings the distinction that emerges is not only one of degree. It is not simply that radical subjectivism is a more *complete*, or extended, subjectivism but, rather, that the "subjectivism of the active mind" starts from different premises. Ontologically, epistemologically, and methodologically, radical subjectivism stands apart.

From a radically subjectivist standpoint, Austrian and neoclassical economics do indeed constitute different paradigms, and to label the latter "subjectivist" is inappropriate. Historically, however, a divide has not always been apparent and there are "Austrian" contributions which are strikingly "neoclassical" in content. Perhaps this is to be expected given the cross-pollination of ideas that occurs in any discipline. Our concern about the historical relationships between the ideas of the schools is not a matter of chauvinism. It arises, rather, in the context of whether some ideas, now accepted as part of the Austrian tradition, can really be accommodated within a radically subjectivist interpretation of that tradition.

Radical subjectivism does involve a reinterpretation of the historical development of Austrian economics. Rather than just building on what went before, and often without addressing directly the points of difference between the views of earlier writers and his own, Lachmann has extracted what he takes to be the essentially subjectivist elements in their contributions. These have been incorporated and developed into an emphatically subjectivist conceptual framework. The ideas are shown to belong together and to constitute foundations of a subjectivist theory. They represent links in a common tradition or heritage. Melding them with complementary ideas, which originate outside the Austrian school, radical subjectivism extends and broadens the compass of this heritage.

One of the results, by analogy, has been to provide a telescope with much greater powers of resolution than existed previously. Focusing that telescope on earlier Austrian writings, we are aware, as no doubt Lachmann has been, in consciously bringing the problems of economics within the ambit of a subjectivist paradigm, that there are elements of these writings—perhaps even important ones—which do not share the same intellectual universe. They belong to a different conception of the scheme of things.

A recent statement by Professor Hahn, in which he defines his position as a neoclassicial economist, provides a starting point for examining the tenets of neoclassical and Austrian economics and for highlighting the relationships that constitute the theme of this paper.[5] Hahn regards "three elements" as denoting his neoclassicism. These are (1) reductionism, or the "attempt to locate explanations in the actions of individual agents"; (2) an acceptance of "some axioms of rationality" as a basis for theorizing about agents; and (3) the view that "some notion of equilibrium is required and that the study of equilibrium states is useful." It is also important to take cognizance of his conception of theorizing in economics, and it is significant that Hahn distinguishes between understanding and prediction. He argues that theorizing involves "an ongoing attempt to bring some order into our thinking about economic phenomena and . . . the creation of a language in which these attempts can be discussed. . . . The attempt at orderly thinking is the attempt to *understand*", (emphasis added).

Now, insofar as these statements obviously represent a personal standpoint, they cannot be assumed to reflect the views of the majority of neoclassical economists as Hahn, himself, recognizes. It may come as a surprise that Hahn's position is similar to one which we believe to be characteristic of many Austrians today. The latter would probably acknowledge that they are 1. "individualists" in much the same way that Hahn is a "reductionist"; 2. that they regard a notion of rationality as central to the understanding of human conduct; and, 3. that the notion of equilibrium, historically important—as seen in the works of Mises and especially Hayek—continues to occupy a place in Austrian theory. Whether, like Hahn, Austrians as subjectivists can "feel secure" that a notion of equilibrium is required is the main question to which we shall return. Finally, Austrians would no doubt agree with Hahn both on the purposes of theorizing and on the importance of drawing a distinction between understanding and prediction.

III THE ENDS AND MEANS OF ECONOMICS

Are the Austrian and neoclassical positions really as close as the aforegoing, and admittedly superficial, comparison suggests? The answer requires an understanding of the "languages" of theoretical discourse in the context of the questions which are being asked and the types of answers which are provided.

Theories, the conceptual frameworks within which scholars interpret the phenomena that they are trying to explain, are necessarily abstract and formal. Attention is often drawn to the problems of the "level of abstraction" and to the consideration that what is abstracted from may ultimately be important in providing a sensible account of the issues being examined. If the theory is too abstract, the explanation will be truncated. What is less often recognized, or acknowledged, is that the process of abstracting is simultaneously one of replacing or substituting. A new language is created which may prove to be inadequate for understanding the problems at hand. If this happens, we may feel a sense of disquiet about the interpretation or explanation that the theory produces. Nor is the discontent necessarily a feeling that the picture is incomplete. It may be a concern that the explanation is intuitively "wrong," that "things do not appear to be, or to work, that way." If so, a new orientation has to be sought—a different way of looking at things—for the problem lies in the nature of the language itself.

Both Hahn and Coddington agree that theorizing involves "the creation of a language" but the latter is more acutely aware of the difficulties inherent in that process.

> The language of economic theory, like any language, provides a framework for thought; but . . . it constrains our thought to remain within that framework. It focuses our attention; determines the way we conceive of things; and even determines what *sort* of things can be said. . . . A . . . conceptual framework is, therefore, at one and the same time both an opportunity and a threat. Its positive side is that . . . it facilitates thought within the . . . framework. But its negative side arises from the fact that thought must be *within* the framework.[6]

The particular framework that economists can employ, the so-called "level of abstraction" and the type of formalism, therefore, is not arbitrary. While there may be latitude in selecting a framework, the language that is chosen must be suited to its purposes. For the language influences what goes into the theory—the phenomena we can attempt to explain—no less than what comes out: the type of explanation that we can provide.

As ends and means of theorizing respectively, the tasks of economics and of theory are logically distinct. The former concern the question of what problems economists wish to study, while the latter deal with the question of developing the most suitable language for studying them. In formulating a program for research, the ends must be defined before the means can be chosen. Once it is widely adopted, however, a particularly conceptual framework tends to be fairly durable. For this reason it must be well chosen. Unless it is consonant not only with the types of problems that economists initially wanted to explain, but also with the new problems that emerge in the course of intellectual inquiry, the difficulties that Coddington refers to will inevitably arise.

What are the problems with which the neoclassicists are concerned? Hahn identifies the purpose of that scheme as casting light on the operation of the "invisible hand" in decentralized economies.

> Adam Smith . . . first realized the need to explain why this kind of social arrangement does not lead to chaos . . . Smith not only posed an obviously important question, but also started us off on the road to answering it. General Equilibrium Theory as classically stated by Arrow and Debreu . . . is near the end of that road.[7]

Obviously Smith was not a general equilibrium theorist and his concern was "plutology" rather than "catallactics." While it may indeed be profitable to transpose Smithian problems into a language of exchanges and market activities, the reason for casting them in general equilibrium terms is apparent when it is recognized that these problems have been *interpreted* in a particular way—as problems of coordination amongst individuals. The task of economics is to show whether, and under what conditions, a set of prices will emerge that will "cause agents to make mutally compatible decisions."[8] Formulated this way, the language of determinism needs no further justification. But catallactic problems can be formulated differently and it is difficult to know which came first. Did the framework—based on a preconceived view of what constituted scientific method—precede the definition of goals, so that these became translated into the analysis of determinate relationships? Or was it the other way round. That is, was the framework consciously adopted as a suitable means for examining certain previously formulated problems?

Arguments could probably be found to support both procedures but this is as far as we need to take the matter. The formalism of neoclassical theory is appropriate in its context. It is simply a reflection of the language itself. The real issue is whether that language is appropriate for the study of catallactic problems. In particular, ought the problems that, now, are of interest to economists be treated in the context of the coordination of different individuals' activities (understood in terms of a notion of equilibrium)?

We can now return to Hahn's characterization of his neoclassicism. The "reductionism" that he espouses is the "attempt to locate explanations in the actions of individual agents" insofar as these "actions" and the "agents" are amenable to the language of general equilibrium theory. The same is true of the "axioms of rationality" that he accepts as a basis of theorizing. Now, the three elements are *logically* independent in the sense that an acceptance of any one does not necessarily imply acceptance of the others (so in principle Hahn is entitled to embrace them with differing degrees of confidence). The unifying factor, in terms of which all three have come to be regarded as elements of a specific paradigm, however, is the third element. By endorsing the fruitfulness of the study of equilibrium states, the theorist circumscribes both the meaning of reductionism and the notion of rationality that will be acceptable in developing the theory.

How these notions are circumscribed by the general equilibrium construct is evident from any modern general equilibrium text. Indeed, an understanding of the conception of "agents" (a particular neoclassical formalization) goes a long way toward revealing the situation. Agents are "functions"; "choosing," "learning," "forming expectations" are purely mechanistic abstractions. Agents are necessarily rational; if they were irrational, they would cease to be agents. Clearly, what is lacking is both a notion of a "mind at work" and, *pari passu*, a logical understanding of the accomplishments (intended as well as unintended) of one or more such "minds." Whether their absence is important depends on the issues that economists seek to resolve with their theories. If these considerations are deemed to be important, it should be recognized that the problem lies in the construction of the theory itself.

IV THE AUSTRIAN TRADITION AND SUBJECTIVISM

Equilibrium, then, is not a notion which can be emphasized or overlooked, added to a theory or taken out, at will. Once the problems of economics are conceived as involving (determinate) equilibrium relationships, the theory has to be tailored to reflect that conception of "the world." If the Austrians can lay claim to a distinctive paradigm—asking different questions and providing different answers—it is surely because the fundamental problems of the discipline are conceived in a different way.[9]

As alluded to earlier, this is only partly true. The Austrian and neoclassical schemes, in many respects, are intertwined. In a number of Austrian contributions, even if the issue of inter-individual plan coordination does not appear to predominate, the analysis proceeds from the standpoint of "the market" as a coordinating device. Individuals' activities in markets—as buyers and sellers, arbitrageurs and speculators—are analyzed in the context of a process. The process may "start" in disequilibrium. Whether it "finishes" with equilibrium depends on the relative strengths of equilibrating and disequilibrating "forces" and the relative speeds with which these forces work.

In the context of this analytical approach, ends-means relationships in decision making are not made manifest. The issue of the coordination/dis-coordination of the interrelated plans of different individuals is central. Yet answers to questions about how an individual formulates his plans—which typically embrace relationships with other people—and when or how these interrelated plans may be consistent, would appear logically to be antecedent. The approach, however, either simply assumes that the market is a coordinating mechanism (whose functioning may be thwarted by changes that occur) or else it is postulated that particular individuals (e.g., "entrepreneurs") fulfill the role of equilibrating agents.

The methodology demanded by an equilibrium framework does not disappear by simply talking about *dis*equilibrium states, or processes. The Newtonian conceptual apparatus remains a means of understanding, even if gusts of wind propel the apple horizontally or hurl it above the branch from which it hung. The language of economics, too, is conditioned by the consideration that the operation of markets is shaped by interactions, or relationships, which, in principle, are determinate. The terminology may change to include "expectations" and "knowledge of market opportunities"; "preferences" may replace "tastes." In each case, however, the meanings of these terms must be congruent with the demands of the underlying conceptual framework.

Within the Austrian school the theoretical approach is identifiable most strongly in the work of Hayek. Hutchison, for example, has drawn attention to the fact that there is more than one Hayek. But the general tenor of Hayek's contribution to economics is aptly summarized in the title which O'Driscoll gave to his book on Hayekian economics: *Economics as a Co-ordination Problem.*[10] Hayek's ideas, influenced by Pareto, in turn have clearly made their impact on the Austrian revival. They have also been adopted, developed, and refined by others. For, as Milgate has argued, Hayek is a progenitor of the neoclassical notion of intertemporal equilibrium.[11]

Another strain within the Austrian tradition, however, poses different questions. It is founded on different premises, and considerations about ends and means are placed at the epicenter of economic theory. Questions concerning the nature and consequences of individuals' interaction in markets, though important, have to be answered in the light of the theorist's understanding of the nature of their plans and choices. Radical subjectivism has been forged out of the identification and development of the elements of this strain, to which Hans Mayer applied the apposite term "cognitive," as opposed to "functional," price theory.

Central to the theme of this paper is the postulate that the two strains are not contiguous for the very reason that radical subjectivism and neoclassicism represent distinct paradigms. Certainly the boundaries between the two approaches have been neither well defined nor well observed by individual writers. As each is developed, however, we come to recognize their independence. It is simply not practicable to address the same problems from either perspective; the languages prevent this. Menger and Mises probably represent the two most important Austrian progenitors of radical subjectivism and it is useful for our purposes to consider the extent of their subjectivism and its significance in their work.[12]

From a present-day vantage point, Menger's subjectivism is irresolute and, given his well-known use of the term "needs," together with a stress on the complementary relationships amongs different goods, one is left with the impression that problems of choice hardly arise. Yet the fact that, for Menger, men do not have to continually "make up their minds" should not obscure the existence of a valuing mind. At the root of answers to questions such as "Does a thing possess 'goods character'?" and "What is the 'order' of a particular good?" are individuals' judgments. It is simply that production and consumption being conceived as relatively mechanical processes, there is little opportunity for exercising judgment.

Others have noted Menger's eschewal of attempts at a mathematical formulation of economic theory as well as his rejection of the notion of general equilibrium.[13] When a notion of equilibrium is used, usually implicitly, it is in the context of explaining logically the implications of individuals' attempts to do the best for themselves (in formulating their plans). Prices depend on individuals' perceptions about different goods and the values they place on them in the sense that these set limits to the terms on which people would be willing to trade. No attempt is made, however, to extend a notion of equilibrium to include situations which involve the decisions of different individuals or to formalize the outcomes of exchange as equilibria involving the compatibility of different plans.

What impresses the reader is that Menger's method of attempting to "reduce the complex phenomena of human economic activity" to the simplest "observable" elements and "to investigate the manner in which the more complex economic phenomena evolve" from these elements is carried through with remarkable consistency. Once it is apparent that the meaning of "observation" includes subjective, or interpretative, understanding (*Verstehen*), the *Grundsätze* represents a logically developed account of how (complex) economic phenomena are related to individuals' "choices." The latter are interpreted within the narrow scope which his approach necessitates. It is not difficult to perceive his efforts as a precursory attempt to "make the social world intelligible in terms of individuals' plans." There is certainly no hint that in order to do so we need to think in terms of equilibrium solutions.

In *Human Action*, the attempts to take Menger's approach further is clearly discernible. The methodology has been crystallized and Mises is far more conscious of his task as a subjectivist. Ends and means, quintessentially subjectivist notions, are the gist of the matter. "Economics is not about things ... it is about men, their meanings and actions" (p. 92). Mises' subjectivism, however, is a long way from radical subjectivism and the notion of equilibrium still features prominently. For example, having stated that the "final state of rest is an imaginary construction," he goes on to argue that it is necessary to

> take recourse to this imaginary construction [because] . . . the market at every instant is moving toward a final state of rest. Every later new instant can create new facts altering this final state of rest. But the

market is always disquieted by a striving after a final state of rest (p. 246)

The reason why Mises views the market process in deterministic terms, we suggest, is associated with his particular approach to the meaning of action as reflected in his lack of concern with the underpinnings of choice and, especially, in his neglect of ends in the planning and decision-making process.[14] There is clearly a *link*, as Lachmann has shown, between economics concerned with men and their meanings and the Shackleian idea of "economics concerned with thoughts." At the same time, we recognize that the considerations which differentiate the positions implied in these statements are not insignificant.

Like Menger before him, but for different reasons, Mises's treatment of individuals' intentions, or goals—as data which are beyond the purview of economists—obstructs enquiry into their nature and, hence, their significance for economic analysis. Though problems of choice are central to the Misesian scheme (and the term itself is used in a nontrivial, nondeterministic sense), the problems that provide the focus of attention are associated with individuals' attempts to choose the "right" *means* in relation to ends which they are assumed already to have formulated.

Now the choosing of appropriate means is always problematic, and Mises reveals the difficulties inherent in such choices. For example, time plays an important role in his analysis and all action is speculative. But Mises does not recognize just how important ideas, expectations, and judgment are in the formulation of plans; how much different peoples' intentions, perspectives, and plans may diverge; and, as a consequence, how difficult it is a priori to say anything about the consequences of specific actions. Radical subjectivism is responsible for these insights, and, in our view, Lachmann's main contribution to Austrian economics has been in clarifying them and in underscoring their practical importance.

V THE SUBJECTIVIST PERSPECTIVE

In arguing that equilibrium does not have a place within a subjectivist framework, two sets of issues appear to be relevant. In the first place, it is a notion which transcends the ordinary perspective of plans and intentions. When people make plans they generally have to take cognizance (at least implicitly) of other individuals' intentions and activities. A producer of components, who sells these to someone else for assembly into a finished product, will probably take a view about his buyer's activities and, perhaps, the "state of the market" before making a decision on whether or not to expand his capacity. His investment decisions and his fixed capital are complementary to the decisions and capital of others. The buyer of a new motor car may give consideration to his spouse's requirements before making a choice while a dealer in the equity market may evaluate a number of offers and bids before establishing the price at which transactions will take place.

In none of these cases, however, are the people involved concerned with the question of coordinating "the market" as a whole and they are certainly not concerned with coordinating all aspects of the plans of all the individuals in whose activities they take an interest. To suggest that their interest in, and sphere of, "coordination" extends beyond attempts to ensure that a *few* interrelated plans are consistent in *some respects* would be an unwarranted assumption belied by an understanding of each situation.

On the other hand, there does not seem to be any justification for arguing that such coordination will emerge (spontaneously) as an *unintended* consequence of individuals' interaction. Again, two sets of considerations appear to be important here. Many processes and institutional arrangements are in fact characterized by divergences of opinion and intention on the part of individuals who participate in the processes. The incompatibility of plans is a necessary condition for their existence. Such incompatibilities arise both within and between markets. Think of the speculative secondary markets for financial assets, commodities future markets, or the rival activities of competitors. Even in those flex-price markets, where through some arrangements—perhaps a broker or auctioneer—the bids and offers made at any time are reconciled, and it is appropriate to speak of a market clearing price, it would be misleading to regard this as plan coordination. In a charitable interpretation, the situation could be viewed as analogous to a very short Marshallian "short run." A price is set at which offers are matched by bids. Beyond this, no demand or supply schedule exist to be discovered, or revealed.[15] Bids and offers will change, possibly very quickly, and possibly in the light of the price which was established. Nor, if the person who intended to sell short at the "right" price finds a buyer, does this mean that he has speculated successfully.

Is there a tendency for plans to be more successful and to become more coordinated over time? Market prices do not serve as "points of orientation" in any deterministic sense. Whatever information is *judged* to be relevant has to be *interpreted.* Its significance has to be evaluated and weighed in the process of forming expectations and making decisions. Not only may different information be "available" to different people, but both on the matter of judging what information is relevant and in interpreting the information people will differ. Even things which some individuals now view as relatively permanent and, therefore, as reliable guides in making plans (and of course, they may change their minds) may be ignored by others who regard them differently or who believe that they will change in the future. In dealing with phenomena that are understood as products of choice or social interaction, we recognize that what is regarded as a "permanent" or "transitory" feature of the world depends not simply on what people think, or expect to happen, but often on their expectations about others' motives and what they think or expect. The most carefully laid plans can go awry. Moreover, an understanding of the circumstances under which plans have failed, and in which resources have been misallocated, may be just as important as those where everything goes according the plan.

There are no concrete circumstances, or "objective data" in the formalistic sense, with which it is possible to pin down a notion of equilibrium. The observable phenomena of markets reflect evanescent thoughts. Economics, perforce, has to be concerned with interpreting and understanding experience. Lachmann has begun to sketch out some of the potentially rich areas that he believes subjectivists should explore in order to "make the world intelligible in terms of human plans" a task which he has advocated for nearly half a century.

No doubt, to some, the idea of pursuing this type of research program would be unattractive, not least because it necessitates a revision of our views about what markets can and cannot do. Coddington is probably not alone in the conviction, expressed shortly before his untimely death, that subjectivism represents a kind of nihilism, and if this is all economists can claim, they might as well shut up shop. The more sanguine will admit that economists unfortunately may have remained silent on issues that matter a great deal. Important questions have gone unasked and, therefore, unanswered. A better understanding of institutions—of the roles which they play in decision making and how they shape, and are shaped by, individuals' interaction—for example, would seem to be worthwhile ends in themselves.

Following from the arguments in this paper, such problems will have to be tackled with the aid of a conceptual framework different from that of neoclassical orthodoxy, the language of which is not up to such demands. Austrians themselves, therefore, will have to decide in which directions they wish their theory to take them. In this context is it not clear what claims can be made for the general equilibrium scheme in particular and the language of equilibrium in general.

For, like Mises, who suggests that the role of general equilibrium is to serve as an *argumentum a contrario*, Hahn has stated on a number of occasions that general equilibrium is a "mock-up." He is evidently disconcerted by the fact that politicians, especially, are busy booking tickets on a structure that will not, and cannot, fly. In the first place, the actions for which the politicians are being chided are, perhaps, not unreasonable given the fact that generations of students have been nurtured on the belief that general equilibrium has something useful to say. More important, however, is that the question of how the scheme constitutes a mock-up has not been addressed. What features of the world, what economic problems, does the theory enable us to understand? Is this understanding complete but for a few, perhaps important, details? Or is the whole thing at a very early stage of development and little more than an empty shell? Whatever the case, surely the least that we, together with the errant politicians, can hope for is a framework which will assist us on our journey.

NOTES

1. In "The Salvage of Ideas: Problems of the Revival of Austrian Economic Thought," Lachmann provides an interpretation of the decline of the Austrian School in the 1930s. A. W. Coats suggests some of the reasons for the revival of subjectivist economics in *Beyond Positive Economics*, ed. J. Wiseman (London: Macmillan, 1983), pp. 94–9.
2. The term is borrowed from Hicks, who distinguishes between (classical) "plutology" and "catallactics." Sir John Hicks, "'Revolutions' in Economics" in *Method and Appraisal in Economics*, ed. Spiro J. Latsis (Cambridge: Cambridge University Press, 1976).
3. This is the tenor of Schumpeter's position. *History of Economic Analysis*, ed. E. B. Schumpeter (London: Allen & Unwin, 1967), p. 918. See also K. J. Arrow and F. H. Hahn, *General Competitive Analysis* (Edinburgh: Oliver & Boyd, 1971), p. 3, where Menger is mentioned as one of the founders of the neoclassical position. Hicks takes the opposite view in arguing that the Austrian and Lausanne "versions of Catallactics . . . , at first distinct, have grown together." Op. cit., p. 214. Seen from a radically subjectivist perspective Hicks appears to be right.
4. I. M. Kirzner, "On the Method of Austrian Economics," in *The Foundations of Modern Austrian Economics*, ed. E. G. Dolan (Kansas City: Sheed & Ward, 1976), p. 40.

5. The views examined here are taken from a typescript of the introduction to the first volume of Hahn's collected papers (forthcoming).
6. Alan Coddington, "Positive Economics," *Canadian Journal of Economics*, 5 (1972), pp. 14–15.
7. Frank Hahn, "General Equilibrium Theory," *The Public Interest*, Special Issue (1980), p. 123.
8. K. J. Arrow and F. H. Hahn, op. cit., p. 16.
9. The point, that the Austrians are asking different questions, is made obliquely by G. P. O'Driscoll, Jr. and M. Rizzo, following the lead given by Joan Robinson. The former, however, do not identify how, or whether, the questions posed by "static subjectivism" differ from those of "dynamic subjectivism." *The Economics of Time and Ignorance* (London: Basil Blackwell, 1985), chap. 2.
10. Gerald P. O'Driscoll, Jr. *Economics as a Co-ordination Problem: The Contributions of Friedrich A. Hayek* (Kansas City: Sheed Andrews & McMeel, 1977).
11. Murray Milgate, "On the Origin of the Notion of Intertemporal Equilibrium," *Economica* (N.S.), 46 (1979), pp. 4–6. Also Fabio Petri, "The Difference between Long-period and Short-period General Equilibrium and the Capital Theory Controversy," *Australian Economic Papers*, 17 (1978).
12. The works specifically referred to are Carl Menger, *Grundsätze der Volkswirthschafslehre* (1871), translated as *Principles of Economics*, trans. and eds. J. Dingwall and B. F. Hoselitz (New York: The Free Press, 1950); Ludwig von Mises, *Human Action: A Treatise on Economics* (London: William Hodge, 1949).
13. Lawrence H. White, "Methodology of the Austrian School," Center for Libertarian Studies *Occasional Paper Series*, 1 (1979), pp. 4–5, Karl Menger, "Austrian Marginalism and Mathematical Economics," *Carl Menger and the Austrian School of Economics*, eds. J. R. Hicks and W. Weber (Oxford: Clarendon Press, 1973), W. Jaffe, "Menger, Jevons and Walras De-homogenised," *Economic Inquiry*, 14 (1976), p. 520; Erich Streissler, "To What Extent was the Austrian School Marginalist?" in *The Marginal Revolution in Economics: Interpretation and Evaluation*, eds. R. D. C. Black, et al. (Durham: Duke University Press, 1973), pp. 172–5.
14. To the subjectivist Mises's argument, that "the only method of dealing with the problem of action is to conceive that action ultimately aims at bringing about a state of ... rest, absence of action" (p. 245), suggests a narrowly formalistic and idiosyncratic view of the individual's motives and notion of rationality.
15. In contrast to the statement of Mises quoted above, such bids and offers merely respresent different peoples' *ideas* about what is the "right thing to do" at the moment. Nor is there any implication that what is "right" is the best of *all* conceivable, or feasible, courses of action.

2 Time and Equilibrium: Hayek's Notion of Intertemporal Equilibrium Reconsidered*

STEPHAN BOEHM

I HICKS AND HAYEK

In doctrinal discussions of significant developments in general equilibrium theory during the interwar period, J. R. Hicks, as he was then known, is customarily credited with having provided an extension of Walras's concept of equilibrium by interpreting it in an intertemporal setting.[1] In what is perhaps the most often-quoted statement from his works Hicks introduces Part III of *Value and Capital* with the well-known definitions: "I call Economic Statics those parts of economic theory where we do not trouble about dating; Economic Dynamics those parts where every quantity must be dated."[2]

However, in an article originally published in the *Zeitschrift für Nationalökonomie* (1933), entitled "Gleichgewicht und Konjunktur," Hicks had already stated the problem of applying equilibrium analysis to the "dynamic" field as follows. "As soon as we suppose that people engage in processes of production that take time, we ought to take account of the influence of future (expected) as well as current prices on their behaviour; for it is with an eye to the future prices of their products that people will embark upon 'indirect' or 'roundabout' methods of production . . . Once we drop the assumption of Stationary Equilibrium, present and future prices are no longer equal."[3]

The immediate starting point for Hicks seems to have been a paper by Hayek on intertemporal equilibrium.[4] In a recently published article Hicks, referring to that paper, recalls: "Hayek was making us think of the productive process as a process in time, inputs coming before outputs; but his completest, and most logical account of intertemporal relations was confined to a model in which everything worked out as intended—a model of 'perfect foresight.' In his *Prices and Production* (1932) . . . things were allowed to go wrong, but only for monetary reasons; it was only because of monetary disturbances that an exception was allowed to the rule that market forces must tend to establish an equilibrium."[5]

Having been asked by Lionel Robbins to translate the model of *Prices and Production* into mathematics, Hicks had great difficulty in understanding what Hayek had meant by an equilibrium not disrupted by monetary disturbances. Picking up a hint from Frank Knight, he perceived that in a perfect foresight equilibrium there was no room for money at all, not even "well-behaving" money. "So there should have been a stage in the model building, in which money as such was brought in; this had just been jumped over by Hayek. One must introduce uncertainty before one can introduce money. That was really the main thing I had to say in my 1933 paper."[6]

Starting out from the problem of extending the Paretian system to incorporate time-consuming production, Hicks became increasingly aware in the course of his reformulation and later abandonment of the Hayek model that there was clearly a glaring need to construct models in which agents did not only not have perfect knowledge of future conditions but also knew they did not have perfect knowledge of the future.

II THE NEO-RICARDIAN CRITICISM

Thanks to the indefatigable efforts of the neo-Ricardians[7] Hayek's role as the originator of intertemporal equilibrium has come to be widely recognized, if not appreciated. In view of both its obvious significance for Hayek's own subsequent work in monetary and capital theory[8] and its crucial position in the neo-Ricardian reconstruction of the history of economic analysis, it may perhaps be worth our while to focus attention on some of the salient issues raised in the 1928 paper as far as they are pertinent to what follows.

In 1928 Hayek was basically concerned with an elaboration of the significance of the element of time for the structure of the price system. He was adamant in his criticism that earlier economic analysis had been conducted along the lines of a fictitious economic system in which all activities were assumed to take place simultaneously.

> Yet as soon as these assumptions . . . are replaced by ones corresponding more to the facts, it becomes evident that the customary abstraction from time does a degree of violence to the actual state of affairs which casts serious doubt upon the utility of the results thereby achieved. From the moment at which the analysis is no longer concerned exclusively with prices which are (presumed to be) simultaneously set . . . but goes on to a consideration of the monetary economy, with prices which necessarily are set at successive points in time, a problem arises for whose solution it is vain to seek in the existing corpus of economic theory.[9]

Hayek clearly felt the need to incorporate in the analysis the import of different prices for technically equivalent commodities available at different points in time for the smooth functioning of the economic system: "Awareness of the necessity for an intertemporal price system to exist is, however, not merely incompatible with the widespread conception that the intertemporal constancy of prices constitutes a precondition for an undisturbed self-reproduction of the economy. It is in fact in the sharpest contradiction to it."[10] Due to differences in the determinants of prices for the same goods available at different points in time, e.g., due to seasonal variations, differences in technical opportunities for production, differences in valuation, and due to the difficulties associated with the transfer of goods through time, it was, according to Hayek, as a rule, not conceivable that the exchange ratio between the same commodity in the physical sense at different points of time would conform to a 1 : 1 relation.

In 1928 Hayek advanced the notion of distinguishing the prices of the same commodity available at different times in analogy to distinguishing the prices of the same commodity available at different locations.[11] Hayek considered equilibrium analysis an indispensable tool for the understanding of intertemporal price relationships; he thus emerged, it seems, as *the* pioneer in intertemporal equilibrium analysis, exerting his influence not only on Hicks but also on Malinvaud, and possibly on Arrow and Debreu.

According to the neo-Ricardian viewpoint,[12] as espoused by Garegnani, Eatwell, Milgate, and Petri, the focus on intertemporal relationships entails a decisive break from the notion of equilibrium entertained by both the classical and earlier neoclassical writers from Adam Smith down to Alfred Marshall, who center their attention on long-period positions of the economy characterized by a uniform rate of profits on the supply price of the stock of capital. This, of course, is in marked contrast to the procedure used in modern neoclassical economics where the determination of $q \cdot t$ market-clearing prices (for $q = 1,2 \ldots Q$ commodities and $t = 1,2 \ldots T$ dates) establishes an intertemporal equilibrium associated not only with different prices for the same commodity at different points in time but also with different rates of return on the value of capital invested in each particular line. When commodities are differentiated in terms of their physical, temporal, and spatial dimensions there is, as a rule, a whole system of interest rates, one for each pair of prices of commodities available at different points in time but otherwise homogeneous in their physical and spatial characteristics. In this framework interest rates are nothing but intertemporal prices; they are derived from previously determined prices for commodities and factors. The calculation of interest rates is therefore merely ancillary to the analysis of prices. In such a system there is usually no such thing as *the* rate of return or interest since there are as many rates as there are commodities. In order to avoid misunderstandings one should therefore heed the sharp conceptual distinction between the classical rate of profits, which can only be defined with respect to capitalist relations of production in the allocation of the surplus output, and neoclassical commodity interest rates, which can be defined without recourse to class relations in production.[13]

The neo-Ricardians further maintain that despite the fundamental changes that economic theory, i.e., the explanation of the object of analysis, underwent in the aftermath of the Marginal Revolution, the method of analysis, the abstract characterization of what is to be explained, was essentially retained. The abandonment of the "traditional long-period method" in the late 1920s and in the 1930s in the works of Hayek, Hicks, Lindahl, and Myrdal, the argument proceeds, had not been due to weaknesses of the long-period method per se, but rather to deep-seated flaws in the orthodox theory of capital and distribution and its underlying conception of capital as a "factor of production," giving rise to the well-known problem of defining the quantity of capital outside a one-commodity world. To put it differently, the method of intertemporal equilibrium had been chosen to fit the theory, i.e., a demand-and-supply approach to the theory of capital and interest. Therefore, the work by the authors aforementioned had not amounted to a mere refinement of Walras' concept of equilibrium. Rather, it had constituted a deliberate departure from the traditional concern with the analysis of the "persistent forces" underlying the classical notion of "centers of gravity" and a move toward the analysis of short-period equilibria and their sequence in time.

The construction of short-period equilibria as the new basis for the theory of value and distribution could not serve as a "center of gravity" of the economic system, because they are not characterized by a uniform rate of profits on the supply prices of the capital goods, thus prompting profit-maximizing entrepreneurs to move away from those positions. The replacement of the "method of long-period positions" with the "intertemporal method" had not only entailed a change in the notion of equilibrium, but it had also meant a separation of the short-period from the long-period problem, which was tantamount to cutting the traditional link between "equilibrium" and "disequilibrium." However, the transformation of the traditional "disequilibrium" into an "intertemporal equilibrium" and the related falling away of the traditional distinction of short and long-period equilibria had created serious problems of its own. Meaning could hardly be attached to the notion of a short-period general equilibrium when "the forces governing it would lack the persistence necessary to distinguish them from those other accidental forces which, at any given time, are likely to keep the economy out of this short-period equilibrium. Thus, before the recurrence of demand and supply flows has been sufficient to correct, or compensate, previous accidental deviations, the equilibrium position itself will have changed considerably, and the equilibrium can then provide little if any guidance to the behavior of the economy."[14]

Now, whatever one may think of the neo-Ricardians' sweeping reading of the history of economic analysis in terms of the central categories of "method" and "theory," which may be called into question both on methodological[15] and substantive[16] grounds, there can be no doubt that Hayek abandoned the long-period framework so defined in his 1928 paper. Hayek also seems to have been fully aware that the intertemporal approach to the theory of capital and interest marked a fundamental break with earlier procedures.

The shift of emphasis is further highlighted in Hayek's exchange with Sraffa, at the heart of which lay two radically different notions of equilibrium: market-clearing demand and supply equilibrium (Hayek) as opposed to long-run cost of production equilibrium (Sraffa).[17] In response to Sraffa's charge of substituting the method of explaining many commodity-own-rates of interest for the method of explaining the general rate of profits, Hayek tellingly remarks: "I think it would be truer to say that ... there would be *no single rate* which, applied to all commodities, would satisfy the conditions of equilibrium rates, but there might, at any moment, be as many 'natural' rates of interest as there are commodities, *all* of which would be *equilibrium rates*."[18]

III HAYEK'S NOTION OF EQUILIBRIUM

It is to Milgate's lasting credit to have drawn attention to Hayek's path-breaking paper on intertemporal equilibrium. While one may be inclined to agree with his evaluation of the thrust of Hayek's reaction to received opinion, i.e., the theory of Böhm-Bawerk and Wicksell describing capital and interest, one may be entitled to take issue with Milgate's claim that "there is no conceptual difference between [Hayek's intertemporal equilibrium] and the notion which characterizes value theory today."[19] That is to say, Hayek's positive contribution amounted to considerably more than the mere introduction of differentiating commodities, not only in terms of their physical characteristics but also in terms of their availability, would suggest.

In any attempt to appraise the significance of the 1928 paper in the evolution of Hayek's thought it must be realized that it represents but the first in a series of efforts to tackle the thorny problem of marrying the concepts of time and equilibrium. Along this path Hayek has persistently urged the need for a conception of equilibrium cut loose from its traditional mechanistic moorings. The first step toward the "subjectivist infusion" of the equilibrium concept was taken in 1928 when it was explicitly divorced from the assumption of stationarity. The next, decisive step[20] occurred in "Economics and Knowledge," in which Hayek was specifically concerned with the meaning of equilibrium in a multiperson context.[21] Equilibrium is here defined not in terms of prices and quantities but rather in terms of the perfect mutual compatibility of individual plans. Referring to his 1928 paper Hayek states:

> For a society, then, we *can* speak of a *state* of equilibrium at a point of time—but it means only that compatibility exists between the different plans which the individuals composing it have made for action in time. And equilibrium will continue, once it exists, so long as the external data corresponds to the common expectations of all the members of the society. The continuance of a state of equilibrium in this sense is then not dependent on the objective data being constant in an absolute sense, and is not necessarily confined to a stationary process. Equilibrium analysis becomes in principle applicable to a progressive society and to those intertemporal price relationships which have given us so much trouble in recent times.[22]

There is a curious passage in that paper to the effect that, since all actions are related to time, "it is obvious that the passage of time is essential to give the concept of equilibrium any meaning."[23] That statement seems to suggest that Hayek was confused over the distinction between *time-to-come*, emphasizing the forward-looking aspect embedded in any plan, and the *lapse of time* in the sense of a historical sequence of events.[24] The former idea refers to a state of *ex ante* coordination, i.e., a *state* of equilibrium characterizing a single moment in time, whereas the latter alludes to the *process* of equilibration. If one defines equilibrium, as Hayek does, in terms of a unity of knowledge then one would have to consider the question: "How can the (subjective) knowledge of each individual, such as bears on his plan, become the same as the knowledge on which each other individual bases a plan of his own?"[25] Hayek does not specifically address himself to the detailed description of the approach toward equilibrium[26] although justification for a concern with equilibrium analysis, we are told, could only be seen in "the supposed existence of a tendency toward equilibrium."[27]

Certainly Hayek's most searching statements on the subject are to be found in Chapter II, "Equilibrium Analysis and the Capital Problem" of his *Pure Theory of Capital.* For any appreciation of Hayek's contribution to the theory of capital and interest it is absolutely fundamental to bear in mind that in the theory of capital his main concern was "to discuss in general terms what type of equipment it will be most profitable to create under various conditions, and how the equipment existing at any moment will be used, rather than to explain the factors which determined the value of a given stock of productive equipment and of the income that will be derived from it."[28] Hayek thus did not pose the Ricardian question reiterated by Böhm-Bawerk: "why and how the owners of 'intermediate products' contrived to draw a permanent income from wealth as if they were factor owners."[29]

Hayek harshly criticized earlier approaches to the theory of capital on the grounds that by focusing on the problem of explaining interest they invariably tended to treat "capital" as some homogeneous substance the quantity of which could be considered a "datum" of the analysis, and to suppress from its purview all those features relating to the dependence of production on the availability of "capital" in various quantities and forms. Hayek's theory of capital is therefore primarily a theory of the use of capital under various conditions and a theory of investment. Consequently, it has to be sharply distinguished both from Solow's suggestion[30] to liberate capital theory from the concept of capital and to restore *the* rate of return in its place as the central category and from Bliss's antithetical proposal[31] that capital theory not only be liberated from the concept of capital but also from the concept of the rate of interest to be superseded by the concept of intertemporal prices.

Hayek not only renounced any attempt to represent the rôle of capital goods in the production process in terms of some single magnitude such as the degree of "roundaboutness" or the quantity of "waiting," but he also cautioned against the futility of analyzing the "dynamics of production," by which he meant "mainly problems connected with the interrelationships between the elaborate structure of productive equipment,"[32] within the confines of long-term stationary equilibrium. For Hayek, the stock of capital at any time does not represent an "amorphous mass" but a definite structure of different capital goods reflecting the underlying network of individual plans, the interdependence of which had been blurred "by the general endeavour to subsume them under one comprehensive definition of the stock of capital."[33] It is surely one of the major ironies in the history of economic thought that Böhm-Bawerk, who went out of his way to stress the heterogeneity of capital goods, should have tried to reduce this complexity by measuring the quantity of capital by the single dimension of time.[34] For the neo-Ricardians, in contrast, there is just one composition of the capital stock that is of paramount importance viz., its long-run equilibrium structure associated with a uniform rate of profits throughout the economic system.

Hayek's formulation of a theory of capital is obviously a far cry from the standard procedure whereby a theory that has absolutely no bearing on the phenomena of capital and interest is miraculously transformed into capital theory by way of a simple redefinition of the concept of a commodity. In *The Pure Theory of Capital* Hayek sought to delineate an appropriate framework for the analysis of capital problems as he conceived them. To *that* end he emancipated the concept of a general equilibrium from the assumption of stationarity and introduced his notion of intertemporal equilibrium, which he considered to be a necessary step in the passage from the economics of the stationary state to a "causal explanation of the process in time . . . the ultimate goal of all economic analysis, and equilibrium analysis is significant only in so far as it is preparatory to this main task."[35]

The abandonment of the "traditional long-period method" was then emphatically not primarily motivated to salvage a supply and demand approach to the theory of capital and interest from the problems posed by the measurements of capital outside the convenient assumption of a one-commodity world, as Milgate alleges, but it rather distinctly reflected Hayek's lifelong crusade against the use of average magnitudes such as the general rate of profits and the average price level.[36]

Moreover, a definition of intertemporal equilibrium as a set of market-clearing prices for both current commodities and for titles to future commodities utterly fails to do justice to Hayek's rich notion of a perfectly coordinated set of individual plans.[37] There are several striking contrasts between Hayek's equilibrium concept and the full intertemporal equilibrium model a la Debreu.[38] In the latter conception the choices of all periods are prereconciled at the outset by way of introduction of a complete system of perfect forward markets. All prices are established and all contracts are entered into "at the beginning of all times"; the "rest of history" merely consists of the execution of previously arranged contracts. As Hahn pointed out: "The assumption that all intertemporal and all contingent markets exist has the effect of collapsing the future into the present."[39] It does not make any sense to speak of a *movement toward* a state of equilibrium, because the intertemporal equilibrium is established once and for all. The "sequential" quality of the allocation process over time has therefore to be interpreted with great care; an intertemporal equilibrium does not describe a sequence in the sense that what happens "next" is dependent on the outcome and plans of the current period, because owing to the availability of all the relevant information at the outset plans need never be revised. Consequently, it is also impossible to give an account of adjustments to changes in market conditions within intertemporal equilibrium models. Alas, such a criticism would be beside the point because intertemporal equilibrium models are primarily supposed to give an account of market clearing of current commodities and titles to future commodities and the efficient allocation of resources over time.[40] In marked contrast to the full intertemporal equilibrium model the Hayekian equilibrium does not require that all transactions occur at a single initial date; the equilibrium is restored every "week." Hayek does not invoke a centralizing agency such as an auctioneer to ensure coordination of plans, but rather "coincident expectations about the quantities and qualities of goods which will pass from one person's possession into another's will in effect co-ordinate all these different plans into one single plan, *although this 'plan' will not exist in any one mind.*"[41] Owing to the absence of any futures markets the Hayekian equilibrium neither qualifies as some kind of temporary equilibrium; it should be classified as an equilibrium sui generis.

Perhaps the most crucial objection to be raised against Milgate's interpretation of Hayek's notion of intertemporal equilibrium concerns the entire neglect of its subjectivist connotation. Hayekian equilibrium does not entail that the unanimously held expectations turn out to be correct in an absolute, objective sense; it is perfectly consistent with error. If the expectations on which individual plans were based are not borne out by the facts, then we may refer, according to Hayek, to a change in the objective data. Indeed, in a subjectivist framework, a change in the objective data can only be defined *relative* to a state of coincidence of expectations, irrespective of whether there is any absolute change. If the expectations "conflicted, any development of the external facts might bear out somebody's expectations and disappoint those of others, and there would be no possibility of deciding what was a change in the objective data."[42]

As a corollary of its subjectivist quality the Hayekian equilibrium carefully distinguishes between the knowledge of the actors and the knowledge of the observing economist, whereas the standard notion of intertemporal equilibrium confounds the distinction between those two perspectives by assuming that the actor's knowledge corresponds to the objective facts. The distinction alluded to comes out most clearly when one considers the meaning of the concept of a "datum." As Hayek notes, economists rarely bother to spell out to whom the data are supposed to be given.[43] Are they assumed to be given to the analyzing economist or to the persons whose actions he wants to explain? If they are given to the latter, do we assume that the same facts are known to all the actors or whether different actors possess knowledge of different "facts"? In Hayekian equilibrium it is not posited that the actors enjoy the knowledge of the omniscient observing economist. The knowledge that is required for the coordination of plans refers to a systemwide correct anticipation of plans such that there is a set of external events which will enable the actors to carry out their plans. From a normative point of view, this entails that the Hayekian equilibrium is not necessarily Pareto-efficient. The normative yardstick in terms of which the system is evaluated touches on the degree to which the coordination between the actions of different members of society is successful.[44]

It is a well-known feature of the Arrow-Debreu general equilibrium construct that it posits a formal identity between atemporal and intertemporal allocation. Time enters the economic system by way of an augmentation of the number of variables over which the actors are supposed to maximize their objective functions. It would seem that Hayek's notion of equilibrium as a set of consistent plans, with its emphasis on the forwardlooking perspective embedded in any plan, would allow for a more appropriate treatment of real time. For Hayek, the distinction between intertemporal and atemporal equilibria does not make any sense; all equilibria are intertemporal equilibria.

As O'Driscoll and Rizzo have recently argued, however, "exact Hayekian equilibrium" is ill-suited to deal with the analysis of processes in real time, and they have therefore proposed its revision.[45] According to O'Driscoll and Rizzo, the basic flaw of exact equilibrium stems from its failure to incorporate endogenous learning by conflating plans with the execution of plans. This revised equilibrium construct, called "pattern coordination," combines Hayek's emphasis on the compatibility of plans with a distinction between "typical" and "unique" aspects of future events. From this perspective, a pattern equilibrium of plans refers to coordination with respect to their typical features but not with respect to their unique aspects. This looser conception of equilibrium explicitly takes into account the distinction between plans and actual activities; planned activities involve the typical ingredients of future action and events, whereas the actual activities embody unique features as they unfold in real time.

IV CONCLUDING REMARKS

Whatever its shortcomings concerning the treatment of real time and endogenous change, Hayek's view of intertemporal equilibrium as the fictitious state of complete compatibility of plans stands in sharp conceptual opposition to the notion of intertemporal equilibrium which characterizes value theory today.

Nevertheless, there remains the question to be cleared up as to why the subtle subjectivist transformation of the equilibrium construct in Hayek's writings should have eluded as careful an expositor as Milgate. This raises, of course, the puzzling problem of placing Hayek's work within the context of the history of economic thought.

For Milgate, there seems to be no doubt that Hayek's feet are deeply rooted in the ground of neoclassical general equilibrium. To be sure, there is some justification for such a view. As Professor Lachmann, in particular, has noted, his early work strikingly reveals the extent to which Hayek was under the influence of the Walras-Pareto system.[46]

For Lachmann, the insufficient attention Hayek paid to the problem of the divergence of expectations is a case in point. There seems to exist a tension in Hayek's work between the dismissal of the *tâtonnement* assumption for both current and futures markets, on the one hand, and his adherence to the assumptions of perfect foresight, on the other. Once the *tâtonnement* assumption is discarded one would think that disappointed expectations should come to the fore. Not so with Hayek. Does this then imply that a complete system of perfect futures markets is introduced through the back door? Not necessarily; there still remains the crucial difference that actors in the Hayek equilibrium construct do not—each for herself or himself without paying attention to what others are doing—form firmly held expectations regarding the prices for current transactions in future periods which happen to coincide. Rather, they form correct expectations concerning each others' plans.

We should also note that in *The Pure Theory of Capital* Hayek was only concerned with the tautological propositions of the Pure Logic of Choice, i.e., equilibrium analysis, whereas the treatment of the causal processes of the real world was reserved for a companion book, which, alas, has never been published.

NOTES

* I am indebted to my colleague Karl Farmer for helpful discussions.

1. K. J. Arrow, "The Potentials and Limits of the Market in Resource Allocation," in *Issues in Contemporary Microeconomics and Welfare*, ed. G. R. Feiwel (London: Macmillan, 1985), p. 116.
2. J. R. Hicks, *Value and Capital*, 2nd ed. (Oxford: Clarendon Press, 1946), p. 115.
3. J. Hicks, "Equilibrium and the Trade Cycle," *Economic Inquiry*, 18 (1980); reprinted in J. Hicks, *Money, Interest and Wages* (Oxford: Basil Blackwell, 1982), p. 31.
4. F. A. Hayek, "Das intertemporale Gleichgewichtssystem der Preise und die Bewegungen des 'Gelderwertes,'" *Weltwirtschaftliches Archiv*, 28 (1928); reprinted in F. A. Hayek, *Money, Capital and Fluctuations*, ed. R. McCloughry (London: Routledge, 1984).
5. J. Hicks, "The Formation of an Economist," *Banca Nazionale del Lavoro Quarterly Review*, 130 (1979), p. 199.
6. Hicks, *Money, Interest and Wages*, op. cit., p. 7.
7. M. Milgate, "On the Origin of the Notion of 'Intertemporal Equilibrium,'" *Economica*, 46 (1979), pp. 1–10; M. Milgate, *Capital and Employment* (London and New York: Academic Press, 1982), chap. VIII.
8. This has already been noted by H. S. Ellis, *German Monetary Theory, 1905–33* (Cambridge: Harvard University Press, 1934), p. 339.
9. Hayek, *Money, Capital and Fluctuations*, op. cit. pp. 71f.
10. Ibid., p. 74.
11. Ibid., pp. 78f.
12. P. Garegnani, "On a Change in the Notion of Equilibrium in Recent Work

on Value and Distribution," in *Essays in Modern Capital Theory*, eds. M. Brown, K. Sato, and P. Zarembka (Amsterdam: North-Holland, 1976); J. Eatwell, "Competition," in *Classical and Marxian Political Economy. Essays in Honour of Ronald L. Meek* (London: Macmillan, 1982); F. Petri, "The Difference Between Long-Period and Short-Period General Equilibrium and the Capital Theory Controversy," *Australian Economic Papers*, 17 (1978), pp. 246–60.

13. V. Walsh and H. Gram, *Classical and Neoclassical Theories of General Equilibrium* (New York: Oxford University Press, 1980), p. 236.
14. Garegnani, op. cit., p. 38.
15. See E. Nell's review of *Capital and Employment* in *Contributions to Political Economy*, 2 (1983), p. 114. Nell argues that the required independence of "method" and "theory" rests on flimsy foundations because the long-period method "depends on an implicit theory of investment." See also E. Nell, "Structure and Behavior in Classical and Neo-Classical Theory," *Eastern Economic Journal*, 11 (1983), p. 147.
16. T. F. Kompas, "Marshall and Keynes on the Long and Short Run: Traditional Notions of Equilibrium Reconsidered," a paper delivered at the History of Economics Society Meetings, May 1983. Kompas distinguishes three distinct notions of long-period equilibria (Wicksellian, Marshallian, static Walrasian), according to whether an aggregate stock of value capital is taken as a datum of the analysis.
17. See L. M. Lachmann, "Austrian Economics Under Fire. The Hayek-Sraffa Duel in Retrospect," unpublished manuscript (1980). Lachmann argues that Sraffa's onslaught presents a prelude to the *Prelude to a Critique of Economic Theory*. See also M. Desai, "The Task of Monetary Theory: The Hayek-Sraffa Debate in a Modern Perspective," and R. McCloughry, "Neutrality and Monetary Equilibrium: A Note on Desai," in *Advances in Economic Theory*, ed. M. Baranzini (Oxford: Basil Blackwell, 1982).
18. F. A. Hayek, "Money and Capital: A Reply," *The Economic Journal*, 42 (1932), p. 245. (Hayek's italics.)
19. Milgate, *Capital and Employment*, op. cit., p. 130, n. 7.
20. In *Prices and Production* (London: Routledge, 1931) and *Monetary Theory and the Trade Cycle* (London: Cape, 1933), Hayek retained the equilibrium notion of the 1928 paper.
21. F. A. Hayek, "Economics and Knowledge," in F. A. Hayek, *Individualism and Economic Order* (London: Routledge, 1949).
22. Ibid., p. 41. (Hayek's italics)
23. Ibid., p. 37.
24. See G. L. S. Shackle, "F. A. Hayek," in *Pioneers of Modern Economics in Britain* eds. D. P. O'Brien and J. R. Presley (London: Macmillan, 1981).
25. Ibid., p. 256.
26. On the competitive-entrepreneurial equilibration process see I. M. Kirzner, *Competition and Entrepreneurship* (Chicago: The University of Chicago Press, 1973); I. M. Kirzner, *Perception, Opportunity, and Profit* (Chicago: University of Chicago Press, 1979).
27. Hayek, *Individualism and Economic Order*, op. cit., p. 44.
28. F. A. Hayek, *The Pure Theory of Capital* (London: Routledge, 1941), p. 3.

29. L. M. Lachmann, *Capital, Expectations, and the Market Process* (Kansas City: Sheed Andrews & McMeel, 1977), p. 27.
30. R. M. Solow, *Capital Theory and the Rate of Return* (Amsterdam: North-Holland, 1964), p. 16.
31. C. J. Bliss, *Capital Theory and the Distribution of Income* (Amsterdam: North-Holland, 1975), p. 10.
32. Hayek, *The Pure Theory of Capital*, op. cit., p. 6.
33. Ibid. p. 6.
34. See Ludwig M. Lachmann, *Capital and its Structure* (Kansas City: Sheed Andrews & McMeel, 1978), p. 73.
35. Hayek, *The Pure Theory of Capital*, op. cit., p. 17.
36. I am indebted to Professor Hayek for pointing this out to me in conversation.
37. On Hayek's definition of intertemporal equilibrium see *The Pure Theory of Capital*, op. cit., p. 22.
38. G. Debreu, *Theory of Value* (New Haven: Yale University Press), chap. 7.
39. F. H. Hahn, "General Equilibrium Theory," in *The Crisis in Economic Theory*, eds. D. Bell and I. Kristol (New York: Basic Books, 1981), p. 132.
40. D. M. Hausman, *Capital, Profits, and Prices* (New York: Columbia University Press, 1981), p. 105.
41. Hayek, *The Pure Theory of Capital*, op. cit., p. 26. (My italics.)
42. Hayek, *Individualism and Economic Order*, op. cit., p. 41.
43. Hayek, *Individualism and Economic Order*, op. cit., p. 39.
44. See Kirzner, *Competition and Entrepreneurship*, op. cit., chap. 6.
45. See Gerald P. O'Driscoll and Mario J. Rizzo, *The Economics of Time and Ignorance* (Oxford: Basil Blackwell, 1985), chap. 5.
46. See Ludwig M. Lachmann, "From Mises to Shackle: An Essay on Austrian Economics and the Kaleidic Society," *Journal of Economic Literature*, 14 (1976), p. 58.

3 Methodology and the Individual Decision Maker

LAWRENCE A. BOLAND

Traditionally, methodology has been of interest to historians of economic thought or to those few economic theorists who view methodology as an instrument to help them explain their theories to other economists. In effect, we might say that methodology has always been "metatheoretical." This instrumental view is in contrast to that which I wish to present in this paper. Here, I argue for a necessary theoretical role for methodology, a role implied to a certain extent in some of Hayek's papers.[1] To be more general, we could say that any economic theory which recognizes a need for knowledge in decision making must in some way imply a role for methodology because, as Hayek explicitly said in 1937, to explain a decision the economist must also explain the "acquisition" of the knowledge needed to make that decision. I have argued previously that while we must recognize the importance of knowledge acquisition, or learning, we must also avoid predisposing our conception of knowledge and its acquisition in favor of only one view of learning methodology, namely, inductive learning.[2]

I shall begin by presenting Hayek's views, which though they are often employed in recent literature, are frequently misunderstood. I will end by presenting my alternative view.

I EPISTEMICS IN HAYEK'S ECONOMICS

In a recent article, Professor Lachmann has argued that one of the neglected contributions of the Austrian School was the view that "the dissemination of knowledge plays a prominent part in the process of competition."[3] Hayek's argument, made in 1937, in favor of capitalist competition depended on the assertion that this competition only requires a minimum amount of knowledge, consisting primarily of easily available private knowledge (of one's personal aims and limitations) and augmented only by the public knowledge disseminated by the market. This view led Hayek, in 1945, to argue that adequate private knowledge is obtainable in practice; but "scientific" knowledge, even if available, is usually inadequate without the individual decision maker's private knowledge. Specifically, the virtue of making decisions based on market-disseminated information arises because even though the day-to-day information from the market can be wrong (e.g., disequilibrium prices), the process that leads to an equilibrium generates the correct information. Hayek thus distinguished between possibly false practical knowledge (Lachmann's "knowledge how") and true "scientific knowledge" (Lachmann's "knowledge that" or "propositional knowledge").

Hayek complained that practical knowledge has always been considered inferior relative to scientific knowledge. More important, Hayek implied that if scientific knowledge were actually true and certain, it would still play no significant role in the economic process because this economic process is concerned with economic problems which arise from changes in such things as tastes. If things like tastes continue as before, there are no allocation problems to be solved. In the absence of new problems, there would be no need to make new decisions or thus to learn anything new. For Hayek, scientific knowledge is knowledge of general rules and thus is inherently static. In effect, scientific knowledge is irrelevant—particularly when it is considered true and certain. Thus, the recognition of possibly false practical knowledge is essential if we want to understand the competitive market process.

This leads Lachmann to conclude that if knowledge is to play an explicit role, Hayek's two types of knowledge must be clearly recognized. Moreover, we need to see that what the Austrians were saying is that "practical knowledge" (or "knowledge how") is what must be explicitly recognized in the explanation of an individual's decision process. According to Lachmann, logicians only recognize knowledge when it is certain. Thus, he argues, whenever "strict logicians" analyze the decision making of market participants they miss the point because, according to Hayek, the market overcomes the problems of (potentially) uncertain practical knowledge.

The importance of the Hayek-Lachmann knowledge distinction

Recognition that any individual's knowledge can be false is central to Hayek's argument in favor of focusing on market-disseminated knowledge that is potentially uncertain rather than on certain scientific knowledge. For Hayek, scientific knowledge is irrelevant for our understanding of the market economy. Whenever an individual's knowledge is false, the empirical evidence generated in the market by actions based on false knowledge actually leads towards the truth about the market. For example, overestimating market supply at the current price leads to some individuals' having to bid the price up and thereby inadvertently reducing the shortage. That is, acting upon false ("disequilibrium") prices unintentionally leads to the creation of true (equilibrium) prices which can be the basis for realizable plans to maximize profits or utility. A competitive market economy thus creates its own adequate practical knowledge. Still, this view of the adequacy of market-generated information presumes that all markets are inherently stable. I argue that it is the presumption of stability and the presumption of the necessity of induction for certain knowledge that together give scientific knowledge a less significant role than practical knowledge.

To understand the importance of Hayek's claim, consider two possible states of one market from the perspective of contrasting the acquisition of "certain" knowledge with the process of "learning by doing," which, as Lachmann notes, underlies Hayek's viewpoint. Let the market be characterized by quantity discount selling. That is, both the supply and demand curves are downward sloping. Following the traditional assumption of Walrasian market behavior, excess demand at a quoted price always leads at least one buyer either to offer a higher price to attract more of the scarce supply or to give up trying to maximize his or her utility for the quoted price. Whenever the supply curve is steeper than the demand curve, the usual conception of the competitive process logically leads to the elimination of the false (disequilibrium) quoted prices. In this stable world, Hayek's practical knowledge is provided coincidentally with the convergence to an equilibrium. However, whenever the demand curve is steeper than the supply curve, Walrasian price competition would only aggravate the situation. Whenever there is excess demand, raising the price causes an even greater excess demand. Nevertheless, if an auctioneer in charge of the market could calculate the respective demand and supply curves and thereby calculate the price at which they intersect, then he or she could simply start the transactions at the intersection where demand equals supply. Thus, even though the market may embody an inherent unstable Walrasian competitive process, all plans would still be realized. That is, everyone could maximize their utility or their profit whenever the price is correctly set in advance. (Note that I could have presented all this with upward sloping demand and supply curves or with excess supply situations.)

The example suggests that the view that Hayek expressed in 1945 meant that true scientific knowledge (when attainable) was like the knowledge required of the successful Walrasian auctioneer. While capable of achieving an equilibrium, true and certain scientific knowledge is unnecessary if the market is stable. In such a market, piecemeal, trial-and-error bidding will always tend towards the equilibrium and never away from it. That is, if the market is stable, the participants will always learn correctly from their mistakes. As my example shows, Hayek must presume the market to be stable—which it would be whenever the demand curve is downward sloping and the supply curve is upward sloping. Furthermore, given the common presupposition that the only method for acquiring the certain knowledge which the auctioneer needs to set the correct price would involve induction, such certainty requires too many observations to be a realistic view of any economy whenever there is the potential of an unstable market.[4] In short, either the market is inherently stable, in which case, in Hayek's view, adequate practical knowledge is provided in the progress of the competitive process, or the market is inherently unstable and thus a viable (equilibrium) price will be provided only if someone (such as an auctioneer) can acquire certain knowledge.

The methodological problem of the Hayek-Lachmann distinction

It is all too easy to criticize neoclassical economics for confusing practical with propositional knowledge. Nevertheless, we still need to appreciate a major difficulty with this Hayek-Lachmann distinction. This distinction is based on a mistake about "scientific" or propositional knowledge. This type of knowledge cannot be distinguished from everyday practical knowledge. Both "types of knowledge" can be true or false. It is necessary to recognize the role of methodology in decision making precisely because the knowledge of the individual decision maker—whether it is scientific or otherwise—can be false.

If one is not careful, the Hayek-Lachmann distinction between practical and propositional knowledge can be used to perpetuate a reliance on a false theory of knowledge—inductivism. For example, Hayek's claim that certain scientific knowledge will always be unattainable (or be otherwise inadequate) presumes that for anyone's knowledge to be true it must have been acquired by some inductive process. That is, there is the presumption that since the knowledge needed by an individual decision maker is more intimate and less general, it can be more certain. Both Hayek and Lachmann have implicitly recognized that knowledge can be false and that, in the absence of induction, there is no need to consider "scientific knowledge" any more reliable than private knowledge. But we need to go further and stress that such a recognition need not imply an endorsement of inductivism.

Today, few would so easily espouse any obvious uses of induction. Rather, most would argue that we can make do with a watered-down approach that replaces inductive proofs or inductive learning with knowledge based on convenient acceptability criteria such as those found in econometric practice. The problem of knowledge acquisition, that Hayek discussed in 1937, can be too easily transformed into a standard conventionalist theory-choice problem. Specifically, it is tempting to think that all individuals participating in the market are conventionalists who are able to participate simply through adopting adequate criteria to determine the equilibrium price so that they can proceed to maximize as usual. That is, even with insufficient evidence all successful decision makers have supposedly employed adequate criteria to choose correctly between imperfect theories. This conventionalist theory of knowledge is only a marginal improvement over the older inductivism. As appealing as choice theory may be to economists, it would be a mistake to think that only one theory of knowledge would ever be chosen at any point in time and hence that the decision maker's theory of knowledge and methodology can be taken for granted.

II THE METHODOLOGY OF DECISION MAKERS

Economic theorists must recognize many different views of knowledge and methodology since the decisions based on them will usually lead to different patterns of behavior. I will try to demonstrate this proposition in the narrow context of the typical neoclassical theory of decision making.

Simple demand depends on the demander's theories

Consider ordinal demand theory. The demand curve for any individual is merely the locus of all price-quantity combinations at which the individual's utility is maximized for the given income and prices as well as the given utility function. How does the individual know all the givens? Prices and income may be sufficiently objective that it is always easy to argue that the individual knows them, at least momentarily, when making planned purchases. However, assuming that the individual knows his or her private utility function begs far too much. A particular bundle of quantities of goods actually can be said to be better than any other (in order to explain the choice of that bundle), only if the individual is presumed to compare that bundle with all other conceivable bundles. Of course, given a typical utility function and a little calculus, such a choice can be justified. But knowledge of the utility function is equivalent to comparing all pairs of bundles. Like any other universal statement, this one cannot be shown to be true in real time since such a demonstration would require an infinity of evidence (and time). But, of course, such an inductive proof is actually unnecessary.

In ordinal demand theory all that the individual needs is an assumption about the nature of his or her utility function. Like any other assumption, we assume that it is true only because we do not know whether it is actually true. In the case of the consumer, the plans for purchases must be made on the assumption of a particular utility function. The assumed utility function can be true or false. How does the individual actually know that he or she is maximizing utility with his or her latest purchase? That is, how does the individual learn what the true nature of his or her utility function is except by making purchases? It is precisely the *learning by doing* situation that Lachmann mentions. The individual's pattern of purchases must over time reflect his or her approach to learning the true utility function. Thus, methodology must play an integral part of our explanation of demand.

Market demand depends on the consumers' methods of learning

Several alternative methodologies might be employed in the process of interacting in the market. Here, we will consider various types of consumers facing the same static market situations (in which, all exogenous variables are fixed). Even more important, all consumers have identical incomes and identical true utility functions. Consumers neither know these functions a priori nor do they share the same opinions about their utility functions.

1 An inductivist consumer. If one has to learn whether one is actually maximizing utility by comparing actual bundles consumed, how does one decide the issue? Some believe that you should not jump to conclusions and thus that you never know the correct utility function until you provide an inductive proof—all done without ever making any assumptions. Such a consumer will always be forced to keep trying new bundles. Although facing a static situation, an inductivist consumer would always appear to be dissatisfied.
2 A sophisticated inductivist consumer. Today few would think that anyone just collects the facts without thinking ahead. But, even if one arbitrarily adopts a theory of the nature of one's utility function, one can still never be satisfied until that theory is proven true. This approach can also lead to the appearance of unstable buying patterns. If the theory is true, we should expect to see the buying pattern converging to a stable point.
3 A conventionalist consumer. Given the many conceivable utility functions, how does the consumer pick one to start with? If one abandons the requirement of a complete proof, various criteria can be adopted to appraise the consumer's theory of his or her utility function. In effect, the consumer need only be a good econometrician. No claim need be made that the true utility function is ever found. Rather, the chosen utility function need only be the best available according to the evidence and the adopted criteria. The pattern of consumption behavior will depend on the method used to process data. For example, how many tests of current theory are required before concluding one knows or does not know the true utility function? Competent conventionalist consumers might test their theory every third trip to the market and still be able to explain away numerous refuting observations before being forced to change their pattern of behavior.
4 A skepticist consumer. At the other extremes there are consumers who are always skeptical about proving any theory true. These consumers will change their mind about their personal utility functions the first time some purchased bundle does not meet their expectations. While the conventionalist consumers can tolerate occasional disappointments and thus seldom alter their consumption patterns, the skepticist will be jumping all over the map.

5 An instrumentalist consumer. It is not always clear what instrumentalist consumers might do since the truth of their theories of their utility functions does not supposedly matter! These consumers might act as if they liked their purchases even when they actually detested them.

The crude examples listed above should be sufficient to demonstrate the potential role for methodology in the explanation of decisions within the domain of neoclassical theory. When it is recognized that one's utility function is not known a priori and must be learned, it must also be understood that an appreciation of methodology is necessary to explain the pattern of behavior in the competitive process of Hayek and Lachmann. In the typical neoclassical model two individuals with identical utility functions, identical incomes, and facing the same prices, would choose the same bundles of goods. The examples above show that this conclusion fails to hold if they try to learn their (identical) utility functions using different learning methodologies.

The methodology of stable markets and convex preferences

If it is now recognized that Hayek's view of the competitive process gets to the heart of the neoclassical market, then it should also be easy to see that his view runs parallel with my alternative view of the decision maker. Hayek's view, unlike those of neoclassical economists does not depend on the actual achievement of an equilibrium. It depends on the progressive learning that must take place by virtue of the presumed stability of the market in question. Hayek did not actually try to explain how individuals learn what is necessary to make a market decision. Instead, as I have argued elsewhere, he took inductive learning for granted.[5] The same thing could be said for the traditional neoclassical theory of the consumer. While convexity of preferences is usually explicitly asserted or assumed, no discussion is provided to indicate how the individual learns which bundle will actually maximize his or her utility. If the individual's preferences are actually convex, then I would suggest that the individual's learning process is taken for granted because neoclassical theorists also take inductive learning for granted. If they do not, then there is no reason to believe that the individual will ever be maximizing his or her utility. If my claims are correct then we can safely predict that much methodological work still must be done even within the otherwise successful neoclassical theory of decision making.

NOTES

1. Friedrich A. Hayek, "Economics and Knowledge," *Economica*, 4 (1937), pp. 33–54, Friedrich A. Hayek, "Uses of Knowledge in Society," *American Economic Review,* 35 (1945), pp. 519–30, both of which are reprinted in *Individualism and Economic Order* University of Chicago Press, 1948).
2. Lawrence A. Boland, "Time in Economics vs. Economics in Time: The 'Hayek Problem,'" *Canadian Journal of Economics*, 11 (1978), pp. 240–62; Lawrence A. Boland, "On the Futility of Criticizing the Neoclassical Maximization Hypothesis," *American Economic Review*, 71 (1981), pp. 1031–6; Lawrence A. Boland, *The Foundations of Economic Method* (London: Allen & Unwin, 1982).
3. Ludwig M. Lachmann, "The Salvage of Ideas," *Zeitscrift für die gesamte Staatswissenschaft*, 138 (1982), p. 636.
4. It is commonly presumed that the ultimate basis of our knowledge is true nontheoretical observations. This includes the extreme view that all knowledge must be based on inductive proofs as well as the more common view that we learn inductively—by experience—without having to make assumptions which go beyond the available facts. See further, Boland, *Foundations of Economic Method*, op. cit., chaps. 1 and 4.
5. See n. 2 above.

4 Toward a Hermeneutical Economics: Expectations, Prices, and the Role of Interpretation in a Theory of the Market Process

RICHARD M. EBELING

> ... the method of interpretation (*Verstehen*) ... is nothing less than the traditional method of scholarship which scholars have used throughout the ages whenever they were concerned with the interpretation of texts. Whenever one is in doubt about the meaning of a passage one tries to establish what the author "meant by it."... It is evidently possible to extend this classical method of scholarship to human acts other than writings ... it is the "natural" method of rendering an intelligible account of the manifestations of the human mind.
>
> Ludwig M. Lachmann, *The Legacy of Max Weber*

INTRODUCTION

Ludwig Lachmann has occasionally recounted in conversation how during the 1960s he was certain that his was to be the lonely role of being one of the last of the "Austrian" economists. Having made major contributions in the periods before and after the First World War, by the time of the Second World War the Austrian school had fallen into eclipse. And by the sixth decade of the twentieth century the particular intellectual tradition that had begun nearly a hundred years before with the publication of Menger's *Grundsätze* appeared to be nothing more than a fading chapter in the evolution of economic ideas. New questions pursued with different methods seemed to have displaced any interest in the particular brand of subjectivist economics that was the hallmark of the Austrian tradition.

Yet, rather than pass away into obscurity on the neglected shelves of the history of economic thought, the Austrian school has experienced an astounding renaissance. It is a renaissance that has proceeded as the "crisis in economics" has progressed. The enthusiasm for the rigors of general equilibrium analysis has subsided and the confidence in a coming "golden age" of quantitative economics has wavered. Both have run aground on the shores of an economic reality that would not permit a permanent neglect of the conundrums of human action in a world of imperfect knowledge and diverse expectations.

Yet, established habits are hard to break. New problems are poured into old frameworks, frameworks that may hinder rather than assist in the advancement of ideas. In the following pages I wish to take the view expressed in the quotation from Professor Lachmann with which this paper began and consider the problem of market coordination from the "interpretive" point of view. My suggestion is that the economic problem can usefully be understood as a hermeneutical problem, i.e., as a problem of interpreting and understanding what another means and intends in his words and deeds, what Max Weber called the problem of "mutual orientation" in the arena of social action. A leading implication of this argument is that, once the assumption of perfect knowledge is dropped, the question, How is market coordination possible? becomes a subset of the question, How is society possible? And, thus, the sociological aspect to market activity that economists have traditionally taken as given or as implicit background to economic analysis rises to the foreground.

RATIONAL EXPECTATIONS AND THE GHOST OF "ECONOMIC MAN"

While the problem of expectations has never been completely ignored by economists (it was discussed by many of the older theorists under the heading of "speculation" or "speculative markets") (McCulloch [1864] 1965, pp. 258–274; Emery [1896] 1969; Hadley, 1904, pp. 97–120; Taussig, 1913, pp.159–169) and while there have been certain groups of economists who especially devoted their efforts to the problem of expectations (such as was embedded in the so-called "period" and "plan" analysis of the Swedish economists of the 1930s) (Lundberg [1937] 1964; Lindahl [1939] 1970; Myrdal [1939] 1965; Ebeling, 1981), it has been the rational expectations theorists who in recent years have given the greatest impetus to the subject.

Part of the monetarist critique of Keynesian economics had been the reliance of the latter upon a persistent money illusion on the part of market agents. The monetarists argued that ultimately agents were concerned with real magnitudes and not nominal ones. As a result, agents would discover declines in real purchasing power due to unanticipated inflation and would negotiate for rates of change in money wages sufficient to keep abreast of observed changes in the price level (Cagan, 1956, pp. 37–41; Friedman, 1969).

However, adaptive expectations, as formulated in most monetarist expositions, was an extrapolation to the future of observed price movements of the past (subject to the "weight" assigned to those price movements). The rational expectations theorists argued that the fundamental flaw in this framework was that agents seemed to possess no theory (or theories) of what made prices move in the way they did. Adaptive expectations were constructed from lagged effects (prices) of a previous cause (e.g., monetary expansion), but the agents did not use any theory of cause and effect to estimate *future* effects from *present* causes.

In the place of adaptive expectations, a "strong" version of rational expectations was proposed. The agents were presumed to use all information available to them and to process and analyze that information in an efficient or optimal manner. Furthermore, agents were presumed to believe in just those theories that were the "correct" and same theories that the analyst would use to predict the equilibrium outcomes of the system in which the agents acted. With the subjective probability distributions of the agents assumed to match the objective probability distributions of the conditional likelihood of occurrence of economic events and outcomes, agents could perfectly predict (in probabilistic terms) everything except the unpredictable, i.e., the random or nonsystematic event (Muth [1961] 1981; Begg, 1982, pp. 28–70; Sheffrin, 1983, pp. 1–17). A peculiar probability version of the perfect knowledge postulate was reintroduced into economic analysis. And just like the earlier versions, the end result of the exercise was to assume that the problem requiring solution was already solved. This problem is: How were expectations formed and changed and how, out of this process, did market coordination emerge? (Frydman, 1983: Haberler, 1980; Machlup, 1983; O'Driscoll, 1984).

The "weak" version of rational expectations came no closer to a solution. The assumptions were loosened so that agents initially did not possess the "correct" theories or all the relevant information. But all that was demonstrated was that agents, being good and efficient utility maximizers, would continue to acquire information and knowledge up to that point at which the marginal benefit of additional information and knowledge would be just equal to the marginal cost. (Shaw, 1984, pp. 47–51). Hence, the optimal knowledge state (in utility-maximizing terms) might be one that fell short of that knowledge state required for correct expectations to be held.

HAYEKIAN PLAN COORDINATION AND THE ROLE OF PRICE

It was a characteristic unique to the Austrians (which I shall come back to) that among the "marginalist schools" they tended to ground their analysis of market activity less frequently upon the assumption of perfect knowledge. As a result, an alternative conception of "equilibrium" seemed in order, one that was formulated by Friedrich A. Hayek in his essay "Economics and Knowledge" (1937). It is a formulation that has served as the starting point for most later Austrian analyses of market phenomena (Hayek, 1948a, pp. 33–56).

The crucial issue for Hayek was the question, To whom is the economic data given? Once it is realized that matching the market's division of labor is a division of knowledge it becomes problematic as to whether the knowledge sets of the respective actors sufficiently overlap, and adjust to various changes in just the right manner, to assure a tendency for equilibrium to emerge. Since the success of each individual's plans is dependent to some extent upon the actions of others, each of their knowledge sets have to include expectations concerning the plans and intentions of those others. *Equilibrium*, both at a moment in time and through time, can only be defined, therefore, in terms of an expectations compatibility:

> It appears that the concept of equilibrium merely means that the foresight of the different members of the society is in a special sense correct. It must be correct in the sense that every person's plan is based on the expectations of just those actions of other people which those other people intend to perform and that all those plans are based on the expectation of the same set of external facts, so that under certain conditions nobody will have any reason to change his plans (Hayek, 1948a, p. 42).

It is interesting, however, that rather than pursuing the question of how expectations are formed about the possible actions and intentions of others, and what the characteristics of those expectations are, Hayek moved the analysis to a different plane in his 1945 article, "The Use of Knowledge in Society" (Hayek 1948b, pp. 77–91). Here the question becomes, How might information about the demands and supplies of others be conveyed to respective actors in the far-flung division of labor so they may effectively bring to bear their special and specific knowledge of time and place that can never be known by a central planner but which is essential to utilize for a solution to society's economic problem?

The structure of market prices is shown by Hayek to be the information-economizing device for the utilization of society's knowledge that exists dispersed among the minds of a multitude of individual actors. The respective market participants need not know either the purposes or plans of all the others in the economic community. All this information is condensed and encapsulated in the various prices for both consumer goods and factors of production. The prices of the market serve as the method for an interpersonal coordination of a vast division of labor and knowledge whose existence and extent would be inconceivable without such a device.

Building upon Hayek's argument, Israel Kirzner has recently suggested two possible meanings to the idea that prices coordinate markets (Kirzner, 1984). In the first, markets may be said to be coordinated when prices are at their equilibrium values. By definition equilibrium prices mean prices at which all actors' plans are compatible and all actions are so mutually adjusted that no expectations are disappointed. However, there is also a potential second meaning in which prices may be said to coordinate markets, i.e., when they are at *dis*equilibrium values. The discovery of disappointed expectations conveys useful information to market participants that plan revisions are necessary. And, furthermore, the type of disequilibrium (disappointed buyers at too low a price or disappointed sellers at too high a price) may suggest the direction in which plan and expectation adjustments should be made to those alert to opportunities in the market.

MARKET COORDINATION: MORE THAN RATIONAL EXPECTATIONS INCLUDES, MORE THAN PRICES CAN SAY

To what extent, however, do either the rational expectations or Hayekian conceptions of market coordination solve the problem of expectations and their formation? Inspection suggests that neither has succeeded. Even if doubts are set aside concerning the probabilistic formulation in rational expectations, e.g., doubts concerning the uniformness and repetitiveness of events sufficient to construct a frequency distribution, or the capacity of the human mind to focus upon and retain knowledge about the entire field of events (Simon, 1983, pp. 3–53), there remains an entire dimension to the problem of expectations not touched upon by theorists supporting rational expectations.

The probability judgments upon which the agents will be guided in their choices are ultimately grounded upon images in their minds concerning the behavioral characteristics of the others pertinent to the decision problem at hand. But these behavioral characteristics are not reducible to quantities. They comprise qualitative attributes from which composite pictures are created on the basis of some form of experiences and interactions with those others in the past. To speak, for example, of "Federal Reserve policy" is to have an "ideal type" of the monetary managers, their typical motives or purposes for undertaking policy, their typical responses to various types of changes in the economic conditions. It is only through such typifications that agents can "size up" the situation, form judgments as to what the Fed may do next, and formulate strategies to nullify through appropriate actions undesired effects likely to otherwise follow from monetary causes. They serve as the behavioral schemas within which an interpretive process may be undertaken for evaluating a possible future course of events influenced by the actions of other men. To speak of theories that agents use to form expectations must refer to theories of human behavior. Yet, such theories of human behavior are ultimately theories concerning intentions, purposes and plans. And this requires going deeper than the distribution of observed events under a normal curve.

The same missing element is discernible in Hayek's theory of market coordination, albeit from a different direction. In recent years, Hayek has referred to the structure of market prices as a vast telecommunications system (Hayek, 1980). This is an extremely apt metaphor, for it clearly highlights the ambiguities in the claim that prices coordinate markets. In equilibrium the information conveyed by prices is unambiguous, equilibrium being defined as that vector of prices at which all plans are mutually compatible and no expectations need be frustrated. But is the information conveyed in prices equally unambiguous in a state of disequilibrium?

A seller finds himself with unsold inventory of a product in excess of desired levels at a particular price. But what exactly is the market telling him at that price? That he needs to relocate his store? That he has failed to advertise the existence or availability of the product sufficiently? That the price is "right" but the quality or characteristics of the product is "wrong"? Or that the quality and characteristics are "right" but the price is "wrong"? What the price has conveyed is information that *something* is wrong, that the seller's plans and expectations are inconsistent with those of others. It has not unambiguously told him in which direction the error lies. The price's information, in other words, needs *interpretation as to its meaning* concerning the preferences and plans of others. Nothing is more "Austrian" than an emphasis upon the temporal character of production, that projects are begun today that will only come to fruition tomorrow. Yet, the pattern of tomorrow's demands must be deciphered from today's prices, and its message is not clear. The problem has been lucidly expressed by Professor Lachmann:

> We may regard the price system as a vast network of communications through which knowledge is at once transmitted from each market to the remotest corners of the economy. Every significant change in needs or resources expresses itself in a price change. . . . But in the world in which we are living change does not follow such a convenient pattern. Here knowledge derived from price messages becomes problematical. It does not cease to be knowledge, but "does not tell the whole story" . . . in a world of continuous change prices are no longer in all circumstances a safe guide to action . . . [price] information therefore requires interpretation (the messages have to be "decoded") in order to be transformed into knowledge, and all such knowledge is bound to be imperfect knowledge. . . .
>
> The formation of expectations is nothing but a phase in this

> continuous process of exchange and transmission of knowledge which effectively integrates a market society. A theory of expectations . . . first task is to describe the structure of the mental acts which constitute the formation of expectations; its second task, to describe the process of interactions of a number of individuals whose conducts is oriented towards each other (Lachmann [1956], 1978, pp. 21–23).

THE HERMENEUTICAL DIMENSION: THE SUBJECTIVELY MEANINGFUL ACT AND STRUCTURES OF INTERSUBJECTIVE MEANING

To suggest that the economic problem has a hermeneutical dimension may initially strike the reader as a peculiar claim. After all, hermeneutics has traditionally been categorized as the discipline concerned with the methods of textual exegesis, i.e., with the interpretation of an author's meaning when time and distance separate reader from writer. Yet, for the last hundred years the hermeneutical aspect to all human understanding has slowly become apparent in both natural and social sciences (Bernstein, 1983). Once "the facts" are seen as theory laden, i.e., bound by context, and once it is appreciated that neither verification nor falsification is unproblematically a matter of empirical testing, then the interpretive element in both evidence and argumentation becomes an essential quality in all understanding. *All* sciences become, in other words, *human* sciences, for it is minds and not matter that serve as the tentative arbitrators concerning the world and its working.

While the hermeneutical character of the natural sciences is still in the early stages of debate (Heelan, 1983) its significance for the social sciences is becoming more widely comprehended (Ricoeur, 1981; Taylor [1971], 1979; Polkinghorne, 1983, pp. 201–204). Its modern development can be traced to the writings of Wilhelm Dilthey in the late nineteenth century. His central argument was that all human activity bears the qualities discernible in the problems of textual interpretation: the meaning of an actor whose doings require interpretation for purposes of intelligibility and understanding. The human spirit, he argued, "speaks to us from stone, marble, musical compositions, gestures, words and writings, from actions, economic arrangements and constitutions and has to be interpreted" (Dilthey, 1976, p. 247).

Each of the manifestations and residues of human conduct bears the imprint of their creators, their meanings are to be found in the intentions of acting men. The importance of the actor's meaning was also emphasized by Max Weber in his definitions of *action* and *social action*:

> In "action" is included all human behavior when and in so far as the acting individual attaches a subjective meaning to it. . . . Action is social in so far as, by virtue of the subjective meanings attached to it by the acting individual (or individuals) it takes account of the behavior of others and is thereby oriented in its course (Weber [1922], 1947, p. 88).

As Weber shows, each of the concepts in the economist's tool kit contains and implies the imprint of meaning—the meaning of actors as they conceive their own doings and their doings in relation to others. The concepts, "market," "buyer," "seller," "mutual agreement," "competition," all represent mutual orientations involving attitudes, conduct, and interpersonal response expected from others and from oneself in the context of particular circumstances. In an exchange, Weber argued, the essential quality of the event is constituted by the meanings the traders ascribe to both their own and the other's behavior. It, in a sense, dictates the mode of conduct expected by each towards the other (Weber [1907] 1977, pp. 109–112).

The fortuitous circumstance for both actor and social analyst is that both are born into an on-going social world already containing structures of *inter*subjective meaning which all in that culture and society share in common. Through a process of inculturation beginning in childhood we are introduced to that world and come to "see" in various actions, things, and situations the same potential meanings that others do, e.g., that man is a "policeman," that object is a "can opener," this experience is "love" or "peer recognition." We orient ourselves in all our doings on the basis of these meanings because for us that *is* what they have come to mean. We, therefore, all come to share a common social world that enables us to understand what each of us means in our words and deeds—to ourselves and to others (Dilthey, 1976, pp. 179–222). These institutionalized meanings become, as Professor Lachmann has aptly described them, the "nodal points of society" for mutual orientation and possible coordination of a multitude of human plans (Lachmann, 1971, p. 50).

IDEAL TYPES AND THE PROCESS OF MUTUAL ORIENTATION

Aspects of structures of intersubjective meaning have been sketched out in some detail by Alfred Schutz under the concept of "ideal types" (Schutz [1932] 1967, pp. 139–214; Schutz [1952] 1973, pp. 3–47; Berger and Luckman, 1967; Natanson, 1970). In the commonly shared "social world" each individual experiences various degrees of intimacy with others, along a spectrum running from total anonymity to a "face-to-face" relationship. The less intimate the relationship the more general the "typical" characteristics ascribable to others. At one end, that of total anonymity, "others" can only be typified as purposeful beings, i.e., as choosers of ends, appliers of means, doers of acts. At the other end, that of the face-to-face relationship, individuals are able to construct composite images not of all men, but of that individual from which expectations are formed as to his behavior in different situations on the basis of his typical attitudes, motivations, and responses as they have come to be seen and analyzed in direct interpersonal contact.

In the wide center of this spectrum stand typifications neither of all men nor of any one specific individual. Rather, these ideal types are composed of various concrete generalizations concerning behavioral motivations and patterns of action to be expected from any individual in the particular social role or situation referred to. Thus, to speak of a "stock broker" conjures up an image (or "ideal type") of an individual (regardless of which real individual) performing certain tasks in a certain typical manner in fulfilling a particular set or type of activities. And to speak of "the stock exchange" is to have a mental image of a particular type of association in which certain types of activities are undertaken by certain types of individuals who have certain typical motives or purposes in mind.

The social standardizations of role and function in the form of typical modes of conduct serve as the foundations for the construction of expectations by agents in the social and economic arenas. They enable each to both understand and *anticipate* to various degrees the conduct of others in various settings and circumstances. They also enable each of us to believe that others will, in turn, have an ability to understand and interpret our own purposes and meanings when we wish to achieve particular ends that require the coordination of our own actions with theirs, and we accordingly act and speak in particular ways. The routinization of behavior along typical patterns introduces *ranges of knowability* about the possible future conduct and motivations of others. It is what makes society and economies possible in lieu of a "perfect knowledge" of each separate individual and his or her unique eccentricities and differences.

AUSTRIAN SUBJECTIVISM AND THE PROCESS OF MARKET COORDINATION

It has generally come to be recognized that the Austrian variation on the marginalist theme had qualities that set the Austrians apart from the other schools of subjective value (Streissler, 1973; Jaffe, 1976). The distinguishing characteristics, it has been argued, are the Austrian emphases upon time, process, and adjustment, in comparison to the mainstream neoclassical focus on equilibrium states and their determination. It can be also argued, however, that emphases by the Austrians were due to their implicit point of departure: a concept of man as an intentional being. Mengerian man, particularly in the *Grundsätze*, is an active plan designer and initiator in an environment of uncertainty (Menger [1871] 1981). Or as Frank A. Fetter described it, man is not merely an evaluator, a chooser of goods, but a doer of acts (Fetter 1915, pp. 171–172). This was restated more formally by Ludwig von Mises, in 1933, in his conception of "purposeful behavior":

> In our view the concept of man is, above all else the concept of the being who acts. Our consciousness is that of an ego which is capable of acting and does act. The fact that our deeds are intentional makes them actions (Mises, 1981, p. 14).

For Mises and other Austrians such as Hayek and Lachmann, the cardinal rule for serious work in the social sciences in general and economics in particular has been adherence to a methodological subjectivism, i.e., that human actions in the social world are outgrowths not merely of the subjectivism of tastes and preferences but of a subjectivism of perspective, perception, and purpose that serve as the steering rods and meanings for the actions undertaken (Mises [1949], 1966; Hayek [1952] 1979, pp. 41–76; Lachmann, 1976). The Austrians' distinction between intentional human plans and the unintended consequences of human action tacitly conceives of a world of actors whose knowledge is less than perfect. Austrian subjectivism, particularly in the twentieth century, is an extension of Max Weber's concept of the subjectively meaningful act writ large. (A point that Professor

Lachmann has seen clearly, as when, in his review of Mises's *Human Action*, he pointed out that "We must never forget that it is the work of Max Weber that is being carried on here.") (Lachmann [1951] 1977, p. 95.)

How, then, is coordination brought about in the market process if each agent acts, and assigns meanings to his actions, on the basis of such a radically subjectivist point of view? The answer is that most of the meanings that actors assign to both their own doings and to their use of things (commodities, factors of production) are not totally private meanings. Many, if not most, of these meanings are shared meanings that actors adopt and express through the structures of intersubjective meaning that we have already discussed. We normally assume we understand what a person intends (his meaning) when he purchases a box of breakfast cereal because, as members of the same "meaning" community, we "understand" the use to which such an object is usually assigned.

But our ability to understand the meanings of others is not perfect. As we suggested earlier they exist as ranges of knowability, rather than determinate points. The reason for this takes us closer to the more traditional conception of hermeneutics. The hermeneutical problem in textual exegesis is seen as one of contextual interpretation. We understand a text through the individual words of which it is comprised; yet, the individual words in the text can frequently have different meanings and connotations. Which is the appropriate meaning, usage, or connotation to assign to the word can only be decided in terms of the overall context within which the individual words appear. There is a non-disintegratable relationship between the parts and the whole. The same applies in the world of action. The same act performed by an agent can have various meanings depending upon the context within which the act is performed. And we form interpretive judgments as to which is the appropriate meaning to assign to the act in terms of how we see the action context within which it occurs.

What, then, of the dilemma of price interpretation, which we saw as a fundamental problem in conditions of market disequilibrium? A solution can perhaps be found in terms of the different ideal-type generalizations, though by varying the conceptualization from that of a spectrum to that of a descending order of specificity from the most general (the generic properties discernible in all choice and action) to the most specific (as at the level of the face-to-face relationship). The more specific the ideal type becomes the greater the detailed knowledge implied in its construction. While all members of the society would share in common a large number of ideal types due to their belonging to the same community, the normal process of the division of labor would bring with it not only a specialization in production skills but knowledge skills as well concerning segments of activities in the market. There occurs a particular form of "social distribution of knowledge" (Schutz [1946] 1964, pp. 120–134). To say that a trading specialist, for example, has informed knowledge concerning a portion of the market is to say that he has, through training and experience, accumulated a stock and structure of knowledge of specific "ideal types" concerning that market and the "others" (to varying degrees of specificity) in it that other people in the division of labor do not possess. His ideal types are less general and more specific in his corner of the social division of labor because contact with certain "others" and their market circumstances and interests has enabled him to fill in the outlines with much greater detail.

Thus, we can see that there is another aspect to Hayek's cogent argument concerning a division of knowledge of the unique circumstances of time and place, an aspect that helps round off rather than contradict his analysis. A vital portion of each individual's knowledge of his unique market circumstances is a set of specific ideal types concerning the buyers and sellers, and typical causes and effects from changing conditions in his market. These specific ideal types are known to him and *structured by him* in his mind and are the implicit background in the forefront of which he makes his market-related decisions. And through the interconnectedness and interdependency of markets in the division of labor there emerges an interconnectedness of overlapping specific ideal typifications where markets "touch."

When a market price changes or when inventory does not "move" at a prevailing price, each trader will have a stock of experience-generated specific typifications which he will draw upon to decide the possible meanings the price change or excess supply might have in the particular circumstance. The *entrepreneurial element* is then to decide which out of this stock of typifications is the one most likely to be the best interpretation considering the market context as the decision maker sees it. It is like the textual scholar who approaches a document with a stock of knowledge concerning his special subject and tentatively assigns appropriate meanings to the words in the overall text. The market test inherent in rivalous competition is, therefore, a competition between interpretive schemas about the message conveyed by the market price signals.

Market prices are used in conjunction with the ideal typifications in the minds of the actors in the social division of knowledge. They give meaning to the prices, just as the prices assist in deciding which meanings may be relevant to the decision problem at hand. Prices, therefore, reside as an element, albeit a crucial element, in the wider social structures of intersubjective meaning. And it is the structures of prices within the structures of meanings that create the potential for market coordination.

CONCLUSION

During the last decade the problems of imperfect knowledge and expectations have risen to the forefront of economic analysis. Yet, when looked at more closely, neither rational expectations nor the Hayekian conception of market coordination through prices successfully solves the problems of expectations and their formation. It may very well be the case that further advancement on this front in economics will require the introduction of certain insights and concepts developed in other social disciplines. I have attempted to suggest in this paper how ideas usually considered in the domains of sociology and textual interpretation may have relevance for the problems of expectations and market coordination, though this is not their only usefulness to economics (Ebeling, 1985; Lavoie, 1985). There emerges a discernible hermeneutical dimension to economic analysis.

The core of Austrian economics has been its focus upon the purposeful human actor and his subjective point of view. Its growing appeal is its greater realism in place of the aridity of neoclassical formalism, a formalism that has more and more reduced man to a functional form, stripped of all human qualities. That the problem of knowledge and expectations blurs the clear, crisp picture drawn by the general equilibrium theorists cannot be denied; but neither can it be denied that the real world is neither that clear nor crisp. The strength of Austrian subjectivism, to generalize Schumpeter's remark concerning Austrian monetary theory (Schumpeter 1954, p. 1090) is that "it tends to replace a simple but inadequate picture by one which is less clear-cut but more realistic and richer in results."

No member of the Austrian school has done more to breathe such realism and richness into the subjectivist framework as Ludwig Lachmann, with his emphasis on the filter of the human mind. With gratitude and affection this paper is dedicated to him.

REFERENCES

Begg, David K. H. (1982), *The Rational Expectations Revolution in Macroeconomics* (New York: Philip Allan).

Berger, Peter and Thomas Luckmann (1967), *The Social Construction of Reality* (New York: Penguin).

Bernstein, Richard J. (1983), *Beyond Objectivism and Relativism: Science, Hermeneutics and Praxis* (Philadelphia: University of Pennsylvania Press).

Cagan, Phillip (1956), The Monetary Dynamics of Hyperinflation, in *Studies in the Quantity Theory of Money*, ed Milton Friedman (Chicago: The University of Chicago Press), pp. 25–117.

Dilthey, Wilhelm (1976), *Selected Writings*, ed. and with an introduction by H. P. Rickman (Cambridge: Cambridge University Press).

Ebeling, Richard M. (1981), "The Stockholm School of Economics: An Annotated Bibliography," *Austrian Economics Newsletter*, 2, pp. 1–12.

—— (1985), "Hermeneutics and the Interpretive Element in the Analysis of the Market Process," *Center for the Study of Market Process, Working Papers Series*, Department of Economics, George Mason University.

Emery, Henry Crosby (1969), *Speculation on the Stock and Produce Exchanges of the United States* (New York: Greenwood Press).

Fetter, Frank A. (1915), *Economic Principles* (New York: Century).

Friedman, Milton (1968), "The Role of Monetary Policy." in *The Optimum Quantity of Money* (Chicago: Aldine), pp. 95–110.

Frydman, Roman (1982), "Towards an Understanding of Market Processes: Individual Expectations, Learning and Convergence to Rational Expectations Equilibrium," *American Economic Review*, 72, pp. 652–68.

Haberler, Gottfried (1980). *Notes on Rational and Irrational Expectations* (Washington: American Enterprise Institute).

Hadley, Arthur Twining (1904), *Economics: An Account of the Relations Between Private Property and Public Welfare* (New York: Putnam).

Hayek, Friedrich A. (1948a), "Economics and Knowledge," in *Individualism and Economic Order* (University of Chicago Press).

—— (1948b), "The Use of Knowledge in Society," in *Individualism and Economic Order* (Chicago: University of Chicago Press).

—— (1979), *The Counter-Revolution of Science* (Indianapolis: Liberty Press).

Heelan, Patrick (1983), "Natural Science as a Hermeneutic of Instrumentation," *Philosophy of Science*, 50, pp. 181–204.

Jaffe, William (1976), "Menger, Jevons and Walras De-Homogenized." *Economic Inquiry*, Dec., pp. 551–524.

Kirzner, Israel M. (1984), "Prices, The Communication of Knowledge, and the Discovery Process," in *The Political Economy of Freedom, Essays in Honor of F. A. Hayek*, eds Kurt R. Leube and Albert H. Zlabinger (Munich: Philosophia Verlag).

Lachmann, Ludwig M. (1977), "The Science of Human Action." in *Capital, Expectations and the Market Process*, ed. Walter E. Grinder, (Kansas City: Sheed Andrews & McMeel).

—— (1978), *Capital and Its Structure* (Kansas City: Sheed Andrews & McMeel).

—— (1971), *The Legacy of Max Weber* (Berkeley: The Glendessary Press).

—— (1976), "From Mises to Shackle: An Essay on Austrian Economics and the Kaleidic Society," *Journal of Economic Literature*, 54, p. 62.

Lavoie, Don (1985), "The Interpretive Dimension of Economics: Science, Hermeneutics and Praxeology," *Center for the Study of Market Processes, Working Papers Series*, Department of Economics, George Mason University.

Lindahl, Erik (1970), *Studies in the Theory of Money and Capital* (New York: Augustus M. Kelley).

Lundberg, Erik, (1964), *Studies in the Theory of Economic Expansion* (New York: Augustus M. Kelley).

Machlup, Fritz (1983), "The Rationality of 'Rational Expectations,'" *Kredit and Kapital*, 16, pp. 172–82.

McCulloch, John R. (1965), *The Principles of Political Economy* (New York: Augustus M. Kelley).

Menger, Carl (1981), *Principles of Economics* (New York: New York University Press).

Mises, Ludwig von (1981), *Epistemological Problems of Economics* (New York: New York University Press).

—— (1966), *Human Action, A Treatise on Economics*, 3rd ed. (Chicago: Henry Regnery).

Muth, John F. (1981), *Rational Expectations and Econometric Practice*, eds. Robert E. Lucas, Jr. and Thomas J. Sargent (Minneapolis: The University of Minnesota Press) pp. 3–22.

Myrdal, Gunnar (1965), *Monetary Equilibrium* (New York: Augustus M. Kelley).

Natanson, Maurice (1970), *The Journeying Self, A Study in Philosophy and Social Role* (Reading, Mass.: Addison-Wesley).

O'Driscoll, Gerald P. (1984), "Expectations and Monetary Regimes." Federal Reserve Bank of Dallas, *Economic Review* (Sept.), pp.1–12.

Polkinghorne, Donald (1985), *Methodology for the Human Sciences* (Albany: State University of New York Press).

Ricoeur, Paul (1981) *Hermeneutics and the Human Sciences*, ed. and trans. John B. Thompson (Cambridge: Cambridge University Press).

Schumpeter, Joseph A. (1954), *History of Economic Analysis* (New York: Oxford University Press).

Schutz, Alfred (1967), *The Phenomenology of the Social World*, trans., George Walsh and Frederick Lehnert (Evanston, Ill.: Northwestern University Press).

—— (1976), "The Well-Informed Citizen: An Essay on the Social Distribution of Knowledge," in *Collected Papers: Studies in Social Theory*, ed. Arvid Broderson (The Hague: Martinus Nijhoff), vol. II, pp. 120–134.

—— (1973), "Common-Sense and Scientific Interpretation of Human Action," in *Collected Papers: The Problem of Social Reality*. ed. Maurice Natanson (The Hague: Martinus Nijhoff), vol. I, pp. 3–47.

Shaw, G. K. (1984), *Rational Expectations* (New York: St. Martin's).

Sheffrin, Steven M. (1983), *Rational Expectations* (Cambridge: Cambridge University Press).

Simon, Herbert A. (1983), *Reason in Human Affairs* (Stanford: Stanford University Press).

Streissler, Erich (1973), "To What Extent Was the Austrian School Marginalist?" in *The Marginal Revolution in Economics*, eds R. D. Collinson Black, A. W. Coats, and Crauford D. W. Goodwin (Durham: Duke University Press), pp. 160–175.

Taussig, Frank W. (1913), *Principles of Economics* (New York: Macmillan).

Taylor, Charles (1979), "Interpretation and the Sciences of Man," in *Interpretive Social Science: A Reader*, eds Paul Rabinow and William M. Sullivan (Berkeley: University of California Press), pp. 21–71.

Weber, Max (1977), *Critique of Stammler*, trans. Guy Oakes (New York: The Free Press).

—— (1947), *The Theory of Social and Economic Organization*, ed. Talcott Parsons (New York: Oxford University Press).

5 A Sympathetic Critic of the Austrian Business-Cycle Theory

JOHN B. EGGER

INTRODUCTION

In 1933, when Ludwig Lachmann went to London, the Austrian theory of the business cycle was near the peak of its popularity.[1] Although everyone knows, in a general way, what happened later in that decade and in those following, the causes of trends in doctrinal history will always be subjects for conjecture. If, as Grinder observes, by the end of the decade "the only consistent and thoroughgoing Hayekians left [in London] were Lachmann and Hayek himself," it may be pertinent that—unlike his new English colleagues.—Lachmann needed no introduction to the Austrian tradition at the beginning of the decade.[2] During the late 1920s and early 1930s, his tutor, Emil Kauder, led Lachmann to augment his acquaintance with Menger's works with the study of Hayek and others. They provided him with a solid grounding in the philosophy and method underlying the Austrian approach.[3]

It is this very foundation which has led Lachmann to criticize the Austrian theory of the business cycle. Like any school, the Austrians have their disciples to whom the phrase "sympathetic criticism" is a contradiction in terms. An examination of Ludwig Lachmann's observation on the business-cycle theory should, however, illuminate the sense in which both his sympathies with, and his criticisms of, that theory flow from his staunch adherence to the philosophy and method of the Austrian School.

Even if Lachmann describes himself as "somewhat skeptical" of the theory, he was and is much more its supporter than critic.[4] The theory's causal-genetic method may be its principal attraction, but the characteristic which made it uniquely appealing to Lachmann was its emphasis on the heterogeneity of capital. This attribute and its implications constitute a standard by which all theories of fluctuation are to be judged and, in most cases, found wanting.

One aspect of the causal-genetic method, however, explains Lachmann's skepticism. Unlike the positivist method espoused by Friedman,[5] the Austrian method cannot dismiss the realism of assumptions.[6] Lachmann approved of the internal logic of the Austrians' theory of fluctuations, but he expressed doubts about both the generality and accuracy of some of the empirical assumptions in the theory. Specifically, he criticized its assumptions about how agents form expectations and its slighting of technological change.

It was important also, Lachmann felt, to emphasize that the Austrian theory was not intended, nor suited, to explain every fluctuation.[7] Some of what readers might consider criticisms of the theory were simply Lachmann's efforts to identify its place in the broader class of theories of fluctuation. In this category are his discussions of "weak booms" and of "secondary depressions."

CIRCUMSCRIBING THE THEORY: THE WEAK BOOM AND THE SECONDARY DEPRESSION

The relevance of a causal-genetic investigation depends on the empirical validity of the assumptions on which it is based. The validity of the "assumptions" underlying the core of Austrian economics cannot be doubted without philosophical absurdity, so its advocates may be right to call them axioms. The analysis of a process as complex as a business cycle, though, requires the repeated specification of empirical preconditions which, however reasonable they seem, can hardly make this claim.

These preconditions, Lachmann argues, have accurately characterized economies in the past.[8] Neither they, nor the theory of fluctuation based on them, is incredible. But the study of aggregate fluctuations should not be restricted to such circumstances. Another type of fluctuation is possible and important. Lachmann calls it the "weak boom."

The Austrian theory is a theory of a "strong boom" which terminates in supply bottlenecks and rising costs. But Lachmann explains, quoting Hicks, that " 'weak booms . . . die by working themselves out' and . . . lend themselves to an underconsumptionist explanation. . . ."[9]

He does not seem to be quite sure how likely weak booms are. His doubt of the relevance of the Austrian "strong boom" theory to modern economies may suggest support for the "weak boom" theory[10] He is unique among Austrians differing sharply with Rothbard, Mises, and Hayek, in identifying "America from 1929 to 1932" as "a prominent example" of a "weak boom which ended when consumption failed to keep in step with production."[11] Identifying the most famous downturn in modern history with the underconsumptionist theory would seem to infuse it with considerable significance, but Lachmann has also asserted that "underconsumption crises are not impossible, but they are unlikely to be frequent."[12] Furthermore, certain strong-boom problems arising from capital complementarity may be "to the untrained observer ... indistinguishable from 'lack of effective demand'."[13]

These observations hardly leave a clear impression of Lachmann's belief in the relevance of consumption-led booms and upper turning points characterized by inadequate consumption. But he does not consider them absurd. This issue, on which Lachmann agrees with Keynes, is not unappreciated by other Austrians.[14] Like Hayek's theory of the quotient,[15] Lachmann's works demonstrate his willingness to embrace multiplier-accelerator types of cumulative processes, in which in periods of widespread idleness of resources a rise in consumption demand may stimulate investment because the latter is temporarily untrammelled by problems of rising cost and scarcity. He rejected, of course, rigid quantitative linkages. Furthermore, perhaps partly to make sure that his support of the possibility of such a process was not misunderstood, Lachmann joined Hayek in defending the Austrian theory against the charge that it worked only under full employment. Hayek vigorously attacked its principal challenger as working only under full *unemployment*.[16] Lachmann added that the critical requirement for the operation of Keynes's theory, with its homogeneous resources, was the uniform scarcity of factors; it worked relatively well either when all were unemployed or in periods approaching the full employment of all factors.[17]

The simple implications of Lachmann's comments is that a realistic appraisal of the Austrian theory requires awareness that economic fluctuations can have other causes, as does the weak boom. Another problem of general fluctuation which Lachmann felt was underappreciated in Austrian works was the so-called "secondary depression."

Both the weak and strong booms, cumulative processes of upswing and upper turning point, culminate in "primary depression." Once a down turn is begun, an economy with a modern fractional-reserve financial system may find its woes exacerbated by the collapse of financial institutions and the resulting deflation of credit and money.[18] To many who discuss "secondary depressions," this constitutes an essentially separable aspect of the primary depression, of questionable benefit and great cost. It is the hallmark of the monetarist history of the Great Depression, for example, that short circuiting the secondary deflation of the early 1930s could have prevented several further years of depressed activity.

Ludwig Lachmann was concerned about the problem of secondary depression. Indeed, he notes that after moving to England in 1933 and becoming Hayek's research assistant,

> I actually worked on secondary depressions ... the process of depression which goes beyond any kind of primary maladjustment. That is to say, that kind of depression that would not be an adjustment process in the Hayekian sense. It was by then (1933) admitted that a depression of this kind could develop and I think everybody admitted that by 1933 the world was in a process of secondary depression.[19]

An article published in 1939 provides reason for Lachmann's special interest. Raising a point recently rediscovered by Auburn University's Don Bellante, Lachmann asserts that the Austrian theory of the strong boom contains no theory of unemployment.[20] Only by linking the "primary crisis," which is "their object of study," to bank deflation and secondary depression does the theory generate "recession in total output and employment."[21] It is not clear that Lachmann is quite fair in this judgment, although explaining how the traditional Austrian primary depression generates unemployment requires the introduction of transaction costs in labor markets, or of structural unemployment caused by distortions of a *human*-capital structure, which are certainly not made explicit in the theory. But to the extent to which he believed it necessary to explain unemployment, his interest in the secondary depression during the 1930s can hardly be considered remarkable.

In 1939 Lachmann noted that "a cumulative process of contraction which nothing but public action will stop, may actually occur."[23] "By 1940," he wrote then, "we have all learned that an 'elastic' monetary system is likely to engender forces which, once our mechanism is set on its downward course, are apt to push it further and further."[24] In his 1951 review of Mises's *Human Action*, Lachmann differentiates Mises from Hicks by noting that "Professor Mises is less afraid than Dr. Hicks of the effects of secondary deflation. . . . This is perhaps a matter for judgment from case to case rather than for theoretical generalisation."[25]

It also suggests that Mises and Hicks may have preferred different policies for dealing with a secondary depression and raises the issue of Lachmann's own advice. His note that "nothing but public action will stop" the downward cumulative process sounds like a clear authorization of a Keynes-Leijonhufvud stimulation of effective demand to bump the economy back into its self-correcting corridor.[26] Seventeen years later, he still was convinced that "such an underconsumptionist crisis may degenerate into a cumulative depression. If so, a budget deficit may help."[27]

This recommendation of a pump-priming fiscal policy to terminate a secondary depression, as tentative as it was, set Lachmann apart from other Austrians and placed him much nearer the mainstream. In 1977 he recounts a letter written in 1932 to the *London Times* by Hayek, Robbins, and Arnold Plant "saying that anything the government did by way of public works or similar methods would only make things worse . . . the 'Austrians' seemed to be committed to a policy of continuous deflation whatever happened."[28] Lachmann interprets this, however, as their disbelief that a secondary depression was in progress, implying that they might not have offered this advice had they accurately identified the situation.[29]

On the issue of monetary policy, the record of Lachmann's advice is even less clear. There are Austrians who prefer not to separate a downturn into primary and secondary aspects, considering the induced deflation and consequent acceleration of the downward cumulative process a healthy quickening of the economy's adjustment. Any monetary measures to stem the deflation would be ill advised.

Unlike these Austrians, Lachmann considered the secondary depression something different, and conceptually separable, from the process of adjustment demanded by the failure of the boom. He firmly agreed with other Austrians that malinvestments engendered by the strong boom would have to be "regrouped." But it is not clear that he agreed that this was facilitated by deflation and secondary depression and that therefore the proper policy was to permit or even to encourage the collapse of the fractional-reserve financial system.

Taking a tough line in 1937, he asserted that "a rigorous banking policy which compels the banks to undertake their immediate reconstruction after the outbreak of the crisis (and which, incidentally, would enforce the early closing of all those banks where this is no more possible) would appear to be the most appropriate method of averting the horrors of the cumulative process of depression."[30] Lachmann's examination of "Investment and Costs of Production," in 1938, is, in part, a thoughtful study of problems of monetary policy, but it does not deal with secondary depressions.[31] In 1940, writing under Hayek as part of his work on secondary depressions, Lachmann makes grudging reference to "whatever the merits of such a ["Cheap Money"] policy in depression or during the early stages of revival" may be. . . .[32]

By 1956, he was trying to devise a monetary policy, apparently credit allocations and restraints, which would complement the imperfections in various aspects of the capital market. "[T]here is much to be said for a 'selective' credit policy which need not be arbitrary if it merely reflects the degree of imperfection of the capital market which is the natural product of the past record of success and failure of individual firms." A " 'severe' credit policy is required" in some sectors to pressure the owners of certain types of capital goods to release them from their current employment, Lachmann suggests, but "a credit policy sufficiently severe to 'crack open' the tougher kind of unsuccessful capital combinations may discourage investment in the critical sectors of the economy."[33] It is not clear how one obtains information, from some source other than the market itself, about whose capital combinations need cracking, and it puzzlingly suggests the kind of industrial policy which finds no home in any Austrian's work. Lachmann's observations demonstrate his sensitivity to problems of intersectoral capital rearrangements, but convey little useful information about policy. Thirty years later, it seems increasingly apparent that the consistent observation of Austrian principles invariably leads to privately provided competing currencies.

THE AUSTRIAN THEORY OF THE STRONG BOOM

Lachmann pays special attention to theories of the "strong boom," largely because problems associated with the heterogeneity of capital are more serious and pervasive here than under weak boom conditions. He identifies only two theories which have "been worked out with any degree of precision":[34] that of Hicks, and that of the Austrians. Those who, familiar with his criticisms of the latter theory, consider him its foe should note that it serves as the standard by which Hicks's is judged, and that perhaps its central feature—the consistent incorporation of capital heterogeneity—is the principal aspect which sets it above Hicks's.

In his own work on capital, Lachmann has upheld a Mengerian approach and expressed disappointment that the development of Austrian capital theory followed certain decidedly non-Mengerian aspects of Böhm-Bawerk's theory.[35] "The Austrian theory is essentially dynamic," he observed in 1940, and "any appearance to the contrary in its first presentation was really due to the upbringing of its protagonists to whom Walrasian equilibrium conditions appeared as the natural jumping-off ground for all excursions into the real world."[36] This refers specifically to Wicksell, who in some respects synthesized the theories of Böhm-Bawerk and Walras,[37] but it could as well be aimed at Hayek's equilibrium models of *Prices and Production.* What is important is that Lachmann found general-equilibrium models unnecessary to process analysis: "in process analysis . . . we need no such assumption . . . that in the 'real world' there does exist a 'tendency towards equilibrium.' "[38] He appears to side with the thoroughly catallistic Arthur W. Marget in holding that the effects of changes can be analyzed by considering their probable ephemerality, without any assumption that either the initial or final position is one of general equilibrium.

As Leijonhufvud has pointed out, the class of Wicksellian theories in which a divergence between the market rate of interest and some sort of natural rate leads to an inequality between *ex ante* saving and investment is quite large.[39] It certainly can be said to include the Austrian theory, although both Hayek and Lachmann noted that the impossibility of developing quantitative measures of "saving" and "investment" outside of general equilibrium makes the formulation of a business-cycle theory which either omits or deemphasizes the role of a divergence between these aggregates highly desirable.[40] Mises preferred to refer to the theory as one of "malinvestment," avoiding the quantitative implications of "overinvestment."[41]

The phenomenon of a business class acting on observed market data which temporarily have ceased to reflect "real" or "natural" preferences is common to saving-investment theories. Despite Hayek's famous explications of how market prices convey information about these preferences, and the causality attributed to policy-induced distortions of this information in the Austrian business-cycle theory, Lachmann wisely chose to emphasize a more detailed and more uniquely Austrian aspect of the theory. "The specifically 'Austrian' element, the link with the theory of capital, has now to be brought into our picture."[42]

Subject to certain qualifications, including one about the "elasticity of expectations" which will be discussed soon, monetary policy which adds to the supply of funds offered to businesses—one of the Austrian theory's empirical preconditions—shifts the supply of loanable funds to the right, lowering their price (the market loan rate) and increasing the quantity of funds loaned. Exactly how the entrepreneurs react to this, Lachmann insists, depends upon their subjective interpretation of the event. Whether or not they resist the temptation, there is a tendency for them to rearrange their productive resources in a manner which takes greater advantage of the new situation.

The capital goods producers have on hand exhibit what Lachmann calls "multiple specificity," usable in a limited variety of ways. Each of these alternative uses requires different cooperating, complementary resources. Before the entrepreneur commits his available capital goods and relatively nonspecific resources to a particular production plan, he must judge the probable future availability of the complementary resources which the successful completion of the plan requires, but which he currently lacks. It is at this stage that market data enter his decision in a critical way.

Lachmann interprets market data, particularly rates of interest, as indicators of the economy's capacity for economic progress.[43] Progress, he observes, normally involves greater degrees of complexity in the combination of capital goods, higher degrees of specificity, and larger numbers of required complementary factors. Lachmann distinguishes between complementarity within a production plan—a simple but familiar example of which would be the relations of complementarity among inputs in a neoclassical production function—and "structural" complementarity—the catallactic relations between the entrepreneur and his suppliers and customers which are just as much required if the plan is to succeed. Economic progress generally involves increasing complexity in both types of complementarity: more complex production plans which are increasingly dependent on highly specific inputs, and greater reliance on market relations to supply a wider range of inputs and to facilitate the sale of increasingly specialized products.

He connects his observations to the Austrian theory of the business cycle by interpreting that theory as an explanation of widespread entrepreneurial error about the economy's capacity for economic progress. "Thus anything which gives a wrong picture of resources available for investment, and of the speed at which the economy as a whole can expand, will lead to wrong decisions about the degree of specialization of the new capital."[44]

Better-known accounts of the business-cycle theory are couched in terms of time preference and voluntary saving, in higher stages of production, and even in degrees of roundaboutness. The skilled expositor of the theory will readily be able to retell Lachmann's story using these more familiar terms. In his discussion of economic progress, Lachmann himself is quick to point out "the strong resemblance of our argument to Boehm-Bawerk's . . ."[45] The value of such a translation is, however, open to some question. It may be that Lachmann's argument requires these concepts, or some of them, as a foundation and that it is incomplete without them. Or it may be that his discussion goes beyond, in complexity and richness, what can be conveyed by these terms; associating his theory with them may have value largely to the historian of doctrine. Lachmann properly expresses respect for many of Böhm-Bawerk's insights on capital, and Hayek's strong and positive influence over his career during the 1930s is undeniable. Yet both of these writers—the latter, at least, largely for expository simplicity—employed primitive concepts which have brought Austrian theories of capital and the business cycle much scorn. One of the virtues of Lachmann's presentation is that it is offered as an application of his own development of Austrian capital theory, which—30 years since its publication—is still "state of the art." A good case can be made that to insist that the insights of Ludwig Lachmann's theory of capital be forced into simplified categories used in earlier expositions constitutes, more than anything, expensive nostalgia.

"We have seen that in a strong boom entrepreneurs, deluded by factor costs which are not equilibrium costs and therefore can say nothing about available supply, embark on investment projects the resources for which do not exist and cannot be created by a transfer of resources from consumption."[46] The Austrian upper turning point is identified by rising consumption. The misled entrepreneurs will experience this largely in the form of the rising costs of the complementary factors they are still attempting to assemble. The rise of these costs gradually dissipates the profits that they originally envisioned.

This forces each entrepreneur to rethink his plans—a phrase which hardly conveys the psychological turmoil and panic which probably accompanies this realization—and to examine alternative uses for the capital goods he has managed to accumulate. Lachmann joins Rothbard and others in highlighting the special problems arising because mistaken overestimating of the economy's capacity for progress involves the production of capital goods which are highly specific to the envisioned plans. This greater specificity of capital goods imposes an asymmetry: by contrast, mistaken *underestimations* of the potential for progress produce errors and losses, but because the complexity of the associated production plans and the specificities of the capital goods are relatively low, the scope for regrouping without great loss is much wider.

Ludwig Lachmann's interest in the Austrian theory of the business cycle stems largely from its ready ability to incorporate the insights of a sophisticated capital theory like his own. But the applicability of that theory is not limited to the Austrian "strong boom." Even in weak booms, and in the depression following their demise, "capital regrouping is just as necessary."[47]

If the virtues of the Austrian theory are many, Lachmann is especially concerned about the realism of one of its empirical specifications. Under what conditions will the monetary authority be able to reduce the rate of interest relevant to the plans of the economy's entrepreneurs? Both the authority's ability to reduce the rate and the entrepreneurs' response to it depend on expectations.

This aspect of the Austrian theory has never been thoroughly investigated. What is required is a thorough knowledge of financial institutions and instruments and the channels through which firms obtain funds. Does the evolution of financial sophistication and the burgeoning of new instruments increase the relevance of the Austrian theory or push it farther into economic history? J. Stuart Wood has paid some attention to these innovations.[48] Much remains to be done. Once these questions are solved, Austrian theorists must examine more closely the decision processes actually followed by corporate planners.[49]

Ludwig Lachmann is a tireless exponent of the subjective nature of expectations. Determined neither exogenously nor by mechanical calculation from market data, an agent's expectations result from a mental processing of that data and a range of other considerations the precise nature of which we must—for philosophical reasons—be ignorant. As carefully as we may be able to describe an observable state, we will never be able to deduce with certainty the different agents' interpretations of it, nor, therefore, its effect on their expectations and actions.

There is some doubt that the Austrian cycle theory takes the problem of the formation of expectations sufficiently seriously. In 1943, Lachmann's provocative "The Role of Expectations in Economics as a Social Science" expressed this doubt.[50] Discussing Hicks's "elasticity of expectations," Lachmann noted that several writers argue that interest expectations are inelastic—that is, an observed change in the rate of interest, if it can be achieved at all, leads agents to expect a reversal.[51] In this view, banking policy cannot be applied to alter the long-term rate of interest.[52] A slight rise would lead to the expectation of an imminent fall, which, through the usual speculative process, would quickly return the rate to its original level.

Lachmann highlights the relevance of such a concept to the Austrian theory of the business cycle. He notes that if that theory's monetary authority is to be able to reduce the long-term rate of interest for a period of time long enough to produce entrepreneurial response, participants in the capital market must hold "elastic expectations." They must, at least, permit the rate to fall and not expect it to rise again soon. The market's Hicksian coefficient must be positive if the rate is to fall, and non-negative if it is to stay down. Lachmann pulls no punches:

> Without fairly elastic expectations there can therefore be no crisis of the Austro-Wicksellian type. . . . Such a gullible capital market we should expect to find in an economy the structure of which is still highly fluid and in which long-run forces have not yet had time to take shape. We tentatively suggest that such a state of expectations may be typical of an economy in the early stages of industrialisation, or of an economy undergoing "rejuvenation" owing to rapid technical progress.[53]

Ludwig von Mises responded, calling attention to his own suggestion that businessmen may learn, from trade-cycle theory, to avoid responding so readily to changes in long-term rates. They may develop increasingly inelastic expectations which limit the relevance of the Austrian cycle theory. But Mises doubts whether most businessmen understand these implications, and hypothesizes that they will continue to act on the basis of observed market data without incorporating knowledge of consequences of past credit expansions into their expectations.[54]

Mises and his followers have a point. It is impossible to determine whether a fluctuation in market data arose from "monetary" or "real" changes, even if one knows that monetary operations have been under way.[55] Entrepreneurs who must contend with temporary fluctuations in tastes have an additional source of confusion, and some are bound to formulate incorrect interest expectations. But the wider significance of this possibility is limited by the operation of a concept Lachmann has emphasized: the more familiar an agent becomes with the facts of inflation and fluctuations of rates of interest, the wider he is likely to set his "practical range," within which fluctuations in the rate of interest are considered normal and have little or no effect on his plans.[56]

If Lachmann wholeheartedly endorses the business-cycle theory's emphasis on heterogeneous capital, with its implications of complementary and substitutability in the context of subjectively formulated plans, he was less than enthusiastic about the credit market story of causality, as his notes on expectations suggest. He has expressed some interest in a story of economic fluctuations which incorporate his perceptive theory of capital but omit the rather questionable chapter on monetary causality.

In his 1977 interview, he expressed the hope that work would emerge on the relation between the Austrian theory of the cycle and the process of technical progress.[57] But there are reasons for skepticism. Technical progress often involves changes in knowledge, rather than capital deepening with already-known techniques. Certainly either type of progress calls for capital regrouping in which patterns of complementarity are *different*, but when there is a change in the knowledge of technique one hardly has any a priori warrant for judging that the patterns of plan or structural complementarity must necessarily be more complex. (This brings to mind the debates about whether new technology necessarily requires "more roundabout" production processes.) Lachmann seems critical of the Austrian theory because "there is no reference whatever to technical progress," and observes that "it is surely clear that in the real world it does matter."[58]

Is this a call for turning the Austrian theory into a " 'comprehensive' trade cycles theory" the day of which, he had argued in 1956, "is long past"? The problem may be important, but increasing specificity and complexity of complementary relationships, a crucial element of the cycle theory, is not a necessary attribute of technical progress. And it is anything but clear that "Austrian business-cycle theory" without its monetary causation any longer deserves the name.

CONCLUSION

Ludwig Lachmann may be better known as a critic than as a supporter of the business-cycle theory. His record suggests that he be considered a sympathetic critic. The theory's principal features are strongly appealing, and his targets have often been precisely those aspects of it which strain the credulity of one who is wholly committed to the philosophy and method underlying the Austrian school. No scholar serious about this approach can take Lachmann's observations and criticisms lightly. Whether they challenge or confirm existing convictions, the thoughtful consideration of his views is bound to produce a better understanding of the validity and limitations of this famous element of the Austrian tradition.

NOTES

1. Walter E. Grinder, "In Pursuit of the Subjectivist Paradigm," in Ludwig M. Lachmann, *Capital, Expectations, and the Market Process* (Kansas City: Sheed Andrews & McMeel, 1977), pp. 9–11.
2. Ibid., p. 13.
3. Ibid., pp. 7–9.
4. "An Interview with Ludwig Lachmann," *Austrian Economics Newsletter*, 1 (fall 1978), pp. 1ff.
5. Milton Friedman, "The Methodology of Positive Economics," in *Essays in Positive Economics* (Chicago: The University of Chicago Press, 1953), pp. 3–43.
6. "An Interview with Ludwig Lachmann," op. cit., p. 15: ". . . contrary to the Chicagoans, we have to be very careful about what assumptions we are making because if we have made assumptions which are unrealistic, we will get results which are unrealistic. In Chicago they don't seem to be interested in what assumptions they make as long as they have the possibility of prediction."
7. Ludwig M. Lachmann, *Capital and its Structure* (Kansas City: Sheed Andrews & McMeel, 1978), pp. 113, 101.
8. Ludwig M. Lachmann, "A Reconsideration of the Austrian Theory of Industrial Fluctuations," *Economica*, 7 (May 1940), reprinted in Lachmann, *Capital, Expectations, and the Market Process*, op. cit., p. 282: ". . . the Austrian theory when confronted with evidence gathered from nineteenth-century fluctuations, comes out well, very well indeed."
9. Lachmann, *Capital and its Structure*, op. cit., p. 101.
10. Lachmann, "A Reconsideration of the Austrian Theory of Industrial Fluctuations," op. cit., p. 284; Lachmann, "The Role of Expectations in Economics as a Social Science," *Economica*, 10 (February 1943), reprinted in *Capital, Expectations, and the Market Process*, op. cit., p. 79.
11. Lachmann, *Capital and its Structure*, op. cit., p. 113; Lachmann, "A Reconsideration of the Austrian Theory of Industrial Fluctuations," op. cit., p.283.
12. Ludwig M. Lachmann, "The Science of Human Action," *Economica*, 18 (November 1951), reprinted in Lachmann, *Capital, Expectations, and the Market Process*, op. cit., p. 106.
13. Lachmann, *Capital and its Structure*, op cit., p. 118.
14. Lachmann once referred to Keynes's "general trade cycle theory," how-

ever, as "an over-investment theory." L. M. Lachmann and F. Snapper, "Commodity Stocks in the Trade Cycle," *Economica*, 5 (November 1938), pp. 452–3.

15. F. A. Hayek, *Profits, Interest and Investment* (New York: Augustus M. Kelley, 1975), pp. 19, 49ff.
16. F. A. Hayek, "Personal Recollections of Keynes and the 'Keynesian Revolution,'" *The Oriental Economist* (January 1966), reprinted in *A Tiger by the Tail* (London: Institute for Economic Affairs, 1972), p. 103: ". . . he based his own argument on what may be called the assumption of full unemployment, i.e., the assumption that there normally existed unused reserves of *all* factors and commodities."
17. Ludwig M. Lachmann, "Some Notes on Economic Thought, 1933–1953," *South African Journal of Economics*, 22 (March 1954), reprinted in *Capital, Expectations, and the Market Process*, op. cit., p. 136, Ludwig M. Lachmann, *Macro-economic Thinking and the Market Economy* (London: Institute for Economic Affairs, 1973), p. 50.
18. Lachmann, *Capital and its Structure*, op. cit., p. 120.
19. "An Interview with Ludwig Lachmann," op. cit., p. 1.
20. Don Bellante, "The Neutrality of Money and Labor Market Distortions: Hayek vs. Friedman," unpublished, 1984.
21. L. M. Lachmann, "On Crisis and Adjustment," *Review of Economics and Statistics*, 21 (May 1939), p. 67.
22. Ibid., p. 68.
23. Ibid., pp. 62–63.
24. Lachmann, "A Reconsideration of the Austrian Theory of Industrial Fluctuations," op. cit., p. 275. By 1956, Lachmann was more sensitive to the mischief that mechanical analogies could cause in the wrong hands: "The reader, we trust, will not expect to be told of an 'adjustment mechanism'; in the realm of human action there is no such thing." Lachmann, *Capital and its Structure*, op. cit., p. 119
25. Lachmann, "The Science of Human Action," op. cit., p. 107.
26. Axel Leijonhufvud, "Effective Demand Failures," *Swedish Economic Journal* (March 1973), reprinted in *Information and Coordination* (New York: Oxford University Press, 1981), pp.109ff.
27. Lachmann, *Capital and its Structure*, op. cit., pp. 125–6.
28. "An Interview with Ludwig Lachmann," op. cit., p. 2.
29. Ibid., p. 3.
30. Ludwig M. Lachmann, "Uncertainty and Liquidity-Preference," *Economica*, 4 (August 1937), p. 308.
31. Ludwig M. Lachmann, "Investment and Costs of Production," *American Economic Review*, 28 (September 1938), p. 481.
32. Lachmann, "A Reconsideration of the Austrian Theory of Industrial Fluctuations," op. cit., p. 280.
33. Lachmann, *Capital and its Structure*, op. cit., p. 122.
34. Ibid., p. 112.
35. Ludwig M. Lachmann, "Sir John Hicks as a Neo-Austrian," *South African Journal of Economics*, 41 (September 1973), reprinted in *Capital, Expectations, and the Market Process*, op. cit., pp. 261–6, especially p. 264: "It was not personal caprice that prompted Menger's dislike of Böhm-

Bawerk's capital theory and Walras's general equilibrium system; it was a conviction that in both a false picture of uniformity disguised the diversity of the world." The American monetary theorist Arthur W. Marget also urged that the profession adopt a Mengerian, rather than a Böhm-Bawerkian, approach to the study of interest and capital; see John B. Egger, *The Monetary Economics of Arthur William Marget* (unpublished doctoral dissertation, New York University,1985).

36. Lachmann, "A Reconsideration of the Austrian Theory of Industrial Fluctuations," op. cit., p. 269.
37. Ibid., p. 268.
38. Lachmann, *Capital and its Structure*, op. cit., p. 40.
39. Axel Leijonhufvud, "The Wicksell Connection: Variations on a Theme," in *Information and Coordination*, op. cit.
40. Lachmann, *Capital and its Structure*, op. cit., p. 114.
41. Lachmann asserts that the Austrian theory cannot "rest upon a stationary model," as critics have claimed, because "saving and investment play a prominent part in it, while of course in a stationary society there can be no such thing." (*Capital and its Structure*, op. cit., p. 114.) The saving and investment in the Austrian theory, however, are gross, not net. A stationary society with a capital stock will have to maintain it, engaging in gross saving and investment simply to remain stationary.
42. Lachmann, *Capital and its Structure*, op. cit., p. 117.
43. Ibid., p. 118.
44. Ibid., p. 119.
45. Ibid., p. 82.
46. Ibid., p. 117.
47. Ibid., p. 125.
48. J. Stuart Wood, *Entrepreneurship and the Co-ordination of Expectations in the Stock Market* (unpublished doctoral dissertation, New York University, n.d.); J. Stuart Wood, "Some Refinements in Austrian Trade-cycle Theory," *Managerial and Decision Economics*, vol. 5, no. 3 (September 1984), pp. 141–9.
49. For a discussion of how the financial management techniques of capital budgeting are relevant to the Austrian business-cycle theory, see John B. Egger, "Shifting Triangles: A Modern Austrian Theory of the Business Cycle," unpublished paper presented at Eastern Economics Association meeting, New York, March 1984.
50. Reprinted in *Capital, Expectations, and the Market Process*, op. cit., pp. 65–80.
51. J. R. Hicks, *Value and Capital* (Oxford: Clarendon Press, 1946), p. 205. By Hicks's definition, a zero elasticity would have agents expecting that the rate of interest would simply be lodged at its current level. Negative elasticity would find agents expecting the rate of interest to come back down, or go back up, perhaps to its original level. Positive elasticity would find them projecting its trend, expecting it to continue up or down. The simple terms "elastic" and "inelastic" are not adequate when the coefficient can be positive or negative.
52. Lachmann, "The Role of Expectations in Economics as a Social Science," op. cit., pp. 76–7.

53. Ibid., p. 79.
54. Ludwig von Mises, " 'Elastic Expectations' and the Austrian Theory of the Trade Cycle," *Economica* (August 1943), p. 251.
55. Arthur W. Marget, *The Theory of Prices* (New York: Prentice-Hall, 1942), vol. II, p. 69: "... the whole point of [Menger's] own distinction was to emphasize the fact that both 'monetary' and 'non-monetary' factors are of such far-reaching importance for price formation that one must be continually on one's guard against specious attempts to explain a given set of price movements in terms of either 'monetary' or 'non-monetary' factors alone."
56. Ludwig M. Lachmann, "A Nøte on the Elasticity of Expectations," *Economica*, 12 (November 1945), p. 249.
57. "An Interview with Ludwig Lachmann," op. cit., p. 11.
58. Ibid., p. 11.

6 Spontaneous Order and the Subjectivity of Expectations: A Contribution to the Lachmann-O'Driscoll Problem

ULRICH FEHL

The first, and most prominent, feature of Austrian economics is a radical subjectivism, today no longer confined to human preferences but extended to expectations.

Ludwig M. Lachmann

I THE LACHMANN-O'DRISCOLL PROBLEM

Littlechild's article "Radical Subjectivism or Radical Subversion?" ends up with the following question:

> Shackle's subjectivism is clearly sympathetic to Austrians, and constitutes a subversion of neoclassical economics quite as radical as the work of Keynes. But is Shackle *too* subjectivist even for Austrians? If we have understood correctly his emphasis on the role of imagination, he calls into question not only their concept of the market process, but even their very definition of economics. Is Shackle's message to Austrians merely one of radical subjectivism, or is it one of radical subversion too?[1]

This alternative is but the radical version of the issue O'Driscoll raises in his article "Spontaneous Order and the Coordination of Economic Activities" with respect to Ludwig M. Lachmann's conception of the market process.[2] While emphasizing the idea of a "spontaneous order" to be common belief in the tradition of Austrian economics he seems to be uneasy about Lachmann who could possibly deny this position, being at least unclear in this respect.[3] The crucial point is whether or not the market process has to have a strong tendency towards an equilibrium if there should result a spontaneous order. Although the latter is not identified with equilibrium, both notions are brought into close connection, "spontaneous order" thus meaning a state of the economy "near" equilibrium:

> If the propensity to discover opportunities is "inseparable from our insight that human beings act purposefully', then we must likewise acknowledge a *tendency* toward equilibrium in all markets. *A fortiori* there exist strong tendencies toward an overall or general equilibrium *at each moment*. Individuals are, then, constantly revising their plans in a way that brings them, into *greater uniformity*. [Emphasis added.] This latter proposition, when thus phrased in dynamic terms, does embody the principle of an undesigned order.[4]

Although conceding that Lachmann "nowhere *explicitly* asserts the contrary position, viz., that we have no grounds for believing that market participants will discover and exploit profitable opportunities,"[5] O'Driscoll tries to make clear that Lachmann does not stick to the notion of the market as a spontaneous order in the just described sense.[6] This interpretation primarily rests on Lachmann's conception of the subjectivity and therefore, in principle, diversity of expectations:

> Experience shows in the real world of disequilibrium different persons will typically hold different expectations about the same future event. If so, at best one person's expectation can be confirmed and all other expectations will be disappointed. . . . The beacon that had been designed to keep entrepreneurs from straying from the narrow path of convergent expectations turns out, on most nights, to be rather dim.[7]

Thus it is the very diversity of subjective expectations that excludes the "greater conformity" O'Driscoll has stressed as a prerequisite for the "spontaneous order" in his sense, i.e., the "near-equilibrium" sense.

In realizing this difficulty O'Driscoll draws the conclusion that Austrian economists, in advocating the doctrine of a "spontaneous order," are faced with a serious problem.[8] If it is impossible to reconcile divergent expectations with a strong tendency of market forces towards an equilibrium one has either to abandon the notion of spontaneous order or, alternatively, to belittle the importance of conflicting expectations. Indeed, O'Driscoll tends to interpret Lachmann as being at least implicitly an adherent of the first alternative while he himself argues in favor of the latter.

In assessing Lachmann's position, O'Driscoll states: "There is no denying the autonomy of the human mind, but one is reluctant to follow Lachmann in his apparent conclusion that we can say nothing about the likelihood that individuals will make consistent and coordinated decisions in the face of new knowledge. If anything, he seems to be saying that they will *not coordinate plans*. [Emphasis added.]"[9] Or, "Indeed, I suspect that there is no coordination in the conventional sense in Lachmann's system. For him apparently, *ex ante* plans bear no relation to *ex post* reality. There is not even reason to believe that actors will move in the right direction in correcting past errors."[10] In order to eschew these conclusions Lachmann has seemingly drawn, O'Driscoll tries to reassess and delimit the importance of divergent expectations:

> Do different and disparate individuals have a common reaction to shared experience? We certainly would not want to say they always do, or there would be little sense in referring to "individuals". Yet, there are obvious cases in which people do react to shared experiences in the same or similar ways: the perception of a fire in an enclosed room will lead to virtually everyone's making for an exit. Each person could form a reasonable expectation about what the others will do.[11]

According to O'Driscoll the same is true with respect to entrepreneurs: "Apparently individual entrepreneurs, experiencing the same signals and trends will often form similar expectations."[12] It is no surprise that O'Driscoll refuses to make, as Lachmann does, a fundamental distinction between knowledge and expectation: "In his most recent work, Lachmann notes that Mises, Hayek, and Kirzner have emphasized the diffusion of knowledge in the market process. But he denies that the market can diffuse expectations in the same way. I believe the distinction between knowledge and expectations is a spurious one."[13] On the whole it seems to be O'Driscoll's firm conviction that the problem of divergent expectations is overcome by equilibrating market forces strong enough to establish a spontaneous order near market equilibrium in the Hayekian sense.

II THE MARKET PROCESS AND ITS ORDER

Both escapes from the dilemma—to abandon the notion of a spontaneous order or to deny that there is an essential distinction between knowledge and expectation—are rather inconclusive. But, fortunately, the relationship between a spontaneous order and the diversity of subjective expectations can be analyzed from a completely different point of view. In this view, "spontaneous order" means an order of the market *process* itself which does not rest upon the latter being near the *state of equilibrium.* Being created by the market forces just in distance from equilibrium this "disequilibrium order" has to be assessed an order sui generis. Now, in this context the subjectivity of expectations and their inherent diversity become a productive power, i.e., divergent expectations are no longer an obstacle to the modus operandi of engendering "order." To see this, at first the working of the market process has to be analyzed and the notion of an "order far from equilibrium" has to be established.

The market process can formally be viewed as being propelled by the simultaneous activity of *arbitrage, accumulation* (or decumulation respectively) and *innovation* as its *driving forces*. Although, as a rule, two or all three driving forces are engaged in human actions, it is convenient to keep them separate for analytical purposes. It can be shown that the driving forces of the market refer to and thus depend on each other: Arbitrage is called the activity of comparing and exchange. This activity would come to an end, if all opportunities were discovered and used. Arbitrage only will go on, if it is supplied with new opportunities to be compared; in short, arbitrage refers to innovation. But it refers to accumulation as a driving force, too, because many actions of "arbitrage" can only be executed if production and investment take place. Arbitrage would be without consequences, if accumulation were not set in motion. But accumulation refers to arbitrage, too, being "directionless" without it. Furthermore there has to be reflected a relationship between accumulation and innovation: Without the latter, accumulation would come to a standstill, because of satiation. Again, innovation as a driving force would have no consequences, were it not diffused by accumulation. Finally, innovation as a driving force refers to arbitrage, because only with the help of the latter (taken in a broad sense) one can make out whether something is "new" and it pays to produce and invest.

Already these few remarks should have made clear that the working of the market process cannot be fully understood without regarding the *simultaneous running* of arbitrage, accumulation, and innovation as driving forces. Nevertheless, economists have restricted their endeavour to the analysis of one or two of the driving forces. By focusing on equilibrium states of economic systems neoclassical economists are mainly concerned with the "logic of arbitrage" (within a framework of fully perceived opportunities). Accumulation and innovation only come into the field of vision by means of comparative statics, the simultaneity of driving forces' activities being thus ignored.

Although analyzing the market as a process Austrian economists, at least partly, exclude from consideration innovation as a driving force of the market. As a consequence they are concerned primarily with the equilibrating process being propelled by the driving forces arbitrage (including the perception of opportunities) and accumulation. This process of equilibration, nevertheless, does not come to a standstill, mainly because there is a continuous change in the "data" of the market. This analytical procedure implies that innovation in the last resort has to be treated as an *exogenous* variable, and is thus analyzed incompletely, i.e., only in its consequences.[14] The above-mentioned desideratum of regarding the simultaneous performance of all three driving forces seems to be a desideratum with respect to the Austrians, too.

Schumpeter's analysis, it is true, comprises all of the three driving forces, but in order to show how, as a consequence of an innovation, the existing state of equilibrium is destroyed and transformed into a new equilibrium, he is concerned with the *successive* performance of innovation, arbitrage and accumulation. At least in his early writings, Schumpeter is not engaged in studying a permanent stream of (new) innovations beyond the scope of a somewhat comparative statics.[15]

It is obvious that there must exist a close relationship between the driving forces of the market and entrepreneurship, the entrepreneur being, so to speak, the driving force of the driving forces arbitrage, accumulation, and innovation. Thus, the driving forces arbitrage and accumulation refer to the neoclassical Robbinsian-type of entrepreneurship or—if arbitrage and accumulation are conceived of, more appropriately in somewhat broader terms including the perception of opportunities—to the Mises-Kirzner type of entrepreneur.[16] Innovation as a driving force of the market has to be identified with the activities performed by the Schumpeterian entrepreneur. It suggests itself that economists' refusal to analyze the simultaneous efficacy of *all* driving forces is reflected in the respective selection of a special type of entrepreneur. For the sake of a full understanding of the working of the market process economists should instead take into consideration the whole spectrum of different types of entrepreneurs. At least they should recognize that market-processes are characterized by the simultaneous activity of the Schumpeterian and the Misesian-Kirznerian entrepreneur.[17] Thus some shortcomings of received theory could be overcome.

The main reason for stressing the proposition that all driving forces of the market (or to say it in other words: different types of entrepreneurs) have to be analyzed with regard to being simultaneously at work is the insight that it is just this "concerted action", by which the market process is kept at a (far) distance from the state of equilibrium in the conventional sense: And it is exactly this distance from the state of equilibrium that makes possible the emergence of a structure which implies an order sui generis, to be clearly distinguished from the order of equilibrium or near-equilibrium.[18]

The process and the structure it exhibits can be illustrated by the model of a homogeneous market. By definition producers offer the same product. Assuming the market process to have the properties just described we can take for granted that the producers will apply different production techniques implying different marginal costs (fixed costs being ignored), the differences being attributed to the continuing process (of innovations) itself. As the introduction of new techniques takes place before the diffusion of the older ones has come to an end, there will coexist by the very notion of the continuing process a whole spectrum of production techniques with differential marginal cost. Thus the marginal cost curves of the producers can be organized to construct the supply curve of the market (see Figure 1). Now suppose innovation as a driving force of the market comes to a standstill. After some periods of time have elapsed the market process will come to a standstill, too, because all competitors will have adopted the technique with the lowest marginal cost, the corresponding market supply curve being shown in Figure 2.

Now, it can be inferred from comparing the supply curves in Figure 1 and Figure 2 that the structure being generated by the ongoing process is destroyed in the state of equilibrium. To say it in different words, the structure under discussion is a property of the continuing process keeping the market in a state far from "equilibrium." Or seen from

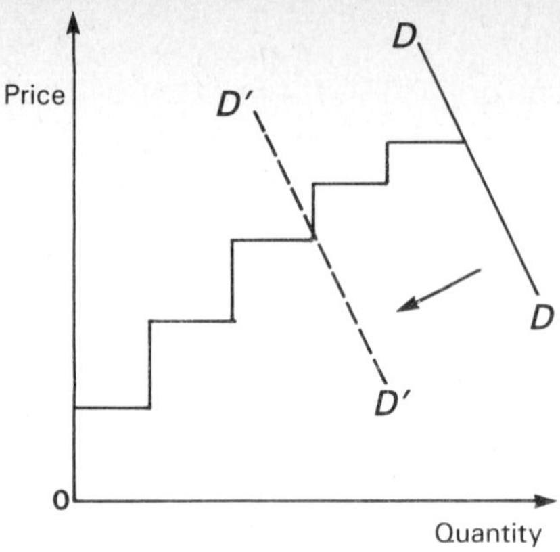

FIGURE 1

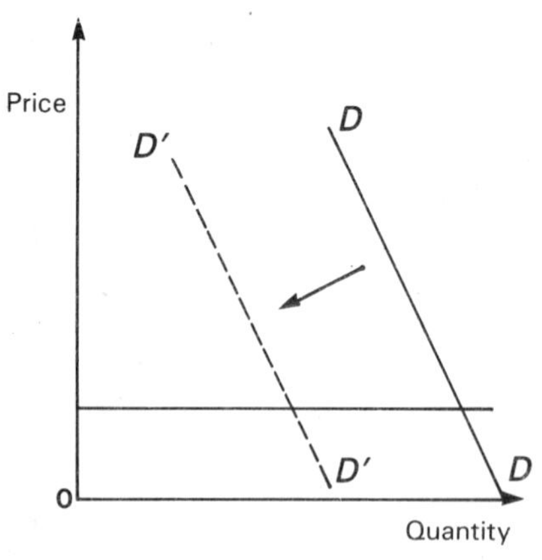

FIGURE 2

another point of view, it is the process which produces *heterogeneity*, while equilibrium is characterized by *homogeneity*.

It is precisely the heterogeneity characterizing the ongoing process which constitutes an order sui generis. To realize this suppose a shift of the market demand curve to the left. In Figure 1 it can easily be seen that some suppliers will become submarginal and will be eliminated.

This leads to the conclusion that the order of the process can be conceived of as a "selection order." The same is not true if the state of "equilibrium" has already been established before the shift of the market demand curve occurs, because in this situation no suppliers can be selected as submarginal, the market does not exhibit an order (of selection) in this case. One is tempted to conclude that the "equilibrium" state of the market in the explained sense reveals a form of "market failure" the market in process does not exhibit.[19] Thus, the latter may be adjudged a higher degree of order in comparison with the market equilibrium or near equilibrium. Seen from this point of view one should be cautious to infer a higher degree of order from the market's approaching the state of equilibrium, being accomplished by the equilibrating forces, a conclusion O'Driscoll obviously draws.[20] Identifying "spontaneous order" with the "order of process" or "selection order" one has to state just the opposite.

It has to be realized that the selection order associated with the market process places at the disposal of entrepreneurs (or market participants in general) a "schedule of orientation" transmitted to them by the working of the price system. The selection profile—together with a system of general rules and other institutions not to be discussed here—constitutes what Hayek has called "*Handelnsordnung*."[21] Thus self organization of individuals in a world of permanent change is rendered possible, without there being necessary any concern to the results of the process or the final state of affairs, i.e., equilibrium, not even in the sense of a vanishing point. This can be seen by the application of the model: If demand shifts—and such shifts have to be judged as regular in an evolving economy—the reallocation of the factors of production can be brought about without any concern to the state of equilibrium or even the approachment of such a state.

Furthermore it should be taken into account that the heterogeneity being generated by the permanent working of the market process is by no means confined to the case of production techniques but applies to the quality of goods and services as well. Permanent creation of new or better goods and their diffusion in the market system produces just another facet of the market's selection order. The same is true with respect to the creation of new markets, the emerging selection order now facilitating orientation for investment processes on a larger scale. These examples may be enough to show how the ongoing market process produces "heterogeneity" and thus the prerequisite for a selection order. But it is important to keep in mind that the selection-profile of the market system as a whole comprises many dimensions.

Finally the fact has to be stressed that the market process does not only generate heterogeneity and thus constitute a selection order and a schedule of orientation, but by its very nature *mobilizes* heterogeneous elements. As all individuals in a market system are allowed to make plans of their own and thus can utilize their skills, differences with regard to skill, creativity, experience, etc., will expand the scope of heterogeneity and thus lead to a refinement of the selection profile. One of these "natural" differences refers to the *expectation* of individuals.[22] The role divergent expectations exert in the context of a spontaneous order—the latter being interpreted after all as an order in a world of disequilibrium, i.e., as a selection order—now can be discussed.

III SPONTANEOUS ORDER AND THE ROLE OF DIVERGENT EXPECTATIONS

The significance of expectations can be derived from the fact that human actions are bound to refer to the future which is notoriously uncertain.[23] Human beings can only produce *imaginations* of future events.[24] Whether these are true or not, depends partially on chance or luck, but on experience and thus judgment, too.[25] As human beings differ in their faculty to judge, and because of their inherent element of subjectivity, imaginations of individuals will be different at least in principle. As a consequence, actions of people will differ, too. But different actions will produce different facts. In short, divergent imaginations and expectations will produce a heterogenous state of affairs. Therefore, a selection order generated by the very diversity of expectations will emerge when the future converts into present time. Clearly, because of the diversity of imaginations and actions not all individuals can have taken the right course. But in the light of the now present knowledge and needs, market participants can choose between the "results" bcing thc outcomes of different actions of different people. Arbitrage as a driving force of the market can work! We can look at this phenomenon to be just a variant of the theorem presented in the market model above.

Subjectivity of expectations (or of imaginations) by no means does exclude learning processes and thus the diffusion of new knowledge. But in the context of an evolving market system the latter does not imply greater uniformity of imaginations. Instead, diversity is maintained, i.e., selection profiles are only shifted in the process.

The diversity of expectations does not lead to a situation in which the actions of the individuals are *coordinated* in the strict sense of the notion, because people will have made "false" plans basing on "wrong" imaginations or expectations, respectively. But this lack of coordination is only the price people have to pay for not being in the position to predict future events. Thus the case in which imaginations and expectations are diverse has to be compared with the case in which expectations are uniform. Then, all of the market participants could, by chance, have formed right imaginations, but the latter can be completely inadequate, too! The diversity of expectations thus serves as a provision that the market will at least be in the middle ground. At least in this sense the generating of a selection order emerging as a consequence of divergent expectations can be interpreted as a coordination process *ex ante*, if one regards the inherent uncertainty of the future. If O'Driscoll cannot make out coordination in the *ex ante* sense in the case of divergent expectations, this may be due to his equilibrium concept of spontaneous order.

Before discussing this point further, it should be regarded that the efficacy of the selection order as a rule does not always imply the elimination of firms. But it should be clear, too, that some firms will have to suffer from losses, while those firms that have formed adequate imaginations will make profits. Thus different impulses to act are transmitted by the market process because the latter exhibits a selection profile. Furthermore, there are cases in which the consequences of divergent expectations and subsequent actions will compensate each other. For example, the entrepreneur with too optimistic expectations will be in the position to utilize his enlarged capacity by the very fact that his pessimistic competitor has underestimated the rate of growth of market demand.

Whereas the existence of divergent expectations or at least a tendency to diversity can be taken for granted, there may be casually more uniformity or homogeneity with regard to both imagination and expectations.[26] As has already been stated, as a rule such a uniformity will prove to be counterproductive for the purposes of coordination, as long as the market process is propelled by the concerted action of arbitrage, accumulation and innovation, i.e., as long as a world of evolution and uncertainty is sustained. Only if innovation has come to a standstill one can conclude, as O'Driscoll does, that a "greater uniformity" of expectations will be a prerequisite for improving the coordination of plans. Outside such a near-equilibrium-situation a greater uniformity of expectations may just lead to discoordination. Imagine, for example, that all suppliers in a market react too optimistically, then errors will not compensate each other, but generate overcapacities. Similar consequences will arise in the case of too pessimistic and uniform expectations. The trade cycle at least can partly be explained by too uniform expectations, and can serve as a further example. Collusion in the market may be possible only, if expectations are sufficiently uniform.[27] Consequently, the full range of possible events is not accounted for and a selection order will not evolve. In this case, the market will reveal expectations to be wrong and at the same time reveal the counterproductivity of uniformity, too.[28]

IV CONCLUSION

Is the subjectivity and diversity of expectations (or better: imaginations) conducive or an obstacle to the emergence of a spontaneous order? This question raised by O'Driscoll obviously is central for economists, especially for Austrian economists stressing the role of subjectivity in general. According to O'Driscoll, Lachmann, by emphasizing the inherent subjectivity and diversity of expectations in the last resort, is bound to negate the idea of a spontaneous order. It can be shown that O'Driscoll's judgment depends on the very notion of spontaneous order. He is right, if the latter has to be interpreted as an "equilibrium"—or "near-equilibrium"—order. In this case, expectations (and imaginations!) by virtue of the equilibrating market forces are bound to become more uniform in the market process, thus favouring the emergence of a spontaneous order in the O'Driscoll sense. (But if the diversity of imagination prevails, spontaneity in this sense is challenged.)

It can be shown, however, that O'Driscoll is forced to treat innovations as exogenous to the market process. Instead, if innovation as a driving force is incorporated in the notion of the market process, the conception of a spontaneous order in the sense of an equilibrium—or near-equilibrium—state has to be replaced by a disequilibrium or selection order, the market process thus being conceived of generating what could be called a "dissipative structure." This structure is the result of the simultaneous working of arbitrage, accumulation, and innovation and can be thought of as being produced by the concerted action of the Schumpeterian and the Misesian-Kirznerian type of entrepreneur. It is exactly this type of the market process Lachmann has in mind:

What emerges from our reflections is an image of the market as a

> particular kind of process, a continuous process without beginning, or end, propelled by the interaction between the forces of equilibrium and the forces of change.[29]

Therefore it is adequate to apply the selection-order variant of the notion of a spontaneous order. Referring to this concept of "order," O'Driscoll's argument breaks down. Lachmann's as well as Shackle's radical subjectivism are not in conflict with the concept of economic and social order. It can be shown, on the contrary, that it is just the very diversity of individual imaginations which—together with general rules in the Hayekian sense and other institutional arrangements—constitutes economic order. Shackle's "kaleidic world" and Austrians' "spontaneous order" thus can be reconciled. There is no radical subversion of Austrian economics by Shackle's radical subjectivism.

NOTES

1. S. C. Littlechild, "Comment: Radical Subjectivism or Radical Subversion?" in *Time, Uncertainty and Disequilibrium* ed. M. J. Rizzo (Lexington, Mass.: Lexington Books, 1979), p. 47.
2. G. P. O'Driscoll, Jr., "Spontaneous Order and the Coordination of Economic Activities," in *New Directions in Austrian Economics* ed. L. M. Spadaro (Kansas City: Sheed Andrews & McMeel, 1976, p. 129.
3. "Those economists who view a system of free exchange—Adam Smith's 'obvious and simple system of natural liberty'—as the solution of the coordination problem in economics face intellectual challenges from at least four sources: first, the continuing challenge of the Keynesian legacy; second, the challenge from what James Buchanan has termed the 'modern Ricardians'; third, the challenge from the new movement for national planning; and finally, the challenge from certain economists in the Austrian school" (O'Driscoll, op. cit., pp. 111–12).
4. O'Driscoll, op. cit., p. 129.
5. O'Driscoll, op. cit., p. 128.
6. In quoting several passages of Lachmann's unpublished paper "Reflections on Hayekian Capital Theory," O'Driscoll demonstrates that Lachmann can indeed be interpreted in this way. For example: "To make confident use of the notion of equilibrium means to imply that the equilibrating forces will always be of sufficient strength to triumph over all obstacles. A skeptic might readily admit that such situations may exist, but he will probably doubt whether they occur with sufficient frequency to warrant our treating as the norm" (op. cit., pp. 128–9). Or: "The human mind is a filter of experience, but each individual's filter is different from every other filter. Divergent expectations are thus as 'natural', a feature of the social landscape, as are divergent tastes" (op. cit., p. 130). Or: "The

future is unknowable, though not unimaginable. Future knowledge cannot be had now, but it can cast its shadow ahead. In each mind, however, the shadow assumes a different shape, hence the divergence of expectations. The formation of expectations is an act of our minds by means of which we try to catch a glimpse of the unknown. Each one of us catches a different glimpse" (L. M. Lachmann, "From Mises to Shackle: An Essay on Austrian Economics and the Kaleidic Society," *Journal of Economic Literature*, XIV (1976), p. 59).

7. O'Driscoll, op. cit., p. 129.
8. O'Driscoll, op. cit., p. 130.
9. O'Driscoll, op. cit., p. 130.
10. O'Driscoll, op. cit., p. 132. In this context O'Driscoll confronts Lachmann's position with that of the "Austrians" in general: "It is certainly not the case that Austrian economists maintain that there ever exists *ex ante* consistency among all transactors' plans. But they have traditionally maintained, as Lachmann himself notes, that there is a *strong* tendency toward diffusion of knowledge and *increased consistency of plans*. (Emphasis added.)" (O'Driscoll, op. cit., p. 132). Furthermore O'Driscoll concludes: "I now believe the apparent semantic confusion is masking real conceptual differences. Kirzner sees any disturbance as developing equilibrating market forces. Lachmann sees change as disequilibrating. The only reason that I can adduce is that Lachmann does not see market forces as being equilibrating in nature" (O'Driscoll, op. cit., p. 134). Finally: "From this, one must conclude that Lachmann is critical even of theories espousing a tendency toward overall equilibrium (i.e., he denies the principle of spontaneous order). I can draw no other conclusion" (O'Driscoll, op. cit., p. 133).
11. O'Driscoll, op. cit., p. 130.
12. O'Driscoll, op. cit., p. 130.
13. O'Driscoll, op. cit., p. 141.
14. Regard for instance, that competitors lagging behind will not always try to overcome their difficulties by means of imitation but also by means of innovation as well. In other words, it seems inadequate to treat innovation as an exogenous variable separated from the process of competition.
15. The crucial point is that new innovations take place, *before* the market system has adapted itself to the preceding innovations, i.e., the process of diffusion has not yet come to an end.
16. With regard to the structuring of the ends–means framework by the entrepreneur see I. M. Kirzner, "Uncertainty, Discovery and Human Action: A Study of the Entrepreneurial Profile in the Misesian System," in *Method, Process and Austrian Economics: Essays in Honor of Ludwig von Mises* ed. I. M. Kirzner (Lexington, Mass.: Lexington Books, 1982), pp. 139–59.
17. That economic analysis can but profit by taking into account a broader range of different types of entrepreneurs is testified by E. Heuss, *Algemeine Markttheorie* (Tübingen-Zürich: J. C. B. Mohr (Paul Siebeck)—Polygraphischer Verlag, 1965).
18. Structures which emerge at some distance from equilibrium are called "dissipative structures." See G. Nicolis and I. Prigogine, *Self-organization*

in Non-Equilibrium Systems (New York, Wiley, 1977); I. Prigogine, *Vom Sein zum Werden: Zeit und Komplexität in den Naturwissenschaften* (München-Zürich: Piper, 1979); ed. E. Jantsch *The Evolutionary Vision, Toward a Unifying Paradigm of Physical, Biological and Sociocultural Evolution* (Boulder, Colorado: Westview Press, 1981); M. Zeleny, *Autopoiesis, Dissipative Structures, and Spontaneous Social Orders* (Boulder, Colorado: Westview Press, 1980). For an economic interpretation of dissipative structures see: K. E. Boulding, "Equilibrium, Entropy, Development and Autopoiesis: Towards a Disequilibrium Economics," *Eastern Journal*, VI (1980), pp. 179–88; U. Fehl, *Die Theorie disspativer Strukturen als Ansatzpunkt für die Analyse von Innovationsproblemen in alternativen Wirtschaftsordnungen*, in *Innovationsprobleme in Ost und West*, eds. A. Schüller, H. Leipold, H. Hamel (Stuttgart: Fischer, 1983), pp. 65–89.

19. Before generalizing the insights to be obtained from the model, its very character as a model should be emphasized, i.e., it should not be taken literally. Of course, the analysis has been carried out in a neoclassical equilibrium framework, and the process of selection, it is true, need not work in a textbook manner. But there will be a tendency in the direction it indicates, a tendency owing to the very existence of arbitrage as a driving force of the market, the latter being set in motion by entrepreneurs of the Mises-Kirzner type. Thus the model and its suggestions may be used for the sake of argument and illumination, so to speak as an ideal standard.
20. It should be clear that the spontaneous order understood as a selection order does not deny the existence of equilibrating forces in the sense of arbitrage activities but takes into account that these are, so to speak, balanced by the forces of innovation as another driving force of the market.
21. See Friedrich A. Hayek, "Rechtsordnung und Handelnsordnung," in *Freiburger Studien*, ed. A. Hayek (Tübingen: J. C. B. Mohr (Paul Siebeck), 1969), pp. 161–98.
22. The statement Garrison makes with respect to knowledge and expectations significantly applies to "natural" differences of individuals as well: "In effect Loasby criticizes the Austrians for not explaining why different people know different things and have different expectations. The issue of differential knowledge is symptomatic of a larger problem faced by any school of thought that does not follow every trend in the way of thinking of the mainstream. The repeated use of contrary-to-fact assumptions, such as perfect knowledge or homogenous products, can blunt our ability to deal with reality as it actually exists" (R. W. Garrison, "Austrian Economics as the Middle Ground: Comment on Loasby," in *Method, Process and Austrian Economics*, ed. I. M. Kirzner, op. cit., pp. 136–7).
23. As a consequence the driving forces of the market (arbitrage, accumulation, and innovation) have to be interpreted as being future oriented; the same is true for the respective activities of the entrepreneurs.
24. Shackle has deeply reflected on this question. See for example G. L. S. Shackle, "Imagination, Formalism and Choice," in *Time, Uncertainty and Disequilibrium*, ed. M. J. Rizzo, op. cit., pp. 19–31. Shackle point out that human action is basing on imaginations. So the driving forces of the market rest on imaginations, too.

25. Judgment as an element of imagination rightly is stressed by J. High, "Alertness and Judgment: Comment on Kirzner," in *Method, Process and Austrian Economics*, ed. I. M. Kirzner, op. cit., pp. 161–8.
26. It has already been stated that O'Driscoll favors the proposition that in certain circumstances even different and disparate individuals will have a common reaction to shared experience. But the example he chooses is not convincing because it refers to a simple situation. Situations that have to be mastered in the market process are far more complex than the actions to be taken for an exit, when a fire in an enclosed room has been conceived of. Thus, more interpretation, more judgment or more imagination is called for. But the simple story of O'Driscoll can demonstrate the advantage of divergent reactions: If all persons in the room will react in the same manner and immediately run to the door, it may well be that the exit will be blocked and no person can get out; divergent, i.e., successive reactions would do better!
27. This is especially the case when the "iterative" factors begin to dominate the "mutative" ones in the market. For a detailed analysis of the resulting consequences see E. Heuss, *Allgemeine Markttheorie*, op. cit., especially chaps 4–6.
28. "Like everyone else, entrepreneurs may seek to conceal the extent of their ignorance, by assuming a degree of continuity between past and future that cannot possibly be assured and that may well be greater than the continuity achieved in the past; alternatively they may place exaggerated reliance on the apparent plans of other entrepreneurs, who are credited with superior forsight. Entrepreneurial competition encourages a variety of opinions and of plans; but faced with the total inadequacy of any basis for rational expectation, we may sometimes find excessive conformity, both in undertaking particular kinds of business strategy and in abandoning such strategies. To rely on one's own imagination, and to await the eventual market test, requires greater resolution, perhaps greater arrogance, than most of us possess" (B. J. Loasby, "Economics of Dispersed and Incomplete Information," in *Method, Process and Austrian Economics*, ed. I. M. Kirzner, op. cit., p. 127). While the picture Loasby draws may be adequate in certain situations or certain phases of the market, on the whole Loasby rather seems to underestimate the vigor of subjectivity.
29. Lachmann, From Mises to Shackle, op. cit., p. 61.

7 From Lachmann to Lucas: on Institutions, Expectations, and Equilibrating Tendencies

ROGER W. GARRISON

I INTRODUCTION

It was ten years ago that Professor Lachmann wrote "From Mises to Shackle: An Essay on Austrian Economics and the Kaleidic Society."[1] The central message of that essay was that while Mises was consistently subjectivist in the context of value theory, Shackle extended the scope of subjectivism from evaluations to expectations. And he did so in such a way as to call into question the existence of a tendency toward equilibrium. In recent years Lachmann's own writing—in terms of both the questions asked and the flavor of the answers given—have been more akin to Shackle's subjectivism than to Mises's.

My own parody in the title to this chapter alludes to modern developments in the treatment of expectations outside the Austrian tradition, developments that are wholly antithetical to Shacklian subjectivism. My message is not that Austrians should embrace Robert Lucas's conception of rational expectations. Rather that it is that by taking only one small step in that direction, the Austrians can provide a more satisfying answer to the question of the existence of equilibrating tendencies, and they can do so without relinquishing their subjectivist outlook.

The objectives of this paper are actually twofold. One is to show that different views about the nature of equilibrating tendencies are not based on articles of faith or on ideology but are a reflection of different understandings of the role of institutions and the formation of expectations in different institutional settings; a second objective is to identify a spectrum of views (from Lachmann to Lucas) on the market's equilibrating tendencies. This spectrum can serve as a basis for interpreting views that lie on different parts of the spectrum, such as those of Keynes and those of Mises and Hayek, and as a tool for enhancing our own understanding.

Section II recasts the question of equilibrating tendencies in the context of intertemporal coordination. Sections III and IV identify the poles of a spectrum of views on the economy's equilibrating tendencies. Section V moves one step away from the Lachmann pole to incorporate an idea that is essential to the Austrian vision of the economy. Section VI anchors these ideas in institutional issues, and Section VII offers a concluding assessment.

II THE PERVASIVE PROBLEM OF INTERTEMPORAL COORDINATION

The general question of whether or not markets work is posed in the context of the Austrian tradition. This tradition does not concern itself with the question of whether a particular pattern of equilibrium prices passes muster on the basis of some standard that lies outside of economics proper. No evolved set of institutions will produce results that coincide with some preconceived norm. Nor is the wisdom—narrowly conceived—of Alfred Marshall and Leon Walras called into question. Under ordinary circumstances (epitomized by the Marshallian fish market), excess supplies put downward pressure and excess demands upward pressure on prices, and at the end of the day all the fish are sold. Both in theory and in fiction, prices that simultaneously clear all markets in a given period could be found by a mathematician (if he had all the relevant data) or by a Walrasian auctioneer.

But general equilibrium as conceived by Walras abstracts from the passage of time. And his theories do not readily generalize to accommodate the temporal element—except in the most formal sense. On this count the concept of partial equilibrium fares no better. Despite the potency of the Marshallian scissors, they often fail to cut cleanly in the time dimension. According to Marshall himself, who was well aware of the limitations of his own analysis, "The element of time . . . is the center of the chief difficulty of almost every economic problem."[2]

More troublesome is the question of the market's equilibrating tendencies in the context of a vision of the economy that makes specific allowance for the passage of time. To make such an allowance, though, is simply to reject the fiction of an atemporal equilibrium—an equilibrium in which economic actions at a particular point in time are coordinated independent of what transpired just before that instant and what may transpire just after. Strictly speaking, such a timeless equilibrium is inconceivable; all economic *actions* take place in time. Thus, the problem of intemporal coordination is not a special problem but one that is fully pervasive throughout any economy.

While the temporal element is present in every economic activity, this element can be highlighted by bringing into focus those activities in which temporal considerations dominate. British contemporaries of Keynes highlighted the market for loanable funds and believed that if this market is properly functioning, the propositions pertaining to equilibrium at a particular point in time could be extrapolated to apply equally to intertemporal equilibrium. Keynes himself focused upon the relationship between spending on (present) consumption and spending on investment (which enables future consumption). He saw no market mechanism that would coordinate these two components of expenditures, and hence he believed that macroeconomic disequilibrium was inherent in the market system.

Theorists in the Austrian school argued that while Keynes had rightly identified the time element as a possible source of discoordination, his level of aggregation would not permit a healthy understanding of the problem, and a fortiori his analysis would not serve as a sound basis for prescribing a remedy. The Austrian alternative involved a disaggregated investment sector, or in the Austrians' own terminology, a structure of production in which a *sequence* of interrelated investment decisions must precede some subsequent consumption decision. This analytical vision was constructed so as to give full play to the ever-present time element, to help identify the possible problems of intertemporal discoordination, and to serve as a basis for showing what institutional arrangements would minimize such discoordination.

Modern economists who take a history-of-thought approach to macroeconomics may well suspect that macroeconomic problems were better understood and the issues were more clearly drawn in the dawn of Keynesianism than they are today. The sharper focus can be largely attributed to the explicit attention to the time element in those earlier days. With noteworthy exceptions, the attention to the intertemporal aspect of the coordination problem in modern macroeconomics is on the wane.[3] Frustration with the thorny issues of capital theory has caused all notions of a temporal structure of production to be jettisoned from the domain of macroeconomics. The now-common practice of reducing the distinction between capital goods and consumption goods to the distinction between a stock and a flow represents a victory of form over substance. Capital and time are no longer seen as central problems but as a basis for classifying theories and models. There are short-run (macroeconomic) models, in which not enough time elapses for capital to grow, and long-run (growth) models, in which capital grows smoothly through time.

Regaining a healthy respect for the temporal element requires that we look at the market process that transforms a sequence of short runs into a long run. Is this process characterized by self-equilibrating tendencies? That is, to what extent does the sequence of short-run equilibria correspond to stages of a market process that tailors the usage of resources over time to the desired intertemporal pattern of consumption? Arguably, modern macroeconomics can be (and ought to be) conceived as the body of thought that attempts to answer this particular question.

Even if we abstract from monetary disturbances and interventions of other sorts, the answers offered range inclusively between two polar extremes: There is no basis for asserting the existence of an equilibrating tendency; the tendency exists; the tendency is so strong that we can assume the equilibrium brought about by this process to be an accomplished fact. Extrapolating from popular terminology, we can dub the three positions identified "equilibrium never" (Lachmann), "equilibrating tendencies" (Mises-Hayek), and "equilibrium always" (Lucas). It will be argued that it is but a short step from Lachmann to Mises and Hayek. But first it is necessary to identify more fully each of the extreme positions. Interestingly, even Lucas, who is far removed from the Austrian theorists on the issue at hand, shares much common ground with Hayek in other fundamental respects.[4]

III LACHMANN: EQUILIBRIUM NEVER

Implicit in Lachmann's writings is the most extreme distinction between the short run and the long run (in the sense that these terms are used in the present paper). The short run is a period over which the passage of time is inconsequential, or over which there is no passage of time an any economically meaningful sense. It is no longer—and is arguably shorter—than Marshall's market period, during which the fishermen sell their daily catch. But for each such short run, traders can strike a balance—whether the object of their trading is a catch of fish or a fishery. Higglers and hagglers in commodity markets and bulls and bears in securities markets can be relied upon to achieve market-clearing prices throughout the economy. If the analysis could somehow be confined to this short run, there would be no question about the existence of equilibrating tendencies.

However, if the analysis is to be meaningful and have application to actual market processes, the passage of time must be taken into account. In Lachmann's view, to introduce time into the analysis is to introduce a fundamental unknowability.[5] This casts doubt on the existence, or at least the effectiveness, of equilibrium forces that work over time to effect an intertemporal equilibrium. We cannot know the future, and we have no reason to believe that the market will behave as if the future were known. We have no reason to believe that today's market for fisheries is coordinated with tomorrow's market for fish.

The fundamental unknowability associated with the time element can best be understood by focusing on the expectations of market participants and how they affect—and are affected by—the unfolding of the market process. For microeconomics as well as macroeconomics, expectations pose a problem every time there is a change in some market condition, every time there is a shift in supply or in demand. We can deduce what price and quantity changes are implied by the new market conditions only by invoking a strict *ceteris paribus* assumption. But, strictly speaking, the state of expectations cannot be impounded in this assumption. The change in a market condition may cause expectations (about future market conditions—and hence about future prices) to change as well. We cannot predict, however, just how these expectations will be formed and reformed. Changes in expectations, then, are neither a truly exogenous nor a truly endogenous variable.[6]

Although we cannot simply assume that expectations are consistent with concurrent prices, we can *imagine* that they are. "The future is unknowable but not unimaginable."[7] If expectations can be so regarded, standard supply-and-demand analysis applies. But we can also imagine that expectations about a particular price, for instance, do change, and we can imagine the change to be in either direction. Suppose an increase in the supply of fish results in a lower price for fish. Expectations that the price of fish will soon return to its previous level will cause demand to increase as buyers attempt to take advantage of an opportunity that is perceived to be temporary. Expectations that the price of fish will continue to fall will cause the demand to decrease as buyers wait to take advantage of an even better opportunity in the future. As Lachmann himself often recognizes, it is possible to categorize expectations as being either inelastic or elastic with respect to price changes.[8] However, it is another matter to predict which will be the case in a particular instance. (It might be noted that Keynes's recommendation that prices and wages should not be permitted to fall in response to widespread unemployment was based upon the fear that expectations are perversely elastic.)

While changing expectations pose a problem for the analysis of the Marshallian fish market, they pose a more serious problem when the analysis is applied to the market for fisheries. On the issues of markets for long-term capital, Lachmann's view is in perfect accord with Keynes's discussion of long-term expectations.[9] The current price of fisheries reflects expectations about the price of fish in both the near and the far future. The mere fact that the object of the expectations lies, in part, in the far future compounds the problem. Prices in the far future are inherently more difficult for market participants to predict. Current prices and changes in current prices may provide little or no basis for such predictions. And further, more time will have to elapse before actual predictions—formed on whatever basis—can be proven correct or incorrect. On what basis can the analyst claim that these expectations will tend to be correct, that market forces based on these expectations will tend to be equilibrating?

The problem of expectations can be recast in a macroeconomic mold simply by extrapolating from fish to consumption goods and from fisheries to investment goods. Investors must invest today on the basis of their current expectations about consumption spending in the relatively distant future. Such expectations may be based in part on the current level—or changes in the current level—of consumption spending. But it is not possible to specify just how current spending gets translated into expectations about future spending.

We can imagine that a reduction in current consumption spending is taken as an indication that consumers are saving now in order to indulge in a greater level of consumption spending in the future. Such expectations, of course, would stimulate current investment spending so as to make a greater quantity of consumer goods available at the very time that consumers are ready to indulge. We could imagine that the abstinence from consumption spending served only to achieve a permanently higher level of cash balances. If correctly reflected in expectations, this increase in the demand for money would have but a transitory effect on real output and real consumption. Or we could imagine that a reduction in current consumer spending is taken as an indication that consumers intend to consume more leisure time. Such expectations would retard investment to the point that the availability of consumer goods falls to a level consistent with the lower level of consumption spending.

If we imagine that the expectations of investors coincide with the intentions of consumers, we have imagined away the problem of intertemporal coordination. If we assert, as Keynes did, that current consumption spending is always taken as the best indication of future consumption spending, we assert the inevitability of intertemporal discoordination. When consumers consume less now in order to be able to consume more in the future, they will be faced in that future with a lesser rather than a greater availability of consumption goods.[10]

Lachmann refrains from imagining the problem away or from asserting the inherent perversity of the market process. He simply leaves us with the open question of whether or not we can count upon equilibrium forces to coordinate intertemporally. The flavor of Lachmann's writings, however, suggests that this question will remain an open one for some time to come. To wit: "Even the assertion of a 'tendency' towards [intertemporal equilibrium] has to be qualified by adding that this is one among others."[11]

IV LUCAS: EQUILIBRIUM ALWAYS

Lachmann makes a categorical distinction between the present, in which market participants know enough to strike a balance in each market, and the future, which is unknowable. Lucas, in effect, denies the distinction by the particular way in which he treats the problem of expectations. The future, both near and far, is dealt with as if it were analytically equivalent to the present. For Lucas, the problem of intertemporal coordination, then, is no different than the problem of, say, interspatial coordination. Time and space may be dimensionally different to the physicist but not to the economist. These polar views of the present/future distinction and of the significance of the passage of time are what put Lachmann and Lucas poles apart on the issue of equilibrium tendencies.

Adopting the terminology and extending the logic of John Muth, Lucas collapses the entire future into the present by claiming that expectations of market participants are "rational."[12] The term "rationality," as used by Muth and Lucas, is not to be equated with rationality either in its ordinary meaning or in the meaning conventionally intended by economists—the transitivity of preference functions. Nor does it correspond with the Austrian meaning of purposive behavior. In the language of probability theory as applied to the possible occurrence of a future event, expectations are said to be rational when the subjective probabilities in the minds of market participants coincide with the true probabilities of the event's occurrence.[13]

For Lucas, the applicability of the rational-expectations assumption spans the entire domain of economic theory. Under conditions of genuine uncertainty, no market participant has a basis for forming subjective probabilities of any kind. But under such conditions, no economist has a basis for applying economic reasoning of any kind.[14] Under all other conditions, economic reasoning is applicable and expectations are taken to be rational. Theoretical formulations incorporate actual prices and price expectations on equal footing.

For Lachmann, of course, this view is wholly untenable. In the absence of genuine uncertainty, economic analysis is reduced to a set of maximization exercises that are more akin to engineering than to economics. The market process—as opposed to the ultimate results of that process under the assumed condition of certainty or its rational-expectations equivalent—is always unfolding in the passage of time and hence always involves genuine uncertainty. Market participants must make decisions without knowing what the relevant true probabilities are and even without knowing what the full range of possible outcomes are. If Lachmann had to adopt terminology conformable with the terminology used by Lucas, he would probably say that expectations, in his own view, are *a*rational.

It might be noted here that the notion of rational expectations does provide a useful basis for identifying alternative theories that are grounded in some explicitly or implicitly alleged *ir*rational behavior on the part of market participants. Theoretical results that depend upon workers systematically overestimating their real wage or investors systematically overestimating future revenues become suspect unless such systematic errors can be accounted for in terms of knowledge possessed and constraints faced by those market participants. The critical view of rational expectations taken in the present paper, then, is not intended to make room for irrational behavior of these various sorts but rather to make room for the arational behavior necessitated by the condition of genuine uncertainty.

While Lachmann remains agnostic on the existence of effective equilibrating tendencies, Lucas takes for granted the ultimate results of those tendencies. In his theoretical constructs, even in those intended to elucidate the problems of the business cycle, prices and quantities are assumed always to be in equilibrium.[15] There is simply no room for the intertemporal discoordination that, in other formulations, characterizes the business cycle. In fact, there is no room for discoordination of any kind.

It remains unclear whether the "equilibrium models of business cycles," to use Lucas's own phraseology, are consistent with regarding cycles as a "problem" in any meaningful sense.[16] But the fact that Lucas can treat business cycles as an equilibrium phenomenon provides further justification for locating him at the opposite pole from Lachmann. For Lachmann, as soon as any elapse of time is taken into account, tendencies toward equilibrium are called into question, for Lucas, not even the elapse of time through a complete business cycle and beyond causes us to depart from the assumption of equilibrium. Lying on the broad spectrum between Lachmann and Lucas are many possible intermediate views on the prospects for achieving intertemporal coordination. One particular view—that of Mises and Hayek—is of special interest because of its specific attention to the problem of intertemporal coordination.

V MISES-HAYEK: EQUILIBRATING TENDENCIES

Such theorists as Mises and Hayek, of course, are not the only ones that occupy the middle ground between Lachmann and Lucas. By the very construction of our argument, all competing views on the question of equilibrium tendencies lie somewhere between the two polar extremes. Textbook Keynesianism, for instance, relies partially on market forces and partially on stabilization policies to maintain a full-employment equilibrium over time. This variant of Keynesianism, however, is concerned not with the prospects for achieving an intertemporal equilibrium but rather with the prospects for clearing the labor market in each period—whether or not investment spending in a given period corresponds to consumer spending in some future period. But Keynesianism, conventionally interpreted, clearly occupies the middle ground: That market forces *can* be effectively augmented by policy makes them more efficacious than Lachmann would have us believe; that they *must* be so augmented makes them less efficacious than Lucas would have us believe.

Hayek's own analysis, as well as his critical evaluation of Keynes, focused squarely on the question of intertemporal coordination. Is there a set of market forces that will transform the desired pattern of consumer spending, which extends into the future, into a corresponding pattern of investment decisions? Hayek argued that Keynes's theoretical construction, in which there is no mechanism to coordinate investment decisions with consumption decisions, was marred by a fundamental deficiency. Critical market forces, which coordinate intertemporally, were overlooked because of the level of aggregation that characterized the Keynesian formulation. In Hayek's own words, "Mr. Keynes's aggregates conceal the most fundamental mechanisms of change."[17]

In Hayek's own formulation, the investment sector is disaggregated.[18] Consumer goods are produced by a market process that involves a temporal sequence of stages of production. The allocation of individual investment goods among the various stages of production affects the composition and time pattern of final output. Analysis based on this construction looks beyond the distinction between the demand for fish and the demand for fisheries. By considering the sequence of individual decisions that gives rise to the creation of a fishery, it gives the fullest play to expectations.[19] Each individual investor at each stage of production must make investment decisions on the basis of his own expectations. Successful investment over time requires that the investor's decisions be consistent both with the subsequent decisions of other investors and with the ultimate demands of the consumers. Theoretical models based on the Hayekian structure of production can illustrate what sequence of investment decisions is consistent with a given pattern of desired consumption. But this exercise is only a preliminary to the more fundamental question: Do we have reason to believe that the investors making these decisions will tend to be the ones whose expectations are correct?

Mises's answer to this question clearly lies between those of Lachmann and Lucas. The Misesian formulation does not allow us to predict in a given situation how an investor's expectations will be affected by some specific change in market conditions. Nor does the formulation require that it simply be assumed that expectations are rational in the Lucas sense. The claim that there is a general tendency toward equilibrium rests on the understanding of a market process in which each investor is investing on the basis of his own expectations. Investors whose expectations about future market conditions turn out to be correct enjoy an accumulation of resources; investors whose expectations turn out to be incorrect suffer a decumulation of resources. Investment decisions of the former become increasingly influential over time; investment decisions of the latter become decreasingly so.[20]

By focusing on the market process within the investment sector, the Mises-Hayek theory can predict that equilibrating expectations will tend to govern, even though it cannot predict what in particular will govern the formulation of expectations. Recognizing the subjectivity and unpredictability of expectations in any given circumstances, then, does not imply the nonexistence or the inefficacy of equilibrating tendencies. The existence and efficacy of equilibrating tendencies does presuppose, however, that correct expectations are rewarded and incorrect expectations are penalized. The realization of such rewards and penalties in turn depends upon the nature of the institutions within which the investment decisions are made.

VI EXPECTATIONS AND INSTITUTIONS

For the views that we have associated with Lachmann and with Lucas, questions about the institutional environment are largely irrelevant. Whatever the institutional arrangements, expectations remain the wild card in Lachmann's view. So long as the future is linked to the present through expectations, there will be an irradicable unknowability, or unpredictability, about the market forces that govern future-oriented investment decisions. For Lucas, the belief that expectations are rational is virtually independent of any institutional considerations. So long as the institutional arrangements are known and so long as policy is, in principle, predictable, rational expectations will prevail and equilibrium will be a reality rather than a mere tendency.[21]

In the view associated with the Mises-Hayek formulation, the validity of the proposition that there is a tendency toward equilibrium depends critically on the nature of the institutional arrangements. So long as the arrangements are such that expectations consistent with underlying economic realities are rewarded and expectations inconsistent with those realities are penalized, the tendency can be expected to prevail. This institutional qualification is what constitutes the short step away from the Lachmann pole.

An illustration that highlights the role of the interest rate in achieving intertemporal equilibrium can serve to illustrate the critical nature of institutional considerations in the Austrian view. The same illustration can serve as well to contrast the Austrian view with the

Keynesian view, in which expectations and institutions interact in a different way.

The rate of interest, broadly conceived, is the market mechanism that allocates resources intertemporally. Determined by the interactions of all market participants, this mechanism works to prevent investors collectively from undertaking more investment projects than possibly can be completed, given the ultimate resource constraints; in a phrase, it keeps the economy from biting off more than it can chew. In a market economy, some investors are better able to "read" the interest rate than are others. If read correctly, the interest rate helps restrict each individual investor to projects whose ultimate completion will not be jeopardized by resource constraints that would be more stringent than expected. Investors who are able successfully to complete their projects gain command over greater quantities of resources. In turn, the subsequent decisions of these successful investors have increased weight in determining the market rate of interest. Investors who overextend themselves get caught in a credit crunch, suffer losses, and their investments possibly are subject to liquidation. Subsequent investment decisions by these investors have decreased weight in determining the market rate of interest. Through this process, the market discipline creates the tendency towards intertemporal equilibrium.

Let us now consider institutional arrangements that override the discipline of the market in order to "deal" with the problem of a credit crunch. Government loan guarantees may be extended to investors who are overextended; low-interest and deferred-payment loans may be made available to investors who would otherwise face liquidation; newly created money may be used to increase the supply of loanable funds. All these policies, of course, will be welcomed by the investors in distress. Because of these policies, which preempt the market process, these investors will be able to maintain command over their resources. And their subsequent investment decisions will have just as much weight in determining the market rate of interest as before.

The credit-crunch policies cut away at the equilibrating tendencies in a double-edged manner. First, investors whose expectations are out of line with economic realities remain in resource-commanding positions. Second, the importance to the individual investors of forming expectations consistent with economic realities is severely reduced if not entirely eliminated: "erroneous" expectations that lead to a crunch and a subsequent bailout may be just as good as—or even better (for the individual investor)—than "correct" expectations. Under such institutional arrangements, there would be no basis to predict a tendency toward intertemporal equilibrium. In fact, by short-circuiting the market process, the credit-crunch policies would virtually ensure intertemporal disequilibrium and hence further credit crunches.

The discussion of the relationship between expectations and institutions allows for a contrast between Keynesian and Austrian views. In the Keynesian view, the intertemporal market process, which coordinates investment and consumption spending, is *inherently* unstable. The interest rate is a baseless convention—a convention that is periodically shaken only to be replaced by another equally baseless convention.[22] Thus, maintaining economic stability requires a stabilization policy, which aims, in part, to control investment spending through monetary expansion and interest-rate manipulation.

In the Austrian view, such policies do not stabilize the economy. On the contrary, they are inherently destabilizing. They nullify the market forces that give rise to equilibrating tendencies thus causing the economy to perform in the very way that Keynes envisioned it. To coin a term, Keynesian stabilization policies serve to "Keynesianize" rather than stabilize the market process that governs investment decisions. Long-term stability requires that no such policies be pursued.[23]

VII A SUMMARY ASSESSMENT

On the fundamental issue of equilibrating tendencies, economic theorists are prone to take a position which denies either the problem (Lucas) or its solution (Lachmann). Arguments for an intermediate view must put heavy emphasis on the role of expectations. While recognizing the impossibility of specifying how correct expectations can be formed, these middle-ground theorists must nonetheless rest their case for equilibrating tendencies on a market process that is based on predominantly correct expectations.

Formulating the problem in this way directs our attention to institutional considerations. If institutional arrangements are such that correct expectations are consistently rewarded and incorrect expectations are consistently penalized, the resulting market process will exhibit equilibrating tendencies. And this happy conclusion is a result of a further extension of—rather than a departure from—the tenets of subjectivism that Lachmann has for so long embraced and so ably defended.

NOTES

1. Ludwig M. Lachmann, "From Mises to Shackle: An Essay on Austrian Economics and the Kaleidic Society," *Journal of Economic Literature*, 14(1) (March 1976), pp. 54–62.
2. Alfred Marshall, *Principles of Economics*, 9th ed. (London: Macmillan, 1961), p. vii.
3. Modern contributions that focus on the problem of intertemporal coordination include Axel Leijonhufvud, *On Keynesian Economics and the Economics of Keynes* (New York: Oxford University Press, 1968); Gerald P. O'Driscoll, Jr. and Mario, J. Rizzo, *The Economics of Time and Ignorance* (Oxford: Basil Blackwell, 1985). These authors draw heavily from the Austrian tradition. In a more limited sense, intertemporal relationships are the focus of the Hyphenless Post Keynesians. See Paul Davidson, "Post Keynesian Economics," *Public Interest*, Special Issue (1980), pp. 151–73.
4. Lucas himself sees a strong affinity between his own views and those of Hayek. See Robert E. Lucas, Jr., "Understanding Business Cycles," in *Studies in Business Cycle Theory*, ed. Robert E. Lucas, Jr. (Cambridge: MIT Press, 1981), p. 215. An enlightening perspective on the relationship between Lucas and Hayek is provided by William Butos, "Hayek and General Equilibrium Analysis," paper presented at the Atlantic Economic Society meetings (Montreal, Quebec, October 1984).
5. Ludwig M. Lachmann, "On the Central Concept of Austrian Economics: Market Process," in *Foundations of Modern Austrian Economics*, ed. Edwin G. Dolan (Kansas City: Sheed & Ward, 1976), pp. 126–32; Ludwig M. Lachmann, "An Austrian Stocktaking: Unsettled Questions and Tentative Answers," in *New Directions in Austrian Economics*, ed. Louis M. Spadaro (Kansas City: Sheed, Andrews & McMeel, 1978), pp. 1–18.
6. Ludwig M. Lachmann, "The Role of Expectations in the Social Sciences," in *Capital, Expectations, and the Market Process*, ed. Ludwig M. Lachmann (Kansas City: Sheed, Andrews & McMeel, 1977), pp. 65–80.
7. Lachmann, "From Mises to Shackle", op. cit., p. 59, and Lachmann, "An Austrian Stocktaking," op. cit., p. 3.
8. Here Lachmann is drawing from John R. Hicks, *Value and Capital*, 2nd ed. (London: Oxford University Press, 1946), p. 204–6.
9. John M. Keynes, *The General Theory of Employment, Interest, and Money* (New York: Harcourt, Brace, 1936), pp. 46–50.
10. For an Austrian perspective on the Keynesian vision, see Roger W. Garrison, "Intertemporal Coordination and the Invisible Hand: An Austrian Perspective on the Keynesian Vision," *History of Political Economy*, 17(2) (Summer 1985).
11. Lachmann, "An Austrian Stocktaking," op. cit., p. 5.
12. John F. Muth, "Rational Expectations and the Theory of Price Movements," *Econometrica*, 29 (1961), pp. 315–35.
13. Robert E. Lucas, Jr., "Understanding Business Cycles," p. 223.
14. Ibid., p. 224.
15. Robert E. Lucas, Jr. "Methods and Problems in Business Cycle Theory," in *Studies in Business Cycle Theory*, ed. Robert E. Lucas, Jr. (Cambridge: MIT Press, 1981), p. 287.

16. Ibid.
17. Friedrich A. Hayek, "Reflections on the Pure Theory of Money," *Economica*, 33 (August 1931), p. 277.
18. Friedrich A. Hayek, *Prices and Production*, 2nd ed. (New York: Augustus M. Kelley, [1935] 1967).
19. Friedrich A. Hayek, "Price Expectations, Monetary Disturbances and Malinvestments," in *Profits, Interest, and Investment*, ed. Friedrich A. Hayek (New York: Augustus M. Kelley, [1939] 1975).
20. Peter Murrell, "Did the Theory of Market Socialism Answer the Challenge of Ludwig von Mises? A Reinterpretation of the Socialist Controversy," *History of Political Economy*, Winter 1983, 15(1), p. 95. Murrell reminds us that this line of reasoning was employed by Ludwig von Mises in the context of the socialist calculation debate. Lachmann acknowledges this reasoning but is not especially swayed by it. "We might say that unsuccessful planners make capital losses and thus gradually lose their control over resources and their ability to engage in new enterprises; the successful are able to plan with more confidence and on a much larger scale. Mises used such an argument. But how can we be sure?" Lachmann "On the Central Concept of Austrian Economics," op. cit., p. 129. Of course, in some absolute sense, we can never be *sure*. But Mises's argument applies to a market economy in a way that it can never apply to state planning, a managed economy, or any other nonmarket system.
21. Alan Coddington provides a useful perspective on Keynesian economics that allows a comparison of both Lachmann and Lucas with Keynes. See Alan Coddington, "Deficient Forsight: A Troublesome Theme in Keynesian Economics," *American Economic Review*, 72(3) (June 1982), pp. 480–7. Coddington shows that is is not expectations per se that drive the Keynesian system, but rather the differential effects that considerations of expectations have on the investment sector as compared to the consumer-goods sector and the public sector. Lachmann virtually eliminates the differentials and treats the entire economy like Keynes's investment sector; Lucas virtually eliminates the differentials and treats the entire economy like Keynes's consumer-goods sector.
22. John M. Keynes, *General Theory*, op. cit, p. 152. The notion that the interest rate and the corresponding pattern of prices form a convention that is periodically upset is what underlies G. L. S. Shackle's *Keynesian Kaleidics* (Edinburgh University Press, 1974).
23. For an elaboration of this perspective on Keynesian policy, see William H. Hutt, *The Keynesian Episode* (Indianapolis: Liberty Press, 1979), pp. 121–33. Lachmann has suggested that " 'public policy decisions' are largely a euphemism for incoherent sequences of disparate expedients" Lachmann, "From Mises to Shackle," op. cit., p. 61. Taking into account the critical role of institutions, we see that Lachmann's suggestion can be pushed further. The incoherent sequence of disparate expedients are precisely what destroy the equilibrating tendencies thus making further disparate expedients appear necessary.

8 Rational Behavior – Observation or Assumption?

JOHN HICKS

I am very well aware that the subject of this paper has been a recurrent theme in recent discussions; it is indeed for that reason that I have chosen it. But I cannot pretend to have followed those discussions as closely as I could wish. I have been unable, for several years, to work in libraries, so I cannot follow up references; my reading, inevitably, has been haphazard. It has nevertheless become clear to me that several of the issues which have been under discussion are closely related to some on which I have myself been thinking for many years—for many years, indeed, before "rational expectations" had been heard of. I have myself been developing, very gradually developing, a view about them. Parts of it have been set out in various of my published writings, but I have never had occasion to pull them together.[1] Perhaps it is not too late to make this attempt.

The obvious interpretation of the statement that an action is rational is that the agent can give reasons for it—that he can explain why he does it, or did it. The clearest instances are those where he has actually set out his reasons, when he has had to make a case for doing this, not that. Consider a chairman (or president) reporting to his board of directors, or a finance minister (in the British system) presenting his budget. There can then be no question but that the decision is rational.

One may nevertheless have suspicions that the reasons presented are not the true reasons—that the finance minister, for instance, has been influenced by pressures from interested parties, more than by the reasons which he gives. But I do not think that we should want to say that a decision, which has been influenced in this way, is any the less rational. The reasons are different, perhaps less respectable; still, they are reasons.

This distinction, between the reasons which are stated by the agent and those which are suspected by the investigator (historian or economist) is nevertheless of quite central importance. Much of what follows will turn upon it. It may be brought out by noticing, still taking the political example, that there may be public reasons for a political decision, set out in speeches or published statements, and that is all that for a time (perhaps a long time) the historian has available to him. But then the time comes when private papers are released that provide additional evidence on what was intended. Even then, however, the historian may still have doubts on whether what has become available shows what was "really" intended. He may have other information, which "must have been" known to the agent, and he cannot believe that it was not taken into account, though it does not appear in the papers before him.

I find it useful to begin with this historical (or historiographical) problem, though it may seem at first sight to be far away from economics. But perhaps it is not so far away as may at first sight appear. For consider the case of banking histories. Bankers, in most countries, are very chary of giving reasons for their actions; they do not give them at the time when they are made, and even when, as sometimes happens, their private papers become ultimately available, they are usually found to be very unrevealing.[2] So the main source of direct evidence on motive, to take the British case as an example, is to be found in statements made by bankers to later commissions of enquiry. But these, of course, are tainted by the witness's knowledge, by the time of the enquiry, of what was to happen afterwards. So the historian of banking is bound to rely, in large measure, on his own reconstruction, on what he can suppose, from his own knowledge of the facts, and from what he can fairly suppose must have been known to the agent, what the motives must have been.[3]

I have deliberately begun with this banking example, though to the economist it is a special case. The decisions of bankers, especially central bankers, have (or may have) what we may call a "macro" quality; the consequences which follow from them can radiate far and wide. Why such a decision was made would be a proper subject for historical enquiry. But the decisions with which, in economics, we are mostly concerned are not like that.

We are mostly not concerned with particular decisions, but with classes of decisions. Even if we had information about the particular dealings of particular traders (as we might have, on occasion, if it came out in legal proceedings), we would not use it. The combined effects of a number of similar decisions are our object of study.

So we proceed at once to what in the "macro" case would have been the final stage in the enquiry—reconstruction, from other evidence than direct witness, what we think that the reasons for the actions must have been. That is more practicable than might appear at first sight, just because we are concerned with classes of actions; so it is enough if we do our reconstruction for a representative case.

It is here that we are helped by using an assumption of rationality, in rather a strong sense. For it is not sufficient to assume that the agent could give a reason for his action; more than that is required. For here it is we, not the agent himself, who have to give the reason. It must be what we ourselves would think to be a good reason, at least an intelligible reason. That is quite a big assumption. I am fully prepared to admit that there are cases, which may be important cases, for which we would not dare to make it. Did the German people have a good reason for voting for Hitler in 1932?

If, in economics, we so often dare to make it, that must be because of something special about economic behavior. We are considering classes of decisions, so it is to the general characteristics of those decisions, and of the people who make them, that we must look.[4]

The simplest class, of the people whose decisions can be analyzed in this manner, is the class of merchants. I define a merchant as one who buys in order to sell again.[5] Whether what he buys is physically the same as what he sells is not important; thus an artificer, who is working for a market, I also reckon to be a merchant.

The simplest kind of mercantile dealing is that in which each transaction (consisting of purchase *and* sale) is separate. It is undertaken for its own sake, without reference to the possibility that the terms on which it is made may influence the terms on which it will be possible to make further transactions. (A sufficient condition for this test to be satisfied is that the parties to a particular bargain are unlikely to meet one another again. That can be judged without asking them questions.[6])

There can here be no question of the rationality of the proceeding. The merchant is in business to make a profit. We do not have to *assume* a profit motive. It is inherent in the nature of the business that is being done.

I find it useful to regard this mercantile behavior as the purest type of economic behavior. The merchant—the pure merchant, who confines himself to such market-oriented dealings—is the original economic man. His behavior is so rational, so clearly rational, that we (economists) can readily reason from it; our reasoning from it is the start of economics.

It may be objected that in the work of what we reckon to be the first great school of economists, the classical economics of Smith and Ricardo, the merchant does not so obviously occupy a leading place. Theirs was an economics of production, not of trading. The farmer and the manufacturer are the people we meet in their pages, not the trader. I believe, however, that the picture looks different if one goes further back.

It was many centuries earlier, in fifteenth-century Florence, that merchants began to study how to keep accounts. They did so long before they were followed by anyone else. The merchant, looking for profit, found that he had to keep his books in order to see how much profit he was making, how successful he was being in making a profit. The appearance of the practice of keeping accounts, which first appears among merchants, is a clear indication that the business is being conducted rationally, with an eye to profit. We do not need to make an *assumption* about a profit motive with that evidence before us.

During the centuries which elapsed between the invention of accounting and the time of Adam Smith, the practice of bookkeeping must have spread quite widely. One need not suppose that it was general practice outside the mercantile sector; but the notions which it bred must have been becoming familiar so that they were available to Smith and his contemporaries. Thus it was natural to assume that nonmerchants, or many of them, would be behaving more or less like merchants. Though it was a simplification to treat them as Economic Men, they would be moving in that direction. That was all the Classical Economics needed, for their use of the profit motive. They were mostly concerned with what we should now call rather long-run equilibria, representative of the general state of the economy as it would be established, on the whole, over rather long periods. All that they needed for that purpose was a rule that when an opportunity presented itself, and continued to present itself, then sooner or later it would be taken.[7]

Afterwards, in several ways, things have become more complicated. I shall not here discuss what happened to the accounting concepts, such as capital and income, when they are applied to more complex situations. Though these are matters on which I have learned from Ludwig Lachmann, so that it would be appropriate to discuss them in a contribution to a volume in his honor, I could not deal with them here save at excessive length.[8] So I pass on to other questions.

There is one which begins to need attention before we leave the mercantile sector. Accounts relate to the past, the decisions of business relate to the future, a future which is always to some extent uncertain and may be very uncertain. It is not sufficient, when judging a project, to judge that it is likely to be profitable; there is also the possibility that for one reason or another it will be a failure. There will be cautious persons who give great weight to the possibility of failure; there will be others, more speculatively inclined, who will give less. We often find the cautious person saying that the speculator is irrational; if the latter is simply relying on a "hunch," the observer may agree. But the risk taker who calculates is not acting irrationally. Especially if he calculates that he is able to stand the loss in the case of disaster, there can be no doubt about it.

The commonest way of making sure that that loss will be bearable is to induce other people to share in the venture, thus spreading the risks. In order to do so, the person who originally decides to take the risk must state his reasons; he must issue what is in fact, if not in form, a prospectus. So what was said about the first form of rational action that we considered will apply. (It is by no means denied that the prospectus may be misleading.)

But as soon as we come to collaboration, even in the simple form of the partnership, other issues arise. Even if there is no more than a single decision that has to be made, it needs to be negotiated. It is only too possible that a negotiated decision may be a "second best" from the point of view of each of the parties to the negotiation; from the point of view of the observer, it is a "bad compromise." One does not need to go far to find examples.

I pass on to the (probably more important) case when there is not a single decision to be made, but when the association is to continue. There will then follow, from each major decision, a number of consequential decisions; and there must often be no time, or opportunity, for each of these consequential decisions to be negotiated. The power to take the consequential decisions must then be delegated.

That is a common situation in modern industry; but it is useful to remark that it came up, in a very strong form, in earlier times. It was then particularly insistent because of bad communications. A trading voyage might then be financed by a consortium, or partnership; but in the course of the voyage, which might well take three years, before the ship returned to Europe from India or Indonesia, the captain of the ship, who was an employee of the owners, had to be left to take the decisions for himself. Such separation has now been much reduced by the airplane and the telephone; nevertheless in a modern business, especially a large business, some of it still persists. In the organization of such a business we still find a system of delegation. There is a "chain of command."

The submanager, who has no more than a delegated authority, cannot be left to seize the opportunity of profit that presents itself to him; for, if each of them did so, they would get in each other's way. So their authority must be limited by rules, formal or informal, which prescribe the limits within which they are to act. It could be that they were left to seize any opportunity for profit within those limits; but to devise such rules as will preserve order and will yet leave a wide opportunity for initiative to the lower ranks in the hierarchy cannot be an easy matter. Rules, by their nature, tend to have a negative bias; it is easier to prescribe what should not be done than to prescribe what should. So the "satisficing," which some have maintained to be a leading characteristic of modern industry, would seem, from this point of view, to have its origin in delegation. The submanager has a task that has been set him; he has a strong incentive to reach his target, but not much to do better.

One can see that applying to the lower ranks; but it should not apply, in the same way, to the "top." But what is the top? In a small concern, where owner and general manager are one and the same, there is no problem of identification, but in a larger concern, especially if it is financed by equity capital, there is. There are two characteristics of the share that are relevant, limited liability and transferability at will (they do not need to go together). It is when both are present, so that the investor can, rationally, spread his risks by diversifying his portfolio, that the separation between control and ownership is so nearly complete.

The shareholders, legally, are part owners of the business; legally, they have power to elect directors. But it is notorious that this is a power which it is hard to exercise. Thus it can readily happen that policy is directed, not in the first place to the pursuit of profit, which is to the interest of the shareholders, but to the maintenance of the organization, the undisturbed existence of the business itself. When this approach is dominant, it tends to defensiveness, the same defensiveness which in the lower ranks derives from delegation.

It is true that against this the market has provided a check. If a firm's policy is such that an outsider can feel fairly sure that it is not doing its best for its shareholders, it may be worth his while to offer high prices for blocks of shares, seeking to acquire enough voting power to change the management, either in person or in policy. Having brought about his revolution, the shares can again be sold; if the prospects of the business, as assessed by the market, then seem to be sufficiently improved, they can be sold at a profit. This sanction, however, is itself dependent on the fact that the share is a liquid asset, so that the value, at any time, is largely dependent on what it is expected to be in the quite near future. A prevalence of take overs is not a sign that the profit motive is working smoothly. It is not in the interest of efficiency that control should be tossed about in the pursuit of short-term gains.[10]

So the take-over sanction works most efficiently if it is an everpresent threat but does not actually occur. In such a world, the controller of business, even of incorporated business, would have no incentive but to work for profit; so the assumption of profit-making rationality would perfectly fit. In practice, it is likely to be less than a perfect fit; it will be tempered by defensiveness. As long as the tempering does not go far, it may be a fair approximation to assume that the representative business man is an Economic Man. Whether or not that is so in a concrete case should be verifiable.

I turn, in conclusion, to other sectors, to Labor and to the Consumer. I do not think that in the case of Labor there is much to be added. We can recognize in the behavior of labor, in a free labor market, the same motives, pursuit of gain, and defensiveness, which we have been considering. Defensiveness must here be relatively more important, especially when the worker has few reserves to fall back on when things go wrong. It is indeed doubtful whether in the strongest cases it is wise to treat the labor market as perfectly fluid.

The case of the Consumer, which our textbooks treat as the most elementary, seems, from the point of view which I have been sketching out, to be less straightforward. It is notable that the classical economists did not treat the Consumer as an Economic Man; they had no need to do so. That comes in with Jevons, with Marginal Utility. The producer was making money, so his goal could be set in monetary terms. The consumer is spending money, so his goal must be defined in a different manner. "Utility" had to be invented in order to give him something in which to do his maximizing.

To treat consumption, or spending, as a maximization against constraints is so appealing, mathematically, that it was bound to carry all before it. But is it any more than a convenient assumption? There can be no question of the service it has performed in fitting statistics into a pattern; but that is just convenience–it does not show that people do act in the way the theory describes.

It has often been remarked that the theory implies that consumers have knowledge of the alternatives before them; but that is a condition which would be better expressed by saying that over a certain field (which is identifiable by the observer) knowledge of the alternatives that are open is easy to get. What should be the test of easiness? The (Paretian) maximization theory is here of little help; it is an issue which is more intelligibly treated by the Marshallian method, of comparing the "utility" of the expected gain with the "disutility" of the cost. So if the gain which is got from a better bargain is highly valued by the buyer, and the trouble which has to be taken to find it is not highly valued, we should expect to find that consumer expenditure would be highly rational; the Paretian scheme would apply very perfectly. These conditions would be satisfied if the shoppers had modest incomes, so that the marginal utility of money to them was high; and if their opportunities for other employment were limited, so that they had time on their hands. I think that such conditions, when they arise, are recognizable.[11]

One should probably add that the shopping needs to be regular, as in the spending of housekeeping money on food and so on, once a week. That gives the shopper repeated experience, from which he learns his "work." It would not appear that irregular purchases can fit so well into the Paretian pattern. Even the consumer whose means are modest, when he has to buy a new coat, does not rethink the whole of his budget in order to see whether the purchase is advantageous. He proceeds in a much more Marshallian manner, considering what he can afford. That is a matter of the marginal utility of money to him, which is derived from his general past experience. When prices, and income, are fairly steady, it is a good guide; but in times of inflation, or great disturbance of relative prices, it can be misleading. One of the costs of inflation is that it causes choices, including consumer choices, to become less rational.[12]

NOTES

1. References are given in notes. I herewith apologize for what I fear will appear to be the self-centered character of those notes, which is to be explained by what is said above. It also explains why I have not been able to say more about the work of others, even of that of our honorand Lachmann. I have not been in a position in which I could identify differences, such as there may be between us. I can just hope that as on former occasions, they will not be found to amount to very much.
2. An outstanding exception is the correspondence between bankers that was so brilliantly utilized by David Landes, *Bankers and Pashas* (Cambridge: Harvard University Press, 1958).

3. Americans, of course, since the formation of the Federal Reserve, are much better placed. The analysis of policy, from documents, which is such an ornament of Milton Friedman and Anna Schwartz, *A Monetary History of the United States, 1867–1960* (Princeton: Princeton University Press, 1963), would hardly be possible in any other country.
4. One can evade this issue by defining economic behavior as being such that it is susceptible of being analyzed in that manner. I gave some countenance to that approach in my *Causality in Economics* (New York: Basic Books, 1979, p. 44), but I have come to feel that it is not good enough.
5. I shall now be drawing quite heavily on my *Theory of Economic History* (Oxford: Clarendon Press, 1969), in which the merchant, as thus defined, is a central figure.
6. Compare the *casual* labor market, as discussed in my *Theory of Wages* (London: Macmillan, 1932), pp. 62–9.
7. This is further discussed in the passage in my *Causality*, op. cit., that was quoted above.
8. Many of the papers in my *Wealth and Welfare* (Cambridge: Harvard University Press, 1981) are relevant. So is the well-known chapter XIV, on income, in *Value and Capital* (Oxford: Clarendon Press, 1939); and so is the less well-known chapter XII of *Capital and Time* (Oxford: Clarendon Press, 1973). Then, on the relations between the economic and the accounting concepts, there is "Capital controversies: ancient and modern" in *Economic Perspectives* (Oxford: Clarendon Press, 1977) and two papers (13 and 14) in *Classics and Moderns* (Cambridge: Harvard University Press, 1983).
9. I have become increasingly convinced that the right way to model behavior, when the outcome of a decision is uncertain is not by mean and variance, as is common practice in portfolio theory, but by concentrating attention on two alternatives: (1) the outcome which is judged to be the most likely (2) the worst that is judged to have a finite possibility. These must be considered, and the estimation of them is manageable; it is hard to see that the estimation of other alternatives will often be worth the bother. (My thinking in this direction took its origin from a paper "The Disaster Point in Risk Theory" which appeared in *Economic Perspectives* , op. cit. republished, in a somewhat improved form, in my *Money, Interest and Wages* (Cambridge: Harvard University Press, 1982), pp. 251–6.
10. I have enlarged on this in my paper on "Limited Liability," in *Classics and Moderns*, chapter 13.
11. I can illustrate by a personal recollection. Just after the time when I had finished *Value and Capital* (the first three chapters of which contain a statement of Paretian theory) my wife and I moved house from Cambridge to the neighborhood of Manchester, where I was to teach for several years. We then found ourselves having to do our weekly shopping in what proclaimed itself to be a "purely working-class town," where most of the shoppers were housewives, who had time on their hands, since there were no extensive opportunities for part-time employment. So they went from shop to shop, comparing prices and talking to the shopkeepers. It was a much more "perfect" consumer market than that to which we had been used in Cambridge.
12. See my paper on "Time in Economics" in *Money, Interest and Wages*, pp. 285–6.

9 Equilibration and Disequilibration in the Market Process*

JACK HIGH

> But a theory of process must establish the determinateness of market events, quite apart from the issue of whether this course of events does or does not tend toward an equilibrium state. (Israel M. Kirzner, *Perception, Opportunity, and Profit*, Chicago: University of Chicago Press, 1979, p. 17)

INTRODUCTION

Austrian economists have long been critical of the neoclassical preoccupation with equilibrium states. Rather than focus their attention on end states, Austrians have concentrated on the process of change that characterizes real-world markets. Nevertheless, most Austrians have also granted equilibrium an important role in the elucidation of the market process. Fink and Cowen[1] have identified four uses to which Austrians have put the equilibrium construct: 1. to explain the market economy's direction of change; 2. as a building block in the analysis of complex phenomena; 3. as a starting point for the analysis of change, and 4. as a foil against which to compare a complex order.

This paper will focus on the first of these uses: equilibrium as a goal toward which the market process moves. Mises, Hayek, Kirzner, Rothbard, and O'Driscoll are among those who have maintained that the equilibrium state tells us the direction in which the market process is moving. These economists see the market as a fundamentally equilibrating process.

Among Austrians, Lachmann has been at the forefront in opposing the conception of the market as a strictly equilibrating process. In keeping with his view that equilibrium is not easily applied to the analysis of markets, Lachmann has stressed that the market process is composed of both equilibrating and disequilibrating forces.[2] "If, with Mises," writes Lachmann, "we reject the notion of general equilibrium, but on the other hand, do not deny the operation of equilibrating forces in markets and between markets, we naturally have to account for those disequilibrating forces which prevent equilibrium from being reached."[3] Lachmann's view has been explicitly criticized by O'Driscoll and Selgin.[4] It is compatible with the view that the market is a strictly equilibrating process. This paper defends Lachmann's thesis that the market is a disequilibrating as well as an equilibrating process.

Our discussion will take place at three levels. First, we will be concerned with semantical questions, especially with the meanings of "equilibrium" and "data." Second, we will be concerned with the status of the claim that the market is a strictly equilibrating process. We will argue that this is an imaginary construction not a description of real world market processes. Third, we will be concerned with the implications for the scientific nature of economics. We will show that the scientific nature of economics is strengthened, not weakened, by incorporating disequilibration into the analysis of the market process.

THE MARKET AS MOVEMENT TOWARDS AN EVENLY ROTATING ECONOMY

There are different meanings of equilibrium as the word is used in Austrian writings, but the one to which we will first direct our attention is the evenly rotating economy, which is similar to the neoclassical conception of general equilibrium. In both constructions there is complete consistency of plans, a single (numeraire) price for each commodity, and no opportunities for profit. The evenly rotating economy has the additional restriction that activities must repeat period after period.

The significance of this construction is the tendency of a market economy to approach this state. According to Mises, one reason for using this equilibrium construction [1963, p. 250], is ". . . the tendency, prevailing in every action, toward the establishment of an evenly rotating economy."[5] Similarly Rothbard claims that the evenly rotating economy ". . . is like the mechanical rabbit being chased by the dog. It is never reached in practice, and it is always changing, but it explains the direction in which the dog is moving."[6] Although Kirzner does not use the conception of the evenly rotating economy, his views are similar to those of Mises and Rothbard. Kirzner looks on the market as a strictly equilibrating process. In contrasting his view of entrepreneurship with that of Schumpeter, he writes, "For me the function of the entrepreneur consists not of *shifting* the curves of cost or of revenue which face him, but *of noticing that they have in fact shifted.*"[7] Kirzner views the entrepreneur as an arbitrageur whose activities successively squeeze out profit opportunities in the economy, thus propelling it towards equilibrium.[8]

ENDOGENOUS AND EXOGENOUS CHANGE

A conception of the market as a process which only equilibrates is incomplete at best; at worst it can distort our vision of the market by presenting as exogenous forces that are really endogenous.

We can best see this point by asking, If the market is always moving toward an evenly rotating state, why doesn't it ever get there? The usual reply is that the end state is always moving. The market is at every instant moving toward a final state of rest, but "[e]very later new instant can create new facts altering this final state of rest."[9] Rothbard puts it even more clearly. "If our *data*—values, technology, and resources—remained constant, the economy would move toward the final equilibrium position and remain there. In actual life, however, the data are always changing, and therefore, before arriving at a final equilibrium point, the economy must shift direction, towards some other final equilibrium position."[10]

If we are to accept the view of the market described above, we must accept any changes in tastes, technology, and resources as *given.* They are given, not only to an individual entrepreneur, but to everyone in the economy, and therefore to the economist. The changes are exogenous to the system, and are therefore not open to economic analysis.

Surely, this is an unnecessarily narrow view of the market and of economics. We know that an open market for ideas will lead people to change their value scales, that the prospect of profits will induce entrepreneurs to seek out new technologies and uncover new resources. These changes are as endogenous to the market systems as changes in prices. As Lachmann has put it, "To speak here of 'random shocks' would be to profess ignorance where we have knowledge."[11]

Hayek's example of a new use for a raw material spreading information through the price system illustrates the proclivity to take entrepreneurial discovery as a given. Hayek writes:

> Assume that somewhere in the world a new opportunity for the use of some raw materials, say, tin, has arisen, or that one of the sources of supply of tin has been eliminated. It does not matter for our purpose—and it is significant that it does not matter—which of these two causes has made tin more scarce. All that the users of tin need to know is that some of the tin they used to consume is now more profitably employed elsewhere and that, in consequence, they must economize tin. There is no need for the great majority of them even to know where the more urgent need has arisen, or in favor of what other needs they ought to husband their supply. If only some of them know directly of the new demand, and switch resources over to it, and if the people who are aware of the new gap thus created in turn fill it from still other sources, the effect will rapidly spread throughout whole economic system and influence not only all the uses of tin but also those of its substitutes and the substitutes of these substitutes, and so on; and all this without the great majority of those instrumental in bringing about these substitutions knowing anything at all about the original cause of these changes.[12]

Hayek takes the discovery of a new use of tin as the starting point in his analysis, and what follows is a concise description of the process by which the market disseminates information. This process is vital to the market, and the Austrians have been fully justified in studying this aspect of the market process. *However, it is not the only important aspect.* What makes the process of dissemination necessary is an entrepreneur who has discovered a new use for tin. Such discoveries do not just "arise." They are not exogenous to the market, but the definite result of profit seeking. To take these discoveries as data is to commit an error similar to the one Hayek warned against.[13] It is to take facts, the knowledge of which should be explained, as given.

Nor is the process which spreads information of the discovery, and moves prices toward its market clearing level, a strictly equilibrating process. As some users of tin watch their supply bid away from them, and see the price bid up, they experience the disappointment of plans. Only if we assume that they somehow knew that the change was coming, could we escape the conclusion that the process disappoints plans that would otherwise have been consistent. But if we postulate that everyone knew the change was coming, there would be no process of adjustment. The market clearing price and redistribution of tin would have occurred at once.

Looking at the market as a strictly equilibrating process requires us to remain silent about changes that Austrian economics is particularly well equipped to explain. If we adopt the view that changes in tastes, technology, and resources are given, that entrepreneurship does not shift curves, but merely notices that they have shifted, we involve ourselves in the same inadequacy that entrepreneurship was supposed to extract us from.

Kirzner has criticized Robbinsian maximizing for its inability to explain the emergence of ends and means.[14] By limiting economics to the study of allocating scarce means among competing means, economics excludes the active mental processes by which these ends and means are formulated. Only by recognizing that action is directed by active mental processes are we able to explain the original formulation, and the continual change, of ends and means.

Similarly, if we look at entrepreneurship as merely noticing changes in revenues and cost curves, then we cannot explain where those changes come from. We are restricted to analyzing adaptation to changes that mysteriously appear.

The fundamental point is this: The same active mental processes which are taken to adjust to change once it has occurred, will also originate change. Changes in cost and revenue curves do not simply happen; they are the results of purposeful attempts by consumers and producers to improve their situations. *If we are not content to take the ends-means framework of agents as merely given, then we should not be willing to take changes in tastes, technology, and resources as given.*

In arguing that the market is not a strictly equilibrating process, we are not necessarily advocating that this concept be eliminated from economic theory. We are simply pointing out that strict equilibration is an imaginary construct. Like the evenly rotating economy, it has no real existence. This interpretation is consistent with the generally recognized fact that the data are in reality always changing.[15]

Perhaps we also should mention at this point our position on the deductive vs. empirical view of the market process. Hayek distinguished between the necessary propositions of the pure logic of choice, which is essentially equilibrium theory, and the empirical propositions of movement toward equilibrium.[16] Kirzner has responded by deducing a movement toward equilibrium from the Misesian notion of entrepreneurship.[17] We are maintaining that both equilibration and disequilibration are deducible from entrepreneurship, and hence we side with Kirzner on the deductive/empirical issue. However, since we are claiming that entrepreneurship both equilibrates and disequilibrates the market, we also have the burden of showing that the net result will be order rather than chaos. We will do this in the next section.

SOCIAL EVOLUTION AND ECONOMIC SCIENCE

There has been some fear among Austrian economists that the admission of endogenous disequilibration into the theory threatens the scientific nature of economics.[18] This fear seems unfounded; many important insights of Austrian economics do not depend on movement toward the evenly rotating state. In particular, the evolutionary aspects of Austrian theory do not depend on a postulated movement toward the evenly rotating state. Moreover, viewing the market as an evolutionary process enables us to explain why an economy composed of both equilibrating and disequilibrating forces results in order rather than chaos.

Austrian economic theory, almost from its inception, has emphasized the spontaneous evolution of institutions.[19] Menger's explanation of the emergence of money is the prototype of this evolutionary theory, but there are other examples as well. Monetary calculations, extensive division of labor, and enterprise firms are examples of practices that evolve from, and only exist in, a system of private ownership of the means of production.[20] Even the property rights that underlie the market economy have been brought within the purview of evolutionary theory.[21]

The evolution of these institutions does not depend on the general equilibrium construct. Evolution is an open-ended process that does not, so far as we know, tend toward any final state of rest. We are able to comprehend, therefore, why money, firms, and an extensive division of labor develop, without any reference to an evenly rotating state. In fact, money and firms are not even possible in general equilibrium.[22]

The evolutionary aspects of Austrian theory hold without any reference to the evenly rotating state, and demonstrate that the scientific nature of economics per se is not at issue here. The framing of scientific laws concerning the market is not dependent on the economy always moving toward a general equilibrium.

Although laws about the evolution of market institutions do not depend on movement toward an evenly rotating economy, laws about the operation of these institutions might. However, we have reason to doubt even this proposition.

The evolution of the market cannot be separated entirely from its operation. The development of market institutions is the result of the operation of the market. The mere fact that money, monetary calculation, business firms, and advertising emerge and persist in the market belies the claim that the market is a strictly equilibrating process. These institutions do not exist in general equilibrium. A theory that postulates a persistent movement toward general equilibrium is a theory that, in an evolutionary sense, can only explain the *disappearance* of these institutions.

A particularly important issue is whether we can, without reference to equilibration, demonstrate that order will emerge from decentralized decision making in a market. If our demonstration of market order depends on movement towards an evenly rotating state, then the scientific nature of economics depends heavily on equilibration in this sense. Interestingly, we can rely on evolution to derive that decentralized market decisions will result in order.

The key to using evolution to explain market order lies in connecting monetary calculation, entrepreneurship, and the division of labor.

The advantage of dividing labor has been recognized since Adam Smith, and has been used by Mises to explain the existence of social cooperation.[23] The superior productivity available through the division of labor gives people an incentive to cooperate with one another through specialization and exchange. As this specialization progresses, exchanging becomes more difficult, which is the impetus for developing a medium of exchange. The development of a medium then facilitates further division of labor, by making exchange easier, and by making possible monetary calculation. This is the process by which a complex economy develops.

The development of a complex economy is, of course, not the result of any overall plan, but rather the unintended consequence of profit seeking. Each further division of labor is undertaken by entrepreneurs hoping to capture profits. For each increase in the division of labor, the entrepreneur must weigh the value of the additional output against the additional cost. One of these costs will be for the additional coordination required. Additional coordination may take place through exchange, or it may take place through supervision in the firm, but each new division of labor necessitates additional coordination somewhere in the social structure. If the value of the increased division of labor outweighs the additional costs, then the division will succeed, and the social structure will become more complex. If the value does not outweigh the cost, then the attempted division will fail, and the complexity of the market will be limited. Thus is the complexity of the market limited by the difficulty of coordinating actions. Order is a byproduct of the competition for profit, which gives entrepreneurs an incentive to discover and implement those divisions that are productive on net. Those divisions that introduce too much disorder into the system and thereby cause monetary losses, will be eliminated.[23]

CONCLUSION

We have argued that characterizing the market as a strictly equilibrating process is an incomplete and misleading way of describing and analyzing the market process. It leaves unexplained those changes in tastes, technology, and resources that upset previously compatible plans. These changes are the result of entrepreneurship and are as endogenous to the market as any other entrepreneurial change.

We have also argued that admitting disequilibration into our analysis does not destroy the scientific nature of Austrian theory. Social institutions have always been considered an important part of Austrian economics, and the theory of their evolution does not depend on movement toward the evenly rotating state. In fact, quite the opposite is true. To the extent that the market homes in on general equilibrium, many market institutions will be destroyed, since those institutions do not exist in general equilibrium.

The conflict between evolution theory and movement toward the evenly rotating economy suggests that we abandon equilibration in the sense of movement toward an evenly rotating state.) Equilibration in this sense is not essential to explaining why plans are largely compatible, nor is this kind of equilibration necessary for explaining the tendency toward market clearing prices and quantities.

The difference between equilibrium in the sense of market clearing and equilibrium in the sense of an evenly rotating state may require some clarification. That the two concepts are fundamentally different can be seen by again considering money, monetary calculation, and enterprise firms. None of these exist in the evenly rotating economy, yet all of them are compatible with market clearing. All market clearing means is that, for a particular period, prices and quantities are such that all expectations are fulfilled.

Since market clearing is a momentary phenomenon, it does not, as an evenly rotating equilibrium does, remove ignorance and uncertainty from the market. The temporary consistency of plans does not require or imply intertemporal consistency the way evenly rotating equilibrium does.[24]

Another way to see this point is to differentiate between Walrasian supply-and-demand curves and Austrian supply-and-demand curves. The Walrasian curves are derived from the auctioneer calling out prices, and consumers and producers responding with quantities derived from utility and profit-maximizing calculations. These calculations are based on complete knowledge of all available consumers' goods, all available producers goods, the best available production techniques, and the knowledge that there is a single, given price for each good. The Austrian curves are based on plans derived from estimated prices, estimated quantities and qualities of consumers' goods, estimated availability of resources, and estimates of the most economical means of production. A great many judgment calls go into the derivation of the Austrian curves, and market institutions are indispensable aids in the formation of these judgments. That is why the market clearing prices and quantities based on these demand curves are compatible with institutions, whereas general equilibrium "prices" are not.[25]

Equilibration in the sense of moving prices and quantities towards their market clearing levels is especially important in a theory that takes disequilibration as an endogenous market force. If we grant that entrepreneurship will shift supply and demand curves in ways not foreseen by everyone in the market, and therefore in ways that upset previously compatible plans, then a process that will move prices and quantities towards market clearing levels is vital. Were it not for this process, the market would not be a process that conveys knowledge about shifting tastes, resources, and production techniques.

We will conclude our argument by claiming two last reasons for including disequilibration as an endogenous force in the market. First, it helps keep economics in that middle ground, which, as Garrison has shown us, is the most fertile for the growth of economic theory.[26] By making changes in tastes, technology, and resources an integral part of our theory, we provide an endless expanse of new knowledge that the market must adjust to.

Second, it is from disequilibration that movements toward market clearing derive much of their importance. Disseminating information through the price system as described by Hayek is vital precisely because the disequilibrating changes of entrepreneurs are so common in the market.[27]

For these reasons, the inclusion of disequilibration strengthens the Austrian analysis of the market process.

NOTES

* I thank Tyler Cowen, Richard Fink, Mary Hirschfeld, Randy Kroszner, and students in the graduate Austrian theory class at George Mason University for helpful comments. Of course, none is responsible for errors.

1. Richard Fink and Tyler Cowen, "Is the Evenly Rotating Economy a Useful Economic Construct?" *American Economic Review*, 75 (1985), pp. 866–9.
2. Ludwig Lachmann, "Methodological Individualism and the Market Economy," in *Capital, Expectations, and the Market Process*, ed. Walter Grinder (Kansas City: Sheed Andrews & McMeel, 1977), pp. 149–50.
3. Ludwig Lachmann, "Ludwig von Mises and the Market Process," reprinted in ed. Grinder op. cit., p. 190.
4. Gerald P. O'Driscoll, "Spontaneous Order and the Coordination of Economic Activities," in *New Directions in Austrian Economics*, ed. Louis M. Spadaro (Kansas City: Sheed Andrew & McMeel, 1978), pp. 128–34; George Selgin, "Praxeology and Understanding," unpublished manuscript, New York University. Selgin criticizes Lachmann in the course of defending the market as a strictly equilibrating process. His defense is interesting for the way it ties together equilibrium, equilibrating, and profit opportunities. However, Selgin's views are much more compatible with those of Lachmann than his paper would suggest. In particular, nothing in his paper (except for the terminology) contradicts the defense of Lachmann presented here.
5. Ludwig von Mises, *Human Action* (Chicago: Henry Regnery, 1963), p. 250.
6. Murray Rothbard, *Man, Economy, and State* (Los Angeles: Nash Publishing, 1962), p. 250.
7. Israel Kirzner, *Competition and Entrepreneurship* (Chicago: University of Chicago Press, 1973), p. 81.
8. Ibid., pp. 15, 27, 85.
9. Mises, op. cit., p. 245.
10. Rothbard, op. cit., p. 262.
11. Lachmann, in ed. Grinder, op. cit., p. 152.
12. Friedrich Hayek, "The Use of Knowledge in Society," reprinted in *Individualism and Economic Order* (Chicago: University of Chicago Press, 1948), pp. 85–6.
13. See Hayek, "Economics and Knowledge," reprinted in ibid., pp. 37–39. The error we are pointing to is not identical to that of Hayek. He objected to economists' assuming that people know things they do not in fact know. We object to leaving the discovery of facts unanalyzed. Both practices treat information that must be acquired as somehow given.
14. Op. cit., p. 33.
15. See, for example, the Rothbard quotation above, p. 4.
16. See Hayek, "Economics and Knowledge," reprinted in *Individualism and Economic Order*, op. cit.
17. Israel Kirzner, "Hayek, Knowledge, and Market Processes," in *Perception, Opportunity, and Profit* (Chicago: University of Chicago Press, 1979), pp. 26–32.

18. See, for example, O'Driscoll, op. cit., p. 132, where he questions the existence of coordination in Lachmann's system. See also Selgin, op. cit., p. 1.
19. See Carl Menger, *Principles of Economics* (New York: New York University Press, 1981), pp. 257–85.
20. Ibid., pp. 212–17. Frank H. Knight, *Risk, Uncertainty, and Profit* (Chicago: University of Chicago Press, 1971), p. 267–8.
21. See, for example, Friedrich Hayek, *Law, Legislation, and Liberty* (Chicago: University of Chicago Press, 1973), chapters 4–5.
22. On the existence of money in equilibrium, see Mises, op. cit., p. 249. For a discussion of why firms do not exist in equilibrium, see Richard Langlois "Internal Organization in a Dynamic Context: Some Theoretical Considerations," in *Communication and Information*, ed. Meheroo Jussawalla and Helene Ebenfield (Amsterdam and Oxford: North-Holland, 1984).
23. See Mises, op. cit., pp. 159–65.
24. See Fink, "Partial Equilibrium and the Analysis of Resale Price Maintenance" (George Mason University: Center for the Study of Market Processes Working Paper Series, July 1983), pp. 9–10.
25. On the derivation of "Austrian" curves, Rothbard, *Man, Economy, and State*, op. cit., pp. 112–18; Jack High, *Maximizing, Action, and Market Adjustment* (unpublished doctoral dissertation, UCLA, 1980), pp. 149–64.
26. Roger Garrison, "Austrian Economics as the Middle Ground," in *Method, Process, and Austrian Economics*, ed. Israel Kirzner (Lexington, Mass.: Heath, 1982), pp. 131–8.
27. O'Driscoll puts the point this way: "The problem of economic coordination is a theoretical and practical issue not merely because decision-making is decentralized, though this is an important aspect of the problem. Of even more importance is the fact that we live in a world of constant change . . . A price system and appropriate market institutions are of practical significance precisely because of the need to register the effects of continuous changes in the data, changes which are given to no one in their entirety." (Spadaro, op. cit., pp. 120–1.)

10 Philosophical Issues that Divide Liberals: Omniscience or Omni-nescience about the Future?*

TERENCE W. HUTCHISON

I

The philosophical issues which divide supporters of economic individualism and the market economy, or, in an old-fashioned sense, economic liberals, are deep and wide, though often not recognized or faced. These divisions exist, for example, regarding such questions as prediction and predictability, falsification and falsifiability, as well as between upholders of critical fallibilism as against those proclaiming infallibilist, or a priorist, apodictic certainties, or between what may be described as more Popperian or more Misesian methodological doctrines.

It has been objected that discussions of such philosophical, or methodological, issues often, or on the average, result in no more than a zero marginal product. Leaving aside questions of measurement, one might, perhaps, observe that a zero marginal product seems quite a respectable one, compared with the vastly negative marginal products which in recent years, according to one school of thought or the other, have accrued from the monetary or macroeconomic doctrines of their opponents, either in promoting disastrous inflation, or in bringing about catastrophic unemployment.

Anyway, this paper is not directly concerned with any particular methodological doctrine or controversy but rather with fundamentally conflicting assumptions regarding economic knowledge, on which has rested, and must still rest, much of the main theorizing from which liberal economists have derived their policy conclusions. Now it reasonably can, and should, be argued that, for all economists, and particularly for liberals, more clarity and realism, and less fundamental disagreement, are as important regarding the nature and extent of economic knowledge and ignorance, as they are regarding any particular policy issue, even that of monetary policy and the monetary framework. Delusions and "pretensions" regarding the nature and extent of economic knowledge have a very long history and have been nourished and propagated by economists of most, or all, schools, types and shades of political opinion, including liberals. Such delusions and pretensions have encouraged overoptimistic, and, often, in the longer run, disappointing, attempts at policy-making, based on excessive expectations which have led either to dangerous disillusionment, or to reactions directly opposed to the original objectives.[1]

II

The opinion has been expressed by that admirably named American legal luminary, Judge Learned Hand that "The spirit of liberty is the spirit that's not sure it's right." The spirit described in the learned judge's apophthegm is hardly to be discerned in the claims of some of the leading exponents of the classical and neoclassical theories from which liberal economic policies have often been, and still are, to a considerable extent, derived. In fact, classical economic theorizing owed much of its confidence and impact to highly optimistic or even Utopian assumptions, or pretensions, sometimes left inexplicit, regarding knowledge, which, in turn, derived, as in the case of the Physiocrats, and to some extent the Philosophic Radicals, from the rosily rationalistic pretensions of the French Enlightenment. Two such assumptions, or pretensions, regarding knowledge are important:

First, there was the pretension regarding the nature, extent, and certainty of economists' knowledge as to how the economy worked, or could easily be made to work.

Second, there was the assumption which gradually, in the nineteenth century, took over a fundamental role in economic theorizing, as to the extent and certainty of the knowledge, and capacity to learn, possessed by individuals, or regarding the correctness and completeness of the expectations, on which they based their economic decisions.

Neither of these optimistic assumptions, or pretensions, had been indulged in to anything like the same degree by Adam Smith, or his great predecessors, such as Mandeville, Tucker, and Galiani, none of whom put forward their policy doctrines in the same unqualified and even extreme terms as some of their leading nineteenth-century successors were to do. (Indeed, both Mandeville and Tucker were so qualified in their views on freedom of trade as to be denounced as benighted mercantilists by the late Jacob Viner.) The *Wealth of Nations*, though expressing a reasonable degree of optimism and confidence, contains many cautious qualifications and stands for an approach to policy distinctly different from that of some of Smith's main classical followers. Smith's system, though mainly and broadly self-adjusting, left significant room for ignorance. He did not claim to be laying down "laws" comparable with those of physics. He himself condemned "the man of system," and criticized for its Utopianism Quesnay's use of the criteria of "perfect liberty" or "perfect justice," recommending simply as an aim, not some optimum or maximum, but the endeavour to establish "the best the people can bear."[2]

The contrast is important, both with the Physiocrats, and with some of Smith's leading classical followers (Malthus excepted). It might be said to constitute much of the contrast between "Individualism: True, and False." For example, regarding the extent of economic knowledge, the Physiocrats asserted that the advance in knowledge which their system represented was comparable in significance with the greatest, all-time human discoveries, like writing, or the wheel. James Mill, Ricardo, and McCulloch claimed that the laws of their new science of political economy possessed "an extraordinary degree of certainty" and were comparable with the laws of physics. Ricardo suggested that his theory of economic progress "is as certain as the principle of gravitation." Moreover, according to the young J. S. Mill, in one of his more pretentious moments, this remarkably advanced state of knowledge had been reached very rapidly and recently and represented an immense advance over Adam Smith.[3]

Of course, the extraordinarily high epistemological quality, indeed certainty, claimed for the new economic laws, justified highly forthright, unqualified, and even, sometimes, extreme doctrines on policy, which were claimed to be justified by the, in many respects, strikingly successful achievements of the British economy in the 1850s and 1860s (Senior, 1878, vol. I, p. 160).

The crisis of English classical political economy in the 1870s brought, for a time, something of a jolt to confidence. Moreover, it was far from clear how far the classical market economy, and the policies derived from the classical "laws," could survive the wider extension of the franchise. Some classical liberals had been highly pessimistic on this question. In due course, however, some forms of neoclassical analysis, in particular the Walrasian, seemed to tighten up classical doctrines regarding the beneficence of the perfectly competitive economy and give them an even sharper edge. This facilitated the formulation of policy objectives in terms of explicitly Utopian maxima and optima (apparently still today regarded as possessing significant, real-world policy relevance or "great practical importance").

Classical confidence thus, to a large extent returned, and was further fortified by comparisons with the natural sciences, expressing an even higher level of confidence than that displayed by James Mill and Ricardo. A doctrine developed by Cairnes and Wieser began to gain ground, according to which the use of introspection provided an *even more* reliable, or certain, basis for economic theory than that available to the natural sciences (Hutchison, 1981, pp. 205–207). This kind of confidence was summed up in Lionel Robbins's celebrated *Essay on the Nature and Significance of Economic Science*, with its assertion of "scientific laws" in economics, together with theories of "immense" or "very considerable prognostic value," based on fundamental generalizations and concepts which there was "much less reason to doubt" than those underlying the natural sciences (1984, pp. 67, 105, and 122–125).

With the boom in the subject after World War II, a further great upswing in confidence took place, based partly on claims for mathematical and quantitative methods. This time, however, unlike on most earlier occasions, most liberals (and, in particular, members of the Mont Pelerin Society) inclined to caution and criticism, though some highly optimistic claims for economics were also expressed. But the last decade and a half, since about 1970, has come to be widely described as one of "crisis," in the subject of economics, as well as in much of the world economy. This has brought, to some extent, a healthy deflation of excessive pretensions and illusions, together with some progress in realizing the extent and inevitability of human ignorance. For its philosophical or epistemological health, political economy is a subject which should regularly be in a state of "crisis." Nevertheless, considerable residues of earlier illusions regarding politicoeconomic knowledge may still survive, alongside new forms, and even extremes, of skepticism.

III

The *second* kind of rationalistic, Utopian pretension, or assumption, about knowledge, with which economists have long, heavily, and often inexplicitly, been involved, is more specific, and concerned with the extent, adequacy, certainty, completeness, or even perfection, of the knowledge which individuals are assumed to possess in coming to their economic decisions. In *The Wealth of Nations*, as we have remarked, there was considerable room for human ignorance. It was with Ricardo that the assumption of adequate or full knowledge was explicitly introduced and began to take on a logically essential role.[4] What is remarkable is for how long, through the nineteenth century and on through much of the twentieth, it was so faintly and fleetingly recognized what a vast simplification this assumption represented, and, at the same time, what a vital role it had to play in so much of economic theory. J. S. Mill, for example, referred to this fundamental abstraction from ignorance and uncertainty in almost casual, throwaway terms, when he appended to his basic postulate that man, "by the necessity of his nature," was, "in all cases," a would-be wealth maximizer, the vital addition that he was also "capable of judging of the comparative efficacy of means for obtaining that end" or, in other words, that human beings possessed a vast amount of knowledge which they certainly do not possess and perhaps *could* not possess, while remaining human beings (J. S. Mill, 1844, pp. 137–138).

Now, of course, this huge general simplification about knowledge made possible a vast development of, up to a point, potentially illuminating analysis, which, if used cautiously and with restraint, could often provide valuable guidance for policy. In some particular cases, or markets, this assumption, or pretension, may well represent a reasonable approximation. But, as a comprehensive generalization, the extent of the abstraction involved seems seldom to have been adequately acknowledged. Nor has it been recognized that, regarding some of the most important, real-world phenomena, such as severe fluctuations, conditions were being postulated, under which such problems, either logically could not, or very probably would not, arise.

The full-knowledge assumption seems first to have been made the target of explicit and extensive criticism by Cliffe Leslie, in his brilliant essay "The Known and the Unknown in the Economic World" (1879). Leslie alleged that the assumptions of orthodox theory included one of "full knowledge," and charged that "the vastness, complexity, and incessant changes" of the real world "are absolutely incompatible with the main postulates of the Ricardian theory." Leslie quoted the question posed by the German historical economist, Erwin Nasse: "Fixed capital—ships, railways, factories, mines—involve production for the future; but how is the future to be known?" (Leslie, n.d. p. 231).[5]

However, on the other side of the *Methodenstreit*, shortly after Leslie's essay, but apparently in ignorance of it, Carl Menger, in his *Untersuchungen*, recognized the same point. Menger observed that there was a gap in the assumptions of theoretical economics. "Error," he pointed out, was "a factor which surely can be separated still less from human action than custom, public spirit, feeling for justice, and love of one's fellow man, can be separated from the economy." Menger observed that historical critics had been too lenient towards their theoretical opponents in not putting more emphasis on this vital limitation:

> The presupposition of a strict regularity in economic phenomena, and with this of a theoretical economics in the full meaning of the word, includes not only the dogmas of ever-constant self-interest, but also the dogma of the "infallibility" and "omniscience" of men in economic matters (1963, p. 84).[6]

Thus Menger argued that the existence, or possibility of theoretical economics, in the full meaning of the word, depended, *and had to depend*, on this simplification. Economic theory, could, apparently, only cope with infallible and omniscient beings.

With the development of business-cycle theory, towards the close of the nineteenth century, there came increasing emphasis (traceable back to Sismondi) on the role of errors of optimism and pessimism in bringing about these vast disequilibria (which had, however, been regarded by leading classicals, such as J. S. Mill, quite logically, on their assumptions, as no more than frictions). Thus more attention gradually and intermittently began to be focused on the question of knowledge and ignorance and on the assumption about them on which economic theory was based.

The next major development in this disconnected story came with F. H. Knight's *Risk, Uncertainty and Profit* (1921). Knight described the abstraction from ignorance and uncertainty as constituting "the most important underlying difference between the conditions *which theory is compelled to assume*, and those which exist in fact" (1921, p. 51, italics added). Thus, like Menger, Knight insisted that economic theory was compelled to limit itself to conditions from which ignorance and uncertainty were excluded, and in which everyone enjoyed, as Menger had put it, "infallibility" and "omniscience."

With the onset of the Great Depression in the 1930s, questions were raised by a number of distinguished writers regarding uncertainty, erroneous expectations, and inadequate knowledge, and about the exclusion of this aspect of the human condition from the assumptions of much of economic theory. Among others, there were the Swedish economists, with their distinction between *ex ante* and *ex post* quantities, as well as Keynes with his accusation that "the orthodox theory assumes that we have a knowledge of the future of a kind quite different from that which we actually possess" (1937, p. 192). In another direction, Friedrich Hayek, in the same years wrote his (already mentioned) path-breaking article on "Economics and Knowledge." He emphasized how "the tautologies, of which formal equilibrium analysis in economics essentially consists, can be turned into propositions which tell us anything about causation in the real world only in so far as we are able to fill those formal propositions with definite statements about how knowledge is acquired and communicated (p. 37)." (In other words, apriorism cannot tell us anything about real-world causation.)[7]

For some time after World War II, however, when many of the leading economies in the world appeared to be enjoying an exceptionally long spell of something like a kind of "equilibrium," with both unemployment and inflation at levels which hardly seemed serious, these fundamental criticisms and questions from the 1930s were, by most economists, disregarded (except as weapons for attacking opposing theories or schools). Alternatively, even if ignorance might be conceded as an important characteristic of individuals, knowledgeable, or even omniscient governments could correct or compensate for their errors and maintain an equilibrium. It was only in the 1970s, when disequilibrium presented itself as an obvious and even overwhelming phenomenon, which governments, perhaps much less than individuals, seemed epistemologically equipped to deal with, that the role of ignorance and uncertainty, and the nature of assumptions on this subject of much of economic theory, began again to receive more serious recognition.

But the full-knowledge assumption still today pervades much of economic theorizing. It is tightly interlocked with the concepts of equilibrium and perfect competition, and it has also received something like a new lease of life in some forms of the assumption of rational expectations. At the textbook level, full and precise knowledge is still regularly on display in the exquisite curves and diagrams, dependent on the availability of just such a Utopian supply of knowledge.[8] In fact, considerable areas of academic economic theorizing could be said, still today, largely to amount to theorizing by the Utopianly knowledgeable about the omniscient. For when economists assume that human beings possess omniscience, or infallibility, in making their economic decisions, they, of course, include themselves, in the everyday business of life, as enjoying this ideal degree of knowledge. Perhaps, when changing to their professional economists' hats, they may sometimes fail to abandon this Utopian pretense of knowledge.

IV

In this last decade or so, however, dominated by disequilibrium and crisis, a libertarian school of economic thought has emerged to prominence which not only rejects comprehensively the assumption of omniscience, or full knowledge, but which has swung over towards an extreme opposite assumption of thoroughgoing uncertainty and unpredictability. This is the Neo-Austrian school, which, inspired by the ideas of Professor George Shackle, insists that fundamental uncertainty and ignorance, together with erroneous or inadequate expectations, or anticipations, dominate economic decisions and the human condition. In the real world of uncertainty and ignorance, decisions, it would seem, have to depend on, or emerge from, a combination, largely of instinct, hunch, inspiration, clairvoyance, or what Keynes called "animal spirits." In such a world, the case for economic freedom and competition has to be based on the desirability of creating and maintaining the widest opportunities for as many as possible to try their luck. For, on these assumptions, it is human ignorance and fallibility which provides the vital justification for free institutions and processes, not human knowledge, and, much less, human omniscience and infallibility.

The argument, therefore, as to the impossibility of economic calculation in a socialist, or planned, economy must, according to the doctrines of Shackle, or the Neo-Austrians, be regarded as fundamentally irrelevant. For, from their standpoint, *any* significant *calculation* is impossible in respect of *any* real-world economic decision making, whether by socialist managers, capitalist entrepreneurs, or by any other kind of economic human being. To regard any important, real-world economic decisions as, to a significant extent, calculable, would seem, according to the doctrine of Shackle and the Neo-Austrians, to amount to a fundamental misconception.[9]

The ideas of Shackle and the Neo-Austrians have brought, or emphasized, important, fundamental insights, and provide a healthy contrast and corrective to the long-standing, though often insufficiently explicit, assumption of full knowledge. They seem, however, to depend on assumptions, or arguments, which constitute too extreme a reaction from conventional, Utopian superrationalism towards a kind of subrationalism, or even irrationalism. These doctrines also seem to contain some paradoxes, or serious ambiguities.

We must first, however, express agreement with Professor Shackle when he insists, like Knight before him, on the gulf which yawns between the assumptions about knowledge underlying traditional economic theory and the actual far-reaching ignorance in which human beings live (even though that gulf may not be as wide and deep as he seems to suggest).[10] Knight observed how, in a world of full knowledge and predictability, human beings would be reduced to automata:

> With uncertainty absent man's energies are devoted altogether to doing things; it is doubtful whether intelligence itself would exist in such a situation; in a world so built, it seems likely that all organic readjustments would become mechanical, all organisms automata (1921, p. 268, quoted by Hutchison, 1978, p. 202).

Though Shackle does not follow the curious view of Menger and Knight that economic theory is somehow *compelled* to assume the absence of uncertainty and ignorance, and concern itself with automata, he does seem to have expressed some doubt as to whether a study based on the assumption of fundamental "disorder" could have the attributes of "science" (1967, p. 134). Moreover, Shackle goes on to observe that "conventional economics" as he calls it, "is not about choice, but about acting according to necessity. . . . Choice in such a theory is empty." At the same time he described equilibrium as "the effective banishment of ignorance" (1961, p. 272, and 1967, pp. 133–134).

As regards the real economic world, however, Shackle insists, as had Knight, on its fundamental and far-reaching unpredictability (though Knight's pronouncements on this point vary somewhat). In fact, "the impossibility of prediction in economics" has been proclaimed in the most emphatic terms by Professor Shackle and by the distinguished Neo-Austrian Ludwig Lachmann.[11] It may be noted that no indication is given in this categorical pronouncement that predictability is confined to individuals and does not apply to economic aggregates (which, in any case, are usually, in principle, highly suspect to Neo-Austrians).

In seeking to interpret the statement by Lachmann and Shackle, difficulty at once seems to arise from the apparently extreme black-or-white terms in which prediction and predictability are presented. In many, or most, actual real-world situations, human beings are not usually to be found in situations either of perfect and precise predictability, or of total unpredictability, just as human situations are not ones either of complete freedom or total lack of freedom. Anyhow, just as complete and far-reaching predictability might, or would, destroy significant freedom by turning human beings into automata, so complete unpredictability would also destroy freedom or render it largely meaningless. For, just as human freedom could hardly be said to survive among omniscient automata, so it could hardly survive if all decisions had to be taken in conditions where ignorance and unpredictability were so profound and complete, and uncertainty so fundamental, that choices amounted to acquiring a ticket in some kind of vast lottery of indefinite extent. Significant freedom can hardly exist at the poles of omniscience and omni-nescience about the future but can only emerge in a mixed world (such as ours blessedly is) which, at any rate in its human and social sectors, combines elements of predictability and unpredictability.

One of Professor Shackle's gnomic apothegms (quoted by Ludwig Lachmann) observes that "*Predicted* man is less than human, *predicting* man is more than human" (Lachmann, 1977, p. 88). Yes: But *totally* unpredictable, *totally* unpredicted, and *totally* unpredicting man would also certainly be as much less than human. Therefore, just as traditional economic theorizing, based on the assumption of full knowledge, the absence of uncertainty, and thoroughgoing predictability (though not devoid of useful lessons) can be, and has been dangerously misleading, so, correspondingly, excessive insistence on far-reaching, or total, ignorance, uncertainty, and unpredictability, may suggest dangerous conclusions. For, if economic decisions resembled those of a player at a vast roulette board, who was ignorant even of the ever-changing and indefinitely wide range of possible numbers, or "choices," on which to put his money, he might well come to feel, indeed it could be "rational" for him to conclude, that it was pointless to insist on himself placing his own bets, and that he might just as well let some authority or other make the pseudochoices for him.

If the Neo-Austrian doctrine that "prediction in economics is impossible" simply means that economists cannot predict with precision or certainty, or even with anything approaching the accuracy attainable in some natural sciences, then such an observation hardly now seems worthy of much discussion. If, however, some kind of distinction is being tacitly assumed between economic "prediction" (which is "impossible") and "forecasting," "prognosis," or "projection," which are recognized as possible, then some precise and significant points of difference need to be spelled out, which, with regard to economics, it seems very difficult to define and sustain. It might obviously seem to be rather begging the question simply to deny the "possibility" of the predictions on which some kinds of governmental policies might be based, while claiming the possibility of the kind of predictive capacity required for the successful establishment of economic or monetary constitutions, or for the effective operation of smoothly self-adjusting markets. Of course, one may believe that some types of prediction about some kinds of processes are generally liable to prove less inaccurate than other types of prediction about other kinds of processes. But it may seem misleading and unjustifiable simply to assert that one kind is, in principle, impossible, while the other kind is intellectually respectable and well worth attempting. For, if a competitive market provides "a discovery procedure" (as Professor Hayek has pointed out), then this procedure is presumably not a purely random one, if it is to work reasonably effectively, but must be based on *some* capacity on the part of successful entrepreneurs to predict not too inaccurately. If (among other things) human preferences were completely unpredictable, then, the claims for the efficiency and effectiveness of markets would have to be highly limited simply to the contention that they produced rather less appalling results than most known kinds of politicoeconomic alternatives. Moreover, it would seem that the, or a, main function of the kinds of politicoeconomic constitutions, to the construction of which such considerable libertarian efforts are devoted, is surely that of reducing unpredictability, or improving some kinds of predictions (one hopes not too Utopianly).

Therefore, a reasonable aim for libertarian economists might be formulated as that of marginally reducing the extent of unpredictability, or of improving the accuracy of predictions, in this or that area of economic activity where such reductions or improvements may enhance freedom. But it must be recognized that these reductions or improvements may not be absolute but are simply relative to the predictive capacity which would have been available without the systematic efforts of economists. For it may well be that the economic world, or important parts of it, is becoming increasingly unpredictable (indeed the work of some economists may have assisted this possibly growing unpredictability). In other words, to maintain such predictive capacity as they have (if it is conceded that they have *some* such capacity) economists may have to run faster and faster up a downward-moving staircase.[12]

The freedoms which civilized societies can provide have always depended on a certain mutual predictability, while leaving vast areas of uncertainty, ignorance, and unpredictability. Presumably there are always, or usually, *some* increases in predictive capacity, at this or that point, which *could* be applied to increasing freedoms, though, of course, other such increases, or even the same increases, *could* be used to reduce freedom. The application to policy of such increases in predictability are, presumably not, or not solely, for the economist, as such, to decide upon. Meanwhile, however, it would seem that the freedom-loving economist should treat with much reserve the conclusions of economic theorizing, ancient or modern, which are based on assumptions either of omniscience about the future, at one extreme, or omni-nescience, or near omni-nescience about the future, at the other. Most of the real world lies well between the two.

V

Public effusions, or pronouncements, on the other side of the Atlantic, whence I come, seem these days to require a "bottom line", or even a "bottom line message." This paper offers two brief bottom lines. First, the world of omniscient economic theorizing (or of economic theorizing about the omniscient) was a world mainly empty of institutions, for most major economic institutions can be said to have come into existence to mitigate certain kinds of ignorance or uncertainty, e.g., money, or (as Ronald Coase observed in his classic article) the firm. Those not satisfied with the assumption of omniscience and certainty, but who are not prepared to fly to the opposite extreme of total uncertainty and unpredictability (which, incidentally, would seem to involve the abandonment of economics as a form of useful knowledge), must be "institutionalists." There has been, historically, but not logically inevitably, quite a strong correlation between theoretical economics and libertarian policies, on the one hand, and "institutionalist" economics and interventionist, or socialist, policies, on the other hand. Institutionalist libertarians have been rather rare birds. This dichotomy should be broken down. There is, after all, the example of Adam Smith, whom Ronald Coase has justifiably described as an institutionalist, not to mention, more recently, Walter Eucken and Ronald Coase himself.

Second, support for libertarian policies can be, and has been, based on fundamental assumptions, on the one hand, of omniscience, and, on the other hand, of far-reaching ignorance, or even omni-nescience regarding the future. Indeed, as alternative particular assumptions, applying to different particular cases, these assumptions, or "pretensions," can and should exist side by side. But, in fact, they are both put forward as comprehensive, *general* postulates (or even as a "rationality *principle*") supporting completely contradictory explanations, or theories, of economic behavior. This is an intellectual situation which hardly seems conducive to the most effective development of libertarian arguments on economic policy. Of course, in different cases, or markets, different degrees, or types, of knowledge and ignorance, certainty and uncertainty, predictability and unpredictability, may be assumed. But to discern which particular assumption may apply at which particular times and places, would require detailed and extensive institutional study. This is simply a more elaborate way of stating the program, set out by Professor Hayek nearly 50 years ago, when he observed (as already quoted) that analysis on the assumption of omniscience, or equilibration, only "can be turned into propositions which tell us anything about causation in the real world," if "definite statements about how knowledge is acquired and communicated" can be supplied.

NOTES

* Ludwig Lachmann and I first saw each other, I think in a seminar of Hayek's in March 1938. We first got to know each other in 1946, when he gave me my first job in an English University. I remember thinking then that our differences about economic philosophy, method, and policy were about as wide and deep as could be. We were colleagues for one academic session only. Since then we have met very seldom and, in fact, have not often been on the same continent at the same time. But if our geographical paths could hardly have diverged more widely, our intellectual paths have converged very considerably. Sometimes it seems to me that what remains of our earlier differences are no more than a few points of terminology and historical emphasis. But there may here be some elements of unfounded, wishful thinking (as Ludwig may complain if he can get through this

paper). Anyhow, what I am sure is another kind of solidly founded wishful thinking, is that of offering our distinguished honorand many happy returns of the day on his eightieth birthday, while expressing the hope that the community of critical economists may long continue to benefit from the contributions of his profoundly cultured, discerning mind.

1. This paper was read at a meeting of the Mont Pelerin Society in March 1985. I am deeply indebted, regarding the questions it seeks to raise, to the writings of Professor Friedrich Hayek, though I cannot too promptly absolve him of all responsibility for the conclusions, or arguments, presented here. The writings to which I refer are (1) the paper of 1937 on "Economics and Knowledge"; (2) the Nobel Lecture of 1974, "The Pretence of Knowledge"; and, in particular, "Individualism True and False" (1945). In this paper, Hayek traced the line of descent of true individualism as coming down from such pre-classicals as Mandeville, Tucker, and Hume, to Adam Smith, and then as continuing in the nineteenth century with Tocqueville and Acton, rather than with the English classical economists, "who came increasingly under the influence of another kind of individualism of different origin," similar in some respects, to that of the Physiocrats, which led on to "the worst kind of despotism" (Hayek, "Individualism True and False," op. cit., pp. 4ff.). (It is interesting to learn that Professor Hayek once favored calling the MPS 'The Acton-de Tocqueville Society'). In his recent essay, which I read while writing this paper, Mr. John Gray has made a similar, or even more comprehensive criticism, remarking that "none of the great classical liberals (with the likely exception of Hume) was altogether free of an uncritical rationalism." He adds that "liberals nowadays must be self-critical and acknowledge the weakness in their own intellectual tradition which have contributed to the debacle of liberal civilization" (1984, p. 35–6). It might be added that *present* philosophical conflicts or contradictions between liberals should also be acknowledged and attempts made to resolve them.
2. Regarding the ignorance of entrepreneurs, Smith observed: "Profit is so very fluctuating, that the person who carries on a particular trade cannot always tell you what is the average of his annual profit" (1937, p. 79).

   Smith's moderate policy ambitions are expressed in *The Theory of Moral Sentiments* where he maintains that "the man whose public spirit is prompted altogether by humanity and benevolence . . . will accommodate, as well as he can, his public arrangements to the confirmed habits and prejudices of the people; and he will remedy, as well as he can, the inconveniences which may flow from the want of those regulations which the people are averse to submit to. When he cannot establish the best system of laws, he will endeavor to establish the best that the people can bear" (Smith, 1797, vol. II, p. 109).

   Smith, indeed, attacked Quesnay for setting up optimal criteria for policy, and for imagining that a nation "would thrive and prosper only under a certain precise regimen, the exact regimen of *perfect* liberty and *perfect* justice. . . . If a nation could not prosper without the enjoyment of *perfect* liberty and *perfect* justice there is not in the world a nation which could ever have prospered" (1937, p. 638).

3. In 1824, McCulloch observed of political economy that "it really admits of such certainty in its conclusions as any science founded on fact and experiment can possibly do" (having just compared its conclusions with those of Newton and Laplace; 1824, p. 9).

   James Mill maintained that there was perfect concurrence on the main doctrines of political economy, and that "there is no branch of human knowledge more entitled to respect" (1836, and 1966, pp. 378–82). In the Preface to his *Principles*, J. S. Mill stated that political economy had "grown up almost from infancy since the time of Adam Smith; and the philosophy of society . . . has advanced many steps beyond the point at which he left it." Mill insisted that "*The Wealth of Nations* is in many parts obsolete, and in all imperfect" (1848 and 1909, p. xxviii).
4. Smith stated his views about human nature and human knowledge in *The Theory of Moral Sentiments*. Self-preservation and the propagation of the species were the great ends of mankind: "But though we are in this manner endowed with a very strong desire of those ends, *it has not been entrusted to the slow and uncertain determination of our reason to find out the proper means of bringing them about*" (Smith, vol. II, p. 129, italics added). The contrast with Ricardo could not be more emphatic. Ricardo recognized the full-knowledge assumption as basic to his method in a letter to Malthus on the theory of international trade: "The first point to be considered is, what is the interest of countries in the case supposed? Now it is obvious that I need not be greatly solicitous about this latter point; it is sufficient for my purpose if I can clearly demonstrate that the interest of the public is as I have stated. It would be no answer to me to say that men were ignorant of the best and cheapest mode of conducting their business and paying their debts, because that is a question of fact not of science, and might be urged against almost every proposition in Political Economy" (Ricardo, vol. VI, p. 64; Hutchison, 1978, p. 48).
5. Erwin Nasse, quoted by Leslie, was one of the German historical economists, together with Schaeffle and Brentano, who early discerned and criticized the inevitably dictatorial nature of socialist economies; "A planned direction of production *without* free choice of goods and jobs would not be inconceivable, but would bring with it a destruction of culture and of everything that makes life worth living. To combine a planned direction of all economic activity *with* free choice of goods and jobs is a problem which can only be compared with that of the squaring of the circle. For if everyone is allowed to decide freely the direction and nature of his economic activity and his consumption, then the control of the economy as a whole is lost" (Nasse, 1879, p. 164).
6. The passage immediately preceding that quoted above in the text reads, in the translation by F. J. Nock: "Even if economic humans always and everywhere let themselves be guided exclusively by their self-interest, the strict regularity of economic phenomena would nonetheless have to be considered impossible because of the fact given by experience that in innumerable cases they are in error about their economic interest, or in ignorance of the economic state of affairs. Our historians are too considerate of their scholarly opponents." (Menger, 1883 and 1963, p. 84).

   Later, Menger observed: "Volition, error, and other influences can, on the contrary, and actually do, bring it about that human agents take different roads from a strictly determined goal of their actions" (Menger, p. 217).

7. Hayek went on to comment as follows on conventional theory: "In the usual presentation of equilibrium analysis it is generally made to appear as if these questions of how equilibrium comes about were solved. But if we look closer, it soon becomes evident that these apparent demonstrations amount to no more than the apparent proof of what is already assumed" (Hayek, "Economics and Knowledge," op. cit., p. 45; Hutchison, 1981, pp. 215–16).
8. Much of conventional theory, based on the absence of uncertainty and ignorance, has been thoroughly rationalist in Oakeshott's sense: "The heart of the matter is the preoccupation of the Rationalist with certainty, . . . with knowledge, that is, which not only ends with certainty but begins with certainty and is certain throughout" (Oakeshott, 1962, p. 11). This certainty includes, presumably, the "apodictic certainty" of Mises.
9. Hutchison, 1937. In the light of nearly half a century of evidence regarding the actual workings of socialist, or planned, economies, I have modified my views somewhat.
10. Some economists seem to have sought reassurance regarding this vast gap of unrealism between the real world and the assumptions of much of economic theorizing, from the complacent, ambiguous, and misleading methodological doctrine, according to which the unrealism of assumptions does not matter, and is not a source of weakness in a theory. On this confusion, see Musgrave, 1981.
11. This pronouncement (from Lachmann, 1959) provides the epigraph for Shackle's *Epistemics and Economics* (1972). Also Professor Kirzner maintains as a basic Austrian tenet the unpredictability of human preferences, expectations and knowledge (1976, p. 42).

    Incidentally, Professor Shackle's interpretation of Keynes, in accordance with the Shackelian doctrine of unpredictability, surely runs completely counter to the reformist beliefs and aims which motivated Keynes's work. According to Shackle, Keynes produced an economics of disorder, when he formulated his "ultimate ground of the possibility of massive general unemployment. . . . To state the ground [of unemployment] was to deny the orderliness of economic society and economic life, and to deny this life the attributes of orderliness was to seem to deny the study of it the attributes of science" (Shackle, 1967, pp. 133–4). But surely Keynes, as an ardent would-be reformer, rejected disorder, and believed (rightly or wrongly) that policies based on *his predictions* as to the effects of government spending, would restore order, for Keynes obviously believed in the predictability of economic behavior, or of some aspects of it, and in the possibility of order, as against Shackelian unpredictability and disorder. However, Lachmann has good grounds for describing Keynes as a subjectivist (which perhaps further demonstrates the ambiguity of that term).
12. As an example of increasing unpredictability, what used to be called "the theory of the foreign exchanges" may be cited. This theory would presumably have been regarded as assisting in the prediction of, say, the

dollar exchange rate. But institutional changes have so transformed markets that the traditional theory seems of much less, and perhaps of little or no, use, as an aid to prediction. Indeed, if applied inflexibly or dogmatically, such a theory could seriously increase the inaccuracy of predictions. It may be that economists are sometimes themselves net increasers, rather than reducers, of unpredictability in the economic world, though this may exaggerate their influence.

REFERENCES

Coase, R. H. (1937), "The Nature of the Firm," *Economica*, N.S., 4, pp. 386ff.

Gray, J. (1984), "The Road to Serfdom: Forty Years On," in *Hayek's "Serfdom" Revisited,* ed. Barry Norman (London: Institute of Economic Affairs).

Hayek, F. A. (1937), "Economics and Knowledge," *Economica*, N.S., 4, pp. 33–54.

—— (1949), "Individualism: True and False," in *Individualism and Economic Order* (London: Routledge & Kegan Paul).

—— (1978), "The Pretence of Knowledge," in *New Studies in Philosophy, Politics, Economics and the History of Ideas* (Chicago: University of Chicago Press).

Hutchison, T. W. (1937), "A Note on Uncertainty and Planning," *Review of Economic Studies*, 5, pp. 72–74.

—— (1953), *Review of Economic Doctrines, 1870–1929* (Oxford: Clarendon Press).

—— (1978), *On Revolution and Progress in Economic Knowledge* (Cambridge: Cambridge University Press).

—— (1981), *The Politics and Philosophy of Economics* (New York: New York University Press).

Keynes, John M. (Feb. 1937), "The General Theory of Employment," *Quarterly Journal of Economics*, 51, pp. 209ff.

Kirzner, I. M. (1976), "On the Method of Austrian Economics," in *The Foundations of Modern Austrian Economics*, ed. E. G. Dolan (Kansas City: Sheed and Ward, Inc.), pp. 40ff.

Knight, F. H. (1921), *Risk, Uncertainty and Profit* (Boston: Houghton Mifflin).

Lachmann, L. M. (1977), "Professor Shackle on the Economic Significance of Time," in *Capital, Expectations, and the Market Process* (Kansas City: Sheed Andrews & McMeel) pp. 81ff.

—— (24 Nov. 1984), "Der Markt ist Kein Uhrwerk," *Frankfurter Allgemeine Zeitung*.

Leslie, T. E. C. (1879), "The Known and the Unknown in the Economic World," in *Essays in Political and Moral Philosophy* (Dublin: Hodges, Foster and Figgis), pp. 221ff.

McCulloch, J. R. (1824), *A Discourse on the Rise, Progress, Peculiar Objects, and Importance of Political Economy* (Edinburgh).

Menger, C. (1963), *Untersuchungen über die Methode*, translated as *Problems of*

Economics and Sociology, L. Schneider, ed., and F. J. Nock, trans. (Urbana, Ill.: University of Illinois Press).

Mill, J. (1966), "Whether Political Economy is Useful," in *Selected Economic Writings*, ed. D. Winch (Chicago: University of Chicago Press).

Mill, J. S. (1844), *Essays on Some Unsettled Questions of Political Economy* (London: J. W. Parker).

—— (1909), *Principles of Political Economy*, ed. W. J. Ashley (London: Longmans, Green and Co.).

Musgrave, A. (1981), "Unreal Assumptions in Economic Theory: The F-Twist Untwisted," *Kyklos*, 34, fasc. 3.

Nasse, E. (1879), "Uber die Verhütung, der Productionskrisen durch staatliche Fürsorge," *Jahrbuch für Gesetzgebung, Verwaltung und Volkswirtschaft*, Dritter Jahrgang, Erster Heft, pp. 145–189.

Oakeshott, M. (1962), *Rationalism in Politics* (London: Methuen).

Ricardo, D. (1952), *Works of D. Ricardo*, ed. P. Sraffa, vol. VI (Cambridge: Cambridge University Press).

Robbins, Lionel. (1984), *Essay on the Nature and Significance of Economic Science*, 3rd ed., (London: Macmillan).

Senior, N. W. (1878), *Conversations with M. Thiers, M. Guizot, and Other Distinguished Persons*, ed. Mrs. M. C. M. Simpson (London) 2 volumes.

Shackle, G. L. S. (1958), *Time in Economics* (Amsterdam: North Holland).

—— (1961), *Decision, Order and Time in Human Affairs* (Cambridge: Cambridge University Press).

—— (1967), *The Years of High Theory* (Cambridge: Cambridge University Press).

—— (1972), *Epistemics and Economics* (Cambridge: Cambridge University Press).

Smith, Adam (1759), *Theory of Moral Sentiments*, 8th ed.

—— (1937), *The Wealth of Nations* (New York: Random House, Modern Library).

11 Another Look at the Subjectivism of Costs

ISRAEL M. KIRZNER

The insight that the cost associated with an item must reflect all the opportunities sacrificed in order to obtain it, has long been fundamental for economists. This opportunity cost doctrine (perhaps the earliest statement of which was made in an 1876 paper by Wieser) is one of the contributions of the Austrian School which has come to be fully absorbed into the contemporary neo-classical orthodoxy.[1] Since Professor Buchanan's incisive treatment of the entire subject, however, economists have learned to appreciate the subtlety of the opportunity cost concept, once its subjectivist implications have been fully drawn, and to recognize the pitfalls which await those who wield the opportunity cost notion without awareness of these implications.[2] A number of contributions to the literature have further explored various aspects of the subjectivism of opportunity costs and have drawn our attention to additional important and valuable insights.[3] This paper seeks to tidy up some remaining issues that appear, perhaps, to warrant further clarification. In attempting this task we will have to review some very elementary and obvious ideas. The need for some tidying up arises from the apparent ease with which ideas are lost sight of as soon as economists move beyond the most elementary of contexts.

COSTS AND COSTS

Let us first review a number of admittedly related, but nonetheless quite distinct, concepts for which the term "cost" might be (and often has been) applied. (Of course the term "cost" has also been used with other meanings as well, but present purposes do not require our attention to more usages than those listed here.) It will be convenient to employ an example introduced by Alchian, in which a homeowner builds a swimming pool; we are inquiring into the cost of the building of the pool.[4]

One concern in seeking the "cost" of the pool may be to establish the array of disadvantages that result from building the swimming pool. Presumably the attendant reduction in the homeowner's bank balance would be one of the disadvantages and thus a component in cost (in this sense). But other disadvantages would have to be included as well, e.g., the "nuisance of noisy, disobedient neighborhood children and uninvited guests."[5] If cost is to be understood in terms of "disadvantages," it will clearly be necessary to distinguish between the sum of the disadvantages that accrue to the homeowner himself (the "private cost" of building the pool) from the disadvantages that may accrue to others (e.g., the nuisance to neighbors of noisy visitors to the pool, invited or not). Or one may seek somehow to assess the sum of disadvantages to everybody (the "social cost").[6]

A different focus of concern may inspire the search for the swimming pool's "cost." One may wish to know what alternative goods that might otherwise have been forthcoming have been precluded through the building of the swimming pool. Here one must consider not so much the disadvantages associated directly with the pool (money subtracted from cash holdings, noise, etc.) as the alternative goods (which may have *their* own disadvantages) that would have been possible if the pool was not constructed. Thus the homeowner might have purchased a car instead of the pool. The pool has "cost" him the car.

This notion of cost is often considered to be an opportunity cost notion, since it refers to the alternative opportunity that the swimming pool has precluded. However, in order to distinguish it from the subjective version of opportunity cost (to be discussed below), we will call this present notion of cost the "objective opportunity cost" notion. It is objective in that the cost of the pool is taken to be a definite good (in this case a car) that might have been enjoyed had the pool not been built. What "might have been enjoyed" in the present context is understood as being a matter of *fact*, objectively determinable, quite apart from anyone's judgments or expectations. It is, for example, held to be an objective fact that the $10,000 expended for the pool, could have (under given factual market conditions) purchased a car.

It should be noticed that the car is the private (objective) opportunity cost of the swimming pool in that it refers to what the homeowner might have *acquired* instead of the swimming pool. But someone might be interested in the objective opportunity of the pool in a different sense. Someone might ask about the alternative goods which might have been *produced* instead of the swimming pool. (If the homeowner built the pool with his own labor, tools and materials this cost would of course also be the private cost of the pool.) One may ask, in the situation in which the homeowner had the pool built by a contractor (who hired labor and tools, and bought the materials), what alternative output might these inputs have produced—possibly in other industries altogether. Suppose they could have produced a summer cottage (which, let us say, our homeowner has absolutely no interest in using at all). Then it might be held that the (objective) opportunity cost of the pool is the summer cottage. The cottage is the potential output "displaced" by the pool. Since our homeowner never did himself possess these physical resources, and since, moreover, he has no interest whatever in the cottage, this cost notion is clearly not the private cost to him of his pool. It would presumably be considered a "social opportunity cost" in that the total output obtained by adding together all the goods and services produced in a society with its available resources, *including* the pool, might have been a different one in that, instead of the pool, it might have contained one more summer cottage. This is the objective social opportunity cost of the pool in that the capability of the labor, tools, and materials (that produced the pool) to have produced the cottage instead is viewed as a matter of objective fact (given the physical requirements for the production of the pool and the cottage respectively).

The final concern which may inspire attention to the cost of building the swimming pool, may be to understand *why the homeowner in fact decided to build the pool.* We know that, in considering whether or not to build the pool, the homeowner was aware that building the pool must entail some sacrifices on his part. Were these sacrifices too great, the homeowner would, it is clear, have reluctantly decided against the pool. To explain economic phenomena, arising as they do out of individual decisions, it is necessary, for each decision taken, to be aware that the relevant sacrifices to the decision maker were considered worthwhile by him. To acquire a swimming pool (to follow Alchian's example again) called for a decision not to buy a car. Only the homeowner himself, however, can know how likely it is that a car *would*, in fact, have been the alternative enjoyed (if the pool were out of reach); only he can know how intense a sacrifice the "loss" of the car means to him. The cost of the pool to the homeowner, then, represents *his assessment at the moment of his decision regarding the pool, of what he would be giving up* in order to acquire it. The emphasis (in this *subjective* opportunity cost notion) is upon the moment of decision, and upon the way in which the decision maker himself sees the alternative opportunity which *he* must sacrifice.

The subjectivity of this notion of opportunity cost flows, of course, directly from its exclusive relevance to the decision. Economists learned long ago that demand behavior cannot be understood without probing beyond the physical objects purchased by the consumer, to the prospective utility which these objects represent for him. In exactly the same way the subjective opportunity cost concept permits us to recognize that costs help explain economic behavior not because costs represent definite objects "displaced," but because they represent perceived utility prospects deliberately sacrificed.

ON THE COSTS OF WIVES AND CHILDREN

A clear understanding of the differences between these various cost concepts can help elucidate points that have sometimes occasioned confusion.

The noisy neighborhood children

Alchian is one writer who has emphasized the sharp difference between the disadvantages of, or the undesirable attributes inherent in a swimming pool, and its opportunity cost. The decision maker must choose among events. Each event is an amalgam of "goods and bads." The opportunity cost of the chosen event is the next most highly valued event—not the undesirable attributes of the chosen event. The nuisance of noisy neighborhood children, Alchian emphasizes, is an undesirable attribute of the pool. It is not part of its opportunity cost. Our discussion may shed a somewhat different light on the matter.

If the idea of the opportunity cost is understood in its subjective version, it may be possible, surely, to find an opportunity-cost-counterpart for the disadvantages inherent in a chosen event. If a homeowner is choosing between building a swimming pool and purchasing a car, then it is very likely that the noisy neighborhood children that will be attracted by the pool enter very definitely into his cost calculations; they may well affect the decision taken. The options considered by the homeowner are, after all, whether to enjoy a car, together with a peaceful backyard, or whether to enjoy the swimming pool, *without* such a peaceful backyard (because of the noisy children). Thus, in choosing the pool, the homeowner is consciously sacrificing the peace and quiet which he recognizes will be destroyed by the noisy children. From the subjective point of view any disadvantage associated with the chosen event (and not with its rejected alternative) represents the sacrifice of the corresponding advantage (or at least the absence of disadvantage) contained in the rejected alternative.[7] (Of course, if a given disadvantage is common both to the adopted option and to its alternative, it cannot enter into the opportunity cost of the adopted option.)

In insisting that for the opportunity cost concept the noisy children represent only one of the undesirable attributes of the pool, not part of its cost, Alchian appears to be understanding the notion of opportunity cost in objective terms. From this point of view the availability of one chosen object may be seen as displacing another definite object. The latter is the cost of the former. In this view each object is seen as an amalgam of desirable and undesirable attributes. In order to perceive that the adoption of the undesirable attributes of one option entails a felt sacrifice (of the absence of these attributes in the alternative option), it seems necessary to emphasize, not displaced physical output, but perceived prospects deliberately sacrificed.

The expensive wife

In 1969 no less serious a scholarly journal than the *Journal of Political Economy* published a semihumorous "Note on the Opportunity Cost of Marriage" by Gary North. This note was remarkable not so much for the very obvious fallacy it contains (which it is very likely that the author deliberately introduced as part of the attempted merriment) as for the fact that several of the subsequent serious comments it elicited utterly failed to take notice of the fallacy.[8] North considered the situation of the man who contemplates marriage to a highly educated woman able to earn a high salary on the professional labor market. Taking it for granted that, after marriage, the wife will give up outside job opportunities and concentrate entirely on running the household, North refers to her shockingly high opportunity costs. A man of modest means, North argues, should never consider courting a woman of such talents; she is simply too costly. "The best kind of wife, from the point of view of contemporary economics, is obviously an uneducated woman . . . [for whom] a man . . . forfeits a small opportunity cost in her lost salary. . . ."

North's article drew comments from several economists, one of them George Stigler,[9] Stigler accepted without question North's analysis to the effect that the opportunity cost of marrying the educated woman is a high one. His criticism of North's conclusion was confined—apparently altogether seriously—entirely to pointing out that if the wife in question indeed stays at home as housekeeper, this demonstrates that the minimum estimate of her revenue equivalent as housekeeper must outweigh the high cost of the foregone professional income. But this clearly concedes the obvious fallacy in North's tongue-in-cheek story which incorrectly counts the forgone professional income as the *opportunity cost of the decision to marry the educated woman* rather than her uneducated sister. Before this marriage decision the prospective groom had no alternative prospect whatever of enjoying the woman's high professional income; his decision to marry her involved no sacrifice by him of her income at all (even if it is understood from the start that marriage calls for her staying at home). To be sure, once the two have married, a *subsequent* decision that she stay at home carries with it the cost of her foregone income. But this is irrelevant to North's injunction to the would-be groom to marry the uneducated girl in order to avoid high costs. Again, if it is understood that marriage necessarily involves forsaking outside employment, then the educated girl's decision to marry carries with it a cost *to her* of the lost professional income. But this is again irrelevant to North's matrimonial advice to the fellow.

That so eminent an economist as Stigler should have failed to point all this out appears to suggest an extreme version of the objective approach to the notion of opportunity cost. Such a version apparently divorces the notion of opportunity cost entirely from the context of the decision. Instead of considering the costs deliberately assumed at the moment of a particular decision, this version focuses on that which has been displaced as a result of a given state of affairs. In this fashion, apparently, it is somehow conceivable to see the educated wife in the kitchen as bearing a cost tag on which is inscribed the professional salary which she might have commanded in an alternative state of affairs. To marry her rather than her uneducated sister is to assume a high-cost option rather than a low-cost one.

That the subjective version of the opportunity cost doctrine is invulnerable to seduction by such a fallacy must surely be counted as one of its merits.

ON THE SUBJECTIVITY OF COSTS

There are several sources for our emphasis upon the subjectivity of opportunity cost (in the context in which cost helps us understand decisions taken). It will be helpful to spell these out. Let us consider a case in which two homeowners in two different (but similar) towns decide to build similar swimming pools in their backyards. To the outside observer it may appear that the two face similar sets of circumstances, that they are called upon to make similar sacrifices. In short, the two pools are built at "equal cost." The subjectivist, however, cannot accept this view.

First, while the situation which the outside observer perceives in each case as facing the homeowner appears identical with that which confronts the second homeowner, we have no assurance that this identity exists in anyone's perception other than that of the observer. An outside observer may presume that the prospect of noisy children from the neighbourhood, which faces each of the prospective pool owners, is taken into account by each of them correctly and equally. But in fact it is possible that one homeowner forgets altogether to consider this undesirable attribute of the prospective pool. In other words, two decision makers may "see" different things despite the fact that they really confront the same objective situation. The costs which enter into the respective decisions can clearly in no sense be said to be equal.

Second, a somewhat different (although closely related) source for the incorrectness of any conclusion by the outside observer that the two homeowners face equal costs is provided by our understanding of the role of entrepreneurship in decision making. Even if two decision makers do see present realities in identical fashion, there is no reason to assume that they will assess future prospects equally. In one sense the preceding case (in which one homeowner forgot about the prospect of a noisy backyard) represents such an entrepreneurial lapse. A clearer example of the importance of the entrepreneurial elements is perhaps provided by the case where the two homeowners each carefully take account of the prospective disadvantage of the noisy children but reach different conclusions concerning its likelihood. Perhaps one homeowner predicts more accurately than the second what other future neighborhood attractions are likely to "compete" with a backyard pool. Both homeowners see present circumstances identically. But they see the future differently. The respective costs of the pool are as different as the two assessments of the future.

Third, another circumstance renders it an error to conclude that the cost of a pool is the same for each of the homeowners. Even if the two arrive at exactly the same predictions concerning the noise to be expected in their respective backyards, they may attach different degrees of significance to this prospective disadvantage. For one homeowner a noisy background may be perceived as a minor irritant; for the second it may loom as a major discomfort.

Finally, our discussion thus far in this section might suggest that the subjectivity of opportunity costs merely makes it impossible *as a practical matter* to rank costs faced by different decision makers. This would be a serious misunderstanding of the position being taken. The truth surely is that costs, as understood in the subjective version, enter into decisions in a strictly private manner. To rank the costs faced by different decision makers is as conceptually impossible a task as is that of comparing utilities interpersonally. (In fact, of course, these two tasks are merely variants of a single impossible undertaking.) Both costs and utilities enter into decisions in a private fashion. They are essentially without meaning except within the context of the private decision.

SUBJECTIVE COSTS, OBJECTIVE COSTS AND EQUILIBRIUM PRICES

The foregoing has important implications for an often-discussed question. Can the private money outlays made by an entrepreneur in the course of producing output serve as a correct, objective measure of the entrepreneur's subjective opportunity costs of production?

Some recent contributions to the literature on the subjectivity of costs have discussed how, under specified conditions (chief among which being the equilibrium state, and the absence of nonpecuniary motivations) money outlays do provide an objective representation of subjective costs.[10] This position reflects the line of reasoning lucidly articulated by Professor Baumol in his 1970 review of Buchanan's book.[11] Baumol's exposition deserves verbatim quotation.

> There surely is a wide variety of circumstances in which the objective cost data do constitute a reasonable approximation to the subjective opportunity costs. This is brought out clearly by the famous argument of Adam Smith, about which Buchanan builds much of his discussion: "If ... it usually costs twice the labor to kill a beaver

which it costs to kill a deer, one beaver should naturally exchange for or be worth two deer." This is plausible even if cost is interpreted as subjective opportunity cost because in Smith's economy hunting is carried on more or less continuously. Assuming that hunting is not done for pleasure, if the objective cost of beaver—the payment to the hunter—were less than twice as high as that of a deer, more hunters would turn to deer slaying and away from beaver trapping until the market costs (prices) were modified to reflect the relative outlay of time involved. The relative marginal valuations of beaver and deer meat by each and every consumer would then also be driven to the same two-to-one ratio, so that to each person the subjective opportunity cost of a pound of deer flesh would be the same, and would be represented correctly by the objective relative cost figure.[12]

For Baumol, then, the result of the market process is that for all consumers "the subjective opportunity cost of a pound of deer flesh would be the same" (since each consumer would face—and would have adjusted the margins of consumption to—the same one-to-two ratio between deer and beaver flesh prices). Also, this common subjective deer flesh cost would be correctly represented by the objective relative cost (of hunting deer as compared to that of hunting beaver). Or, as Buchanan sums it up, "marginal opportunity cost, measured in the numeraire, is equal for all suppliers."[13]

Now, there is nothing in these discussions described above to which exception can be taken. It does, however, appear important to emphasize the limited sense in which it is correct to describe money outlays as constituting "objective costs," either in the sense of somehow translating subjective, private, interpretations and valuations, into interpersonally visible, comparable and measurable terms, or in the sense of being publicly observable cost *to society* (rather than merely a common representation of distinct *private* sacrifices). Let us take up these limitations in turn.

Comparing costs interpersonally

It would, for many economists, doubtless be highly desirable to be able to map the private, subjective costs perceived by different decision makers upon an external and interpersonally valid scale. It is tempting, but of course quite wrong, to believe that money outlays—even under equilibrium conditions and without nonpecuniary distractions—constitute such a mapping.

In equilibrium, output and consumption decisions with respect to pairs of products have been adjusted to bring both marginal rates of substitution and of transformation into equality with relative prices for each consumer and producer. It may even be loosely claimed that for each consumer a dollar's worth of each commodity at the margin provides the marginal utility of one dollar. In this special sense, then, it is not incorrect to say that both utilities and subjective costs are the "same" for all consumers. But all this does not, of course entitle us to view a dollar as an objective, interpersonally valid yardstick of utility. For you, as for me, a marginal dollar's worth of bread provides approximately the same utility as does a dollar. This does not mean that you and I attach equal "significance," in any absolute sense of the word, to the given physical quantity of bread. It is certainly highly important to understand how, under equilibrium conditions, *rankings* at the margin are, for all market participants, brought into uniformity. But this does not imply that private, subjective appraisals have been rendered publicly visible.

Quite similarly the subjectivity of costs has not been magically suspended merely by the circumstance that, both for you and for me, a pound of deer flesh can be acquired only at the same dollar outlay. What I believe that I must sacrifice for deer flesh is a mental picture which I have of possible future enjoyments, a picture which is inaccessible to anyone else. There is no straightforward meaning that can be attached to the question whether or not this picture is the same as that which for you constitutes the subjective cost of similar deer flesh. And this is not affected by the feeling that *each* of us may have that the sacrificed prospect is identical in significance with that which would be made possible by the expenditure of a marginal dollar.

Now one can readily understand a tendency to shrug off this kind of purism. For you, as for me, the sacrifice called for in order to enjoy a unit of deer flesh is a given quantity of beaver. Then, surely it is the case, it may be objected with some impatience, that for you the opportunity cost of deer *is* the same as it is for me. You must give up exactly what I must give up. A prospective marginal unit of beaver may be associated with a private picture for you; it may be associated with an equally private prospective picture for me. But since for each of us these (admittedly incommensurable) pictures are mental representations of the same physical object (a given quantity of beaver), it may seem unfruitful pedantry to insist on reserving the term "opportunity cost" for the incommensurable subjective mental representations of a given commodity sacrificed, rather than for the objective commodity itself. And if a given outlay of money might have purchased that commodity (both for you and for me), why should that sum of money not be recognized as the objective measure of the common opportunity cost to each of us of what we buy with that outlay?

The recent writers on subjective costs (cited above) have emphasized the unrealism of the equilibrium construct as thoroughly undermining the suitability of money outlays for service as such an objective measure of opportunity cost. Here we wish to draw attention to one aspect of equilibrium which is particularly important for understanding the unsuitability of money outlays for such service. In equilibrium analysis it is taken for granted that, while you and I may differ about the significance of a given objective prospect, we are nonetheless disagreeing about what we both recognize as being the *same* object. In other words, the state of equilibrium is one in which all market participants correctly perceive that which is objectively perceivable. It is precisely this aspect of equilibrium to which we wish to draw critical attention.

As discussed in an earlier section, the subjectivity of opportunity costs derives, in part, from the circumstances that different individuals perceive different things even when they are looking at the same object. If two individuals were always to see the given object (or prospect) that is before them correctly, then we might indeed wish to replace discussion about differing prospective utilities to be sacrificed by reference to the identical object (the prospective sacrifice of which is at issue). But wherever we wish to take into account the extent to which decisions reflect highly personal views not only concerning the significance of the facts before one's face, but also concerning the very facts themselves, we dare not talk of sacrificed *objects* apart from the private *perceptions* of these objects. A given amount of money does not, except under highly artificial assumptions, represent the same purchase possibilities to two individuals exploring the same supermarket. It is certainly unhelpful to focus on analytical models in which such artificial assumptions have been made, to an extent that permits us to overlook the crucial difference between the following statements. You and I have expended equal amounts of money. You and I have sacrificed the prospective utilities which we respectively attach to the given sum of money. The statements are simply not completely interchangeable statements. There may, it is true, be imaginable sets of circumstances under which some might be content to use the first statement as a workable (and more easily manageable) substitute for the second. Our point is that, if the cost notion is to serve as an *explanation* of why a person made the decision he did, it will not do to invoke a statement such as that made in the first statement, as such short explanation (in place of the more complete second statement) unless we can rely on the assured, complete awareness of the objective facts that enter into the first. Most economists would agree that such complete awareness is likely to be achieved, in general, only through learning process which involve decisions based on *faulty* awareness. If *these* decisions are to be explained, as they surely can and must be, on the basis of relevant costs, we dare not confine discussions of cost to contexts in which the possibility of faulty (or otherwise idiosyncratic) awareness of facts has been assumed away. The use of money outlays provides no justification for so confining the discussion.

Money outlays as measuring costs to society

The use of money outlays to serve as objective measures of cost is often suggested in order to assess the "social cost" of a particular undertaking. It is useful to emphasize that, strictly speaking, such attempts can have nothing at all to do with the subjectivist notion of opportunity cost. *The subjective notion of the term "cost" is necessarily always private*. It has no meaning outside the context of a decision. All decisions are made by individuals; hence all costs (in this usage) are private costs. While decisions may be made that affect society, or even be made on behalf of society, they are nevertheless made by individuals (whether as private citizens, voters, public officials, or members of governing groups) and hence involve only private costs, that is, sacrifices which the decision maker sees *himself* to be making. (Of course a public official may consider the effect of a course of action upon the public, but such considerations enter into his decision, after all, only to the extent that *he* considers them to be important.) For us to be able to talk of the (subjective) *social* opportunity cost of a decision, it would be necessary to imagine society *as a whole* making decisions. In any but a metaphorical sense a society simply cannot make decisions. Hence, there can be no notion of social cost (in the sense of a subjective opportunity cost).[14]

One may indeed wish to discuss the alternative volume of goods that might have been forthcoming in a society had resources been allocated for purposes other than those in fact pursued. It may seem not inappropriate to describe these goods as the social cost of the project pursued. And, if money outlays might have commanded such a volume of goods, it seems natural to see these outlays as being but the monetary expression of this social cost. But the truth is that for no individual entrepreneur can this volume of goods be described as the subjective opportunity cost of his decision to acquire the resources for the purposes pursued. If these alternative goods are described as social cost, this can only be in a sense for which no actual decision can have been relevant. If such social cost is held to be an opportunity cost, this can only be in a nonsubjectivist meaning of this term. Money outlays may, under assumed conditions of equilibrium, measure this quantity of alternative goods that might have been produced. But to use such outlays as a measure of social cost cannot, *even though these outlays are made by individuals*, succeed in erasing the conceptual gulf that separates the objective notion of social cost from the subjective, private, notion of opportunity cost. Even under equilibrium conditions the money outlays of individual entrepreneurs cannot at the same time represent both private and social "costs"; money outlays may indeed be taken to represent alternative outputs (and hence social cost (in the objective sense discussed above)), but private (subjective) opportunity costs are not these alternative outputs, and certainly not these money outlays. They are the *significance* of the perceived purchases foregone by these outlays.

We may put the matter quite briefly. Money outlays for a particular project, are, of course, objective. They may, under specified conditions, be held to represent the objective opportunity costs to society of that project. But money outlays cannot serve as an objective counterpart for any *subjective* notion of social cost simply because, in strict terms, the notion of a subjective social cost is without meaning.[15]

One may, as noted, wish to use the term "cost" in an objective sense, or, with Professor Buchanan and the Austrians, one may wish to reserve the term to refer only to subjective sacrifices. If it is the latter usage which is being followed, then money outlays are simply not, in and of themselves, costs; they certainly do not translate subjective costs into objective costs.

CHOICE, HYPOTHETICAL CHOICE, AND SOCIAL COST

We may in fact go further in our contention that money outlays cannot provide an objective translation of subjective opportunity costs. Thus far our discussion has left unchallenged at least the insight that money outlays may be seen as an objective expression of *social* opportunity cost. We merely pointed out that the latter term must itself then be used to refer to costs in an objective, decision-irrelevant, sense. But in fact, we will now argue, there are grounds for the assertion that the term social cost, as widely used, does indeed imply a truc opportunity cost in a decision context (and thus ultimately in a quasi-subjective sense), albeit in very limited and special terms. So that, we will point out, if money outlays are indeed held to measure social costs, we shall have to reinterpret these outlays as costs in a less than completely objective sense. All this may appear to be quite confusing and paradoxical and indeed to involve an abrupt about-face from our earlier insistence that social cost can under no circumstances be recognized as a cost in the sense of the subjective opportunity cost. These matters do deserve elucidation.

Until now we have recognized (among the various meanings different economists have attached to the term "cost") objective as well as subjective opportunity cost interpretations. One might well question the felicity of using the term "cost" to denote the objective disadvantages or objective output losses in fact imposed on society by the construction of a swimming pool, whether or not these disadvantages were taken into account prospectively by the homeowner. But we did not question the possible interest and importance attached to the volume of such disadvantages or losses. Whether or not we wished to refer to the sum of such disadvantages or losses as the cost of the swimming pool, we recognized that it might well be important, for normative purposes, to take cognizance of these disadvantages or forgone social outputs even if the homeowner himself did not do so. We wish now to argue, however, that, in referring to such disadvantages, or forgone alternative social outputs as "costs," economists are, in fact, whether they are completely aware of it or not, implicitly treating these disadvantages and lost outputs *in the context of hypothetical decisions*.

We maintain, that is, that all the cost concepts we have considered do ultimately depend upon the subjective opportunity cost notion (which we have endorsed as the only version capable of rendering individual decisions intelligible). Even the apparently objective notion of displaced social output and the like *are treated as cost only because one is imagining a decision through which these alternative advantages are deliberately being sacrificed.*

If the cost of a particular process of production is being discussed, this is presumably because the worthwhileness of the project is under examination. For the decision maker responsible for the project this is of course a matter of obvious and immediate relevance (and is the reason why we have emphasized the role of cost in explaining decisions). For those other than the decision maker himself, consideration of the cost of a project is presumably taken in order to make a judgment on its worthwhileness, either from the point of view of the decision maker himself (i.e., a judgment by another of whether or not the decision maker made a wise decision) or from the point of view of "society" (e.g., whether the project's full "cost" to society is being taken into account). These judgements may be either prospective or retrospective, but they are all judgments concerning efficiency. Such judgments, then, answer the following kinds of question: "*Should* this project be undertaken, or are its expected benefits outweighed by the costs?" "Should this project have been undertaken, or were its expected benefits outweighed by the costs?" These questions are questions about decisions, either actual decisions or hypothetical decisions.[16] In reviewing hypothetical decisions the reviewer may imagine himself to be responsible only for himself ("If *I* were the prospective producer. . . ."), or for society at large ("If *I* were in charge. . . ."). However, the reviewer may imagine a decision "by society" (regardless of whether he is aware of the strictly metaphorical character of "decisions by society") whether or not to permit a private entrepreneur to decide to initiate the project.

Into all these hypothetical decisions, then, costs enter in exactly the same way as they do into actual decisions by individuals. The objective social costs of a project enter into such hypothetical decisions in the following way. Let us imagine that a privately built swimming pool increases the noisiness of a neighbourhood (a matter by which, let us say, the homeowner himself is unaffected). Then an economist may argue that, after taking the externalities imposed upon neighbors fully into account, the social cost of the pool renders its construction a mistake, from the point of view of society. This means that the economist is making the judgment that if "society" were choosing whether or not to have the pool (or whether or not to permit the homeowner to build the pool), a negative decision would be in order, since relevant costs are held to outweigh relevant benefits. But all this means that the so-called "objective costs" to society of the pool, are being imagined to be taken into account by a hypothetical decision maker. As such, such costs must be imagined to be *perceived* and evaluated by this hypothetical decision maker. As a result, these objective costs turn out to be at least quasisubjective, after all.

Now we have indeed argued throughout this paper that *actual* decisions are made only by individuals, not by 'society'. It is for this reason that we have insisted that "social costs" (as something apart from private decision making) cannot be true subjective opportunity costs. We certainly still maintain this position. Nonetheless our present discussion is designed to emphasize that such social costs, while indeed not true subjective opportunity costs in the straightforward sense, can be imagined to be meaningful only in the context of *imagined* decisions, possibly by altogether *imaginary* decision makers. The cost notion, even in its apparently objective versions, ultimately expresses an implicit subjectivism.

While, for purposes of such discussions of social efficiency, economists may be indulging in questionably legitimate stretches of their imagination, we must understand them as after all implicitly treating costs as quasi-subjective.[17] It follows, as stated earlier, that while money outlays may be used to measure "social cost" under relevant equilibrium conditions, the ultimate subjectivity that is inherent in the cost notion, cannot even then be thoroughly exorcised.

Let us sum up our position. In explaining actual decisions the only costs that are relevant are private, subjective perceptions of required sacrifices. Conversely, the use of cost in judging the actual efficiency (to relevant decision makers) of particular projects, can refer only to subjective costs as they appear to these decision makers. For costs in this true sense, attempts to find objective measures or counterparts—whether in terms of money outlays or anything else—to subjective costs, are doomed to failure. Moreover, we have found, the subjective element is so deeply engrained in the notion of cost, that even truly objective versions of cost turn out ultimately to reflect an implicit quasisubjectivism. Notions of social cost are, as has been amply demonstrated in the recent literature, totally illegitimate in the strict context of subjective cost. We have found that, in addition, such ostensibly objective notions of cost turn out to conceal a quasisubjective element, after all.

NOTES

1. T. W. Hutchison, *A Review of Economic Doctrines, 1870–1929* (Oxford: Clarendon Press, 1953), p. 156.
2. J. M. Buchanan, *Cost and Choice* (Chicago: Markham, 1969). The numerous debts to which the writing of this paper owes to Buchanan's discussion will be apparent to every reader of that book. A recent paper offering an excellent new exposition of similar insights is J. Wiseman, "Costs and Decisions," in *Contemporary Economic Analysis*, eds. D. A. Currie and W. Peters (London: Croom Helm, 1980), vol. II.
3. S. C. Littlechild, "The Problem of Social Cost," in *New Directions in Austrian Economics*, ed. L. Sparado (Kansas City: Sheed Andrews &

McMeel, 1978); E. C. Pasour, Jr., "Cost and Choice—Austrian vs. Conventional Views," *Journal of Libertarian Studies* (Winter, 1978); E. C. Pasour, Jr., "Cost of Production: A Defensible Basis for Agricultural Price Supports?" *American Journal of Agricultural Economics* (May, 1980); K. I. Vaughn, "Does it Matter That Costs are Subjective?" *Southern Economic Journal* (March, 1980).

4. A. A. Alchian, "Cost," in *Encyclopedia of the Social Sciences* (New York: Macmillan, 1969) vol. III (also in *Economic Forces at Work: Selected Works by Armen A. Alchian* (Indianapolis: Liberty Press, 1977), pp. 404ff. (Page references are to *Encyclopedia*).
5. Alchian, op. cit., p. 404.
6. Of course such attempts may raise serious questions concerning the very meaning of such a sum.
7. Let the advantages of the adopted and the rejected options be represented by *A, C,* respectively; and let the disadvantages of the adopted and rejected options be represented by *B, D,* respectively. Then one may say that the net utility of the adopted alternative is *A-B*, and its cost is *C-D* (with the latter term not including reference to *B* at all, confirming Alchian's position). However, it seems entirely in order to say that in choosing the first option the decision maker is embracing the utility *A* plus the "freedom from disadvantage *D*," and that the sacrifices called for are made up of the forgone utility *C* plus "freedom from disadvantage *B*." It must be readily conceded that such accounting considerations may sometimes appear arbitrary and even forced. If I choose to sit on a hard park bench rather than on the soft grass, it may seem artificial to say that the hardness of the seat enters into the cost of my decision (in the form of the sacrificed softness of the grass). It certainly may seem more natural to say that the hardness of the bench merely reduces its utility. But it should be emphasized that this is not because disadvantages cannot in fact be represented as associated sacrifices, but because they may under given circumstances not be perceived as such. Where such perception is not lacking, the point being made in the text comes back into full relevance.
8. This does not apply to the insightful comment by Madelyn L. Kaflogis, "Marriage Customs and Opportunity Costs" *Journal of Political Economy* (March/April, 1970), pp. 421–3.
9. "Opportunity Cost of Marriage: Comment" *Journal of Political Economy* (September/October, 1969) p. 863.
10. Vaughn, op. cit.; Pasour, op. cit.
11. See, for a discussion of Baumol, Vaughn, op. cit., pp. 709ff.
12. W. J. Baumol, "Review of *Cost and Choice*," *Journal of Economic Literature* (December, 1970), p. 1210.
13. J. Buchanan, op. cit., p. 85.
14. See however the final section of this paper for a somewhat different way of stating this.
15. See the following section for a discussion in terms not so strict.
16. See Littlechild, op. cit., p. 85 for a discussion of the role of hypothetical choices.
17. For example, there may be problems with the internal consistency of such imagined choice situations.

12 Conceptions of Equilibrium: The Logic Choice and the Logic of Production*

J. A. KREGEL

> If I am right, the whole problem of applying monetary theory is largely one of deducing changes in anticipations from the changes in objective data which call them forth . . . once the connection between objective facts and anticipations has been made, theory comes again into its rights. . . . Nevertheless, it does seem to me most important that . . . we should bring out very clearly the assumptions which we are making about the genesis of anticipations. For this seems to be the only way in which we can overcome the extraordinary theoretical differences of recent years, which are, I think very largely traceable to this source.[1]

This passage from Hicks' "Suggestions for Simplifying the Theory of Money," published in 1935, is not only testimony to Hayek's influence on monetary economics, it also represents the "method of anticipations" which Hicks imputed to Keynes' *General Theory* in his review of the book a year later.[2] While expectations played a central role in both the neo-Austrian theory built on Hayek's work and Keynes' *General Theory*, Hicks' presumption that the "objective facts" generating anticipations were similar in the two approaches appears to have been mistaken. Present day neo-Austrian and post Keynesian theories also seem to have a great deal in common when it comes to recognizing the importance of the genesis of anticipations, but it is still the case that fundamental differences exist over what constitutes the "objective facts" characterizing the equilibrium of the economic system. Since Professor Lachmann's work in particular represents an important synthesis of Austrian and Keynesian elements, it will be exploited in this essay to identify the source of these differences.

I ANTICIPATIONS, OBJECTIVE FACTS AND EQUILIBRIUM

In an essay published some eight years after Hicks' monition cited above, and despite the publication of Keynes' *General Theory* and Hicks' summary of it, Professor Lachmann noted that "It has to be admitted that hitherto the scope of economic theory has been unduly restricted to the formal characteristics of the economic problem and its implications. Equilibrium economics (what Hayek has termed 'The Pure Logic of Choice') studies the full implications of a set of data, the 'conditions of equilibrium'; it does not study the ways in which these logical implications are translated into human action, which is thus conceived as a quasi-automatic response to an external stimulus."[3] The equilibrium based on the "logic of choice" to which Lachmann refers would seem to be Walrasian general equilibrium, the "set of data" comprising the "conditions of equilibrium" the endowments, preferences, and technology which permit the existence of a vector of prices at which all agents' individual plans are mutually compatible. Modern general equilibrium theory has shown unequivocally that the purely formal characteristics of the conditions of equilibrium produce a determinate solution, but, as Lachmann notes, the existence of "a determinate solution does not entail that those attempting its solution will actually succeed."[4] Indeed, modern general equilibrium theory has been singularly unsuccessful in demonstrating how an economy of independent individuals might achieve equilibrium conditions if they did not already exist. The Rational Expectations Hypothesis proposes a solution to the problems which assumes that the implications of the logical conditions are automatically translated into human action. Lachmann's lamentation concerning the failure to analyze how logical implications may be translated into human individual action capable of achieving equilibrium has lost none of its currency.

For the Austrians, as Lachmann puts it, the problem is that equilibrium economics does not "study the ways in which these logical implications are translated into human action, which is thus conceived as a quasi-automatic response to an external "stimulus." But in the theory of economic action no such mechanistic preconception is admissable, a point which the introduction of expectations brings out with all necessary clarity."[5] What is needed is to "fill in those formal propositions with definite statements about how knowledge is acquired and communicated."[6]

Hayek, in "Economics and Knowledge," initiated this; he based it on the presumption of the existence of the knowledge of the "objective data" of the conditions of the (general) equilibrium so that in the tendency to equilibrium "the knowledge and intentions of the different members of society are supposed to come more and more into agreement or, ... that the expectations of the people and particularly of entrepreneurs will become more and more correct."[7] Thus, "it is only relative to the knowledge which a person is bound to acquire in the course of the attempt to carry out his original plan that an equilibrium is likely to be achieved."[8] Thus, not only is an equilibrium presumed to exist, it is assumed to be independent of the process of acquiring the knowledge necessary to achieve it.

The problem is thus not viewed as the objective conditions which require individuals to form expectations or the genesis of expectations per se. Rather, "the question why the data in the subjective sense of the term should ever come to correspond to the objective data is one of the main problems that we have to answer."[9] Here subjective data refers to the individual's conception of the objective data necessary to produce the tendency to equilibrium. It is this problem of the translation of the logical implications of the conditions of equilibrium into human actions by filling in the formal propositions with definite statements about how knowledge of existing and available objective data is acquired and communicated as subjective data that Lachmann refers to in the passage cited above as not having been sufficiently studied. While the absence of knowledge of the necessary objective data is admitted, the objective data defining the equilibrium is presumed to exist. Expectations enter only to the extent that they link the objective data defining the conditions of equilibrium and the subjective data necessary for human action to lead to equilibrium.

In Keynes' theory, on the other hand, expectations were important because of the conditions facing the entrepreneur in taking investment decisions: "All production is for the purpose of ultimately satisfying a consumer. Time usually elapses ... between the incurring of costs by the producer ... and the purchase of the output. ... Meanwhile the entrepreneur ... has to form the best expectations he can as to what the consumers will be prepared to pay when he is ready to supply them ...

after the elapse of what may be a lengthy period; and he has no choice but to be guided by these expectations, if he is to produce at all by processes which occupy time."[10] There can be no tendency to equilibrium based on a relation between expectations and the objective data of what the consumer will demand and the price he will pay which describes the conditions of equilibrium because the incomes available to consumers will be determined ultimately by the very decisions taken by entrepreneurs on the basis of these expectations.

The post Keynesian approach is thus influenced by Keynes' insistence that the level of output and employment cannot be considered as objective data determining the conditions of equilibrium because they will be endogenously determined by entrepreneurs' decisions. The conditions of equilibrium thus cannot concern the coordination of plans in "a society consisting of several independent persons"[11] if the actions of those independent persons only determine the exchange equilibrium of exogenously given scarce means in order to satisfy a multiplicity of exogenously given ends. Rather, Keynes is concerned with the role of expectations in the coordination of individual production plans in a society consisting of several independent producers whose expectations determine the means available to satisfy an uncertain multiplicity of future demands. Expectations themselves determine the objective facts of the conditions of equilibrium. Post Keynesian theory is little concerned with the dissemination of knowledge necessary for the tendency to equilibrium because the "objective facts," independent of the process by which they are acquired, are presumed not to exist at the point in time when they are required for investment, output and employment decisions. The problem is not whether the objective data necessary to achieve equilibrium will be reflected in subjective data available to the individual, but the very definition of the objective data. Indeed, even its objectivity is questioned.

Thus, despite the similarity of the importance attached to the genesis of expectations, the neo-Austrian concern with expectations does not necessarily imply the post Keynesian conception of uncertainty. Even more important, the neo-Austrian introduction of uncertainty to explain the tendency toward a general equilibrium implies acceptance of the specification of equilibrium in terms of the "Pure Logic of Choice." This is impossible in Keynes' theory, for the existence of expectations implies existence of uncertainty concerning the very objective facts which determine the conditions of equilibrium of the "Logic of Choice." The similar concern for expectations thus stems from divergence concerning the definition of the conditions of equilibrium and of the objective data which generate expectations upon which Hicks' proposal is based.

II THE LOGIC OF PRODUCTION AND THE LOGIC OF CHOICE

Keynes' "principle of effective demand", formulated to explain the objective datum of the constraint of means available to satisfy ends, is a theory of "economic action," as defined by Lachmann, for expectations determine individual behavior. The difference is that these expectations do not produce a tendency to reflect the objective data of an independently determined equilibrium; instead, they determine the equilibrium. Keynes called his early efforts to work out his new approach the theory of a monetary *production* economy to stress its difference from the conditions of neutral exchange equilibrium of the logic of choice.[12] Keynes attempted to produce a theory to determine endogenously the relevant output constraints by proceeding directly to the crucial role of expectations in the genesis of production and investment decisions. He thus started from a theory based on "human action," rather than working out a separate "Logic of Production" to replace the existing "Logic of Choice". It was only with the publication of Sraffa's *Production of Commodities By Means of Commodities* that what one might call the full implication of a set of objective data related to production and investment decisions, and its conditions of equilibrium, that is, a "Logic of Production" that would be applicable to all possible levels of output, became available to replace the neoclassical "Logic of Choice."[13] In this respect the Sraffa system may be interpreted as representing all the objective factors relevant to investment: input costs, technology, relative rates of return; it may thus be interpreted as demonstrating the logical relations of an equilibrium in which production plans are mutually consistent at the maximum possible uniform rate of return, independent of the level of output and employment. These latter elements can only be determined by introducing expectations of future costs, technology, profitability. In short, it is a theory of human action to determine investment which Keynes called the theory of effective demand.

Thus, post Keynesian theory is not concerned with the failure to specify the relation between objective data and the subjective data motivating the human actions which are supposed to produce the tendency to equilibrium. Rather, it argues that the objective factors themselves cannot be unambiguously defined within the particular Logic of Choice which is retained as the basis for the neo-Austrian approach. It is the criticism of the logic itself, not of the specification of the human action which might or might not accompany it, which defines the fundamental difference between the two approaches. Prior to the question of knowledge and its relation to uncertainty, the post Keynesian refuses to accept that the knowledge that Hayek takes as his starting point exists or can be generated by the model he adopts.[14]

It is interesting to note that many Austrian economists, including Professor Lachmann,[15] have sharply criticized much of the post Keynesian theory (in particular the theory of long period growth which sets aside the problem of knowledge and the tendency to equilibrium by assuming that you must be in equilibrium in order to get there) and Sraffa's theory because of the failure to specify the processes by which the subjective data are generated by the objective data without noticing that these works are concerned with the formulation of a different basic "logic" upon which economic analysis of the economic problem might be grounded. These theories are, rather, attempting to identify a consistent economic logic by identifying categories of objective data (primarily in relation to the investment decision) about which expectations must be formed, rather than seeking the objective conditions which may form the basis for, in Hicks' words, the genesis of expectations. The criticisms appear misplaced, for they fail to recognize that the different specification of the basic logic of the economic problem requires a different specification of the problem of human action in terms of the relation between expectations and fundamental uncertainty rather than objective and subjective knowledge. The study of the relation between objective and subjective data stressed by the Austrians within the logic of choice is not applicable to the logic of production, nor is it the same problem as that between uncertainty and the necessity to formulate expectations about future events stressed by post Keynesian analysis of human action in a monetary production economy.

III UNCERTAINTY AS A BASIS FOR HUMAN ACTION

The change that a different "logic" of the economic problem implies for the way expectations and uncertainty enter the theory of human action separates the views of Austrians and Keynesians. Here, Professor Lachmann's work is of fundamental importance, for he has been particularly aware of the difference in the place of expectations, emphasizing that Shackle's contribution to Austrian economics extends "the scope of subjectivism from tastes to expectations"; while "Professor Hayek ... dealt with expectations ... but not with the causes and consequences of their divergence. In fact, expectations were ... regarded as being of analytical interest only to the extent to which they converge. They were, on the whole treated as a mode of foresight, a rather unfortunate but inevitable consequence of imperfect knowledge."[16] But, as Lachmann notes, if individuals generate information through their actions, rather than just acquiring it, there is no reason for expectations to converge. This is an even more powerful criticism of equilibrium theory than its failure to study the ways conditions of equilibrium are translated into human action. It has implications similar to those of the Keynesian criticisms of the "Logic of Choice": "It is this view of the market process as at least potentially terminating in a state of long-run general equilibrium that now appears to require revision."[17] The interesting fact is that the Keynesian criticism has been based on an alternative conception of the conditions of economic equilibrium, while Lachmann reaches a similar position on the basis of an alternative specification of expectations in human action. Both routes reach the same conclusion: The conception of equilibrium and of human action must be changed together.

For post Keynesian economists the "revision" suggested by Lachmann leads to an alternative specification of equilibrium in terms of those factors relevant to the investment decision that does not presume a unique constraint on the level of activity, as represented, for example, in Sraffa's "Logic of Production" in terms of uniformity of rates of return. This specification has the advantage of allowing the introduction of individuals' divergent production expectations as determinants of the level of output and employment in a way which is compatible with Keynes' introduction of the essential properties of a monetary production system in Chapters 16 and 17 of the *General Theory*.[18] In this way, the Logic of Production provides a basis for a theory of economic processes based on the competitive process and the formation of expectations in conditions of fundamental uncertainty which results from the fact that individuals can never attain subjective data required to produce the tendency to equilibrium because the objective data defining the conditions of equilibrium do not exist when they are required to formulate decisions. As Sraffa pointed out in his criticism of Hayek, "under free competition ... divergence of rates [of return] is as essential to the effecting of the transition as is the divergence of prices from costs of production; it is, in fact, another aspect of the same thing."[19] Since each individual will form expectations of future prices and implied rates of return, which determine their investment and expenditure decisions, that, in turn, determine the conditions governing prices in the future, there is no reason for expectations to "converge" to a common value even though they will produce actions which eliminate potential for profit represented by divergences between prices and costs or relative rates of return so as to produce a tendency to the maximum possible expected rate of return.

IV NEO-AUSTRIANS, POST KEYNESIANS AND NEO-RICARDIANS

It is with reference to a particular development of Sraffa's work, which Professor Lachmann identifies as "neo-Ricardian," that the neo-Austrian and post Keynesian views are most similar.[20] The problem is not the meaning or implications of the logical relations which Sraffa defines between relative prices and the distributive variables.[21] Rather, it is Garegnani's claim that these relations "may provide better support than was provided by Keynes himself for establishing the principle of effective demand in long-period analysis" by identifying "the error of orthodox theory ... at a more fundamental level than simply the obstacles which uncertainty and expectations might raise ... for equilibrium of demand and supply of labour."[22] Since the long-period equilibrium of the classical theory, as defined by Sraffa in terms of natural prices producing uniform rates of return, does not rely on supply and demand and is not associated with full employment, Garegnani argues that uncertainty and expectations, which were of importance as short-period frictions preventing supply and demand from producing full employment, "may be dispensed with."[23] Keynes' short-period analysis is thus relegated to the random or accidental deviations of the system caused by uncertainty and expectations which impede the adjustment or gravitation of the economy to its long-period position.

In contrast to Hayek, who argues that only by filling in the formal propositions with statements about how knowledge is acquired and communicated can scientific propositions be produced, Garegnani instead argues that such propositions may be omitted because they may be made implicit in more general scientific propositions.

Garegnani refers to the classical economists to support his position that expectations can be omitted from long-period analysis by noting that

> a particular treatment of price expectations was ... implied [in] ... Smith's argument about the tendency of the market price to fall when it exceeds the natural price ... producers should expect the high market price to last long enough for them to reap an extra profit by acting now in order to produce more of the commodity later. But the important point of Smith's procedure is precisely that this effect upon the minds of people of a market price exceeding natural price appeared to be so inescapable as to permit proceeding directly to its objective consequence, increased production. This would seem to be the procedure to be aimed at with respect to "expectations" in the theory of value: to relate them uniquely to objective phenomena, so as to bypass them and relate the facts explaining the expectations directly to the actions of the individuals.[24]

Thus, in agreement with Hicks' quotation at the beginning of this essay, Garegnani's long-period theory of effective demand is based on the belief that once the "inescapable" links between expectations and the objective facts which produce them have been established, "a plausible respondence of expectations to experience"[25] may be assumed so that expectations may be omitted and objective facts explain the actions of individuals.

Since this "long-period" theory of effective demand depends on the permanence of less than full employment in the long-period position, it also depends on the "gravitation" of market prices to natural prices, i.e., on the production decisions of individuals being an inescapable objective consequence resulting from divergence of market and natural prices or market from natural rates of return. But, as Parrinello shows, this process of gravitation depends crucially on three propositions: an explanation of why market prices diverge from natural prices, a proof that an increase in the market price above natural price will indeed produce "extra profit by acting now," and an identifiable relationship between realized and expected profits if these are to guide producers' decisions.[26] Restricting his analysis to the first two points, he concludes that both are simply assumed but not demonstrated in neo-Ricardian theory.

With respect to the third point, Garegnani has explained that in the long-period theory of effective demand, investment decisions are determined with respect to the "normal rate of profits" which

> corresponds to the rate which is being realised *on an average* (as between firms and over time) by the entrepreneurs who use the

> dominant technique. This is so because these firms (like all other firms) will receive, on an average, the normal price for their product and pay, on an average, beside normal wages and rents, normal (supply) prices for the means of production to be replaced. But because this is the rate of profits which is being realised *in the present* under the stated conditions, it is also the rate of profits which that present experience will lead entrepreneurs in general to expect *in the future* from their current investment.[27]

But individual decisions can be taken on the basis of average rates of return, which are determined by those decisions, only if "normal profit" is determined independently of those decisions. This requires not only that entrepreneurs have a uniform idea of the normal rate of profit, but that they believe that their actions have no impact on normal returns. Yet, if deviations from the normal position are purely random or accidental, they should not generate changes in production for normal prices will be restored simply by the return of normal conditions. The impact on production of the "objective" circumstances of a deviation of price from its natural value will depend crucially on entrepreneurs' expectations of both the determinants of the natural position and their assessment of the causes of deviation from it. Absence of specific explanation of the first two of Parrinello's requirements for gravitation listed above implies absence of the third.

Cartelier has also analyzed Smith's process of gravitation by using a sequence of periods in which entrepreneurs, who do not know the "natural rate" established over all markets, compare their realized return on investment with the rate that they require to invest for sale in the market in the next period.[28] He concludes that gravitation of market to natural price requires that the entrepreneurs' "state of expectation must be such that a small change in the realized rate of return does not lead to large changes in their decisions to invest."

Professor Lachmann had already made the same point noting that the "normal level in the minds of the people . . . is determined by what are believed to be permanently operative forces. . . . A market will exhibit inelastic expectations only if it believes that price is ultimately governed by long-run forces, and if it has a fairly definitive conception of what these forces are."[29] Thus, it is not enough to postulate normal prices or rates of profits based on average values, for the stability of the averages and the conception of normal must rest on individuals' having "a fairly definite conceptions of what these forces are," which will allow them to distinguish whether deviations from these values present opportunities for profit or whether they will be automatically corrected by the disappearance of the factors of disturbance. For example, a bad harvest causes prices to deviate from normal, but it is the return of normal weather conditions, not increased production, which brings about the return of normal prices. Indeed, increased production moves market prices away from natural values and creates cyclical fluctuations.

The "inescapable" or "unique link" between objective facts and actions thus seems to depend crucially on the assumptions made about the knowledge available to each individual concerning the normal forces determining the conditions of equilibrium and his beliefs concerning the causes of disturbances which will generate expectations which determine actions. Thus, even the long-period demonstration of unemployment equilibrium requires, as Hicks reminds us, careful specification of the assumptions concerning expectations.

Further, Sraffa's analysis, upon which the long-period position is based, presumes one of the distributive variables (the normal rate of profit) and the dominant technique are given, while the very act of investment is usually considered to be directed to changing either one or both of these; investment decisions produced by gravitation of market prices to natural values consistent with uniform rates of return will then change the normal rate of return. An explanation of the long-period rate of investment which relies on an exogenous normal rate of profit cannot also determine that rate. Both the Austrian and Keynesian criticisms point to the impossibility of identifying an a priori link between objective facts and expectations that can be considered "so inescapable" as to be eliminated from the analysis.

Garegnani[30] defends his approach to expectations by reference to Pareto's statement that the best science can do is to predict what "the consumption of alcohol will be in France next year" while it will never be able to predict "the consumption of alcohol of a particular individual at a given time or day."[31] Although Pareto affirms that abstract theory can only be judged with reference to "general and average facts, not happenstance occurrences"[32] he goes on to emphasize that "The classification of phenomena as principal and secondary [more and less general, or in Garegnani's interpretation, long and short period] is not the same from the general point of view of science and from the particular point of view of an individual. A traveller is not interested in knowing the length of the geodesic arc which links the point on the earth where he is and the one where he wants to go, what he wants to know is the route which will get him from one place to the other."[33]

But the point at issue is not the defense of abstraction in theoretical analysis, which requires the exclusion of random events, but rather whether the geodesic arc can be considered to be of any use to the traveler in reaching his destination. The Austrian would give a positive answer only if some mechanism by which the traveler can base his travel plans on the arc can be identified, for example competition leading profit seeking entrepreneurs to the production and sale of geodesic maps. For the post Keynesian, on the other hand, the very assumption that the spheroid shape of the earth may be taken as given is questioned, for the decisions of the individual may change its very nature, indeed are intended to do so. Thus the necessity of forming expectations about the likely shape of the world.

Thus, Pareto does not argue that theory ignore the determination of individual decisions. The classification of long-period phenomena on Pareto's "principal" level does not then imply that the analysis of individual behavior capable of explaining the level of activity which will actually prevail should be considered as "secondary." Both comprise the principal level necessary to a long-period theory of effective demand.

Despite this substantial agreement between the post Keynesian and neo-Austrian criticism of Garegnani's attempts to eliminate explicit consideration of expectations from the long-period theory of effective demand, there still remains a difference over the status of the objective data and the conditions of equilibrium. Here Professor Lachmann's criticism goes beyond the Austrian position to question the very existence of the objective data which subjective data reflects. This is not only a criticism of Garegnani's general proposals for the treatment of expectations in the theory of value, it is also an implicit criticism of Hicks' proposal which opens this essay. Clearly, his reference to the genesis of expectations implies an underlying conception of equilibrium characterized by objective data. Theoretical differences between neo-Austrians, post Keynesians and neo-Ricardians seem to be less concerned with the problems of expectations and knowledge than the specification of the objective factors representing the conditions of equilibrium.

NOTES

* I would like to thank J. Snippe for many helpful comments and suggestions without making him responsible for the final result.

1. J. R. Hicks, "A Suggestion for Simplifying the Theory of Money," (1935) reprinted in John Hicks, *Collected Essays on Economic Theory, Money Interest and Wages* (Oxford: Basil Blackwell, 1983), vol. II, pp. 58–9.
2. J. A. Kregel, "Microfoundations and Hicksian Monetary Theory," *Economist*, 130 (1982).
3. L. M. Lachmann, "The Role of Expectations in Economics as a Social Science," (1943) reprinted in *Capital, Expectations and the Market Process*, ed. W. E. Grinder (Kansas City: Sheed Andrews & McMeel, 1977), pp. 69–70.
4. Ibid., p. 69.
5. Lachmann, op. cit., pp. 69–70.
6. F. A. Hayek, "Economics and Knowledge," (1937) reprinted in *Individualism and Economic Order* (London: Routledge & Kegan Paul, 1949), p. 33.
7. Ibid., p. 45.
8. Ibid., p. 53.
9. Ibid., p. 39.
10. J. M. Keynes, *The General Theory of Employment, Interest and Money* (London: Macmillan, 1936), p. 46.
11. Hayek, op. cit., p. 37.
12. J. M. Keynes, *Collected Writings* (London: Macmillan, 1973, 1979), vol. XIII, pp. 408–11 and vol. XXIX, pp. 50ff.
13. P. Sraffa, *Production of Commodities by Means of Commodities* (Cambridge: Cambridge University Press,1960).
14. Thus the post Keynesian criticism of general equilibrium was not limited to the importance of expectations or the relation of objective to subjective knowledge but, with the help of Sraffa's Logic of Production, also concerned the logical impossibility of generating the functional relations of supply and demand between quantities and prices which produce the objective market prices which form the data of the logic of choice. This criticism was most evident in the theory of capital. Thus, Lachmann's theory of capital discussed "what type of equipment it will be most profitable to create under various conditions . . . rather than to explain the factors which determined the value of a given stock of productive equipment and of the income that will be derived from it" *Capital and its Structure* (Kansas City: Sheed Andrews & McMeel, 1978), p. vii. Joan Robinson, in contrast, argued that capital had no meaning outside the conditions of equilibrium upon which the logic of choice was based. Indeed, Joan Robinson's early complaints about equilibrium were linked to the problem of capital: "There is only one case where the quantity of capital can be measured . . . that is when the economy as a whole is in equilibrium. . . . Never talk about a system *getting into* equilibrium, for equilibrium as no meaning unless you are in it already." Joan Robinson, "A Lecture Delivered at Oxford By a Cambridge Economist," in *On Re-Reading Marx* (Cambridge: Students' Bookshop, 1953), p. 16.
15. L. M. Lachmann, *Macroeconomic Thinking and the Market Economy* (London: Institute of Economics Affairs, 1973).
16. L. M. Lachmann, "From Mises to Shackle: An Essay," *Journal of Economic Literature*, 15 (1976) p. 58.
17. Ibid., p. 60.

18. See, for example, J. A. Kregel, "Effective Demand: Origins and Development of the Notion," in *Distribution, Effective Demand and International Economic Relations*, ed. J. A. Kregel (London: Macmillan, 1983); "Hamlet without the Prince: Cambridge Macroeconomics Without Money," *American Economic Review*, 75:2 (1985); and M. Tonveronachi, *J. M. Keynes: Dall'instabilita ciclica all'equilibrio di sottoccupazione* (Rome: Nuova Italia, 1983).
19. P. Sraffa, "Dr Hayek on Money and Capital," *Economic Journal*, 42 (1932), pp. 50–1.
20. C. Torr, *Equilibrium, Expectations and Equilibrium* (unpublished doctoral dissertation, Rhodes University, 1983), chap. 7.
21. See, for example, the interpretation given by A. Roncaglia, *Sraffa and the Theory of Prices* (Chichester: Wiley, 1978).
22. P. Garegnani, "Notes on consumption, investment and effective demand: a reply to Joan Robinson," *Cambridge Journal of Economics*, 3 (1979), pp. 181–2.
23. Ibid., p. 182.
24. P. Garegnani, "On a Change in the Notion of Equilibrium in Recent Work on Value and Distribution: A comment on Samuelson," in *Essays in Modern Capital Theory*, eds. M. Brown, K. Sato, and P. Zarembka (Amsterdam: North-Holland, 1976), p. 39.
25. P. Garegnani, "Two Routes to Effective Demand: Comment on Kregel," in *Distribution, Effective Demand & International Economic Relations*, ed. J. A. Kregel (London: Macmillan, 1983), p. 78.
26. S. Parrinello, "On the Role of Demand Schedules: A Comment," (Trieste: Centro di Studi Economici Avanzati Mimeo, 1983), p. 2.
27. Garegnani, "Notes on consumption, investment and effective demand," op. cit., p. 185.
28. J. Cartelier, "Marché et concurrence dans la 'Richesse des Nations,'" *Cahiers d'Economie Politique*, 8 (1982), p. 151.
29. L. M. Lachmann, "The Role Expectations in Economics as a Social Science," op. cit., p. 78.
30. Garegnani, "Notes on consumption, investment and effective demand," op. cit., p. 184.
31. V. Pareto, *Corso di Economica Politica* (Torino: UTET, 1971), para. 37, p. 142.
32. Ibid., quoted in Garegnani, "Notes on consumption, investment and effective demand," op. cit., p. 185.
33. Pareto, op. cit., paragraph 36, pp. 141–2.

13 Coherence and Flexibility: Social Institutions in a World of Radical Uncertainty

RICHARD N. LANGLOIS

> In our view the central problem of the institutional order hinges on the contrast between coherence and flexibility, between the necessarily durable nature of the institutional order as a whole and the requisite flexibility of the individual institution.
>
> Ludwig M. Lachmann

INTRODUCTION

Professor Lachmann is prominent among the leaders of the recent revival of Austrian economics. Not without justification, most students of his work would also likely assign him a particular role within that vanguard. Professor Lachmann has been the scourge of determinism, the apostle of disequilibrium, the prophet of the kaleidic. Thus, in many, if not most eyes, Lachmann's role has appeared as that of gadfly—or, at best, of methodological conscience—to his fellow theorists. His has been the salutary, albeit annoying, task of reminding us that the future is unknowable, that expectations must diverge, and that there are forces of discoordination as well as of coordination.

My objective in this essay is not to dispute this interpretation of Professor Lachmann's influence. Even less do I wish to take a position in the long-standing controversy over the existence of a tendency toward equilibrium. Rather I propose to reflect on another, perhaps somewhat neglected, aspect of Professor Lachmann's contribution: the theory of social institutions.

In *The Legacy of Max Weber*, much of which is devoted to the topic of social institutions, we find no absence of concern with the problems of expectations and radical uncertainty, no lack of acknowledgement that the forces of discoordination are strong and change inevitable.[1] But we also find—surprisingly?—the outlines of a theory of plan coordination in which social institutions serve to align expectations and in which these institutions themselves may weather successfully the forces of change.[2]

This essay is an attempt to return to and develop some of the themes Professor Lachmann articulated in *The Legacy of Max Weber*. In particular, it will try to reinterpret some of his suggestions using ideas and modes of expression from a now expanding literature devoted to the economic theory of social institutions. The first section will discuss the connection between institutions and the plans of individuals, and will examine the notion that institutions can act as signposts in a world of uncertainty. The next section offers a hierarchical portrayal of plans and institutions—one inspired, in part, by Professor Lachmann's distinction between fundamental and secondary institutions. And the final section turns to the problem of change and the response of institutions to it.

PLANS, COORDINATION, AND INSTITUTIONS

This volume takes as its theme the role of subjectivism in the social sciences. It is a theme that runs throughout Professor Lachmann's work, one that forms the starting point for his theory of social institutions.

For Lachmann, subjectivism has its roots in the Weberian tradition of *Verstehen* or understanding, which in turn finds its origins in the ancient methods of textual and historical interpretation. In the context of the social sciences, subjectivism consists in the interpretation of human action and, more importantly, of human interaction. Rejecting Weber's well-known concept of the "ideal type," Lachmann offers the method of praxeology, which he associates with the notion of the plan.[3] "To act at all," he says, "men have to make plans, comprehensive surveys of the means at their disposal and the ways in which they might be used, and let their actions be guided by them."[4]

The success of any individual plan depends, of course, on the extent to which that plan is adapted to the environmental conditions the agent will face in carrying out the plan. This environment includes nature and its vagaries such as the weather, for example, or the constraints of physical laws. But the environment also means the actions of other individuals: successful plans are in large measure those that are compatible, that dovetail, as the Austrian writers like to say, with the plans of others. Indeed, as Lachmann suggests, the uncertainties thrown up by the actions of others are in general far more worrisome for planning than are the uncertainties of nature. Human action, he points out, is more volatile than the conditions of nature, and thus far less easy to predict. This means that "we have here a source of danger to successful action, the importance of which grows as society grows more complex."[5]

It is at this point that social institutions enter the picture. A social institution is a "recurrent pattern of conduct" that helps an individual plan by reducing the volatility in the plans of others.[6] "An institution provides a means of orientation to a large number of actors. It enables them to co-ordinate their actions by means of orientation to a common signpost."[7]

What Professor Lachmann provides in outline is both an understanding of the role of social institutions and an approach to studying them. In order to fill out this outline, I propose to draw on some recent literature that has taken up many of these same themes.[8] Happily, my task will be made easier by the congruence—both in approach and in substance—between this literature and Professor Lachmann's work.

To say that the economic agent must confront in his planning both nature and the actions of his fellows is to say, in the modern argot, that he "plays a game" against nature and other social agents. Thus the conceptual framework of game theory comes to mind as a useful way of thinking about the nature and role of social institutions. Like most potentially mathematical formalisms, game theory is, of course, frequently given to fits of unilluminating technical excess. But in its simpler manifestations it is not inconsistent in spirit with the methodological approach Professor Lachmann recommends; indeed, the notion of a plan, disguised in this case as a strategy, is arguably the central analytical tool.

The distilled essence of social institutions, and of their role as aids to the coordination of plans, emerges from a consideration of what are called, appropriately enough, coordination games.[9] Here the agent finds himself confronted with the sort of situation depicted in Figure 1. He can choose any of the three actions (or plans, if you will) represented by the rows of the matrix. His opponent faces the same choice of three actions, represented as the columns of the matrix. The entries in the matrix, or payoffs, as they are called, are an indication of the extent to which the agent's actions are coordinated with those of others. In this case, coordination—a high payoff for both—occurs when both players choose the same action. A standard illustration is the problem of choosing the side of the road on which to drive. It is irrelevant which side, left or right, one chooses, except that it had better be the one all other drivers choose.

Suppose that the actions of Agent B are very volatile, that B is given to shifting among the three actions over time in a more-or-less unpredictable fashion. Clearly, this makes A's task of planning a difficult one. Agent A may often be wrong in his anticipation of what B will do, and their payoffs will suffer. Yet, if both happen to hit upon the same action (Action 1, let us say) at the same time, and, moreover, find themselves continuing to pursue the same action over time, they will have solved their coordination problem. Neither will have the incentive unilaterally to deviate from the established pattern. Thus the behavior pattern "always take Action 1" emerges as a social convention, becoming one of those "successful plans which have crystallized into institutions through widespread imitation."[10]

All of this is fairly elementary. It is also a rather stark portrayal of the culturally and historically rich process by which institutions take shape. But it does provide an intuitively appealing schematic for talking about the interaction of plans.

We can already see here the outlines of the signpost function of institutions. By reducing the volatility of other people's actions, an institution can provide an agent with useful information. To put it another way, an institution creates predictability—it brings order out of relative chaos. Indeed, our simple game-theory representation permits us to make this assertion in a slightly more formal way that connects with conceptions of order and chaos familiar from other disciplines. Suppose that we stand back from the game in figure 1 and watch the play of the two agents. A glance at the figure confirms that there are nine possible squares on which the players might land on any play. If Agent A takes Action i and Agent B takes Action j, call the square s_{ij}, with $i, j = 1, 2,$ or 3. Suppose further that, after observing for a while, we decide that f_{ij} is the frequency with which we observe s_{ij} to occur. Using the familiar formula, we can talk about the *entropy* of the game. It is defined as

$$\sum_{i,j} f_{ij} \log f_{ij}$$

		Agent B		
		Action 1	Action 2	Action 3
	Action 1	3 3	0 0	0 0
Agent A	Action 2	0 0	3 3	0 0
	Action 3	0 0	0 0	3 3

FIGURE 1

It turns out that entropy is highest when all the squares are equally likely. Therefore, a high-entropy game is one in which the agents' behavior is chaotic, in which the agents move about unpredictably from square to square. By contrast, entropy is least when the players always stick to one particular square and never land on any others. Thus, a low-entropy game is one in which the agent's behavior is completely orderly, completely predictable.[12]

A social institution, then, is a mechanism to reduce the entropy of the environment. The presence of such a mechanism means coordination, high payoffs, and, in this context at least, a rigid and predictable pattern of behavior by both agents. Moreover, a state of minimum entropy means a situation that is fully informative. That is, continuing to observe the play of the game can teach us nothing useful to predicting the agents' behavior, since that behavior is already perfectly predictable.[13]

In order to clarify the ideas a little more, consider a slightly different representation of the game the agent faces. Now, we will let Agent B play first. We may take B to represent all the other agents in the economy or the environment in general. Agent A's task is now to respond to what B does. Unfortunately for A, though, his competence to respond adequately may be limited in a couple of ways that I will make more precise shortly. For the moment, Figure 1 will continue to hold our attention.

We discussed the entropy of a game from the point of view of an outside observer. But we can also take the point of view of the agent. As A sees it, B can take any of three actions. If he is as likely to take Action 1 as to take Action 2 or Action 3, then B's actions are maximally unpredictable and A's environment is a high-entropy one. If B invariably takes the same action every time, A's environment is a predictable, low-entropy one. A's goal, of course, is to maintain coordination—to maintain a nonzero payoff. This means that A wants to make sure that, irrespective of what B does, the same outcome occurs every time. And that, in turn, means, in effect, that A wants to maintain the set of payoffs in a low-entropy state. He wants to make sure that the payoff he receives is predictably positive and infrequently zero. How does A accomplish this? As Figure 1 suggests, A must adjust his behavior constantly to the behavior of B. If B picks Action 1, A must do likewise; if B picks action 2, so must A; and so on. In Figure 1, such adjustment is always possible. But consider Figure 2. Here A is barred from ever taking action 3. As a consequence, he no longer has complete control of the situation. If B takes Action 3, A can never match, and the entropy in his payoffs must increase (that is, he must sometimes get zeroes as well as ones if B sometimes chooses Action 3).

The discussion so far suggests the outlines of a well-known principle in cybernetics: the so-called "law of requisite variety."[14] Let us call the entropy of B's moves "environmental entropy" and the entropy of A's behavior "behavioral entropy." In these terms, the law of requisite variety says, roughly speaking, that, in order to maintain the set of outcomes at a state of minimum entropy, A's behavioral entropy must be at least as great as the environmental entropy. To see this, consider first a world in which B takes Action 1 with certainty. The environmental entropy is zero. To maintain a favorable outcome, A need only follow suit with Action 1. His entropy is also zero, as is that of the outcomes. Suppose now that B changes his behavior and begins alternating randomly between Action 1 and Action 2. B's entropy increases to log 2. If A continues to take only Action 1, his entropy remains zero, but the entropy of the outcomes increases to log 2, since

		Agent B		
		Action 1	Action 2	Action 3
Agent A	Action 1	3	0	0
	Action 2	0	3	0

FIGURE 2

the payoff is one for half the time and zero half the time. In order to keep the entropy of the payoffs at zero, A has to increase his own entropy to log 2 by switching back and forth between Actions 1 and 2 with the same frequency as B. In short, then, the only way to fight entropy is with entropy.

In the type of coordination game we have been considering here, the presence of a social institution reduces the entropy of the agent to exactly the same degree that it reduces the entropy of the environment. A social convention to drive on the right-hand side of the road constrains other drivers and makes their behavior more predictable, but it also constrains my own behavior since I, too, now always drive on the right. At the same time, though, the existence of this convention does not remove my *ability* to drive on the left. I decide to follow the convention in order to avoid the crash of metal that would attend the discoordination of my driving plans. However, I can still drive on the left if I have to—to avoid an obstruction, or when I find myself in England. Thus a social institution reduces the *observed* entropy of the agent but not necessarily the *potential* variety in his actions.

We might think it reasonable to suppose that the agent is always better off with a greater variety of actions—a larger repertoire of possible plans—at his disposal. In some interesting recent work, Ronald Heiner has suggested that this is not always the case.[15] To the extent that the agent is unreliable in his responses to the environment, he is sometimes better off limiting or reducing the set of actions at his disposal.

Heiner's analysis works this way. Consider again the coordination game in which Agent B plays first and Agent A must respond. Now ask the following sort of question about each possible response at Agent A's disposal. Is A well served by having this action in his repertoire or is he in fact better off debarring himself completely from ever taking action? The answer will depend upon how reliable Agent A will be in using this action, that is, the extent to which he is able to use the action when appropriate and refrain from using it when inappropriate. If π is the probability that it is the right time to use the action; r is the probability that the agent takes the action when it is the right time; w is the probability that he takes the action when it is the wrong time; g is the gain from taking the action at the right time; and l is the loss from taking the action at the wrong time, then the agent should include the action when $\pi rg - (1 - \pi)wl > 0$. Rearranging gives Heiner's "reliability condition," $r/w > [(1 - \pi)/\pi](l/g)$.

The left-hand side is the "reliability ratio," which reflects the agent's competence in responding to the actions of Agent B (or of the environment). The right-hand side is the "tolerance limit," which sets a lower bound on the reliability the agent must be able to claim before allowing the action into his repertoire will do him more good than harm. If, as Heiner maintains, reliability decreases as the volatility of the environment increases, then fewer and fewer actions will satisfy the reliability condition as the environment becomes more volatile. This means that high environmental entropy can lead to lower potential (and therefore lower observed) behavioral entropy.[16]

At first glance, we would seem to be left with a paradoxical result. A stable environment leads us to expect rigid and predictable behavior in our agent—but so does a highly volatile environment. There is, in fact, no paradox, of course, merely a spectrum. At one extreme we find predictable behavior arising as an adaptation to an unchanging environment. If the environment becomes more volatile, the agent benefits from the ability to alter his behavior in response. But once the environment becomes sufficiently volatile, its demands begin to exceed the agent's ability to respond, which causes the agent to retreat again to a more predictable pattern. At this second extreme, the agent actually benefits from self-restraint, from foreclosing options that he cannot trust himself to use reliably.

There are also some differences between rule-following behavior in a placid environment and predictable behavior in a volatile environment. For one thing, it remains true that the agent's performance, his ability successfully to coordinate his plans, always deteriorates as the environment becomes more volatile (at any rate, it never improves). More importantly, though, we can expect a difference in the *type* of actions the agent would undertake at each extreme. Consider the variant of our standard game depicted in Figure 3. Here the structure of the payoffs is a bit more complex. Agent A can respond to B's moves in the usual way by matching Actions 1, 2, or 3. But he can also resort to a "generic" action, Action 4, that achieves the same payoff no matter what B does. If A can respond reliably to B, we would expect him to keep all the actions within his repertoire; and we would expect him to rely exclusively on Action 1, 2, and 3 since they provide the highest payoff. If B plays Action 1 every time without fail—which is to say that the environment is entirely placid—Agent A would follow the rule "always play 1." If B becomes less predictable, we would expect to see A jump around among Actions 1 through 3 in response. But if B became so unpredictable that his play thrust A beyond the "tolerance limit," A might eliminate some of the actions from his repertoire. More to the point, A might restrict himself to a repertoire consisting entirely of Action 4. Thus A would again display rule-following behavior, but the rule would be a quite different one.

We can perhaps see this best in light of the entropy formalism. Once again, A is trying to maintain his payoffs in a low-entropy state. He can do this—at first at least—by increasing his own entropy to match that of B. But as A's response becomes unreliable, he can turn to another strategy: he can choose an action that has inherently lower entropy. (Actions 1 through 3 have a maximum payoff entropy of log 2 because they contain two possible payoffs; action 4 has only one payoff, which gives it a maximum entropy of zero.) In a sense, then, increased flexibility is always desirable as the volatility of the environment increases, but that flexibility comes increasingly in the form of "state flexibility" rather then "action flexibility."[17]

Actions that are flexible across states are general actions, and, as Adam Smith reminds us, such actions are likely to be less productive—to have lower payoffs—than more specialized actions. Thus it seems reasonable to suppose that, *ceteris paribus*, increased volatility in the environment brings with it a decrease in the division of labor, while increased stability in the environment has the opposite effect.

		Agent B		
		Action 1	Action 2	Action 3
	Action 1	3	0	0
	Action 2	0	3	0
Agent A	Action 3	0	0	3
	Action 4	2	2	2

FIGURE 3

THE HIERARCHICAL NATURE OF PLANS

We now have at hand most of the ideas we will need to talk about the response of institutions to change. Oddly, perhaps, we have not yet said much about radical uncertainty. We have talked about uncertainty indirectly, of course, in the guise of environmental volatility; but I have been deliberately vague about how volatility as seen by an outside observer translates into subjective uncertainty as seen by the agent. In the conventional paradigm, the transition is an easy one. The agent knows all the possible states of the world (i.e., B's moves) and can assign subjective probabilities to them; these probabilities take the place of observed frequencies in the entropy formulas, and everything goes through as before.

But what about radical uncertainty? How does that change the picture? The answer depends on what one means by radical uncertainty. Radical uncertainty accepts a more open-ended world than the standard paradigm will admit to. That is, the radically uncertain agents can be uncertain not merely about which possible state of the world will occur but also about which states are even possible. In the standard formulation, this is taken implicitly to mean that the future is populated by two kinds of events: foreseeable events and unforeseeable events. To modify our original game accordingly, we could associate agent B's moves with the future events or states of the world and divide those events into foreseeable and unforeseeable. Figure 4 does this. The columns of the matrix represents the states of the world; x_1 through x_k are foreseeable states and x_{k+1} through x_n are unforeseeable. (To capture the idea of a truly open-ended world, imagine n as very large.) For good measure, we can also divide Agent A's actions, in the rows of the matrix, into those actions the agents know about (a_1 through a_l) and those yet to be discovered or invented (a_{l+1} through a_m). P_{ij}, of course, represents the payoff to taking action i in state j.

This is surely a useful way to look at radical uncertainty. It turns out, though, that adding this kind of radical uncertainty does not change the conclusions of the previous section, even though it does tend to strengthen them.[18] For our purposes, the interesting implications for social institutions of radical uncertainty emerge from looking at that kind of uncertainty in a slightly different way.

In discussing radical uncertainty—especially with aficionados of the conventional probability calculus—I often find myself confronted with what I call the category problem. That is to say, if we view radical uncertainty in the way I suggested above, it is always possible to *redefine* the set of events so that what was an unanticipated event falls into an anticipated category. "Give me an example of an unanticipated event," my interlocutors demand. How about the Trojan Horse?[19] "That's just a military 'trick'; tricks are a concept the Trojans were familiar with, and they could have anticipated that kind of strategy and assigned a probability to it." Well, consider the many possibilities attendant on the introduction of a technical innovation. Surely some possibilities can't be anticipated? "Just divide the world into two events: 'innovation succeeds' and 'innovation fails.' These are well-

	x_1	x_2	x_3	• • • •	x_k	• • • •	x_n
a_1	P_{11}	P_{12}	P_{13}	• • • •	P_{1k}	• • • •	P_{1n}
a_2	P_{21}	P_{22}	P_{23}	• • • •	P_{2k}	• • • •	P_{2n}
•	•	•	•		•		
•	•	•	•		•		•
•	•	•	•		•		•
•	•	•	•		•		•
a_l	P_{l1}		P_{13}		P_{lk}	• • • •	P_{ln}
•	•	•	•		•		•
•	•	•	•		•		•
•	•	•	•		•		•
•	•	•	•		•		•
a_m	P_{m1}	P_{m2}	P_{m3}	• • • •	P_{mk}	• • • •	P_{mn}

FIGURE 4

defined, collectively exhaustive, and naturally exclusive events over which we can define probabilities." I had always consigned this kind of discussion to the realm of "paradigmatic" mutual incomprehension.[20] But the point, of course, is that the category problem is not just an intellectual game. It reflects the fact that events are normally *both foreseeable and unforeseeable at the same time.*

To put it more accurately and less mysteriously, we might say that all events have both foreseeable and unforeseeable *aspects.* In fact, it might be most useful to talk not about foreseeability at all but about what Gerald O'Driscoll and Mario Rizzo call *typicality* and *uniqueness.*[21] Interestingly, the inspiration for this distinction is the work of Alfred Schutz, who championed the Weberian tradition of the ideal type in the methodology of the social sciences. Typification in this case is not, however, a methodological notion so much as a model of the process by which the economic agent perceives the economic landscape in which he acts. Thus, it is a model of the process by which the agent plans and, moreover, an approach to understanding the nature and structure of those plans. Typical features are the relatively stable elements of reality, those that we discover to be repeatable in principle. Unique features, by contrast, are the idiosyncratic, nonrepeatable aspects of reality—that are tied to history and to the particular concrete circumstances in which they occur.

But we should not think of these aspects of events as coexisting, as it were, on the same level. The process of typification, it seems to me, is inherently a hierarchical operation. "We anticipate events as to their typical features," O'Driscoll and Rizzo wrote, "but we cannot fill in the 'details' beforehand."[22] And, as Herbert Simon notes, the way we fill in the details is normally a hierarchical operation.[23]

> If you ask a person to draw a complex object—such as a human face—he will almost always proceed in a hierarchic fashion. First he will outline the face. Then he will add or insert features: eyes, nose, mouth, ears, hair. If asked to elaborate, he will begin to develop details for each of the features—pupils, eyelids, lashes for the eyes, and so on—until he reaches the limit of his anatomical knowledge. His information about the object is arranged hierarchically in memory, like a topical outline.

In order to visualize this structural or hierarchical conception of typicality and uniqueness, consider Figure 5. Instead of immediately dividing the set of events X into typical and unique events (as we did in Figure 4), we instead divide X into subsets X_1 through X_n. Each subset contains both typical events and unique events. If we think of the subset X_i as itself an event, then we can think of the subevents $\{x_{ij}\}$ as characteristics or aspects of X_i. Some of these subevents will be foreseeable and others not. Those that are truly typical may in fact serve as defining characteristics of X_i. Moreover, we can view the x_{ij} themselves as being composed of subevents $\{x_{ijk}\}$. Some of the subevents are typical (and may serve to define the subevent x_{ij}), and some are unique. As Figure 6 suggests, we can imagine a hierarchy of events in which lower-level events (or their typical features) define higher-level events. (The solid lines represent typical, foreseeable events, and the dotted lines indicate unique or unforeseeable events.)

We can also think of the agent's actions as organized in hierarchical fashion, with the set of actions A divided into subsets A_i composed of

		X_1		X_2	X_3	X_4
		$X_{11} \ldots$	X_{1n_1}	$X_{21} \ldots X_{2n_3}$	$X_{31} \ldots X_{3n_4}$	$X_{41} \ldots X_{4m_4}$
A_1	a_{11}	$P_{11'11} \ldots$	$P_{11'1n_1}$	$\ldots$	$\ldots$	$P_{11'}{}^{4m_4}$
	a_{12}	$P_{13'11} \ldots$	$P_{13'1m_1}$	$\ldots$	$\ldots$	$P_{12'}{}^{4m_4}$
	$\vdots$	$\vdots$	$\vdots$			
	a_{1m_1}	$P_{1m,11} \ldots$	$P_{1m_1 1n_1}$	$\ldots$	$\ldots$	$P_{1m'}{}^{4m_4}$
A_2	a_{21}					
	a_{22}	$\vdots$				
	$\vdots$					
	a_{2m_2}					
A_3	a_{31}	$\vdots$				
	a_{32}					
	$\vdots$					
	a_{3m_3}					
A_4	a_{41}	$\vdots$				
	a_{42}					
	$\vdots$					
	a_{4m_4}					
	$\vdots$	$\vdots$				
	a_{mm_n}	$P_{mm_m,11}$		$\ldots$	$\ldots$	$P_{mm_m,}{}^{4n_n}$

FIGURE 5

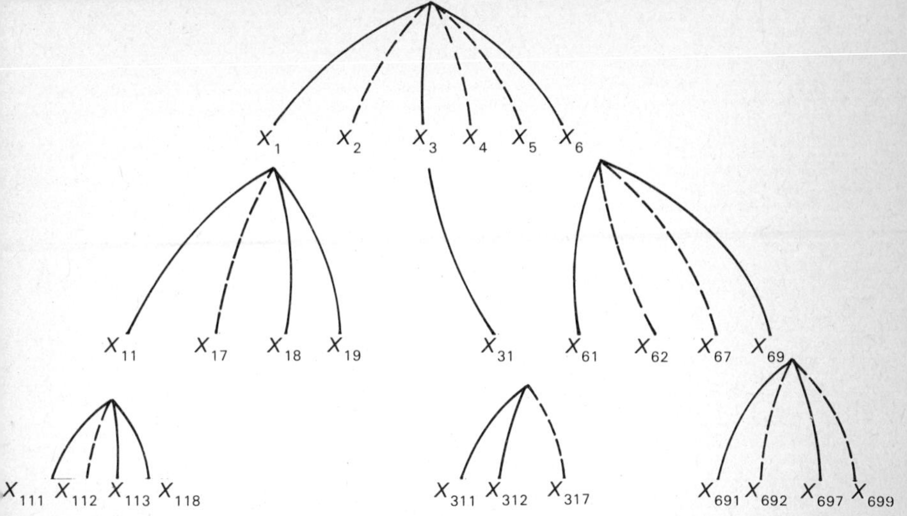

FIGURE 6

subactions a_{ij}, which are, in turn, composed of sub-subactions a_{ijk}, etc. The hierarchical structure of events (of the X_i) reflected the hierarchical nature of the agent's perception of the world. The notions of typicality and uniqueness, borrowed from Alfred Schutz, seemed most appropriate to describing the perceptual process. When we talk of actions, however, we might more sensibly use the terms "abstractness" and "concreteness" as analogous to typicality and uniqueness. An action or plan at the highest level of the hierarchy is abstract in the sense that it is oriented toward a typical situation and consists in a general pattern of response.[24] As we examine the plan at lower levels of the hierarchy, we see that more details have been filled in. The plan is increasingly more concrete in its orientation and more specific in the response it embodies.

If both the agent's plans and his perceptions of events are hierarchical in nature, so also are institutions. Highest-level institutions coordinate the highest level of plans. Institutions at lower levels coordinate lower-level or more concrete plans. In Professor Lachmann's terminology, the higher-level institutions are external institutions, and the lower-level ones are internal institutions.[25]

> In a society in which it is generally known that frequent change of undesigned institutions is inevitable, the designers of designed institutions may deliberately confine their activity to designing a frame-

work which leaves room for a good deal (in principle an unlimited amount) of change which, since it takes place within the framework, will not affect the latter as such. . . . This idea is not a mere figment of our imagination. The legal framework of modern Western societies has in fact achieved something similar to the model just envisaged by leaving a wide sphere of "freedom of contract" to individuals acting in pursuit of their respective interests. The modern market economy would not be possible without it.

In such a society it might be said that the undesigned institutions which evolve gradually as the unintended and unforeseen results of the pursuit of individual interests accumulate in the *interstices* of the institutional order. The interstices have been planned, though the sediments accumulating in them have not and could not have been. In a society of this type we might distinguish between the *external* institutions which constitute, as it were, the outer framework of society, the legal order, and the *internal* institutions which gradually evolve as a result of market processes and other forms of spontaneous individual action.

The issue of which institutions—the external or the internal—are designed and which undesigned is a complex matter into which I can't enter here. I should note, however, that followers of Hayek might object to viewing the legal system as a designed institution; indeed, they might be more likely to suggest that the spontaneous order consists in the growth of designed institutions (like firms) within the interstices of an undesigned legal framework.[26] However this may be, the hierarchical logic is the same. And we can use some of the ideas we developed above to reinterpret this notion that lower-level institutions "grow" on the trellis of higher-level institutions. Recall that I made a point of distinguishing *observed* behavioral entropy from *potential* behavioral entropy. In a highly stable evironment, the agent displays little variation in his behavior. But he may remain competent to deal with a much more complex environment than he actually faces. What becomes of that unused potential? I would suggest that the agent's potential entropy gets pushed down to lower levels of the hierarchy of actions. To put it another way, the existence at higher levels of institutions that stabilize the environment and reduce environmental entropy effectively frees behavioral entropy for use at lower levels. In a stable regime, the agent's reliability is high enough that he can add new actions to his repertoire. But, precisely because the regime is stable, the agent does not need a large repertoire *at that level.* He needs only to follow the rules dictated by the coordinating institution. Thus, I propose that he adds new actions at lower levels.

It follows that a stable high-level environment—one coordinated by stable external institutions—is conducive to the increasing division of labor for two reasons. It permits the use of highly adapted, state-specific actions, *and* it allows for the filling out, as it were, of the agent's hierarchy of plans. In terms of the diagram in Figure 6, we would expect the passage of time to shade in more solid lines at the lower levels. But it may also lead the agent to remove some lines (convert them to dotted lines), particularly at the higher levels. The events, after all, are the agent's conjectures about the future shape of the world. Experience would lead him to reject some conjectures (in a Popperian sense) as well as to ignore some possibilities because they are rare in experience (a very un-Popperian thing to do).

To the extent, then, that experience provides stable feedback, we would expect the passage of time to reduce genuine uncertainty or to shift genuine uncertainty to lower levels of the event hierarchy. With time and learning, the maker of a complex product is no longer genuinely uncertain about whether his product will work or sell; in fact, he also probably has a good idea about the typical subcharacteristics that are necessary to a successful product. His concerns have progressed from very general ones to very specific ones like, "Which approach to the subassembly widget will prove most successful?" or, "Should we split the southeast sales region in two?" This means, as we would expect that the agents plan hierarchy is also taking on a more complex, detailed, concrete structure in response to his learning about the environment.

We see, then, that constraints on individual behavior at the highest or most abstract levels can assist in the coordination of plans and facilitate the extension of the division of labor. These constraints are the external institutions that stabilize the high-level environment and channel the agent's potential for change and innovation to the more concrete levels. At the same time, it should also be clear that constraints on individual behavior at the *lower* levels can obstruct the coordination of plans and block the extension of the division of labor. This is so because lower-level constraints reduce the agent's potential entropy without creating any corresponding gain in environmental stability. As we saw above in the framework of the coordination game, constraints can have a stabilizing effect when they are universally and abstractly applied (e.g., never drive on the left). But constraints on concrete actions have little effect on the overall environment.[27]

The way of looking at things described above finds some corroboration in history. The French historian Jean Baechler, another student of Max Weber, has argued that the development of capitalism in Western Europe can be traced to the conjunction of two factors. "The ultimate explanation for the expansion of economic activity in the West is the coincidence between the homogeneity of the cultural space and the multiplicity of political units sharing that space. *The expansion of capitalism owes its origins and its* raison d'etre *to political anarchy*."[28] That Western Europe was culturally homogeneous suggests the existence of high-level coordinative institutions.[29] That Western Europe was politically anarchic suggests that government was unable to restrict economic behavior by interfering in voluntary exchange or by destabilizing the environment through war.

THE RESPONSE OF INSTITUTIONS TO CHANGE

Now, we must consider the issue of institutional change. Here we will find our task an easy one, since the groundwork is almost fully laid.

How do institutions respond when genuine uncertainty increases? The answer depends upon *where* in the hierarchy the genuine uncertainty appears. The appearance of genuine uncertainty at a newly recognized lowest level of the hierarchy causes no problems. It is in fact consistent with learning and with a movement toward more state-specific actions. It is the appearance of genuine uncertainty at the higher levels that is troublesome. Suppose we are concerned with a decision contingent on events at the x_{ij} level of Figure 5. If we are genuinely uncertain about the x_{ijk}, that is, we cannot list all the relevant x_{ijk}, this causes no problems since we know we can fit any event at that level into one of the x_{ij}. But if we are uncertain about whether we know all the relevant x_{ij} themselves, we would respond in the manner suggested earlier: moving to less state-specific actions. And genuine uncertainty at the X_i level would likely call for even more drastic retrenchment.

We might say loosely that, whereas a more-or-less predictable environment moves genuine uncertainty further down the hierarchy and creates structure, unreliable feedback and novelty move genuine uncertainty back up the hierarchy and destroy structure.

It is in this light that we can interpret the various devices that, in Professor Lachmann's view, help to maintain the coherence and permanence of an institutional order. The first two we have already seen: the maintenance of firm "outer institutions," coupled with more flexible "inner" institutions that grant individuals "a fairly wide sphere of 'contractual freedom,' a sphere in which change must be expected to be frequent and which may be regarded as the main source of undesigned institutions."[30]

Professor Lachmann's third device—the "widening" of institutions in response to change—fits in just as naturally with the schema I've outlined. This device

> takes the form of meeting a situation requiring change not by the creation of a new institution, nor by replacing an old by a new, but by "widening" an existing institution in such a way that it can serve new interests without upsetting the plans which have thus far made use of it. The widening of the conception of property in the modern company, in such a way that the relationships between directors and shareholders can be brought within its province, appears a good example.

In our terminology, widening an institution means defining the relevant level of action in a more abstract way and the relevant level of events according to features of experience that are more broadly typical. This keeps the disturbing events at a lower or more concrete level and ensures the maintenance of coordination at the higher levels.

NOTES

1. Ludwig M. Lachmann, *The Legacy of Max Weber* (Berkeley: The Glendessary Press, 1971).
2. It is often forgotten on both sides of the controversy that attacks on the possibility of equilibrium or coordination are focused—in Keynes and Shackle as well as Lachmann—on a particular set of institutions: centralized asset markets like the Stock Exchange. The claim is that, because of the particular structure of these institutions, asset prices are inherently "restless" in a world of radical uncertainty. It thus seems to me a mistake to argue about the "tendency to equilibrium" (or coordination) in the abstract without reference to institutions. To do so, I would argue, is to carry over from general-equilibrium theory precisely the feature that many writers on both sides of the controversy find most objectionable: its wholly non-institutional character.
3. Lachmann's argument for rejecting the Weberian ideal type is that it "lacks any specific reference to human action and seems as readily applicable to the animal kingdom or the plant world as to the human sphere" (*Legacy of Max Weber*, op. cit., p. 29). In other words, it is not a sufficiently

subjectivist concept. This may be true of Weber's version of the ideal type; but I would argue that the version of this concept developed by Alfred Schutz and Fritz Machlup not only withstands Professor Lachmann's strictures but actually comes very close to his own notion of the plan. On this see R. N. Langlois and R. G. Koppl, "Fritz Machlup and Marginalism: A Reevaluation," working paper no. 14, Center for the Study of Market Processes, George Mason University (1984). Of course, Professor Lachmann does indicate that he sees the ideal type as "naturally linked to our concept of Plan." (*Legacy of Max Weber*, op. cit., p. 33.)

4. Lachmann, *Legacy of Max Weber*, op. cit., p. 30.
5. Lachmann, *Legacy of Max Weber*, op. cit., p. 45.
6. Lachmann, *Legacy of Max Weber*, op. cit., p. 75.
7. Lachmann, *Legacy of Max Weber*, op. cit., p. 49.
8. In broad terms, the literature to which I refer is a joint product of economics and philosophy. From the latter vantage point see especially Edna Ullman-Margalit, *The Emergence of Norms* (Oxford: Oxford University Press, 1977). From the economic point of view, see Andrew Schotter, *The Economic Theory of Social Institutions* (New York: Cambridge University Press, 1981).
9. Another important class of games relevant to the analysis of social institutions are called "prisoner's dilemma games." These are games in which the interests of the agents are not quite so well aligned in the sense that individuals often have the short-run incentive to deviate from an established social institution in a way that can undermine the institution. This class of games is thus extremely relevant to the problem of what Professor Lachmann picturesquely calls "the deformation of social space." For a fascinating recent study of such games—which, unhappily, I will have to neglect in this essay—see Robert Axelrod, *The Evolution of Cooperation* (New York: Basic Books, 1984).
10. Lachmann, *Legacy of Max Weber*, op. cit., p. 88. I have not been careful in telling the story of how a coordination game between two individuals might be extended to the problem of an individual coordinating his actions with all others in the relevant society. But this problem, however interesting, is not central to my main point. For discussions, see note 8 above.
11. The information-theory version of the entropy formulation traces back to Claude Shannon, "A Mathematical Theory of Communication," *Bell Systems Technical Journal*, 27 (1948). The notion of entropy has a much older history in thermodynamics and statistical mechanics, of course.
12. Schotter, *The Economic Theory of Social Institutions*, op. cit., pp. 140–3.
13. Ibid.
14. W. Ross Ashby, *An Introduction to Cybernetics* (London: Chapman & Hall, 1956), chap. 11. I am indebted to Ronald Heiner for calling this literature to my attention.
15. Ronald Heiner, "The Origin of Predictable Behavior," *American Economic Review*, 73 (1983), pp. 560–95.
16. There is, of course, a selection argument operating behind the scenes. Those agents who have repertoires containing many actions that violate the reliability conditions will do worse *ceteris paribus* than agents who have fewer actions in their repertoires; therefore the agents with over-large

repertoires will be selected out, will lose relative command over resources, and/or will recognize the need to imitate their more successful rivals. The result is a decrease in the average size of repertoires. Such an argument is subject to all the usual cautions that attend selection stories.

17. See my "Kaleidic and Structural Interpretations of Genuine Uncertainty," photocopy (September 1984), p. 17; Richard Bookstaber and Joseph Langsam, "Coarse Behavior and Extended Uncertainty," photocopy, Brigham Young University (1983), p. 9, who talk about "general" actions versus "state-specific" actions.
18. Langlois, "Kaleidic and Structural Interpretations," op. cit., p. 12.
19. An example from Bookstaber and Langsam, "Coarse Behavior and Extended Uncertainty," op. cit., p. 2, n. 1.
20. See the recent "paradigmatic" interchange on this topic between Nitzan Weiss and Douglas Vickers in the *Eastern Economic Journal*, 10 (1984), p. 71.
21. Gerald P. O'Driscoll and Mario J. Rizzo, *The Economics of Time and Ignorance* (Oxford: Basil Blackwell, 1985), chap. 5.
22. O'Driscoll and Rizzo, *The Economics of Time and Ignorance*, op. cit.
23. "The Architecture of Complexity," in Simon, *The Sciences of the Artificial*, 2nd ed. (Cambridge: MIT Press, 1981), p. 218.
24. F. A. Hayek, *Law, Legislation and Liberty* (Chicago: University of Chicago Press, 1973), vol. I, p. 30.
25. Lachmann, *Legacy of Max Weber*, op. cit., p. 81.
26. See, for example, Hayek, *Law, Legislation, and Liberty*, op. cit., chap. 2.
27. The point this paragraph makes is, of course, closely related to Hayek's argument in favor of rules that are general and universal. See especially Hayek, *Law, Legislation, and Liberty* (Chicago: University of Chicago Press, 1976), vol. II, chap. 7.
28. Jean Baechler, *Les origines du capitalisme* (Paris: Gallimard, 1971), p. 126, emphasis original, translation mine. For a similar argument about the transition from mercantilism to liberalism in England, see R. B. Ekelund and R. D. Tollison, "Economic Regulation in Mercantile England: Heckscher Revisited," *Economic Inquiry*, 18 (1980), pp. 567–99. The related arguments of Mancur Olson are also relevant here. See Mancur Olson, *The Rise and Decline of Nations* (New Haven: Yale University Press, 1982).
29. On the role of culture as a social institution, see Thomas Sowell, *Knowledge and Decisions* (New York: Basic Books, 1980), pp. 100–10.
30. Lachmann, *Legacy of Max Weber*, op. cit., p. 90.

14 Euclideanism versus Hermeneutics: A Reinterpretation of Misesian Apriorism*

DON LAVOIE

INTRODUCTION

> Now the determination of economic quantities, as far as this is possible, is obviously a goal of any economic theory and thus of any market theory. But for a method of analysis that is also concerned with the interpretation of the meaning of action, this determination is only the first step. The real task is to explain how relations between quantities derive from mental acts.
>
> Ludwig Lachmann (1977, p. 113)

Perhaps the most significant event propelling the modern revival of Austrian or subjectivist economics in the United States in the 1970s was the arrival at New York University of Ludwig Lachmann. First drawn to Austrian ideas by the methodological writings of Ludwig von Mises in the 1930s, Lachmann had already maintained a lifelong dedication to the advancement of subjectivism. Yet his arrival at NYU was tumultuous. This was an Austrian of a different stripe. Many of us were at first alarmed by his radical critique of what he called "formalistic" neoclassical theory, a critique that seemed to come perilously close to a complete rejection of all economic theorizing, that is, to historicism.[1] We were confused by his injection of names like Max Weber, Paul Davidson, and George Shackle into our discourse, and we continue to quarrel with him over the nature of Keynes' contribution. The American followers of Mises seemed to have developed a very different brand of Misesian economics from that brought to New York by Professor Lachmann.

While it would be much too strong to say we are all Lachmannians now, it is clear that after ten years of his influence American Austrians will never be the same again. It is not that fears of some historicist tendencies in Lachmann's work have been altogether dispelled. But he has challenged us in several important ways that forced us to improve our economics. We now take more seriously the difficulties with neoclassical economics to which he drew our attention and this has led us to reexamine many aspects of our own theories. He has forced us to go beyond theoretical discussions of the market and to examine real-world market institutions. He has made us never forget the importance of expectations in economics. And perhaps most significantly of all, he has directed our attention at what I now believe is the chief obstacle to progress in contemporary economics, the overexalted respect for formalistic at the expense of interpretive modes of explanation.

This paper is offered to Professor Lachmann as an attempt to extend this last theme, the critique of formalism. I believe that Lachmann's antiformalism, unlike that of historicists, does not deny the need for systematic theory. Here I will not, however, be trying to substantiate this interpretation of Lachmann as a nonhistoricist. Rather, I will try to show that the literature that drew Lachmann into economics, Mises' methodological work, which has been widely interpreted as itself a kind of formalism (which I will call Euclideanism), may instead be seen as a kind of antiformalism along broadly Lachmannian lines (which I will call hermeneutics). Although the textual evidence is mixed, there are discernible, if heretofore almost completely ignored, antiformalist strands in Mises' methodological thought which should attract followers of Mises toward some of the very methodological directions in which Lachmann has been pointing us.

In view of the fact that both friends and foes of Mises from Hayek to Hutchison have agreed in seeing his methodology as a Euclidean one, some justification seems appropriate at the outset for this exercise in reinterpretation. There are two general considerations that suggest that the strictly Euclidean interpretation may be an incomplete view of Mises' apriorism. First, the distinction, upon which Mises vigorously insisted, between theory and history, has been frequently misinterpreted as a strict dichotomization that isolates these two cognitive processes completely from each other. But, in fact, Mises not only mixed historical observations in with all his own theoretical expositions but even explicitly said that theory and history are absolutely necessary for one another. They are described as two incomplete halves of the human sciences. There is, indeed, a difference between the particularizing intent of history and the generalizing and systematizing intent of our cognitive processes. Mises called these aspects, respectively, understanding and conception. All he was saying is that "What has happened?" questions are not the same thing as asking: "What can happen?" questions. But the theory and history are nevertheless two inescapable aspects of what is ultimately one integrated intellectual endeavor. Good theory cannot be developed without a background of information about "what has happened," just as telling the story of what has happened requires drawing conclusions about what can. We necessarily construct systematic theory by a continuous weaving back and forth between these complementary halves of cognition. When this complementarity between theory and history is kept in mind, many otherwise objectionable aspects of Mises' apriorism appear much more reasonable. History cannot refute theory, Mises says, but then he goes on to point out that it is precisely history that tells us what parts of our theorizing are applicable to the real world. Thus, theory is not nearly as insulated from "the facts" as some of Mises' own pronouncements suggest. Moreover Mises' description of his apriorism as "strictly deductive," taken in light of this complementarity between theory and history, can be seen as an answer to historicists. Mises may not have desired his "strict deduction" to restrict cognitive processes to a linear, Euclidean form of argument, but rather to insist on the power of the conceptual process, of discursive reasoning in its wider sense as opposed to empirical fact finding.

The second general consideration that raises some doubt about the strictly Euclidean interpretation is the ambiguity surrounding Mises' use of the two words *praxeology* and *apriorism*. The first word was coined to substitute for his earlier use of the word *sociology*, which he believed came to be too contaminated with positivism and Marxism. He borrowed the second from neo-Kantian philosophers but put it to his own use. Most interpreters have assumed that Mises intended these words narrowly to refer to his own brand of economics, in which case a statement like "All economics must be aprioristic and praxeological" is taken as an exclusivistic prejudice. We shall see, however, that in some contexts Mises uses these words in a much wider sense, to refer not to how he thought economics should be, but how it is and has been, throughout the history of the science. Many of Mises' most Euclidean-sounding passages take on a whole new meaning if these two considerations are borne in mind.

If I am right that there is a hermeneutic way of reading Misesian apriorism, then many of the harshest criticisms of Mises' methodology become problematic. The dogmatism and rigidity, the antagonism to empirical work, and the confident air of completeness and apodictic certainty that has infected some of his admiring followers and infuriated some of his fiercest enemies are all symptoms of the Euclidean style of thought. To the extent that Mises' apriorism can be recast as hermeneutic instead, to that extent, I believe, his methodology takes on a new power and eloquence for today. And, incidentally, Lachmann's distinctively hermeneutical brand of economics correspondingly takes on a new significance for the American followers of Mises who had found Lachmann's work so outlandish a decade ago.

TOWARD A NON-EUCLIDEAN MODEL OF COGNITIVE SYSTEMATIZATION

> From Aristotle's day until the Age of Reason—and well beyond—it was generally thought that all of our knowledge of the observable world could eventually be organized into a single vast deductive system along the lines envisaged by the Euclidean model. ... In modern times, this Euclidean picture of scientific cognition was first seriously questioned in the wake of the era of Romanticism by those who sought to uphold the existence of distinct scientific methodologies, differing as between the sciences of man and the sciences of (extra-human) nature. ... German participants in this *Methodenstreit* as Wilhelm Dilthey, Wilhelm Windelband, and Heinrich Rickert held in effect that the ahistorical, analytical, and nonevaluative *Naturwissenschaften* are committed to a Euclidean model of systematization, whereas the historical, synthetic and evaluative *Geistewissenschaften* required something along the lines of a network model.
>
> Nicholas Rescher (1979), pp. 56–7.

Many of the subjectivist followers of Ludwig von Mises, including Professor Lachmann and most of Mises' methodological critics, have expressed a certain dissatisfaction with the language in which Mises cast his method for a general science of action. Mises sometimes presents his apriori science as what Imre Lakatos called a Euclidean system, a privileged category of knowledge, uniquely certain and immune to all criticism. It was built from a set of self-evident axioms from which strictly deductive arguments can be cranked out mechanically. Mises and his followers like to insist that since in economics any investigation of historical facts necessarily presupposes a theory that is able to make sense of those facts, therefore theory is *prior* to, rather than tested by, history. An apriori approach is distinguishable from an aposteriori one in that while the former primarily strives to test the intelligibility of a conjectural historical account against believed theories, the latter strives primarily to test the applicability of conjectural theories against believed facts. Sophisticated proponents of each can today admit that theories and facts test one another in different phases of scientific research. But there was a time when a naïve version of aposteriorism dominated the natural sciences completely and seriously impinged upon economics and other social sciences. Naïve aposteriorism holds that theories are strictly subsidiary to the facts which neither should, nor need to, be theory laden.

It was in this environment, in which the successful natural sciences were thought to build their theories from a neutral accumulation of facts, that Mises declared his economics to be apriori. The argument he used to support this claim—that all facts in his discipline are theory laden—is today widely accepted to be true of facts in the natural sciences as well. In this sense we can almost say we are all apriorists now.

But there is, so to speak, both more and less to Mises' apriorism than this rather uncontroversial view that facts are theory laden. The "less" is an implication Mises leaves (which I will call Euclidean) that no historical account can ever cause us to go back and reconsider our apriori theory, thus suggesting that theories are somehow epistemically privileged and safely dichotomized from history. This view makes economics seem too different from the natural sciences. The "more" is the insight (which I will call hermeneutic) that for any economic explanation to be acceptable it must relate the observed phenomena to their underlying meaning in terms of the individual purposes whose interplay constitutes an economic system. That is, social sciences like economics must not only explain what happens, as a physicist might explain the motion of a planet, they must also understand the meaning of what happens to those to whom it happens. This view shows in what respects there are genuine differences, at least in degree, between the natural and social sciences.

Unfortunately while the Euclidean aspects of Mises' apriorism have been well documented and appropriately criticized, the more promising hermeneutic aspects have not. As a result, Mises' whole methodological contribution is dismissed for its Euclidean vices without any recognition that its hermeneutical virtues exist. Thus, much depends on how the textual evidence stacks up concerning these alternative readings of Mises' apriorism. But before examining this textual evidence it is necessary to state somewhat more directly if perhaps a bit simplistically just what these alternatives will be understood to entail.

Euclideanism and hermeneutics can be seen not so much as alternative methods but as two contrasting views of the relationship between methodology and science, and more broadly as contrasting styles of thought. Euclideanism is a more prescriptive methodology while hermeneutics is a more descriptive one. Euclideanism is represented as a fixed deductive structure into which economists are told they ought to fit their arguments in order to keep up with the philosophers' standards of true scientific objectivity. Hermeneutics is rather what Rescher calls a network model, an approach that bases its assessment of what is scientific by a reliance on the pragmatic judgments of systematicity, coherence, clarity, etc., by members of the scientific community. Here what is acceptable is not what meets the preestablished epistemological criteria of the methodologists but simply what works, i.e., what persuades effectively.

The difference between these styles of systematization is not simply that Euclideanism dares to recommend methods while hermeneutics timidly abstains from doing so. The difference is rather that the Euclidean methodological prescription is logical (from one mind), ahistorical, and confining, whereas the hermeneutic one is dialogical (from the scientific community as a whole), historical, and open ended. Hermeneutics derives its standards from examining the history of thought and from the living "conversation" that is science, while Euclideanism strives to stand above the practicing scientist and judge his work by extrahistorical, logical standards.

If Euclideanism takes its model to be axiomatic geometry what is the contrary model of hermeneutics? The Dilthey/Weber tradition is an extension into the social sciences of the methods of textual interpretation, mainly Biblical and legal exegesis and language translation, which trace back into ancient times. Its modern revival, in the able hands of such writers as Clifford Geertz, Hans-Georg Gadamer, and Paul Ricoeur, has turned this interpretive approach to explanation in the social sciences into an extremely powerful philosophical school with important implications for contemporary economics.[2] Thus this paper, a textual reinterpretation of Mises, is both about and an example of the hermeneutical method. Understanding the meaning of a written text often requires a sustained effort; a tentative formulation of the meaning of the whole (say, Mises' life work) is checked against the meaning of particular parts (say, his methodological chapters at the beginning of *Human Action*, or that book's opening sentence). The revision of the meaning of these parts then requires a new hypothesis about the meaning of the whole, and the dialogical process continues.

To support the need for systematic theory in the cognition of social phenomena need not, then, demand a Euclidean procedure for establishing systematization. In his book *Cognitive Systematization*, Nicholas Rescher advances a general case for non-Euclidean procedures for ensuring, as far as possible, that our scientific explanations are integrated, coherent systems of knowledge. Euclideanism takes as its ideal a fully axiomatized, linearly constructed system of strict deduction along the lines of Euclid's geometry. What Rescher calls the "network model," while it too strives to uphold knowledge as an integrated, coherent system, constitutes a fundamentally different path for cognitive systematization. He refers (1979, p. 46) to three critical points of difference between these two models of systematization.

> (1) The network model dispenses altogether with the need for a category of basic (self-evident or self-validating) foundational or "protocol" theses capable of playing the role of axiomatic supports for the entire structure.
> (2) The structure of the arrangement of theses within the framework of the network model need not be geological: no stratification of theses into levels of greater or lesser fundamentality is called for. . . .
> (3) The network model accordingly abandons the conception of priority or fundamentality in its arrangement of theses. It replaces such fundamentality by a conception of enmeshment in a unifying web—in terms of the multiplicity of linkages and the patterns of inter-connectedness with other parts of the net.

The Euclidean model has extremely stringent requirements which have made it increasingly difficult to uphold, even in its domain of geometry. It requires a linear construction from the most fundamental axioms toward the less fundamental derivation such that, as Rescher (1979, p. 52) puts it, "Nothing whatever that happens at the epistemically later stages of the analysis can possibly affect the starting-point of basic truths." These basic axioms are thus rendered completely "exempt from any retrospective re-evaluation in the light of new information or insights." By contrast, the network model of cognitive systematization permits a recursive movement between its parts, none of which need have any absolute epistemic priority over any others. In the face of a variety of devastating criticisms from philosophy, mathematics, and cognitive science, Euclideanism, once the dominant model of science, has been all but defeated in virtually every field of thought. Lakatos (1978, p. 90) shows that Euclideanism even in mathematics truncates the critical process by artificially injecting "intuitively indubitable first principles" and perfect reasoned "facts" into science where only more or less tentative conjecture properly belongs.[3] It retains a foothold, as Imre Lakatos pointed out, only in mathematics (where it seems to be only a minority view) and "in those underdeveloped subjects where knowledge is still trivial, like ethics, economics, etc."[4]

Lakatos refers to Ludwig von Mises (along with a methodological follower of Mises, Lionel Robbins) as his example of a Euclidean economist.[5] Indeed, the esteemed historian of economics, T. W. Hutchison, has shown that many of Mises' own statements about his methodology lend fairly strong support to Lakatos' interpretation.[6]

The thesis of this paper is that, Hutchison and Lakatos, to the contrary notwithstanding, Ludwig von Mises' methodology can at least as readily be interpreted as a network as it can as a Euclidean model of cognitive systematization. In particular, a direct influence upon Mises' thought can be found from the very continental tradition of hermeneutics which Rescher calls the first to seriously question Euclideanism. Hutchison's textual evidence for Mises' Euclideanism cannot be lightly dismissed, nor can it be argued that Mises' own explicit descriptions of his methodology are free of some Euclidean "contamination". When in the next section Hutchison's textual case is examined closely, however, and set against other textual evidence, it is far from conclusive.

This is a paper whose chief purpose is "merely" exegetical. I ask the doctrinal question what Mises "really meant" when he called economics aprioristic. Today such backward-looking questions are deemed quite secondary to the forward-looking development of economic theory. Hence, I should clarify, before commencing with the exegesis, that I do not accept this received view of the secondary nature of exercises in the history of thought. I view doctrinal history as paradoxically forward looking in the sense that its proper goal is not the historicists' one of attaining an empathic understanding of what was in somebody's head in the past, but rather reworking the latent meaning of a text in terms of its relevance for today. My aim is to see how Mises' methodology "speaks to us" as the hermeneutical philosophers say, and what can be done in the future with various insights.

TEXTUAL EVIDENCE FOR THE EUCLIDEAN INTERPRETATION

> The theorems attained by correct praxeological reasoning are not only perfectly certain and incontestable, like the correct mathematical theorems. They refer, moreover, with the full rigidity of their apodictic certainty and incontestability to the reality of action as it appears in life and history. Praxeology conveys exact and precise knowledge of real things.
>
> Ludwig von Mises (1966, p. 39)

Evidence for the Euclidean interpretation of Mises is by no means superficial. The methodology of the science of *Human Action* which Mises explicitly formulated in his economic treatise of that name, was cast in Kantian terms and often described as a special category of knowledge that was inherently beyond any criticism. It is boldly presented as if it represented a completely unique category of knowledge. In its purely formal and deductive character, praxeology is described as similar to logic and mathematics; it is even directly compared with Euclidean geometry. In the passages that surely provide the best evidence for the Euclidean interpretations of his method, Mises writes

> Aprioristic reasoning is purely conceptual and deductive. It cannot produce anything else but tautologies and analytic judgments. All its implications are logically derived from the premises and were already contained in them. Hence, according to a popular objection, it cannot add anything to our knowledge.
>
> All geometric theorems are already implied in the axioms. The concept of a rectangular triangle already implies the theorem of Pythagoras. This theorem is a tautology, its deduction results in an analytic judgment. Nonetheless nobody would contend that geometry in general and the theorem of Pythagoras in particular do not enlarge our knowledge (1966, p. 38).

The stance of apriorism as knowledge that is uniquely unquestionable or as Mises liked to put it, "apodictically certain," is the position Hutchison understandably finds so offensive to the sensibilities of contemporary methodologists. At the very least it has to be admitted that Mises is a bit free with his pronouncements of economic theorems that are "perfectly certain and incontestable, like the correct mathematical theorems."

Moreover he seems to be claiming not only uniqueness but also an exclusivity for his approach, as when he declares that "For the comprehension of action there is but one scheme of interpretation and analysis available, namely, that provided by the cognition and analysis of our purposeful behavior" (1966, p. 26). Such exclusivity would suggest an insulation from criticism which, Hutchison rightly reminds us, would certainly violate the spirit of the growth of knowledge literature.

Hutchison says that Mises "traces the impossibility of questioning *a priori* judgments back to introspection," by which Hutchison means some sort of purely private knowledge that is essentially beyond criticism. To show that this was Mises' meaning, Hutchison supplies a quotation where Mises uses the word introspection and emphatically insists on the unique unquestionability of praxeological knowledge:

> What we know about our own actions and about those of other people is conditioned by our familiarity with the category of action that we owe to a process of self-examination and introspection as well as of understanding of other peoples' conduct. To question this insight is no less impossible than to question the fact that we are alive.[7]

Furthermore, Hutchison says that Mises "completely rejects" Karl Popper's demarcation principle between science and non-science, and Hutchison supports this charge in another rather emphatic quotation:

> If one accepts the terminology of logical positivism and especially also that of Popper, a theory or hypothesis is "unscientific" if in principle it cannot be refuted by experience. Consequently, all a priori theories, including mathematics and praxeology, are "unscientific." This is merely a verbal quibble. No serious man wastes his time in discussing such a terminological question. Praxeology and economics will retain their paramount significance for human life and action however people may classify and describe them.[8]

Aside from again misleadingly lumping praxeology and mathematics together, Mises can be charged here with treating Popper's point with less respect than it deserves. There are, after all, such things as dogmatic systems of thought which can explain everything that can imaginably occur and therefore can really explain nothing. Most branches of Marxism/Leninism would undoubtedly be classified by both Mises and Popper as unscientific in this sense. Every empirical science deserving of the name must be ready to deny the possibility in the real world of some imaginable states of affairs.[9]

Moreover, Mises' view of the natural sciences appears to modern eyes to be somewhat naïve, as when he remarks that the history of the natural sciences, unlike that of the human sciences, "is a record of theories and hypotheses discarded because they were disproved by experience" (1966, p. 41). This interpretation of the natural sciences led him in general to exaggerate the differences between these and the human sciences, and in particular to concede that the natural sciences "have no use for understanding" (1966, p. 61), which is "the specific mental tool of history" (1966, p. 51). In light of the writings of such philosophers of the natural sciences as Popper, Lakatos, and Michael Polanyi this concession to positivism for the natural sciences can no longer be accepted.

Mises also could be charged with exaggerating the difference between disagreements among scientists, on the one hand, which he thought were "open to a settlement by 'objective' reasoning," and, on the other hand, disagreements among historians. In the latter, in so far as the argument is over "judgments of relevance," he says, "It is impossible to find a solution which all sane men must accept" (1966, p. 58). Although he recognized that the "understanding of the historian is always tinged with the marks of his personality" and "reflects the mind of its author," he was under the illusion that knowledge in the natural and social sciences was categorically different, purely aposterioristic or aprioristic, and unsullied with any such personal tinges. It seems to me that Michael Polanyi (1958a; 1958b) has now shown, beyond any reasonable doubt, that all knowledge is unavoidably tinged with a personal component.

In all these respects, to the extent that praxeology is presented as uniquely unquestionable knowledge, Mises does, in my view, leave himself open to Hutchison's charge of dogmatism. If praxeology is to be a science, it must reject Euclideanism and permit its first principles, its chains of deductive reasoning, and its modes of application to the real world, to be challenged by serious criticism. If Mises' insistence on the certainty of the axioms and derived conclusions of praxeology is an exclusionary device, employed to remove his ideas from the threat of challengers, then the scientific community has no responsibility to take him seriously.

TEXTUAL EVIDENCE FOR THE HERMENEUTIC INTERPRETATION

> Reasoning and scientific inquiry can never bring full ease of mind, apodictic certainty, and perfect cognition of all things.
>
> Ludwig von Mises (1966, p. 25)

But is this Euclideanism really what Mises' apriorism is supposed to be all about? Even in the evidence just provided for the Euclidean interpretation, there are intimations that an altogether different reading of Mises is possible.

Take, for example, the opening two quotations for these sections where Mises first refers to praxeological theorems as apodictically certain and then denies that any scientific process can yield apodictic certainty. Although there is no question but that the first quotation has a distinctively Euclidean tone, Mises only explicitly says here that the true theorems of praxeology are apodictic, leaving unanswered the question: How do we know for certain that any praxeological theorem is true? Perhaps this sounds like hairsplitting, and maybe in this case we simply have Mises contradicting himself. But it seems conceivable that Mises was trying to insist emphatically on the possibility of true knowledge from praxeological reasoning against those forms of historicism which leave no room for this possibility, not to assert a unique, Euclidean uncriticizability for the products of such reasoning. True theorems in mathematics are genuine additions to human knowledge even though they come from within the mind as a product of deductive effort and not from without the mind as a product of empirical observation. Perhaps Mises' aim was to open his readers to the possibility of such knowledge from within in the case of praxeology, not close it off in Euclidean fashion from rational criticism.

When Mises said there is "but one scheme of interpretation" open to the study of human action the scheme that treats it "as meaningful and purposeful behavior"—he may not have been claiming exclusivity for his particular economics. He may have only been pointing out what Dilthey, Weber, and Schutz had stressed, that it is impossible "to grasp human action intellectually ... without entering into the meaning which the acting parties attribute to the situation" (1966, p. 26). The way Mises describes the earliest realization that there are regularities in economic phenomena is that people discovered that "there is another aspect from which human actions might be viewed than that of good and bad, of fair and unfair, of just and unjust" (1966, p. 2). This suggests that Mises views economic theory as providing us with a workable scheme for the subjective interpretation of human conduct and one which is not the only such perspective possible.

When Mises talks about introspection or "knowledge from within" it is presented not as private knowledge but as what hermeneutical philosophers call "intersubjective." The realm of the intersubjective is, for hermeneutics, definitely, not insulated from rational criticism. Mises, moreover, does not trace the supposed certainty of his apriori axioms to introspection alone, but adds the phrase "self-examination and understanding . . . other peoples' conduct," suggesting that he may have meant by the apriori what in the hermeneutics literature is also called "knowledge from within." And when Mises asserts that to question the apriori "is no less impossible than to question the fact that we are alive" he might be read as saying no more than that, as contributors to the hermeneutics literature such as Schutz argued, those who try to suspend judgment on whether other minds are intelligent will in any case contradict themselves in practice by arguing their behavioralistic case to other "minds" in the scientific community. The level of practical, common-sensical reasoning in the day-to-day affairs of men, the level of already existing meaning which some writers in the hermeneutics tradition calls "the intersubjective life world," is taken for granted by all active scientists when they try to persuade one another. In the sense it is apriori but it is not immune to criticism. The foundation of all our scientific knowledge lies in the fact that when we learn to speak we all enter this life world and learn to share its tacit meanings, but science begins with a questioning and refinement of our common sense. The hermeneutic apriori, unlike the Euclidean, is not a list of explicit, self-evident intrasubjective axioms from which a science is deduced but a level of pregiven intersubjectivity, of common understanding which precedes and sustains science.

As for the rejection of Popper's criterion of falsifiability, it is notable that Mises sees this criterion not so much as incorrect, but as insignificant. It is only a verbal quibble. This admittedly terse remark might be read as referring to the distinction between theory and history. It is true that praxeology, the incomplete theoretical half of the science of human action, is unfalsifiable by any particular historical event. The empirical element of science simply comes with the other half, its application in history, when the applied economist decides what parts of theory are relevant to the case at hand. In this sense it does seem a verbal quibble to call the theoretical half of the human sciences unscientific, as it would be to complain that the Pythagorean theorem cannot be falsified by any instances of real world triangles. In physics we ask which of several valid geometries is relevant to our space. Where Euclidean geometry is relevant, the theorems in it are true and applicable. Similarly, in the human sciences we ask which of several interpretive schemes or theories is most applicable to the comprehension of an episode of history.

Admittedly Mises' quoted comments about the natural sciences show a genuine misunderstanding of these disciplines on his part from which no effort of reinterpretation can rescue him. The growth of knowledge tradition has shown that Mises, along with nearly everyone else of his day, had a seriously flawed picture of the natural sciences. But after all, the natural sciences were not the concern of Mises' methodological writings except as an illustration of what the human sciences were not. The belief that the natural sciences are free of any personal tinges appears today to be unwarranted, but it should be noted that Mises did not see these tinges as opening the door to relativism in history. "In the exercise of understanding," he wrote, "there is no room for arbitrariness and capriciousness" (1966, p. 57).

A more serious difficulty arises with the language of axioms and theorems in which Mises' theory is cast. The reader can easily get the impression that Mises meant for economic theory to be forced into a fixed, hierarchically deductive structure, like the theorems of geometry. Yet, even here, the Euclidean interpretation is by no means the only reading of Mises possible. Although he thought of praxeology and geometry as similar in that all their "theorems" are "already implied in the axioms" (1966, p. 38), he also stated explicitly that "Economics does not follow the procedure of logic and mathematics" (1966, p. 66).

They are different, in the first place, in that "The starting point of praxeology is not a choice of axioms and decision about methods of procedure, but reflection about the essence of action" (1966, p. 39). Second, unlike geometry, praxeology "does not present an integrated system of pure aprioristic ratiocination severed from any reference to reality." Instead it adopts "a form in which aprioristic theory and the interpretation of historical phenomena are intertwined" (1966, p. 66).

Each of the differences between praxeology and Euclideanism can be seen linking Mises to the tradition of hermeneutics. The fact that the point of departure for praxeology is reflection upon the essence of action recalls Dilthey's, Weber's and Schutz's points of departure for their "interpretative sociology" far more than Russell's or Hildreth's formalizations of mathematics or for that matter, Debreu's of economics. And Mises' intertwining of theory with history in such a way as to view theory not as an elegant construction of formal, intellectual beauty, like mathematics, but as a practical device through which the facts of history are to be interpreted, sounds much more like the hermeneutical than the Euclidean variety of apriorism.

The language Mises uses in the following passages to explain the "apriori" and "deductive" character of praxeology suggests more a pragmatically based, open-ended, and reflective form of reasoning than any sort of strictly linear deductive structure of Euclideanism:

> The scope of praxeology is the explication of the category of human action. All that is needed for the deduction of all praxeological theorems is knowledge of the essence of human action. It is a knowledge that is our own because we are men . . . The only way to a cognition of these theorems is logical analysis of our inherent knowledge of the category of action (1966, p. 64).

In calling his method aprioristic, Mises uses the language of Kantian philosophers, but he does not attempt to supply any sort of metaphysics or ontological argument for apriorism. Instead, he relies on a pragmatic argument, saying simply that circumstances enjoin upon us not a metaphysical but a methodological apriorism (1966, p. 35):

> Everybody in his daily behavior again and again bears witness to the immutability and universality of the categories of thought and action. He who addresses fellow men, who wants to inform and convince them, who asks questions and answers other people's questions, can proceed in this way only because he can appeal to something common to all men . . . (1966, p. 36).

We must also accept not only the existence but also the significance of the already interpreted life-world or involve ourselves in self-contradiction. We accept the assumption that we share an intersubjectivity with one another not because of firm philosophical foundations but because this procedure works in everyday life and in science. Mises says the emptiness of positivism becomes manifest "precisely when we accept this pragmatic point of view" (1966, p. 24).

In a passage to which a reference to Schutz (1932) is attached, Mises shows that his defense of the validity of the apriori is that, practically speaking, all of us are already taking the life world for granted. Apriori propositions, such as that all humans share the same common sense logic, are to be employed because they are already in extensive use and they "work in practice and in science":

> [T]he positivist must not overlook the fact that in addressing his fellow men he presupposes—tacitly and implicitly—the intersubjective validity of logic and thereby the reality of the alter Ego's thought and action, of his eminent human character (1966, p. 24).

If Mises had meant his praxeology to be a variety of Euclideanism, it would be difficult to make sense of his statement that "In asserting the a priori character of praxeology we are not drafting a plan for a future new science different from the traditional sciences of human action" (1966, p. 40). Traditional economics, sociology, and history can be said to have been hermeneutically apriorist in that they took the already interpreted life world as the pregiven object of their investigations, but they could hardly be called Euclidean. Even "regular citizens eager to comprehend occurring changes" resort to an aprioristic approach in this sense. If Mises had meant by *reasoning* the kind of strictly linear deduction favored by Euclideanism, this statement would have to reflect a peculiar misunderstanding on Mises' part of the nature of the mundane reasoning of the common man.

The so-called "purely deductive" reasoning of Misesean apriorism can be read as fundamentally different from that of Euclideanism. The latter aims at achieving a deductive structure made up of a sequence of purely logical steps which could have been arrived at by a Turing machine. For Mises, however, "Cognition from purely deductive reasoning is also creative and opens for our mind access to previously barred spheres." The task of "aprioristic reasoning," he says, is "to render manifest and obvious what was hidden and unknown before" (1966, p. 38). Moreover, contrary to the Euclidean aspirations for conclusiveness and completeness (and some of his own pronouncements), Mises admits that science "can never bring full ease of mind" and that "All that man can do is to submit all his theories again and again to the most critical re-examination" (1966, pp. 25, 68).

The only way to choose among competing interpretive theories is to try to see reality through them, one by one, to try to debate where disagreements seem crucial, and ultimately to make a judgment about which perspective renders the best grasp on the flow of events. In arguing for the aprioristic method Mises may not have been claiming special validity to his own particular development of aprioristic theory, much less his own understanding of history, but may have only been trying to echo the hermeneuticists' point that all social theorists in practice and each of us in our everyday lives view social phenomena as already interpreted, or from within. Although he emphasized differences between theory and history he did not wish to, and did not himself, dichotomize them. He insisted, as does the hermeneutics literature, that theory is a framework for the interpretation of the facts of history, more than an hypothesis to be tested by those facts. Nevertheless, there is no way to be certain in this life that one's own interpretive perspective is the best. This need not imply a retreat to a theory-less historicism but only reinforces the fact that our only way to eliminate errors is, as Mises put it, to submit our own and our fellows' work to the most critical reexamination.

NOTES

1. George Selgin's (1985, p. 1) critique of Lachmann and Shackle, which interprets them both as historicists, points out that since the Austrian school began with Menger's devastating criticism of the historicists of his day, it would be unfortunate if contemporary Austrians were to revert to this antitheoretical stance. While I agree with much of this critique, I am not convinced that Lachmann is an example of historicism.
2. I have elaborated at more length on the meaning and significance for economics of this modern hermeneutics literature in my paper "The Interpretive Dimensions of Economics: Science, Hermeneutics, and Praxeology" (1985) from which some passages in this paper have been borrowed. Some other attempts to relate the literature of hermeneutics to that of economics include Lachmann (1971), Grinder (1977), Langlois and Koppl (1984), Ebeling (1985), and O'Driscoll and Rizzo (1985).
3. However in the wake of the work of such mathematicians as Gödel, Church, Cohen, Lowenheim, and Skolem, Euclideanism seems doomed even in mathematics. See Lakatos (1978) and Kline (1980). As Kline (1980, p. 271) pointed out, "the Lowenheim-Skolem theorem tells us that a set of axioms permits many more essentially different interpretations than the one intended." The choice among such interpretations must be done by procedures not specified within the axiomatic system. Therefore even Euclidean systems need to be defended by non-Euclidean arguments.
4. Lakatos (1978, p. 10) exhibits here a bit of the holier than thou attitude of many philosophers of the natural sciences. In response to such claims that economic reasoning is trivial, Mises answers that economics, although "tautological" nevertheless "transforms, develops and unfolds" our comprehension of reality, telling us things which without this effort would remain unknown. Before the development of systematic economics, Mises points out, "A long line of abortive attempts to solve the problems concerned shows that it was certainly not easy to attain the present state of knowledge" (1966, p. 38).
5. An argument could be made that the mathematical analysis of the general equilibrium theorist Gerard Debreu represents a less ambiguous example in economics of what Lakatos calls Euclideanism than Mises' apriorism does.
6. See especially Hutchison (1981, pp. 203–32; 266–307).

7. From Mises (1978, p. 71), quoted by Hutchison (1981, p. 210).
8. From Mises (1978, p. 70), quoted by Hutchison (1981, p. 210).
9. In this connection it is noteworthy that Mises' magnum opus ends by dramatically stressing that praxeology forbids some conceivable states of affairs: "Man's freedom to choose and to act is restricted in a threefold way. There are first the physical laws to whose unfeeling absoluteness man must adjust his conduct if he wants to live. There are second the individual's innate constitutional characteristics and dispositions and the operation of environmental factors; . . . There is finally the regularity of phenomena with regard to the interconnectedness of means and ends, viz., the praxeological law as distinct from the physical and from the physiological law . . ." (1966, p. 885).

REFERENCES

Dilthey, Wilhelm (1976), *W. Dilthey, Selected Writings*, ed. and trans. H. P. Rickman (New York: Cambridge University Press).

Ebeling, Richard M. (1985), "Hermeneutics and the Interpretive Element in the Analysis of the Market Process" Center for the Study of Market Processes Working Paper 16, George Mason University.

Gadamer, Hans-Georg (1975a), *Truth and Method*, eds. and trans. Garrett Barden and John Cumming (New York: Seabury).

—— (1975b), "Hermeneutics and Social Science" *Cultural Hermeneutics*, 2, pp. 307–16.

—— (1976), *Philosophical Hermeneutics*, ed. and trans. David E. Linge (Berkeley: University of California Press).

—— (1982), *Reason in the Age of Science*, trans. F. G. Lawrence (Cambridge: MIT Press).

Geertz, Clifford (1973), *The Interpretation of Cultures* (New York: Basic Books).

Grinder, Walter E. (1977), "In Pursuit of the Subjective Paradigm," in L. M. Lachmann (1977), *Capital Expectations and the Market Process: Essays on the Theory of the Market Economy* (Kansas City: Sheed Andrews & McMeel.

Hutchison, T. W. (1981), *The Politics and Philosophy of Economics, Marxians, Keynesians and Austrians* (New York: New York University Press).

Kline, Morris. (1980), *Mathematics: The Loss of Certainty* (New York: Oxford University Press).

Lachmann, Ludwig M. (1971), *The Legacy of Max Weber* (Berkeley: Glendessary Press).

—— (1984), "Economic Theory in Tempestuous Season" (unpublished English translation by Cornelia Dorfschmid) copyright by Frankfurter Allgemeine Zeitung.

Lakatos, Imre (1978), *Mathematics, Science and Epistemology* (New York: Cambridge University Press).

Langlois, Richard N. and Roger G. Koppl (1984), "Fritz Machlup and Marginalism: A Re-Evaluation," Center for the Study of Market Processes Working Paper 14.

Lavoie, Don (1985), "The Interpretive Dimension of Economics: Science, Hermeneutics, and Praxeology," Center for the Study of Market Processes Working Paper 15.

Mises, Ludwig von (1966), *Human Action: a Treatise on Economics*, 3rd ed. (Chicago: Henry Regnery).

—— (1969), *Theory and History: An Interpretation of Social and Economic Evolution* (New Rochelle, N.Y.: Arlington House).

—— (1978), *The Ultimate Foundation of Economic Science: An Essay on Method* (Kansas City: Sheed Andrews & McMeel).

—— (1981), *Epistemological Problems of Economics*, trans. George Reisman (New York: New York University Press).

O'Driscoll, Gerald P., Jr., and Mario J. Rizzo (1985), *The Economics of Time and Ignorance* (Oxford: Basil Blackwell).

Polanyi, Michael (1958a), *Personal Knowledge Towards a Post-Critical Philosophy* (Chicago: University of Chicago Press).

—— (1958b), *The Study of Man* (Chicago: University of Chicago Press).

Rescher, Nicholas (1979), *Cognitive Systematization: A Systems-theoretic Approach to a Coherent Theory of Knowledge* (Oxford: Basil Blackwell).

Ricoeur, Paul (1965), *History and Truth*, translated by C. A. Kelbley (Evanston, Ill.: Northwestern University Press).

—— (1981), *Hermeneutics and the Human Sciences*, ed. and trans. J. B. Thompson (New York: Cambridge University Press).

Schutz, Alfred (1970), *On Phenomenology and Social Relations*, ed. and trans. Helmut R. Wagner (Chicago: University of Chicago Press).

Schutz, Alfred and Luckmann, Thomas (1973), *The Structures of the Life-World* (Evanston, Northwestern University Press).

Selgin, George A. (1985), "Praxeology and Understanding: An Analysis of the Current Crisis in Austrian Economics" (unpublished manuscript, New York University).

Weber, Max (1949), *The Methodology of the Social Sciences*, eds. and trans. Edward A. Shils and Henry A. Finch (New York: The Free Press).

—— (1980), *The Interpretation of Social Reality*, ed. J. E. T. Eldridge (New York: Schoken Books).

15 Economic Policy and the Capital Structure

PETER LEWIN

I

For almost 40 years Professor Lachmann has explored the nature of the capital structure of market economies.[1] He has provided us with unique insights into the dynamic connections between individual plans, social institutions, the distribution of income and wealth and the capital structure.[2] He has always emphasized the role of expectations in human decisions. These themes are of enduring relevance and interest.

This essay explores the relationship between monetary policy and the capital structure. In particular, I examine how the logic of modern political processes and the nature of capital can lead to what we perceive as business cycles.

II

The capital structure can only be understood in terms of the individual plans from which it derives. A production plan involves the combining of individual capital goods and labor resources in order to produce particular outputs. These capital goods stand in a complementary relationship to one another within the plan. As individual bits of machinery, raw materials, buildings, and so on, they make little sense. But when seen as part of an overall plan, they assume immediate significance. Though their individual contributions may not be disentangled, they contribute jointly to the fulfillment of the plan.

The significance of understanding capital in terms of the plans from which it derives is twofold. First, the plans provide the reference points for interpreting any given capital structure. We understand the role of capital goods in terms of the plans that they help fulfill; that is to say, have helped, are helping, or will help to fulfill. And as long as the plans indeed continue to be fulfilled, the capital structure will be maintained. But, second, and perhaps more important, when plans fail, completely or in part, or succeed beyond the planner's expectations, they will be revised and the capital structure will be changed. And it is in understanding this change that we must, once again, refer back to individual production plans. Change (by which we must mean the occurrence of something unexpected) necessitates a regrouping of the established capital combination, and this will obviously have implications for labor resources as well.

The success or failure of an individual production plan depends crucially on the nature of other individual plans in the market. Only if all plans are consistent with one another will they all succeed. Plan inconsistency implies plan failure. Plan failure implies plan revision which implies capital reshuffling. Every plan is based on the expectations of the planner. If the plan fails, it will be revised and a new plan, based on new expectations, will emerge. Plan revision is thus the root of changes in the capital structure.

The perfect consistency of all individual production plans is a most unlikely occurrence. In any modern economy production plans are almost certain to be, at least in part, inconsistent. This means that producers will experience less than complete fulfillment of their expectations. Disappointed expectations may take such forms as inability to obtain necessary supplies, or to obtain them at the expected price, inability to sell the expected quantities of goods at the expected prices, inability to obtain the expected labor services at the expected prices and so on. Whether or not such disappointments will lead to significant changes in the production plan depends on just how unexpected they are. Every plan has a set of contingencies. Thus, some events will cause minor adjustments while others entail more drastic measures. It all depends on the nature of the change in expectations that the event produces.

Lachmann has analyzed this revision of expectations in a manner that anticipates the modern notion of "rational expectations."[3]

> The business man who forms an expectation is doing precisely what a scientist does when he formulates a working hypothesis. Both, business expectations and scientific hypothesis serve the same purpose; both reflect an attempt at cognition and orientation in an imperfectly known world, both embody imperfect knowledge to be tested and improved by later experience.[4]

Furthermore:

> . . . the formation of expectations is incidental to the diagnosis of the situation as a whole in which one has to act. How is this done? We analyse the situation, as we see it, in terms of *forces* to which we attribute various degrees of strength. We disregard what we believe to be *minor forces* and state our expectations in terms of the results we expect the operation of the *major forces* to have. Which forces we regard as major and minor is of course a matter of judgment. . . . In general, we shall be inclined to treat forces working at random as minor forces, since we know nothing about their origin and direction, and are therefore unable to predict the result of their operation. We treat as major forces those about whose origin and direction we think we know something. This means that in assessing the significance of price changes observed in the past for future changes we shall tend to neglect those we believe to have been due to random causes, and to confine our attention to those we believe due to more "permanent" causes.[5]

Thus, some price changes, if they are regarded as signaling fundamental permanent causes, will produce significant plan revisions, while others, those regarded as random events, will produce no such revision and thus have no resource allocation implications. The applicability of this to situations of inflation should be obvious

> . . . the really operative forces will [not] be recognized at once. That must depend on the insight, vigilance, and intelligence of the market. Experience shows, for instance, that an inflation is hardly ever recognised as such in its initial stages, at least in a society which has no prior experience of it.[6]

Whatever its motivating cause, a plan revision entails the *substitution* of some resources for others. Substitutability is a phenomenon of change. It is part of the process of capital regrouping that follows upon the revision of disappointed (or surprised) expectations. Thus, while complementarity is an aspect of any given plan, substitutability is an aspect of contemplated *changes* to the plan.[7] Together these two concepts characterize different aspects of the capital structure, namely its coherence and its adaptability. Whether or not the capital structure is able to successfully adapt to change is a question to which we shall have to return.

III

It is possible to describe a plan in terms of some common components. Each production plan entails the use of specific resources in combination with one another. This capital (including human capital) combination is accomplished for the purpose of producing and selling particular outputs. The capital resources are of two types: operating assets (like machines, buildings and automobiles) and reserve assets (like inventories of raw materials and, most importantly, cash balances). These reserve assets serve to increase the adaptability of the plan to changes. Changes in inventories or in cash balances are the natural response to other unexpected changes. And if the latter are seen as a result of random nonpermanent causes they may be the only responses. Other aspects of the plan, notably its operating assets and the labor attendant to them, may be left intact.

However, in addition to performing this well-known "shock absorber" role, changes in reserve assets also serve as barometers of plan success or failure. Unsold stocks and unused materials are indicative of problems as are unplanned stock shortages and cash drains. If they persist they suggest the need to alter the structure and composition of the operating assets.

Following Lachmann we may imagine a firm that makes production decisions once every period.[8] During period t_1, it has a capital combination of the form

$$kA;\ lB;\ mC;\ \ldots$$

where $A, B, C \ldots$ are different types of equipment and $k, l, m \ldots$ are positive constants. At the end of t_1, as a result of its experience, the firm decides to alter this combination for period t_2 to

$$l'B;\ m'C;\ n'D;\ \ldots$$

where $l < l'$ and $m > m'$, and D is a type of equipment not hitherto used by the firm. The firm will therefore have to sell kA and $(m - m')C$ and buy $(l' - l)B$ and $n'D$. What this will imply for the firm's cash balances depends on the market prices of A, B, C, and D, and these depend upon the actions of other firms. However, in general there is no reason to expect that the proceeds of the assets sold will just suffice to buy the ones acquired. It must then be true that

$$kAp_A + (m - m')Cp_C + Z = n'Dp_D + (l' - l)Bp_B \qquad (1)$$

where $p_A \ldots p_D$ are prices and Z is the fall in cash reserves. Changes in

$p_A \ldots p_D$ from period to period reflect capital gains and losses that indicate the value of the resources in this and alternative uses. Z (relative to its expected level) is an indicator of the firm's success or failure in producing and selling its outputs. If n firms reshuffle their capital combinations in a similar way and sell their discarded equipment to each other (i.e., we imagine a closed market), then

$$Z_1 + Z_2 + \ldots + Z_n = 0 \qquad (2)$$

implying a windfall for some firms. A negative Z implies greater financial strength. Changes in money holdings are thus not necessarily an indication of changes in the demand for money. It is often more meaningfully interpreted as a *result* of unexpected change and plan revision.

In addition to the operating and reserve assets which constitute the essential components of the structure of the firm's production plan, there exist financial assets (of which money is really an element). Financial assets serve as instruments for the obtaining of the necessary physical assets, and, in an important way, the value of the firm's financial assets reflects the value of its physical assets which, in turn, reflect its degree of planning success.

In the economy as a whole many firms will be acting in the manner described, planning and replanning their production activities. Out of the interaction between them and the economic environment, will emerge a flow of goods and services. It is as a result of the individual production plans that production occurs. The logic of these interacting plans provides the logic of the capital structure. At the firm level, the entrepreneur-manager establishes the plan structure. At the market level, the market process establishes the capital structure. Successful plans are rewarded, unsuccessful plans are punished. In this way, those capital combinations that prove themselves survive at the expense of those that do not. In a perfectly stable economic environment this would mean that a stable capital structure, consisting only of sustainable capital combinations, would eventually be established. All production plans would be consistent with one another. No surprises or disappointments would occur. The capital structure would be perfectly integrated. We may refer to it as a "sustainable capital structure."

In reality, no capital structure is perfectly sustainable. Its existence would imply a world devoid of technological progress. The latter necessarily implies capital reshuffling as some resources are rendered obsolete and others find unexpected uses. The normal course of economic progress implies the unavoidable failure of some plans and the reallocation of resources. In this way, the market process tends towards the integration of capital into a sustainable structure. But, because change is incessant, the process is never complete and never works perfectly. "Success" of a plan is in part a matter of interpretation, and "failure" may lead to "inappropriate" action. Signals have to be subjectively interpreted and acted upon. Thus, the stability of a market economy rests, in the final analysis, on the dominance of capital integrating forces over forces of disintegration. The latter exist, but we should normally not expect them to predominate. There should, by the law of large numbers and the law of markets, be at least as many gains as losses. Successes should at least balance failures.

The predominance of failures in one period followed by the predominance of successes in another, is one way of characterizing an economic cycle. It is thus something of a mystery.

The problem may be posed another way. The failure of a plan may be characterized as an economic error. It appears, in retrospect, as a misallocation of resources. In general, though we expect errors to occur, we should not a priori expect them to occur en masse. What then explains the "clustering of errors" characteristic of a recession?

IV

Part of an answer surely has to do with the existence of *plan complementarities* and *capital specificity and durability*. Insofar as plans depend on each other for their success, some more so than others, the failure of one set of plans may set in motion a series of failures. Since plans embody specific durable capital that cannot be rapidly depreciated, plan failures imply capital losses. There is thus a cumulative process of the kind that Keynes envisioned, that accompanies the capital regrouping process. In normal circumstances, however, similar processes should work in reverse as some planners exceed their goals and experience capital gains. Still, an observed cluster of errors may often be the chance result of simple uncertainty inevitable in the capital formation process. Cycles, in the sense of retrospectively identified coherences of selected economic aggregates, are probably an inevitable feature of market economies.

There is reason to believe, however (and this is the greater part of our answer), that economic policy exaggerates the concentration of errors in time and space. The logic of modern political processes suggests that biases exist that push the economy towards the successive adoption and abandonment of unsustainable capital structures. In more familiar terms economic policy causes malinvestment.

In a majoritarian democracy, with frequent elections, the incentives facing policy makers favor the sponsorship of specific investment projects. Elected politicians face the problem of reelection. Votes can be "bought" with promises of subsidies for the needy projects of their constituencies. Promises will not be believed in the absence of a track record. The individual politicians will thus attempt to secure for his/her constituency the largest possible subsidies consistent with the demands of other politicians and consistent with constitutional financial constraints. Though appointed government officials may balk, they serve at the pleasure of the elected officials. In the long run they must therefore spend the funds appropriated. In fact, since their salaries depend on it, they have an incentive to spend all funds appropriated lest their needs appear too modest.

Catering to the interests of particular constituencies implies attempting to distribute wealth in a particular way. It involves supporting the production plans of some producers at the expense of others. It is entirely rational for the producers so favored to respond by investing in capital combinations whose success depends on the promised support, as long as they believe that that support is likely to be enduring. The capital structure will thus be affected. Resources will be attracted to the subsidized sectors. The fate of these subsidized activities is importantly related to the logic of the government financing process.

The appropriation of funds for specific projects is a two-step affair. The projects are decided upon, then the revenue is found. Revenue raised to pay for government expenditure is, in general, not earmarked for specific projects. The latter are paid for out of general revenues. This means that it is impossible to tie a particular tax to a particular expenditure. It is never clear who actually pays for a project financed out of general revenue. Thus, if the project should fail it is not clear who really pays the price besides those immediately affected. Losing other peoples' money is naturally less painful than losing one's own, especially when the "other people" don't know who they are. The incentive for cost control is thus less intense for public than for private projects. In this way expenditures are biased upwards.

In addition, however (because of this free rider problem), there is a tendency for the total demand for expenditure by politicians (to meet their commitments to their constituents) to exceed the revenue available from taxation and fees. Even after the total of such claims has been pared down, there is likely to remain a deficit between income and expenditure. This deficit can be financed in two ways; by borrowing from the private sector or by money creation, i.e., inflation. If the government elects the former the result will be higher interest rates. This effect is reinforced by the fact that a government borrower may be inclined to pay more for loans than private investors in the knowledge (or expectation) that future interest payments can (in the last resort) be financed by increased taxation or money creation.

However, since higher interest rates are politically unpopular, there remains a strong temptation to resort to the second method of deficit financing. Money creation leads naturally after a while to price increases in general, including the prices of the capital and labor resources used in the projects that it financed. Thus, the real value of the original subsidy tends to diminish over time. Even if this is anticipated, however, the production plan may still be implemented. First, the short-term gains may still be attractive. Second, and more important, once a project has been started, higher than anticipated costs may lead to increasing appropriations rather than to abandonment—at least for a while. If this happens, expenditure will tend to accelerate.

This effect is reinforced by another factor. That is, those projects financed by government subsidies tend to be losers. In other words, they are less likely than other projects to survive the market test. If this were not true, they would not use the political process, as opposed to the market process, to the extent that they do. At least we may say that those projects, or those parts of projects, whose viability depends on government sponsorship, would not survive in the private marketplace. This means that, as their costs rise as a result of general inflationary financing, their viability disappears unless more financing is forthcoming.

We may now draw some implications of the argument of this section so far. To the extent that politicians are interested in winning reelection they will rationally tend to concentrate on the specific effects of their policies. Inflation may thus be seen to result from the efforts of economic interest groups in using the political process to improve their relative positions. It is rational for them to do this even if it implies trying to divide up the total value of production into shares that sum to more than 100 percent. Obviously this struggle to divide up the whole in this way must fail in part. Even so, no influential political group will find it reasonable to withdraw. For to do so would impair its share even more. Likewise, it is rational for politicians to continue to support the claims and to rely on money creation as the finance of last resort, even though they know that this behavior on the part of all will lead to a vicious spiral.

Money creation is a politically attractive form of government finance because its costs are not obvious or at least are less obvious than the alternatives of taxation and high interest borrowing. Congress votes deficits because a majority of its members favor (or do not oppose) the spending programs involved. These spending programs are on specific projects for the benefit of specific groups of people. The beneficiaries are fairly clear. But the general nature of government revenue, and the option of money creation, imply that the cost bearers are not easy to identify. In a nutshell

> Government monopoly over [money] severs [the] link between [benefits and costs]. It now becomes possible to enact or expand a program designed to benefit one set of citizens without having to curtail a program designed to benefit another set or having to increase taxes. Positive promises can be made without negative offsets, for the excess of the desire to spend over the means to pay for such spending can be bridged through money creation.[9]

V

There comes a point, however, when the financing spiral must be broken. If, as we have argued, the efficacy of the original subsidy tends to diminish over time as inflation proceeds, or simply because costs tend not to be contained, the periodic amounts necessary to keep the project going tend to grow. At first, writing off sunk costs, commitment to the project leads to accelerated financing. If there are many projects in this category, this will imply growing budgetary pressures. Rising taxation, accelerating inflation and high interest rates are the likely long term results. Avoiding or curing these must imply cutting expenditures. And cutting expenditures must imply abandoning specific projects. Eventually pressure will build up to bring this about. In nations anxious to avoid the costs of inflation it will happen sooner. In those that try to spend their way out of the dilemma it will happen later but be more severe. In those nations that never get the budgetary process under control the collapse is extreme.

This then is the answer we seek. By encouraging the formation of a capital structure that cannot be sustained policy makers sow the seeds of recession. The "cluster of errors" is inherent in the cluster of government supported projects. The projects rise and fall together.

Individual producers are led to establish capital combinations whose profitability depends on government support. Though they may know that in the long run they will not be able to rely on this support, each historical episode is unique enough that the precise course and timing of cyclical events cannot be predicted. Short run capital gains are made in the boom phase and with some astute forecasting and a little bit of luck, the losses that come with the recession can be avoided. Indeed they are often borne by the taxpayer. Entrepreneurs are quite rational in gambling with the political process. They form capital combinations in the pursuit of profit, but under the assumption of a particular policy regime. And when the regime changes they must reshuffle these capital combinations, discarding some goods and disemploying labor in the process. The total of the Z's of these projects is positive and constitutes a negative cash drain on the rest of the economy (see equation 2 above). When the history of the period comes to be written a "cycle" is observed.

NOTES

1. Ludwig M. Lachmann, "Complementarity and Substitution in the Theory of Capital," *Economica*, 14 (May 1947), pp. 108–19.
2. Ludwig M. Lachmann, *Capital and Its Structure* (London: London School of Economics and Political Science, 1956), reprinted with a new Preface (Kansas City: Sheed Andrews & McMeel, 1978); Ludwig M. Lachmann, *Capital, Expectations, and the Market Process* (Kansas City: Sheed Andrews & McMeel, 1977).
3. See Lachmann, *Capital and Its Structure*, op. cit., chap. II.
4. Ibid., p. 23.
5. Ibid., pp. 23–4. Emphasis in original.
6. Ibid., p. 32.
7. See note 1 above.
8. *Capital and Its Structure*, op. cit., pp. 44–6.
9. Richard Wagner, "Boom and Bust: The Political Economy of Economic Disorder," *Journal of Libertarian Studies* 4 (Winter 1980), pp. 1–37. "I have concentrated on the distortion of the capital structure, produced by explicit subsidies. Similar effects, however, result from implicit subsidies like tariffs, quotas and credit guarantees. With implicit subsidies the price is paid by the consumers and producers and does not involve taxpayers directly. However, the effects are similar to those of direct subsidies. In particular, the costs tend to rise over time, especially since the industries involved tend to fall further behind the competition against which they are protected (witness the steel industry and the farm sector). Thus, the degree of protection must either be increased or adjustments must be made and the longer the latter is postponed the larger it will be."

16 Beyond Choice

WILLI MEYER

I KNOWLEDGE, IGNORANCE, AND PSYCHOLOGY

One outstanding characteristic of Austrian economics is the stressing of the causal role of knowledge and of human mind in all human and social affairs. Hayek and Mises pointed to the much neglected role of knowledge as the main weakness of equilibrium theory.[1] They tried to show how the market process is likely to produce most of the information which is needed by economic agents and they claimed that such useful knowledge as the market provides cannot otherwise be got. Morgenstern attacked the idea that social scientists should, like physicists, aim at the prediction of economic and social variables. He stated the strong impossibility theorem: Any prediction of social events which is a causal factor for the predicted events must necessarily go wrong.[2] That this theorem is not true for logical reasons, as Morgenstern hoped to demonstrate, can today easily be shown in applying Brower's fix point theorem.[3] Nevertheless, as a synthetical proposition, the following conjecture of Morgenstern might be true: No publicly announced (and believed) prediction of economic events will come true if the prediction changes the information set on which individuals base their future actions.

Usually one assumes that utility maximizing choices presuppose full information about the available alternatives. Let us take this for granted. However, in most real cases the decision maker lacks some needed piece of information. Assume he can get all relevant information about some wanted objects by spending a certain amount of his resources. Is the fact that one knows precisely the information costs sufficient for utility maximization? I do not believe so.

To clarify, let us for example assume that there are two different objects, each believed to provide the same utility to the potential buyer.

The demand price for each of the different objects (say a library and a yacht offered by the widows of two late colleagues) may be $20,000. The two selling prices are not announced but information concerning each can be purchased for $500. In this case, where full information is available at a known price, the decision maker has to choose one out of four alternatives: a_1, buying information for object 1; a_2, buying information for object 2; a_3, buying information about both; a_4, keeping the money in his pocket. What can he do in order to maximize his utility? Let us for the sake of the argument disregard a_4. Probably, he can rank the three alternatives and a likely preference order would be a_1 indifferent to a_2; a_1 and a_2 preferred to a_3 (because the information which he can get choosing a_3 can as cheaply be gained if he chooses a_1 and thereafter, if he likes, a_2 or vice versa). But he has no rational reason to choose a_1 rather than a_2.

What the example demonstrates is that our decision maker cannot avoid risk: He may spend $500 to learn that he can or cannot afford to buy the library; in either case he may go on and spend another $500 to learn that he can or cannot afford buying the yacht or to learn that the yacht (or the library) is after all the better option. *After* each decision to invest $500 for information, he may regret or rejoice at his choice, but, in advance, he has nothing but hope or fear to guide his choice. Thus, when reason cannot help, the irrational faculties of man will probably dominate his tendencies to act and that means: one has to look for some *psychological* mechanism or force in order to explain the ensuing behavior.[4]

However, the research program of subjectivism seems to advise economics not to go beyond the plainly given fact of human choice.[5] For Mises, causal explanations of human actions are *not possible* and search for motives to act is *unnecessary*. It is not that Mises believed in uncaused events of any kind, quite the contrary: "All that happens was, under the prevailing conditions, bound to happen ... because the forces operating on its production were more powerful than the counteracting forces"[6] But Mises was convinced that there are *unknowable* causes that give rise to those ideas which induce man to make a decision.[7] And since "there is only one motive that determines all the actions of all men, viz., to remove, directly or indirectly, as much as possible any uneasiness felt" further search for human motives is superfluous.[8] The methodological reason for this waste-of-time proposition is Mises' belief in his apriorism.[9]

Popper has recently shown that neither in the case of human action nor in the case of classical physics is the principle of accountability universally satisfied.[10] That is, we can in neither case "calculate from our prediction task (in conjunction with our theories, of course) the requisite degree of precision of initial conditions."[11] In other words, we nowhere are able to account for all causes of a certain event. By analogy to natural science one can therefore say that Mises' epistemological impossibility proposition as to causal explanations of action is in no way sufficient to prove that one never can discover some laws of how the working of the human mind might affect human choice.

As to Mises' view that we already possess the relevant knowledge of human motivation due to his principle of praxeology I only would like to say that this principle is presumably a true metaphysical proposition but that it lacks empirical content. It is the responsibility of science to go *beyond the obvious*, the bare fact of choice, and to rise *above the metaphysical* in order to approach some worthwhile truth about human nature, i.e., one should try to invent hypotheses on the whys and hows of human action.[12]

As Lachmann[13] has already observed there is within the camp of the subjectivists at least Shackle's impressive work on decision making[14] that demonstrates how one can go beyond Mises' subjectivism. Shackle has shown that one *can* build a nonvacuous theory of the working of the human mind. This theory starts with the fact the people usually lack perfect knowledge about future events. Under these conditions Shackle supposes everyone to concentrate his attention only upon certain elements, focus gain and focus loss, of one's set of imagined and strictly competing conjectures of what is possible. The focus elements are derivable from assumptions of how interest in prospective gain (or fear of prospective loss) combines with degrees of possible surprise (a measure of the subjectively felt likeliness of a future event) to produce in the mind of the individual a certain amount of attraction. Focus elements are characterized by maximal attractiveness (ascendancy).

This "language of expectations"[15] may, like any human-made theory, entail true and false ideas about the nature of the human mind. Anyway, it is remarkable to note that the subjectivist Shackle who stresses the creativity of human choice nevertheless seems to favour a methodologically unified approach to scientific knowledge when he states: "Physical law and psychological law can both be looked on as parts of natural law."[16] On the basis of this naturalism, Shackle holds that economics is refined psychology. "Economic theory", he says, "is an endeavour to systematize part of psychological law."[17] Let us now take a look at some other hypotheses of social scientists that may shed some light on how human mind, embedded and somehow connected with human body, might work.

II COGNITIVE NEEDS

Believe it or not, psychology had lost its mind for years and is now on the road to get it back. This is in one crude sentence the content of the cognitive revolution in psychology.[18] One aspect of this revolution is the recognition that the older view of the brain as the servant of the stomach cannot be upheld; instead of this one-way relationship, one has to assume a more symmetrical relation. At times cognition is an end in itself. And, most important, the *content* of the ideas which satisfy the cognitive needs is sometimes so powerful a motive that it is able to override all other motivational influences, even the impulses to self-preservation. How can one otherwise account for the countless religious martyrs and political prisoners undergoing torture and death in the service of their faith or their party? Or, how can one otherwise understand stories like the following? An assistant pastor and a layman of the Holiness Church of God in Jesus Name, of Carson Spring, Tennessee, died after drinking a mixture of strychnine and water to test their faith in the Bible, where in Mark 16: 16–18 it is asserted that "if they drink any deadly thing, it shall not hurt them" (*Newsweek*, April 23, 1973).[19]

Looking not only at the behavior of a single subject, like some psychologists, but at the history of mankind, like Max Weber, one cannot but recognize the importance of the cognitive needs of the human breed.

As is well known, Max Weber tried to give an explanation of some salient features of the cultural and economic development of the whole of mankind from the dark days of the past up to our century. How is it that we have rational capitalism in some and not in other cultures? How is it that we observe at certain places of our earth the combination of a legal state, bureaucratic organizations and rational managed business firms? How is it that the productivity of human beings is so fantastically high in some and so desperately poor in other parts of this planet? To these deep questions he gave a complicated answer: The details of this historical process can only be explained by some millions of singular historical facts. But *one* of the main causes of the various economic and cultural states of our day has been the particular kind of interaction of the *practical beliefs* of certain influential societal strata—

warriors and knights, civil servants, peasants, intellectuals, tradesmen, and craftsmen—with the great religious belief systems. This is really a bold conjecture.[20]

One basic theoretical idea of Max Weber is, in my view, the assumption of a strong need for a cognitive order of all things of vital importance which happen in this world and which resist an easy or natural explanation. In those as in our days the world was full of sorrow, grief, and pain; there were wealthy and healthy people as well as the poor and sick; death was the sure lot of all of them. In such a situation it seems quite natural that people ask for the legitimation of this unequal distribution of happiness in those days as in ours. Besides, the need for good reasons to account for their own happiness will be felt by the rich and healthy people too, perhaps somewhat less urgently than by the poor. One is not content with the good luck one has; one tries to make sure, i.e., to provide good reasons, that one deserves what one possesses.

Where there is a demand there will be a supply; furthermore, when public goods, which then were provided by the tribal gods, rain, sunshine, victory over enemies, good quarry, cannot fulfil individual needs such as salvation from individual sorrow, then eventually there will emerge a supply of the relevant private good. And, to extend the market analogy, as there are usually more people on the lower end of the happiness-unhappiness or rich-poor spectrum, the market for this private good could be expected to boom. Weber explicitly uses the market analogy to explain the emergence of the great salvation systems.

Yet, there is a second basic theoretical idea in Weber's argument. It is the *content* of the various religious beliefs, he says, which governs the ways in which people manage their conduct of life. Of course, Weber knew that not ideas but interests (material as well as immaterial) will determine the daily actions of man. But the general direction of these actions, the particular way in which they are exercised, will be mainly influenced by the content of the accepted world view. For it is this world view that defines what constitutes the relevant salvation good and that defines the states from which one will be redeemed. Moreover, the accepted world view tells one the efficient means to get the salvation goods. Thus, it makes a difference whether a religious doctrine makes one believe that contemplation, mystic worldflight and the like will bring one the possession of unity with God and eternal happiness or whether one's faith makes one feel that one is God's tool in this world and that one has been commanded to change this world into God's beloved place. The motive to show restless activity will be much enhanced when there is no promise that one will be redeemed one day and when the only proof of one's predestination is success in one's daily work.

In our days the old world views have lost much of their power. There are new ideas or ideologies to give this world a firm meaning. We can observe today new prophets and new followers. Whatever they may do, for good or bad, will not be understood if we disregard Weber's two ideas; that man has cognitive needs and that the intellectual products—the very content of the accepted ideas—which are determined to satisfy the cognitive needs may have far-reaching consequences for the human behavior.

III INDIVIDUAL AND SOCIAL PERSPECTIVES

There is in social science a suggestive idea which says that what a person does rests highly upon his definition of the situation. To this one should add with Shibutani that the manner in which he consistently defines a situation depends on his perspective.

"A perspective," to quote Shibutani, "is an organized view of one's world, what is taken for granted about the attributes of objects, of events and of human nature. The environment in which men live is an order of things remembered and expected as well as perceived. It includes assumptions of what is plausible and what is possible. . . . [One's] perspective is an outline scheme which, running ahead of experience, defines and guides it."[21]

The first thing I would like to note in regard to the idea that perspectives are relevant to human behavior is that it makes every man a scientist. The one author I have found to make this view an explicit basis of his theorizing is G. H. Kelly. "Let us then," Kelly says, "instead of occupying ourselves with man-the-biological-organism or man-the-lucky-guy, have a look at man-the-scientist."[22] Kelly believes that man can best be understood as a being that proceeds by permanently using, developing and elaborating on alternative constructs of his external as well as his internal world. As a general point of departure he takes the position of what he calls "constructive alternativism", and as the basic postulate of his theory, followed by eleven corollaries, he takes the proposition: "A person's processes are psychologically channelized by the ways in which he anticipates events."[23]

A second point to make with respect to the perspective-paradigm is that it naturally leads to the question where the perspective of a person comes from. Are perspectives impressed upon people by their reproductive conditions, by the brute requirements for survival, by their location within the social strata of society, by mere contact with other people, by contact with certain other people—mothers, teachers, party leaders, priests, scientists (real and self appointed ones), methodologists—or by contact with dead people in reading their books? Further, do people passively accept what they listen to or do they reject or change transmitted perspectives? Are there various degrees of commitment to one's accepted perspective? Do people change their perspectives like their shirts? What are the relations between different existing perspectives? Do they give rise to peaceful coexistence, cold war, hot war, or emotionless segregation? Are perspectives really powerful or are they simply the invention of mildly schizophrenic social scientists? These are a lot of questions, certainly more than I will try to answer.

It may be helpful to distinguish *explicit perspectives*—the result of preaching and teaching—and *implicit perspectives*—mainly the result of tradition or of simply being with others. Of course, what today is accepted as a matter of course could have been the very central element of preaching years or centuries ago. This remark may serve as a reminder that implicit perspectives or implicit parts of an explicit perspective can be as important for guiding human behavior as explicit perspectives. Moreoever, one can argue that implicitly held convictions may be, on occasion, more powerful than explicitly held convictions because they block the ability to imagine alternatives. In other words, one of the important things one can know about a person is what he takes for granted.

The only way to become infected with a perspective is through social intercourse of a kind. Sociologists believe therefore that the participation in various communication networks will account for the existence of different perspectives because it seems unthinkable that, even in quite totalitarian regimes, all communication channels can be centrally controlled. And as one can assume that anyone who doesn't want to hear the music can switch off the radio, it seems safe to assume that he who keeps tuned to some broadcaster probably shares to a certain degree the perspective of that broadcaster. Thus, we should expect in each society the existence of various and different shared perspectives which give rise to various reference groups to address oneself to and various social worlds to live in. These perspectives do have behavioral consequences. Thus, in level of aspiration experiments, Negro college students, when informed that white college students had achieved a certain level in the task, reduced their aspiration levels more than the control group of Negro students did, when informed that the same fictitious standard of achievement had been achieved by other Negroes. The same, but in opposite direction, held true for white college students. The information of a fictitious Negro mark caused white students to increase their own estimates.[24]

As an example of what power an explicit perspective is sometimes able to exercise one could point to radical political groups in Western capitalistic societies, perhaps also to the so called dissenters in some communist countries. As Kornhauser has observed,[25] the radical who is effectively insulated from influences outside the radical movement does not simply change jobs to gain more money, nor does he expend major energies to gain promotion and to advance his career. He cuts ties to all people who are not radicals as well. He terminates ties outside the party not merely because he is constrained to do so, but also because he feels uneasy with people who do not share his central mission in life. Among the members of the radical groups there usually develops warm bonds, brotherhood, sisterhood and the like. It needs, apparently, no more than bread, sex and an emotion-loaded, eschatologically oriented perspective to make young people happy, at least for a while.

An equally important, although less spectacular, way to study the formation and development of perspectives and their consequences for human behavior, i.e., thinking, feeling, and acting, is to consider the history of scientific ideas. Instead of referring time and again to Thomas Kuhn's view of history of knowledge as a permanent change of paradigms, I would rather like to draw your attention to the ideas of his proper forerunner, the physician Dr. Ludwig Fleck. This totally unknown author, rarely quoted except by Kuhn, invented in 1935 the notion of a *Denkstil* (style or mode of thinking) by which he meant the shared perspective of a *Denkkollektiv* (community of scientists). Fleck uses this concept in pretty much the same way as Kuhn uses his paradigm concept. In order to fight eighteenth- and nineteenth-century philosophers' subject/object quarrel in epistemology, earlier Carnapism, and the layman's veni-vidi-vici-theory of knowledge—one wants to know something, one makes an observation or exercises an experiment, and, hocus pocus, one knows—Fleck tries to show what it takes for a scientific fact to be eventually established. As a very instructive case he uses the Wassermann-reaction for the diagnosis of venereal disease. (I will not comment on the details of this reaction.)

As to the process of knowledge formation and as to the proper understanding of this process, Fleck argues that one has to distinguish three factors: the individual, the *Denkkollectiv* and objective reality. By *Denkkollektiv* he means a community of people exchanging ideas and sharing perspectives, the *Denkkollektiv* is the carrier of a special *Denkstil*. Knowing (*Erkennen*) is for Fleck the most social conditioned activity of man, and knowledge (*Erkenntnis*) has to be regarded simply as the social product. Thus he notes that all leitmotives of scientific theories tend to originate in community related concepts; one of his examples is the medieval conception of syphilis as punishment for lust (syphilis was then labeled lust contagion). Moreover, as Fleck rightly notes, the very foundation of our scientific discourse, the language, implies a philosophy of our culture. Even single words are marks or cores of complex theories. Whose philosophy and whose theories do these linguistic entities represent?

The social character of scientific activity is not without consequences. Words, which were originally used simply as labels, will become slogans; sentences, which originally were meant simply as statements, will become battle cries. After their transformation, they gain magic power (Fleck's wording); their main impact is not on behalf of their logical structure or theoretical content but because they are with us. Examples which come easily to one's mind are critical rationalism, positivism, dialectical materialism, logical empiricism, socialism, liberalism, methodological individualism, methodological holism, historicism, subjective value theory, labor value theory, consumer sovereignty, consumer manipulation, and so forth. (Fleck quotes, of course, examples from biology and medicine.) Meeting such concepts or phrases in scientific contexts makes at once friends and foes. This very social character of scientific activity generates new emotions and motives: propaganda, imitation, authority, competition, solidarity, hostility, friendship. All this is not very crucial for the logical aspects of theories, and it is not of much importance for the abstract truth content of a theory, but it will influence the factual assessment of competing theories by individual scientists and, anyway, it must not be forgotten if one wants to understand scientific activity and the stage science has reached so far. Fleck's and Kuhn's view may help us to recognize the similarities of fashions, ideologies, religious beliefs, and scientific theories as well as their differences. The central notion behind all these insights is the idea that man's living will be guided by perspectives.[26]

IV CULTURAL VALUES AND RISK TAKING

In addition to moral obligations and selfish inclinations there are various grades of normlike expectations which are based unwittingly on a widely shared system of values of a society. These values refer to various traits of human behavior and come normally to people's mind as an idealization of some kind: to be a brave man, to be a good catholic, communist, or citizen, to be a good husband, and the like. The problem is, do the implied cultural values of these and of other idealizations exert a sensible and measurable influence even on the behavior of those who have not explicitly committed themselves to these values? Sociologists and social psychologists believe that they do.

The piece of work I would like to describe now is quite interesting because it is not one of the merely descriptive variety. It originated from theoretically unexpected experimental outcomes and developed from the endeavors to explain them. The unexpected outcome is the "risky-shift" phenomenon of group decisions; the one explanation I will briefly mention is the cultural value explanation.[27]

Up to the early 1960s any good sociologist and social psychologist believed in the theory that in order to reach a compromise or consensus group members should direct their influence to the most deviant among them. Group dynamics were understood as averaging individuals' opinions. In 1961 Stoner demonstrated that a person's willingness to take risks increases after participating in group discussion of a problem. The risky-shift phenomenon was born and aroused much experimental work thereafter. However, the subject's "risky decisions" which were at stake in the experiments were not real decisions implying real profits or losses but mere thought experiments, so to speak. This is apt sharply to reduce an economist's interest in this kind of research, but this aspect of the experiments is not relevant for my purpose now.[28]

The cultural value explanation which is originally due to Brown assumes that people are led in their (verbal) behavior by the prevailing cultural values if they deal with problems for which the respective value is of some importance.[29] In other words, if a certain stimulus situation elicits a cultural value, then people tend to orient their (verbal) behavior to this abstract standard and not to the stated opinion of other people, similar to them or not. Ideal, not empirically lived standards are assumed to be the fix points for human beings. This general hypothesis is accompanied by another one which relates to the basic need of positive self-evaluation. In regard to this need the cultural value explanation entails the view that everyone likes to think of himself as being much nearer to the ideal than most other people. Should he observe himself not to be one of the leading ones in respect to the relevant ideal then there will be a strong pressure to speed up in order to catch up. In short: the maxim is not keeping up with the Joneses, but striving to be the best Jones. The real Joneses are needed nevertheless to define one's own position.

Now, if the experimental design which produced the risky shift could be shown to elicit the cultural value of risktaking or caution, as the case may be, and if group discussion could be shown to make the respected elicited value more salient, then the observed risky shift is explained, because it is the logical consequence of the just mentioned initial conditions and the two general hypotheses.[30] (Incidentally, previously observed exceptions from the risky shift could be explained as caution shifts). The discussion with other people is needed not mainly for comparative purposes, as in Festinger's theory of social comparison processes, but to be able to define what adequate risk really means under specific circumstances. The abstract ideal that one should be daring will not tell one whether one's own behavior accepts the proper degree of risk.

The researchers were able to confirm the singular hypotheses about the initial conditions. This is equivalent with providing the required explanation, provided that the two general hypotheses could be accepted as true. However, further research showed some unexpected problems. The theory predicts that homogeneous as well as heterogeneous groups—in terms of the initial willingness to take risk—should produce the risky shift, the more heterogeneous the group the more marked the shift. In fact, there is considerable evidence for a positive relationship between the range of the initial risk scores among group members and the magnitude of risky shift produced. But homogeneous groups did not shift at all! Moreover, if the experimenter engineered a group majority consensus which was more conservative than naïve subject's initial decision, subjects exhibited marked conformity to the artificially established group consensus. As stated by Dion, Baron and Miller, "These results suggest that, when the effects of value are pitted against those of normative influence [i.e., pressure of majority, W.M.], the latter primarily determine risk taking."[31]

As it stands, the quote above would serve as a nice example of an ad hoc explanation, were it not for the famous Asch experiments which demonstrate how much an individual's independent opinion can be changed through the firm stated view of a majority. However, the explanation of this empirically demonstrated effect is far from satisfactory. The view of Asch that majority views tend to overcome the individual's independent judgment has been criticized by Moscovici and Faucheux.[32] All experiments have been reinterpreted in terms of the needs of an individual for cognitive stability, intrapersonal as well as interpersonal. This view interprets the Asch experiments as a certain kind of a bargaining process between the deviant and the majority. It stresses the cognitive work done during the influence process and fights primarily the conformity bias in the earlier interpretation. The underlying theoretical approach leads one to predict that a determined minority may influence a majority to change its opinion. Experimental evidence for this prediction is provided which demonstrates that it is not the mere number of opponents but the property of their stated view which may exert the greater influence. The greater the internal consistency of a view and the less the doubts in the correctness of the view the more likely other people tend to accept this view. This interpretation of the influence process sheds another light on the nature of the miraculous human mind.

V CONCLUDING REMARKS

Good science should tell the truth about the nature of the objects it deals with. Thus, economics should entail some truth about the nature of human beings because the actions of millions of people constitute the facts and events economists try to explain.

Modern economics models man as a choosing machine that is able to use available resources optimally in order to get the most utility. In these models necessary knowledge is known or can be bought from the environment, and the uncertainty about the future outcomes of present actions can be accounted for by substituting certain knowledge about a distribution of the relevant variables (profits, wages, interest rates, exchange rates, length of own life, own health status, etc.) for the unknowable singular values of those variables.

Models which use the aforementioned simplifications can, up to a certain degree, account for a lot of observable facts. But the compatibility of a theory with some facts is no guarantee for the truth of the assumptions of that theory. For example, the proposition that utility maximizers respond to an income compensated increase in price with a reduction of demand cannot be confirmed by the observation of a decreasing *market* demand curve. The same observation, reduced market demand with increased market price, can be deduced on the assumption of nonrational behavior.[33] Generally, any finite set of observations can be derived from numerous different assumptions. Moreover, false assumptions may entail true conclusions.[34] In short, the instrumental value of a theory for the explanation and prediction of observations gives no certainty as to the truth value of the premises that logically entail the sentences which describe those observations.

Because of the methodological principle, due to David Hume, that facts cannot prove theories, everyone who wants social science to tell the truth or to come near the truth should argue against all the unbelievable aspects of man as the choosing machine, if he can. The speculations, observations, and experimentations of sociologists and psychologists cannot, in fact, refute the economic theory of behavior because there is, after all, much truth in this theory.[35] But the views developed within the social sciences outside of economics give rise to some doubts whether human action can really be understood if one does not go beyond choice.

NOTES

1. F. A. von Hayek, "Economics and Knowledge," *Economica*, IV (N.S. 1937), 33–45. L. von Mises, *Nationalökonomie. Theorie des Handelns und des Wirtschaftens* (Geneva: Editions Union, 1940), pp. 284, 397ff.
2. O. Morgenstern, *Wirtschaftsprognosen* (Vienna: Julius Springer, 1928), p. 96.
3. E. Grunberg and F. Modigliani, "The Predictability of Social Events," *Journal of Political Economy*, 62 (1954), pp. 465–78; H. Simon, "The Effect of Prediction," *Public Opinion Quarterly*, 18 (1954), pp. 245–53.
4. If optimization of resource use requires that marginal benefits of an activity equal (or are not less than) its marginal costs then the existence of positive information costs will prevent an optimal use of one's resources. The argument is simply that, if the benefits of an information activity are related to the *content* of the information searched for, then one cannot in advance know what marginal benefits a certain search will produce. Therefore it is not possible to state in advance whether incurred information costs will pay. Of course, this is very similar to part of Lachmann's argument against the possibility of predictions in economics. I would like to quote from Shackle who used Lachmann's argument as the leitmotiv of his *Epistemics and Economics* (Cambridge: Cambridge University Press, 1972): "... The impossibility of prediction in economics follows from the fact that economic change is linked to change in knowledge, and future knowledge cannot be gained before its time ... Ludwig M. Lachmann, Metroeconomica, vol. xi (1959)." For related arguments against the possibility of maximization or optimization see Sidney G. Winter, "Optimization and Evolution in the Theory of the Firm," in *Adaptive Economic Models*, eds. R. H. Day and T. Groves (New York: Academic Press, 1975), pp. 81–5; P. Zweifel, "Identifizierung kommt vor Optimierung," *Zeitschrift für Wirtschafts- und Sozialwissenschaften*, 103 (1983), pp 1–26.

5. See my paper, "Ludwig von Mises und das subjektivistische Erkenntnisprogramm," *Wirtschaftspolitische Blätter*, 28 (1981), pp. 35–50.
6. L. von Mises, *The Ultimate Foundations of Economic Science* (Princeton, N.J.: D. van Nostrand, 1962), p. 59.
7. Mises, ibid., pp. 57–9. The basis for Mises' epistemological impossibility proposition is the presumed absolute individuality of any person.
8. Mises, ibid., p. 76.
9. For a methodological evaluation of Mises' apriorism see my paper mentioned in note 5 and Hans Albert, "Modell-Denken und historische Wirklichkeit," in *Ökonomisches Denken und soziale Ordnung*, ed. H. Albert (Tübingen: J. C. B. Mohr (Paul Siebeck), 1984), pp. 47–53.
10. K. R. Popper, *The Open Universe: An Argument for Indeterminism* (Totowa, N.J.: Rowman & Littlefield, 1982).
11. Popper, op. cit., p. 12.
12. For a modern treatise that shows how one can use scientific knowledge and philosophical arguments to understand the human mind see Mario Bunge, *The Mind-Body Problem. A Psychobiological Approach* (Oxford: Pergamon Press, 1980).
13. Ludwig M. Lachmann, "From Mises to Shackle: An Essay," *Journal of Economic Literature*, 14 (1976), pp. 58–60.
14. G. L. S. Shackle, *Decision, Order, and Time in Human Affairs*, 2nd ed. (Cambridge: Cambridge University Press, 1969).
15. Shackle, *Epistemics and Economics*, op. cit., chap. 34.
16. Shackle, *Decision, Order, and Time*, op. cit., p. 274.
17. Ibid.
18. W. N. Dember, "Motivation and the Cognitive Revolution," *American Psychologist*, 29 (1974), pp. 161–8.
19. Besides, there is some grain of truth in Mark. Schachter and Singer demonstrated that cognitions can control the emotional impact of neural arousal induced by an adrenalin injection; subject's pleasant or unpleasant feelings depended upon their perceived environment. Subjects looked presumably for a cognitive interpretation of their internal states. See S. Schachter and J. E. Singer, "Cognitive, Social, and Physiological Determinants of Emotional State," *Psychological Review*, 69 (1962), pp. 379–99.
20. M. Weber, "Einleitung in die Wirtschaftsethik der Weltreligionen," in *Max Weber: Soziologie, weltgeschichtliche Analysen, Politik*, 4th ed., ed. J. Winckelmann (Stuttgart: Alfred Kröner, 1968), pp. 398–441.
21. T. Shibutani, "Reference Groups and Social Control," in *Human Behavior and Social Processes*, ed. A. M. Rose (London: Routledge and Kegan Paul, 1962), p. 130.
22. G. A. Kelly, *A Theory of Personality. The Psychology of Personal Constructs* (New York: Norton, 1963), p. 4.
23. G. A. Kelly, op. cit., p. 46.
24. H. H. Hyman, "The Value System of Different Classes," in *Class, Status, and Power*, 2nd ed., eds. R. Bendix and S. M. Lipset (New York: Free Press, 1966), p. 496.
25. W. Kornhauser, "Social Basis of Political Commitment: A Study of Liberals and Radicals," in *Human Behavior and Social Processes*, op. cit.
26. L. Fleck, *Entstehung und Entwicklung einer wissenschaftlichen Tatsache:*

Einführung in die Lehre vom Denkstil und Denkkollektiv (Basel: Schwabe, 1935), chap. 2, sect. 4.

27. K. L. Dion, R. S. Baron, and N. Miller, "Why do Groups make Riskier Decisions?" in *Advances in Experimental Social Psychology*, ed. L. Berkowitz (New York: Academic Press, 1970), Vol. 5, pp. 305–77.
28. To describe the experimental design: Subjects were presented twelve hypothetical real-life situations which consisted each of two alternative courses of actions, a conservative and a risky one that was said to have a greater expected income. The task was to indicate what the odds for success would have to be before the subjects would advise a fictitious person to attempt the risky alternative.
29. R. Brown, *Social Psychology* (New York: The Free Press, 1965).
30. "To give a *causal explanation* of an event means to deduce a statement which describes it, using as premises of the deduction one or more *universal laws*, together with certain singular statements, the *initial conditions*." K. R. Popper, *The Logic of Scientific Discovery* (London: Hutchinson, 1959), p. 59.
31. K. L. Dion, R. S. Baron, and N. Miller, op. cit., p. 358.
32. S. Moscovici and C. Faucheux, "Social Influence, Conformity Bias, and the Study of active Minorities," in *Advances in Experimental Social Psychology*, ed. L. Berkowitz (New York: Academic Press, 1972), vol. 6, pp. 149–202.
33. See Warren C. Sanderson, "Does the Theory of Demand Need the Maximum Principle?" in *Nations and Households in Economic Growth*, eds. P. A. David and M. W. Reder (New York: Academic Press, 1974), pp. 173–221.
34. For example: From the false assumption: "all Germans know Bach's birth year" one can deduce the true conclusion: "there is at least one German who knows that Bach was born in 1685." Moreover, as logic teaches us, from a contradiction *any* statement can be derived.
35. See my paper "The Research Programme of Economics and the Relevance of Psychology," in *Social Psychology and Economics*, eds. W. Stroebe and W. Meyer (Leicester: The British Psychological Society, 1982), 3–13.

17 Mechanomorphism

KARL MITTERMAIER

I

It should not be hard to see what is meant by the made-up word which serves as the title of this paper. The word came to mind when Professor Lachmann winced visibly at the reference in a conversation to the reaction of a person, not in the sense that by common convention it was the person's turn to do something, but in the sense which may be suggested by the formulation of economic theory in terms of dependent and independent variables.

The physical sciences have been largely purged of anthropomorphisms, i.e., of implications of the influence of mind and purpose where in the perception of scientists there is no such influence. So high, apparently, is the esteem in which the physical sciences are held that the purge has been carried over even into intellectual fields concerned specifically with human actions and purposes. Mainstream economics endeavors to clarify economic issues by means of theories which are so unmistakably conceived along mechanical lines that economists sympathetic to a subjectivist outlook have good reason to complain of mechanomorphisms and to wish to carry out a counter purge.

However, as is so often the case, the matter is not quite so simple. Given the universal and pervasive use of metaphor and analogy, we do not really have a very strong argument against mechanical metaphors if that argument amounts to little more than stating that the world is not like that. It will be suggested below that it is worth our while to distinguish between an ontological subjectivism and a logic of subjectivism and that the latter may lead us to a rule or an ideal which may allow the former to have a more definite case against mechanomorphism. The rule or ideal may also suggest what it is in physical science that may be emulated with advantage even in the social sciences.

II

A scientist engages in anthropomorphism when he ascribes human attributes to what is otherwise recognized as inanimate or at least not human. By analogy we may say that an economist engages in mechanomorphism when he ascribes mechanical properties to what is otherwise recognized as an aspect of human affairs or when he treats an economic system as though it were a mechanical system. In its most general sense we may understand mechanics to be concerned with matter in motion. In the Newtonian formulation, a mechanical system involves concepts of space, time, force, point mass, and derivations from these.[1] Equilibrium clearly comes from this domain of thought and talk of equilibrating or market forces must be regarded as mechanomorphic. Consumption and saving, which normally are regarded as activities, acquire a mechanical aspect as macroeconomic aggregates. They are treated as though they were quantities of a substance, perhaps a liquid flowing through some kind of system—the conception Coddington called hydraulicism.[2]

It would be quite correct to say that these are metaphors, but misleading to say that they are merely metaphors. In the traditional view, metaphors are mere ornaments, picturesque ways of saying things that may also be expressed literally. In some cases this may be so, but in general metaphors are not quite so superficial. The subject of metaphors has been coming increasingly under the scrutiny of linguists and philosophers in recent years and though no consensus view appears to have been reached, there are some interesting analyses. George Lakoff and Mark Johnson argue convincingly (since the evidence is available to anyone with a tolerable command of English) that metaphorical expressions form coherent systems which reflect metaphorical conceptions.[3] For instance, we *set out* to prove something, *proceed* in a certain way and *arrive* at conclusions, as though we were on a journey. A theory needs a *solid foundation*, like a building, so that it is not easily *demolished*. It will *stand or fall* on the *strength* of an argument, which, if it is *shaky*, may *fall apart* or *collapse* and so on. Metaphors are not merely a matter of "rhetorical flourish," nor even of words alone, but also of thought and action. As the title of the book indicates, we live by metaphors; we perceive the world in terms of them and act accordingly. In our culture we not only pay and are paid by the hour, day, week, or month, but we say that we *spend*, *save*, or *waste* time, *spare* a little time for someone, and even live on *borrowed* time.

If there is something to all this, mechanical metaphors in economics take on added significance. They are more than mere expressions. They involve conceptions of the nature of economic affairs and consequently also certain attitudes of mind when economic questions are dealt with. When policy advisers go home in the evening they no doubt regard spending and saving, looking for bargains and looking for customers as ordinary human activities. But when they are sitting behind their desks or speaking at conferences they may well conceive the problems of policy as though there really were a macro-economic fluid whose flow sometimes has to be augmented and sometimes diminished or as though there really were an autonomous market mechanism which sometimes operates smoothly and sometimes breaks down.

When mechanomorphism is seen to be more than skin deep, its actual scope becomes problematical. How deep does it go? Shackle has argued extensively that the concept of time to which economists often turn, and which is essentially that of classical mechanics, is inadequate for economics. Then there is the question of prediction. Since time is one of the terms in which a logical inference or the result of a calculation in classical mechanics is expressed, such inference or result is easily interpreted as a prediction. Such prediction differs of course from the foretelling of soothsayers and the revelations of prophets and in mainstream economics as elsewhere has become the ideal of science. Should one regard this ideal as a mechanomorphism? What of the apparent conviction of mainstream economic theorists that their task is to find the determinants of this, that and the other? Classical mechanics is the generally acknowledged paradigm of a deterministic theory. But perhaps the notion is derived from mathematics. The use of mathematics is another issue. Mathematics in general has no necessary connection with mechanics, but differential and integral calculus does. It was developed initially by Newton, and independently by Leibniz, apparently so that he could deal with time and space as archetypes of continua. It was developed further by others specifically for dealing with problems in celestial mechanics. It is not surprising that its transplantation into economics required some conceptual adaptations, such as that people had to be seen to *react* rather than to do things and even to be subject to mutual reaction, as one is sometimes asked to represent to oneself the process of solving simultaneous equations. Mutual determination makes sense when one wonders how bathwater comes to an even level if one keeps perfectly still, but is quite baffling when it is meant to enlighten one on economic affairs.[4]

III

In the extended sense we have been considering, mechanomorphism is an aspect of what Hayek has spoken of as *scientism*, i.e., the "slavish imitation of the method and language of Science" and the "uncritical application of habits of thought to fields different from those in which they have been formed."[5] To Hayek, as to most subjectivists, scientism is a derogatory term. But in the history of economics this was not always so. For some, mechanomorphism was even a high aim or, at least, when accomplished, something to be proud of.

J. S. Mill thought that "the backward state" of the social sciences could "only be remedied by applying to them the methods of Physical Science, duly extended and generalized." In this way one could "hope to remove this blot on the face of science." The "science of human nature" fell short of the exactness of astronomy but could achieve that of the study of tides or that of astronomy when it had "mastered the main phenomena, but not the perturbations."[6] Jevons described his theory as "the mechanics of utility and self-interest." Economics "thus treated presents a close analogy to the science of Statical Mechanics, and the Laws of Exchange are found to resemble the Laws of Equilibrium of a lever as determined by the principle of virtual velocities." He noted with pride that it was "curious" that his equations were "exactly similar in form" to those of the lever.[7] (It hardly was curious when the theory of value was conceived in mechanical terms.) Marshall agreed with Mill that the "method of combination" of the "forces with which economics deals" is that of mechanics. In characteristic fashion, he hedged this about by observing that the matter with which economics deals is sometimes more like that of biology. But he seemed to take it for granted that analogies were useful.[8] In his published correspondence with Croce, Pareto expressed himself distinctly: "I look for a theory which may include and present economic facts. For my part, I know only the system of equations of pure economics as being capable of attaining that end, just in the same way that the system of equations of celestial mechanics explains and represents the movements of celestial bodies."[9] Nearer to our own day, Samuelson described the deterministic theory-form derived from mechanics and observed that any part of economic theory which cannot be cast into that mould "must be regarded with suspicion as suffering from haziness."[10]

Subjectivist economists should perhaps reassure themselves that they really are the only ones in step by enquiring more deeply into what really is wrong with mechanomorphism. What is wrong with copying a great intellectual achievement? After all, Hayek also has stressed, in another context, the importance of emulation in the process of cultural evolution.[11] What is wrong with metaphors? Their use is so universal that one may presume them to be an essential part of language and thought. How else does one venture into new fields of thought if not with the equipment used in older fields? Thought about economic systems and economic order is surely a very new field when seen against the sweep of a conjectured history of thinking. One could also speculate differently. Perhaps we apply a standard of sharp delineation in articulating our thoughts. Some articulated subjects may measure up to this standard better than others and so we apply the former to the latter. For instance, smells and tastes are notoriously difficult to talk about, but wine lovers have many thoughts about their wines. How far can they articulate them with a three-word vocabulary (sweet, sour and bitter)? They get by with references to the visible sources of odor and with an amazing array of metaphors. To a lesser extent this also is found in articulated thoughts about the mind and mental activities. One may be referring to mental prowess when one says that someone has lost his momentum or is a bit rusty. Physical location is not at issue in the question: "What did she have in mind, what was behind it all?" Nor is physical force in: "He was struck by her beauty, it made a deep impression on him. When she left him, he went to pieces; it was a shattering experience." Even subjectivism in economics may be explained with a little help from physical metaphors. Economic phenomena, one is told, must have an identifiable source in some mind or be generated by human action.

It would therefore be difficult to maintain that there is something wrong as such with using metaphors, analogies and allusions to apparently other departments of being. But perhaps one may find fault with the way they are used. What comes most readily to mind, especially if one subscribes to the ornament view of metaphors, is a distinction between figurative and literal uses of expressions. Mechanomorphism may then be confined to the transposition of expressions in their literal senses. In other words, one may give free rein to rhetorical flourishes since they are harmless as long as they are recognized for what they are. Only if they are taken seriously, i.e. understood literally, can they do harm. The problem with this, however, is that it is not always easy to tell which are the literal, primary, original or most usual usages of expressions. What is the literal sense of *force* or *cause*, for instance?

The problem is not unsurmountable. The approach may be taken further since its purport is to downgrade the importance of language, of the actual form of expression, and to focus on what things are really like.[12] One adopts an attitude which may perhaps be expressed as follows: "There is a state of nature and there are human beings. I am in daily contact with both and I know what they are like. I can tell the difference between physical events and mental phenomena and their derivatives such as economic phenomena. The language in which they are expressed hardly matters at all. *Mist is rising out of the valley* is a physical event. *Their expectations are rising* and *consumer prices are rising* are not physical events. The fact that the same verb is used in all three cases is unimportant. If you were to tell me that *mist is rising* is a metaphor, that we use the expression because rising mist reminds us of rising prices, I would not believe you. But it hardly matters."

We may follow Husserl in calling this attitude the *natural attitude*.[13] With it, one cannot regard mechanomorphisms as transposed expressions taken literally because an appeal is made directly to what is perceived as real, rather than to the way in which that which is perceived as real is expressed. But the point may be made in another way. One may regard mechanomorphisms as mongrel conceptions which refer neither to physical phenomena nor to mental phenomena and their economic derivatives and therefore correspond to nothing that is real.

It would seem that the case which subjectivist economists bring against parts of neo-classical economics is quite often based in effect on the natural attitude and mechanomorphism as a mongrel conception. That is fair enough since such criticism must, in the nature of the case, be based on a commitment to what the world is really like. But as a procedure, as a method of analysis, the approach is rather limited. The following example may help to bring this out.

IV

Modern economists are people who have spent many long hours gazing at functional relations represented in diagrams or in mathematical notation. So deep is their preoccupation that they say "is a function of" where others say "depends upon." In itself, this parlance is quite innocuous. It is, in this case, a rather unpicturesque way of saying something that may also be said differently. But metaphors run deeper than that. We have seen that we may live and act by them.

An economist has the job of advising a central bank on what to do about interest rates. He pictures to himself a diagram in which a one-to-one continuous function is represented. On one axis there is the rate of interest, on the other something else conceived as a quantity, the nature of which depends on the school of thought to which the economist owes allegiance. A slight alteration in the interest rate of perhaps half a percentage point, the diagram shows him, would result in such or such a variation in expenditure, money supply or whatever. It is a useful device. It could also be used to represent the effect, with the corresponding reaction read off the function, of a slight twist of a knob on a radio receiver or of a slight alteration of pressure on the accelerator of a car running on level ground.

That the actual reaction is not as certain and regular in the case of interest rates as in the other two cases is well known. To those who all along have stressed the importance of expectations in economic affairs, notable among them Ludwig Lachmann, it is furthermore not at all surprising. Their point has been taken up widely by other economists but seemingly not in the subjectivist spirit in which it was intended. If the omission of expectations is a defect in models, then the models may be rectified by putting expectations into them. The judicious addition of some further parameters or perhaps a more extensive reconstruction of models should effect the desired accommodation. This is most unlikely to be what subjectivists have in mind. The reaction (to changes in interest rates, etc.) has been modified in so far as it has become more complex, but it still remains a reaction. The models are still mongrel conceptions.

Let us, however, consider the following statements. "In order to achieve their policy objectives, monetary authorities should raise interest rates in one great leap to levels at which they have not been for a long time and the authorities should do this in a manner that indicates that they mean business, as the expression goes. In these circumstances, many people would expect interest rates to be lower again in the not too distant future and therefore would postpone some of their expenditure." Is this a reasonable thing to say about one's fellow human beings or is it the idea of mechanical reaction dressed up in a garb of greater reasonableness? If it is also a mongrel conception, could economic policy ever be expected to succeed, could even the ordinary individual decide on a plan of economic action with a fair chance of success? But then, economic policy has never been remarkably successful and one could at least argue the point whether it is calculation or luck that leads to great success in business.[14]

One may hazard the guess that there would not be unanimity on this question even among members of the modern Austrian school who hold the subjectivist position in economics. Perhaps this particular question could never be settled. But as long as one relies only on the natural attitude, one does not even have a means for trying to settle it. One has only a belief, in this case, about what people are like. But what are they like? There may be a multiplicity of beliefs and when these are merely stated one may not come to any agreement other than to differ.

V

It would be useful to distinguish between ontological subjectivism and a logic of subjectivism. Ontological subjectivism is the commitment to a subjectivist *Weltanschauung* or a subjectivist ontology, i.e., a set of beliefs or tenets. (This is the current usage of *ontology* which Quine appears to have popularized.) Different people may of course be committed to different subjectivist ontologies. They may also be committed to mechanistic or physicalist ontologies. Ontological subjectivism is reflected in the unself-conscious natural attitude to life. We know that there are people out there, that they have some knowledge, beliefs and expectations, that they make decisions, make plans, act purposefully and so on. Ontological commitment is necessary in any field of study but does not in itself provide a method of analyzing what one is committed to.

We may speak of a logic of subjectivism which is a logic in the sense that it deals with the language in which subjectivist ontologies are expressed. One speaks about the terms in which one speaks about people, economic affairs and so on. As philosophers put it, one uses a metalanguage to talk about or mention the terms which one uses in an object language. For example, let us consider the statement "Economic phenomena must have an identifiable source in some mind or be generated by human action." One may make much the same point, and incidentally avoid, the obvious mechanical metaphors by using a metalanguage thus. "*Economic phenomena* are properly expressed or defined in the terms in which *mental attitudes* and *human action* are expressed." The words in italics are in the object language and the rest is in the metalanguage. One is no longer speaking about economic phenomena but about the expression *economic phenomena.*

When a writer's intention is not only to state but also to analyze his subjectivist ontology, he ventures into the logic of subjectivism. But he may do so without using the distinction between metalanguage and object language, making use instead of metaphors and possibly other devices in what would be the object language. The original statement about economic phenomena above may be a case in point.

Let us consider, by way of example, one of Shackle's interesting discussions of *decision*, where he seems to waver between discussing the activity of making decisions and the usage of the term *decision*. He says that in a determinist world, in which "history is a book already written, whose pages the hand of time is merely turning, not composing," human beings "only seem to themselves to be the source of any current of events" and decision is illusory. In a world of certainty, of perfect foresight, decision is empty since it is really calculation. In "a world without discernible order" where one has no idea what will be the sequels to one's actions, decision is powerless. He went on to ask: "What kind of world can we find, wherein decision will be none of these things . . . ?"[15] Shackle uses metaphors effectively to talk about the activity of making decisions, but he is really concerned with the usage of the term *decision*. He also poses the problem in a more metalinguistic way: "How to find a scheme of thought about the basic nature of human affairs, which will include *decision* in the meaning we give to this word in our unself-conscious, intuitive attitude to life, where . . . we take it for granted that a responsibility lies upon us for our acts; that these acts are . . . *creative, inceptive*, the source of *historical novelty*."[16]

To look for a scheme of thought is, in our metalanguage, to inquire into which terms hang together and how they are interlinked. (Metalanguages also use metaphors.) In a way, this is what Shackle has been doing in most of his work. But it is a voluminous work. What is admirable about the physical sciences, and mechanics in particular, is that they have formulated their domains of thought succinctly. Shackle is able to say that decision in a determinist world "belongs to a conceptual world where morality, ethics, wisdom and, above all, creative thought have no place,"[17] because it is quite clear what does have a place in the conceptual world or domain of thought of mechanics. There is evidence in the Menger-Mises tradition in the Austrian school of a groping for the same clarity in the subjectivist domain of thought. To this we now turn.

VI

There has been much argumentation over whether Newton's famous three laws of motion are concealed or implicit definitions.[18] It is unlikely that Newton regarded them as such, but they may be interpreted as statements which show how certain terms are interlinked and which helped in this way to articulate and codify the preexisting thought domain of mechanics.

Let us consider the law of inertia. Every body perseveres in its state of rest, or of uniform motion in a right line, unless it is compelled to change that state by forces impressed thereon.[19] This original formulation by Newton is full of anthropomorphic metaphors: *persevere, rest, compel*, and even *force* with its old usage in the context of human effort and muscular exertion. But, while the metaphors are suggestive, the main terms in the law of inertia mutually define each other and nothing more than their stated mutual interconection may be deduced from any one of them. It has sometimes been said that the law of inertia states that a body continues to move in a straight line at a constant velocity except when it does not. When it does not, one says that forces are acting upon it. In the thought domain of classical mechanics, force is a measure (as implied by the second law of motion) of change of velocity or direction and no more than that. The limited meaning of *straight line* or of *uniform motion* are derived similarly. When the latter is elaborated into *equal distances in equal time intervals* the meaning of these terms (e.g., equal time intervals) in mechanics may also be derived. How the law of inertia may be used in practical applications is not our concern here. What interests us is the way it shows what belongs and what does not belong to the thought domain of mechanics and how the terms are interlinked. One may call the law of inertia a part of a codification of the thought domain of mechanics. One could also refer to a paradigm or a Wittgensteinian language game in the sense of a stipulation of the usage of terms.[20]

Though it is a tall order, it would be useful to develop a codification of the subjectivist domain of thought, the subjectivist language game, which would, for instance, stipulate the usage of Shackle's *solitary present* or *time lived in* and of *decision* in the required sense. It would not show us what people and the world are really like, but, by more clearly delineating the implications of what we are committed to ontologically, it may make decisions in this regard easier. The current discussion of uncertainty, for instance, seems to involve (though one cannot be sure of this) quite different domains of thought when some economists treat uncertainty as a feature of the environment and others as a mental state of those who have doubts about the environment.

It is common in economic writings to provide ad hoc clarifications of concepts by such devices as the Crusoe economy or Adam Smith's "early and rude state of society."[21] Menger and Mises, however, are rather special cases. Though their respective philosophical tenets made them express themselves differently, they may be seen to have advocated a systematic codification of the thought domain of economics, to have held it up as the ideal form of economic theory.

In the preface to the *Grundsätze*, Menger touched on mechanomorphism when he spoke of an empty playing with superficial analogies between the phenomena of economic life and of nature. Yet he insisted that his method was the same as that which had led to great success in the natural sciences.[22] His position became clearer in the *Untersuchungen* when he explained what he meant by "exact science."[23] Still later he said that sciences differ by subject matter but that a certain direction of cognitive endeavor (*Richtung des Erkenntnisstrebens*) or way of looking at things (*Betrachtungsweise*) establishes exact branches in each and allows, for instance, the formulation of the morphology of economic phenomena.[24] Though space does not permit it here, it may be shown that when Menger is translated out of the Aristotelian into a modern style of philosophizing, his phenomenal forms (*Erscheinungsformen*) become something like terms and the exact laws based on them something like a codification of the economists' language game, or, as we may say, of the thought domain of economics. For instance, he spoke of exact laws in economics as laws of economizing (*Wirtschaftlichkeit*).[25] Then in a book review of 1887 he described them as laws of rational economic means-ends relations (*Gesetze der rationalen ökonimischen Zweckbeziehungen*).[26]

Mises, it would appear, translated Menger into a neo-Kantian and later an ever more radically rationalist framework and in this way was led to praxeology. Trimmed of its claims of apodictic certainty and incontestability, the category of action and hence praxeology translates into our metalanguage as the thought domain of human action. Perhaps because he conceived action as a Kantian category which all of us carry around with us all the time, he nowhere, as far as one can tell, tried to set out in a few propositions what praxeology entails apart from means and ends, i.e., he made no attempt to codify it. His discussion, in one of his books, on the logical character of praxeology was over and done with in about 300 words.[27] This is a pity. Even if we do all have a good idea of what it is to act, it is not easy to articulate the further reaches of the implications of that idea. Mises said, for instance, that the "category *means and ends* presupposes the category *cause and effect*" and even that "causality is a category of action."[28] But, as is evident from Shackle's problem with *decision*, it is not so obvious how the troublesome idea of causation fits in with the idea of human action. What of private property? It seems somehow to imply means and ends, but not vice versa. Perhaps all the material for a codification of praxeology may be found in *Human Action*, if someone is prepared to go through it with a fine-tooth comb. There have of course been excellent commentaries on praxeology.[29] But something else is needed: a few succinct propositions in which the main terms are intended to be mutually defined, not with the arbitrariness of some axiomatic systems, but so that at least commonly found ways of thinking are reflected. It would by no means be an easy task.

VII

Let us imagine that we have available to us codifications of various domains of thought or, more likely, competing versions about which argument continues. We would then be in a position to suggest what we may call the *coherence rule*. The rule stipulates that a question should be posed in terms which all belong to the same domain of thought and that the corresponding answer should be composed in terms which all belong to the same domain of thought as the terms of the question.

With the aid of the coherence rule, the logic of subjectivism would be able to reformulate the case which ontological subjectivism brings against mechanomorphism. This case usually has the form: The real world is not like that. The *that* which by implication is unreal or nonreal is a proposition of a theory, conjecture, intended representation or anything which (as the metaphor has it) exists only in the mind. It is intended as an explanation or a solution to a problem or a representation for which one of these is the ultimate goal. Loosely it may be called an answer. To every answer there must correspond a question. When the *real world* is brought into relation with theory (i.e., answers in our loose terminology) in the case against mechanomorphism, we must mean some question, problem or issue in the real world. In any case, we could not be concerned with a description of the world as a whole; the real world is a concept without bounds. With the real world as question and theory as proposed answer, the coherence rule may be applied. The case against mechanomorphism is that the coherence rule should be applied.

The remarkable success of classical mechanics and of the physical sciences in general may owe much to the fact that something like the coherence rule is followed. However complex and full of life a situation may be, one is able to pick out the mechanical aspects (if there are any) and explain them entirely in mechanical terms. One does not go on a detour through thought domains where, say, gremlins, fate or the forces of darkness are at home, nor does one end up in the subjectivist domain of thought. Similarly, when an issue is expressed entirely within the subjectivist domain of thought, one should ensure that its explanation remains in that domain and does not end up in the thought domain of mechanics.

This is the strictest form of coherence rule. There may be less restrictive versions. Let us imagine a street map which is fixed to a wall and has on it an arrow with a notice stating: *You are here*. It is a device which establishes a connection between a here and now and a point in a representation of mechanical space. If here and now is something like Shackle's time lived in, it establishes a connection between the thought domain of Shacklean mental life and that of mechanics. This may require a reformulation of thought domains or allow a relaxation of the coherence rule. It is hard to tell.

More broadly, however, the coherence rule may be regarded as unduly restrictive. Some writers on economic methodology have lately been taken with the notion of Pluralism.[30] They see it, it appears, as a welcome liberation from positivism and falsificationism. But it has the potential for creating a free for all in which no intellectual rules apply. In this spirit we may well ask why we should lumber ourselves with a rule. Indeed, there is no profound reason in the grand design of things why we should apply the coherence rule, or why we should not seek our explanations by whatever means we can think of.

The coherence rule is an ideal. It is a version of the ideal which has come down to us from ancient Greece, not of a simple Monism, but of distinct but internally coherent intellectual disciplines. Let us take an example. On separate occasions we may say: *Leave the decision to the market, the new regulation has paralyzed the market* and *the market is operating smoothly*. On their respective occasions, each of these statements is no doubt quite meaningful. But if someone were asked to develop an intellectual discipline called economics in which the three statements may be shown to be part of a coherent conception, he would not know whether the market should be treated as a mind capable of making decisions, as a biological organism or as a machine. The metaphors, however, need be no more confusing than those in Newton's original formulation of the law of inertia if they are tied together by mutual definition into a single domain of thought. The coherence rule may then be applied.

What is disconcerting about textbook expositions of economics, at least to one who is not impressed by the idea of testable hypotheses, is that the coherence rule is not followed. The student is introduced to a topic reeking with the richness of social life. He is then taken by a little legerdemain through a blur and suddenly finds himself in an eerie world of continuous functions. He watches the functions shift about and, when they have stopped, notes down the coordinates of their points of intersection. He is then taken again through the blur and, behold, he finds himself once more among familiar human faces. The recommendation of this paper is that the subjectivist case against mechanomorphism be based on the ideal that such blurs be removed. In itself, however, that is not enough. One should also be able to show how it may be done.

NOTES

1. For a discussion of various aspects of classical mechanics from the point of view of the philosophy of science, see Ernest Nagel, *The Structure of Science* (London: Routledge, 1979) pp. 153–214 and 278–85.
2. A. Coddington, *Keynesian Economics: The Search for First Principles* (London: Allen & Unwin, 1983) pp. 100–5. He may have borrowed the term from Shackle. See his review of Shackle's *Epistemics and Economics* in *British Journal for the Philosophy of Science*, 26 (1975) pp. 151–63, especially p. 162, n. 2.
3. G. Lakoff and M. Johnson, *Metaphors We Live By* (Chicago: University of Chicago Press, 1980).
4. See also the discussion of metaphors in economics in D. N. McCloskey, "The Rhetoric of Economics," *Journal of Economic Literature*, 21 (June 1983), sect. VI, pp. 502–8.
5. F. A. Hayek, *The Counter-Revolution of Science* (Glencoe: The Free Press, 1952). The quotations are from pp. 15 and 16. The book is devoted to the subject but Hayek has used the term in other of his writings.
6. J. S. Mill, *A System of Logic*, ed. J. M. Robson (Toronto: University of Toronto Press, 1974), Book VI, pp. 833–4 and 846.
7. W. S. Jevons, *The Theory of Political Economy*, 5th ed. (New York: Kelley & Millman, 1957), pp. vii, 21, and 104.
8. Alfred Marshall, *Principles of Economics*, 8th ed. (London: Macmillan, 1949), Appendix C, par. 2, p. 637.
9. V. Pareto, "On the Economic Principle," *International Economic Papers*, No. 3 (Macmillan, 1953), p. 207. Originally in *Giornale degli Economisti*, 1901.
10. P. A. Samuelson, *Foundations of Economic Analysis* (Cambridge: Harvard University Press, 1963), pp. 8–9.
11. See, for instance, F. A. Hayek, *Law, Legislation and Liberty* (Chicago: University of Chicago Press, 1979), vol. III, pp. 155–8.

12. McCloskey, op. cit., p. 503. McCloskey pointed out that the idea of removing a metaphor like an ornament to reveal meaning is itself a metaphor.
13. Husserl used the term extensively. He described the natural attitude in *Ideas Pertaining to a Pure Phenomenology* First Book, trans. F. Kersten (The Hague: Martinus Nijhoff, 1982), pp. 51–7.
14. On this topic, see I. M. Kirzner, *Perception, Opportunity, and Profit* (University of Chicago Press, 1979) chap. 10, pp. 154–81. It is, of course, not a simple either-or question, and entrepreneurial judgment is not the same as calculation. See also, I. M. Kirzner, "On the Method of Austrian Economics" in E. G. Dolan, *The Foundations of Modern Austrian Economics* (Kansas City: Sheed & Ward, 1976), pp. 40–51.
15. G. L. S. Shackle, *The Nature of Economic Thought* (Cambridge: Cambridge University Press, 1966), pp. 72–4.
16. Ibid., p. 73.
17. Ibid., p. 72.
18. For a discussion of this question, see Ernest Nagel, op. cit., pp. 174–202.
19. Quoted in Ernest Nagel, op. cit., p. 158. The law of intertia is the first law or axiom of motion.
20. When Kuhn introduced the term *paradigm* in the sense now common, he mentioned Newton's *Principia* as one of the works which implicitly defined problems and methods for succeeding generations of scientists. When he dissected the term in his *Postscript 1969*, he used Newton's second law ($f = ma$) to illustrate paradigms as implicit definitions and as group-licensed ways of seeing situations as like each other. The latter could be taken to refer more generally to the ability to use metaphors effectively. See T. S. Kuhn, *The Structure of Scientific Revolutions*, 2nd ed. (Chicago: University of Chicago Press, 1970), pp. 10, 182–4 and 188–91.
21. Adam Smith, *The Wealth of Nations*, Book I, Chapter VI, first sentence. The drawback of ad hoc clarifications is illustrated by the fact that the beaver-and-deer case, which is introduced with these words, has often been taken, perhaps even by Ricardo, as the basis of a labor-content theory of value. It can also be understood to introduce the simple idea that prices resolve themselves into factor earnings.
22. Carl Menger, *Grundsätze der Volkswirthschaftslehre, The Collected Works of Carl Menger* (London School of Economics Reprint No. 17, 1934), vol. I, p. xlv.
23. Carl Menger, *Untersuchungen, Collected Works* (London School of Economics. Reprint No. 18, 1933) First Book, chaps. 4 and 5, pp. 31–59.
24. Carl Menger, "Grundzüge einer Klassifikation der Wirtschaftswissenschaften" in *Collected Works* (London School of Economics, Reprint No. 19, 1935), vol. III, pp. 189–92 and 197–8.
25. For example, in *Untersuchungen*, pp. 59 and 265.
26. Menger, *Collected Works*, op. cit., vol. III, p. 105. See also p. 192 where he speaks of an understanding of the inner connection (*inneren Zusammenhanges*) of the results of scientific research.
27. L. von Mises, *The Ultimate Foundation of Economic Science*, 2nd ed. (Kansas City: Sheed Andrews & McMeel, 1978), pp. 44–5.

28. L. von Mises, *Human Action* (New Haven: Yale University Press, 1949), pp. 22–3.
29. Professor Lachmann's review in *Economica*, 18 (Nov. 1951); L. M. Lachmann, "The Science of Human Action," in *Capital, Expectations, and the Market Process* (Kansas City: Sheed Andrews & McMeel, 1977), pp. 94–111; Murray N. Rothbard, "Praxeology: The Methodology of Austrian Economics," in E. G. Dolan, *The Foundations of Modern Austrian Economics* (Kansas City: Sheed & Ward, 1976), pp. 19–39. Rothbard, among others, explores praxeology as a logic.
30. As opposed to monism, i.e., the assumption that there is a single ultimate principle or kind of entity. See B. Caldwell, *Beyond Positivism* (London: Allen & Unwin, 1982) chap. 13, pp. 244–52; L. A. Boland, *The Foundations of Economic Method* (London: Allen & Unwin, 1982), Part IV, especially chap. 12, pp. 188–96.

18 Subjectivism, Uncertainty, and Rules*

GERALD P. O'DRISCOLL, JR. AND MARIO J. RIZZO

I THEORY

Dynamic subjectivism

The concept of subjectivism entered modern economics through the marginal utility revolution of the 1870s. Except for Menger and the Austrians, however, subjectivism was confined to the domain of consumer tastes.[1] The fundamental goal of modern subjectivists, including most Austrians, is to complete the revolution by widening its application in economics. James Buchanan has contrasted the subjectivism of tastes with a more thoroughgoing variant that underlies the very structure of economic explanation.[2] In this view, subjectivism then becomes the methodology of economics. Moreover, it permeates analysis in the treatment of, for example, time, uncertainty, entrepreneurship and rules.

Subjectivist economics systematically recomposes market phenomena in terms of typical structural components of everyday decision making.[3] Accordingly, subjectivists reject explanations that abstract from purposes, make unreasonable computational demands on the agents being modeled, or impute knowledge to them that they could never acquire. They portray individuals as deciding and acting in real or historical time, under conditions of genuine uncertainty and change. The linkage of overall market outcomes to individual decisionmaking, not some arbitrary precept, determines the methodology.

Subjectivism is incorporated in neoclassical economics solely in the theory of consumer preferences. It is, moreover, fundamentally static in conception. In contrast, modern subjectivists emphasize that subjectivism's relevance derives primarily from the effects of time and uncertainty. In this essay, we present the modern development of subjectivist economics. We then apply subjectivist insights to explain two important phenomena: entrepreneurship and the adherence to rules. Each reflects the response of individuals to uncertainty. We discuss entrepreneurship briefly and then emphasize rule-following behavior as a mode of adaptation to uncertainty.

Fundamental characteristics of subjectivism

There are four major features of subjectivist analysis. First, the analyst employs the method of mind constructs by modeling a fictitious consciousness endowed with goals, knowledge, expectations and constraints. The specificity and complexity of these endowments depends on the problem at hand. In all cases, however, the mind is portrayed in an understandable relation to the phenomenon being explained. This method encompasses but is broader than traditional neoclassical choice-theoretic analysis. The latter assumes that all behavior can be modeled as continuous utility maximization under known constraints. The former also includes, however, other purposeful activity, such as entrepreneurship and rule-following behavior. Later in this part we discuss the circumstances in which continuous utility maximization is impossible or inappropriate, and why this requires scope for both creative activity and rule-governed behavior.

Second, the mind construct is portrayed as existing in real time. Real time, or more precisely, the subjective perception of the passage of time, is inextricably linked to ineradicable uncertainty, irreversibility of processes and a continuous flow of information. The passage of time and changes in knowledge are necessarily associated. Moreover, information flows do not merely add to each individual's existing stock of knowledge, but render some of the already accumulated stock obsolete. The fact that individuals are continuously acquiring information reflects the incompleteness of their knowledge. The fact that this continuous information flow leads to obsolescence of existing knowledge prevents any asymptotic approach to an informational equilibrium.

Third, agents are seen to be capable of creative and not just passive decisionmaking. While this creativity limits the predictive capacities of economic models, it by no means implies theoretical nihilism. All creativity takes place within a context and the analyst's specification of the context bounds the decisionmaker's creativity. These bounds are the source of the stability of patterns of behavior and of social structures, and they enable the economist to render "pattern predictions."[4] Further, as Heiner has forcefully argued, it is uncertainty not certainty that is the source of predictable or stable behavior.[5]

Fourth, there is a recognition that different individuals have different knowledge. Just as there is a division of labor in society, so too there is a division of knowledge. Indeed, this informational heterogeneity is inherent to the very concept of a decentralized economy. Much of what is interesting about market processes consists of the transmission of knowledge from one individual to another. Certainly there have been contributions by neoclassical economists to the analysis of decentralized information.[6] Recent neoclassical work has tended to ignore, however, the heterogeneity of information and to obscure the distinction between knowledge of the observer (i.e., the modeler) and that of the observed (i.e., the economic agent). This occurs whenever the individual's knowledge, beliefs or expectations are assumed either to be identical with or to converge toward an objective knowledge set (or probability distribution) determined solely by the model's structure.[7]

Time

In this section, we contrast two fundamentally different perspectives on time: neoclassical spatialized and subjectivist real time. Neoclassical economics has adopted the Newtonian conception of time in which time is analogized to points on a line. This implies that time has certain convenient mathematical properties, of which the first is that it is homogeneous. Each point is identical to all others, save for its position. Changes then occupy these points just as matter occupies space. One corollary of this is that, since space can be empty, time can pass without anything happening. This is equivalent to saying that time can pass without agents learning. Spatialized time thus forms the basis for the concept of stationary equilibrium.

Newtonian time is also mathematically continuous, in the sense of continuous divisibility. No matter how finely subdivided or how close the points are to each other, there is always space between them. Each instant of time is isolated, or independent of all other points. Thus mathematical continuity implies the absence of a dynamic continuity among events or successive points on the time line. The practical importance of this is that adjustment tends to be modeled as a series of comparative static equilibria rather than a process in time. This modeling distinction is a fundamental difference between neoclassical and subjectivist economics.

Finally, Newtonian time is causally inert. The mere passage of time produces no novelty or impetus for change. Any change that occurs is completely determined by some exogenous force at the end of each period or in the interstices of the temporal model.

Building on foundations laid by the philosopher Henri Bergson,[8] subjectivists have stressed the dynamic continuity, heterogeneity and the causal efficacy of time. Dynamic continuity means that successive temporal phases are structurally related by the memory of elapsed time and the expectation of what has yet to come. In principle, there are no isolated points of time.

As time passes our memory is enriched and our expectations changed. Each new experience changes our perspective on both what has happened and what we expect to happen. Thus, time is made up of heterogeneous instants. Only by accident, then, would expectations remain constant as time elapsed. (The implication for the practical applicability of rational expectations is obvious.) The causal efficacy of time follows immediately from its heterogenity. Since the mere elapse of time is a source of novelty, then the passage of time and the absence of change are incompatible.[9]

Neoclassical economists certainly recognize that the Newtonian framework does not do well at accommodating spontaneous change and surprise. This is, however, viewed as a factor affecting only the applicability of a model and not as having implications for the way models should be constructed. For example, Machlup argued that all well-designed economic models are deterministic and that indeterminism enters at the applications stage. If, however, change and novelty are inherent to the passage of time, then this indeterminism or element of surprise ought to be incorporated in economic models. On this point, there is a fundamental difference in method or approach between subjectivists and orthodox neoclassical theorists.[10]

The implications of indeterminism and surprise for individual decisionmaking are twofold. First, since not all decisionmaking is determinate, economists must turn their attention to the creative or entrepreneurial behavior that is crucial for market processes. Second, in response to the surprise and uncertainty permeating the environment, many individuals follow rules of thumb, rather than engage in maximizing behavior. While entrepreneurship and rules of thumb are different modes of behavior, they are not incompatible. Indeed, they are mutually reinforcing. Entrepreneurial altertness, for example, may be the source of the perception of an opportunity, but rule following may be the only feasible way of exploiting it in an uncertain world.

Entrepreneurship

A real-time framework puts the informational content of prices in a more balanced perspective. Neoclassical models postulate the logical simultaneity of prices and exchanges. The process of exchange does not bring about the vector of prices in existence. Indeed, to the extent that there are any temporal lags "the formation of prices must *precede* the process of exchange and not be the result of it."[11] As a result, prices are generally "correct" from the outside.

In contrast, subjectivists view exchange as the causative force bringing about market prices. The exchange process is a trial-and-error process taking place in time. There are built in corrective mechanisms but it would be a sheer act of faith to treat market prices as always conveying accurate information. Indeed, in a world of endogenous change and uncertainty, it cannot be demonstrated that reliance solely on the information conveyed by prices will result in a systematic approach to equilibrium.[12] This is precisely why market economies do *not* rely solely on prices but depend on entrepreneurial activity, rules of thumb, contracts and other institutions to convey information and coordinate behavior.

Neoclassical economics studies behavior in only one form—continuous utility maximization. The neoclassical framework thus implicitly denies the very existence of entrepreneurship. At the individual level, entrepreneurship consists in establishing the very means-ends framework that is a precondition for maximizing behavior.[13] At the market level, entrepreneurship can be characterized in a number of ways. For instance, Kirzner emphasizes the role of entrepreneurs in discovering hitherto unnoticed arbitrage opportunities. Schumpeter emphasizes the role of entrepreneurs in literally creating new opportunities. For Schumpeter, entrepreneurship is a creative leap, the success of which depends on "the capacity of seeing things in a way that afterwards proves to be true, even though it cannot be established at the moment."[14] This characterization points to the inconsistency of entrepreneurial activity with the assumption that agents are endowed with a preordained means-end framework or a given opportunity set. What entrepreneurial theories have in common is that they focus on market phenomena that are strictly outside orthodox economic models.

The approaches of both Kirzner and Schumpeter remove entrepreneurial discovery from the confines of maximization models. The latter imply that, given the data, the outcome is inevitable. It is in this sense that these models are deterministic. Entrepreneurial discovery or creativity is not, however, a determinate outcome of the data. If it were, it would not be entrepreneurship!

The market function of entrepreneurial activity is to fill gaps in the knowledge of market participants. This function is linked with our previous argument on the insufficiency of prices as a source of information. Outside Walrasian general equilibrium, reliance on prices alone will not equilibrate or coordinate individual activity. In a real-time context, entrepreneurial activity consists in *outguessing* market prices when the prices do not seem consistent.[15] Entrepreneurial profit derives from exploiting inconsistencies in market prices. Entrepreneurship is thus the driving force of the market process, a crucial force coordinating individual plans.

Hayek first articulated the proposition that "the price system is a mechanism for communicating information."[16] In neoclassical economics, however, his point has been taken out of context. It has been transformed into the assumption that prices alone convey information in competitive markets. Of course, if prices are the only source of information for competitive firms, then prices must be assumed to be correct or at their general equilibrium level. If they are not, then there will be sub-optimality or market failure of some kind. Hayek's insight has thus unfortunately been used to construct an impoverished view of how markets operate.

In this section, we briefly showed that entrepreneurial activity brings nonprice information to markets, filling informational gaps left by the price system. Despite the informational content of price signals, agents have incomplete knowledge. Entrepreneurship is one form of market activity that supplements the price system in coordinating behavior. In the next section, we begin our primary focus on another, equally important coordinating mechanism.

Rules and uncertainty

The recognition of real time and genuine uncertainty is among the most important consequences of adopting a subjectivist approach. Accordingly, the methods by which agents adjust or adapt to their nonstatic environment must become a central emphasis of economic analysis. In this essay, we focus on rule-following behavior as a theoretically interesting issue with great practical significance. Specifically, we explore the relationship between genuine uncertainty and several kinds of rules. Uncertainty makes optimizing behavior either impossible or inappropriate, and thus agents are led to standardize their behavior in terms of rules.

Before proceeding to a general analysis of the interrelation between rules and uncertainty, it is necessary to define precisely what we mean by rules. If, in situations of the general type *X*, a relatively specific action or a limited set of actions *A* is observed, then the agent's behavior can be characterized as "rule following." The more general *X* is and the more specific *A* is (or the more limited the set *A*), the more rule oriented is the behavior. Thus, individuals who in a wide variety of circumstances pursue the same specific course of action, or who draw from a very limited repertoire of actions, are said to be adhering to rules. This type of behavior is not generally the result of optimizing decisions. Although an individual may (and in the cases we discuss below will) know he is following a rule, he usually will not know the precise reasons he is following any particular one. Consequently, if rules are, in some limited sense, optimal, they are so by virtue of evolutionary mechanisms rather than of conscious decision processes. Attempts to explain rules as if they were the result of individual maximizing behavior seriously misconstrue the phenomena at hand. Rules are followed either because agents lack the knowledge necessary for solving a particular maximization problem or because individual maximizing is self-defeating in the context. Rules may therefore produce more satisfactory long-run results insofar as they reduce the errors attributable to fine tuning without sufficient knowledge, or insofar as they prevent destabilizing behavior.

The idea of genuine uncertainty implies both the endogeneity of the source of uncertainty and the perceived unlistability of all the potential outcomes of a course of action. Each of these features of uncertainty provides a basis for the adoption of rules. By "endogenous uncertainty," we mean that attempts to cope with uncertainty by independent, optimizing behavior can itself generate additional uncertainty. In the context of a "cooperative game," for example, individuals will intentionally disguise their preferences in order to achieve a better result. This activity increases the level of uncertainty as the participants in the game seek simultaneously to create uncertainty about their own intentions and to uncover the true intentions of other parties. In some admittedly extreme circumstances, the sole form of uncertainty may be of this type. This is the case in the famous Keynesian beauty contest.[17] Here the problem is that individuals must guess what average opinion believes average opinion will be. Expectations formulated in this way are really expectations about expectations. Consequently, the source of uncertainty is purely endogenous, that is, changes in expectations induce further changes without logical limit. As both Keynes and Morgenstern understand, the only stopping point will be some sort of conventional behavior.[18] The process stops by a simple arbitrary act of will on the part of one individual or mutually reinforcing acts of will on the part of two or more individuals (i.e., a convention).

"Unlistability" refers to the agent's perceived inability to list all of the possible future outcomes of his actions. The alternative courses of action are not well-defined or, more precisely, their possible outcomes are not well defined. In this case, optimization in the usual sense is not possible: The agent does not have the requisite information to maximize his objective function.[19]

The overall effect of uncertainty can be understood as increasing the gap between the agent's competence and the complexity of the decision problem.[20] As uncertainty and the gap increase, the probability that a given action will be selected at an inappropriate time increases. Thus, the number of actions in an agent's repertoire that, on net, produce beneficial outcomes will fall.[21] To the extent that there exist efficient evolutionary selection processes, the no-longer beneficial actions will tend to be dropped from the set of possible actions. This in turn reduces the agent's flexibility and produces apparently rigid responses. The actions remaining in the repertoire will perform satisfactorily in many states of the world. For these courses of action the probability that the eventual state will be right for their selection is relatively high.

II APPLICATIONS

The Coase theorem and bargaining

Suppose that entrepreneurial alertness has resulted in one or several parties noticing an opportunity for mutual gains from trade. Specifically, let us assume that a factory would accept a minimum of X to reduce pollution by a certain amount, while the residents of the neighboring area would be willing to offer a maximum of Y, where Y

exceeds X. The difference between Y and X constitutes the potential gain from trade and the surplus over which there can be conflict. On a perfectly competitive market, however, there will be no such difficulties. The "market" will set the price of a unit of pollution, and the agents will merely adjust the quantities they wish to buy or sell at that price. But, in the absence of perfect competition, the price and consequent division of the surplus will arise from the process of bargaining. As we show below, this process cannot be frictionless even if transactions costs are zero. The absence of transactions costs implies that there are no obstacles to any desired acquisition or communication of information. It does not imply that agents will always desire to communicate accurately.[22]

Bargaining involves making an offer in the anticipation of a counteroffer. Bargainers must each form some expectations about what the other(s) will do in response to an offer. If these expectations are rational, that is, if they correspond to the underlying objective frequencies of the other bargainer's counteroffers, then there will be an equilibrium. Each party will choose an optimum bargaining strategy on the basis of the rationally expected response of the other party. On the average, this equilibrium will result in the parties coming to an agreement and effectively exploiting the opportunity for mutual gains. If expectations are rational from the outset, the equilibrium will be immediately and costlessly achieved. Rational expectations are not, however, consistent with a subjectivist approach for reasons that we have discussed at length elsewhere.[23] It is not useful to postulate an underlying objective frequency of responses in the presence of unlistability and endogenous uncertainty.

A pure bargaining model, without rational expectations, will not necessarily result in an equilibrium exploitation of the surplus. Agents will disguise their true preferences with regard to minimum acceptance and maximum offer prices in order to capture more of the surplus. Even if the cost of communicating their preferences is zero, they will not wish to do so. Active strategic disguising of preferences, however, creates additional uncertainty. The path followed by each party in bargaining depends on what the expected response is. Because this response is not fixed in either a deterministic or stochastic sense there is nothing to anchor expectations. As a result, there is an unending gamelike process in which one party's adjustment to the expectations of the other results in changes in that party's expectations and hence in further changes in the first party's expectations, ad infinitum.[24] This is a manifestation of the endogeneity of uncertainty: attempts to cope with uncertainty merely enhance it.

In order to exploit potential gains from trade in a setting without perfect competition, some kind of expectational equilibrium is necessary. If expectations are rational, independent optimizing behavior by each party is sufficient to effect an equilibrium. If, on the other hand, they are not rational, optimizing behavior will not be effective in exploiting the potential gains from trade. Under these circumstances reciprocal rule-following behavior, that is, the mutual adoption of a convention, may lead to a satisfactory agreement among the parties. For example, in the factory-residents case the parties might follow the rule that each reveals his true preferences and then the surplus is simply shared in equal (or any other fixed) proportion. This may be an outcome upon which each party believes he could improve if he were able to dominate the bargaining process. But protracted bargaining may result in no agreement or in a very costly one.

In the long run, a rule-oriented approach may, in fact, maximize the surplus obtained by each party as the number of failures to agree is reduced. Recognition of this long-run gain implies, however, that the parties are conscious of the specific advantages of following particular rules. More importantly, however, even if they were aware of those advantages, independent behavior would not be sufficient to generate a mutually acceptable rule. One party might insist on a division of the surplus that is different from what the other party desires. To argue over the rule would eliminate the advantages of following rules. Thus, it seems more plausible to suggest that rules evolve rather than are deliberately constructed.

If evolved rules of the division of the surplus are followed then, within certain limits, the prices established as a result of the bargaining process are a matter of convention. Obviously, the maximum offer price and the minimum acceptance price need not be determined by conventions, but where exactly within that range a price is established will be. Prices are therefore partly determined by evolutionary processes rather than exclusively by the instantaneous or even long-run forces of supply and demand for the particular good in question. The role of rules or conventions will be more significant the greater the degree of uncertainty created by the bargaining process itself. As that uncertainty rises attempted individual maximization will increasingly lead to failure to exploit gains from trade and the behavior of individuals will become more rule oriented.[25]

Collusion

We have seen that in a bargaining situation where the actions of the parties are unconstrained by rules, there may be a failure to exploit the potential gains from trade. In this section we show that even outside the classical bargaining context rules may be necessary in order to ensure the proper exploitation of profit opportunities.

Consider several independent firms in a given industry who simultaneously perceive an increase in demand and a profit opportunity associated with an expansion in capacity. In a completely frictionless system each firm will seek to expand capacity to the full extent permitted by the industry-wide opportunity. But if each firm tries to satisfy the entire new demand, the aggregate result will be excess capacity. The potential profits would thus be transformed into actual losses. Knowing this, each firm would refrain from expanding capacity at all because, in effect, there are no profits to be captured. In general, a profit opportunity equally and frictionlessly available to all is paradoxically available to none.[26]

Each firm's decision about whether to expand capacity depends on its expectations about what others will do. In the absence of rational expectations, frictions, and agreements among firms, there will be no way to anchor these expectations. The endogenous uncertainty produced by the potential expansion of other firms will paralyze the decisionmaking of each. There will be an endless series of conjectural reactions and counter-reactions as the adjustments of one firm to the adjustments of another produce further adjustments by the first firm.

If expectations are not rational there are only two circumstances in which this problem can be reduced or eliminated.[27] First, if frictions exist or can be created then individual firms will be able to make decisions largely free of concern about what their rivals will do.[28] For example, when knowledge of a potential opportunity is not widespread the threat of excess expansion will be less. Similarly, where products are differentiated and consumer loyalty is high, there will be greater certainty of demand facing each firm. Hence there will be less anxiety about the effects of competitive increases in investment.

When, however, knowledge of a profit opportunity is widespread, the product is not differentiated, and other frictions do not exist or cannot be created, agreements among competing firms may be the only solution to the problem of endogenous uncertainty. In this second circumstance, firms may tacitly or explicitly follow rules that allocate shares in the new investment opportunity. Division of territories and market share quotas are among the devices by which expectations about what rivals will do can be anchored. This, in turn, permits more effective exploitation of the opportunity.

Although tacit and explicit collusive arrangements decrease endogenous uncertainty and increase the coordination among firms, they also tend to reduce output and raise prices for the usual reasons explicated by static analysis. This tendency may, however, be overwhelmed by the efficiency-promoting properties of collusion. Thus the across-the-board condemnation of collusion by neoclassical economists is unwarranted.[29] In the first place, the *expected* returns from any given level of investment will be greater with coordination, and hence with less endogenous uncertainty, than without coordination. (The probability of a disastrous transformation of a potential profit into a large actual loss is greater when the probability of competitive oversupply is high.) As a result, collusive arrangements increase the flow of investment into the industry relative to the noncollusive, uncoordinated state of affairs. Furthermore, this effect is reinforced to the extent that firms exhibit risk-averse behavior. Even without an increase in expected returns a reduction in uncertainty will increase investment by risk-averse firms.

The beneficial results of collusion are more likely to dominate in the final analysis, the fewer "natural" frictions are present in the particular market under discussion. Endogenous uncertainty is high when frictions are absent and so the social returns to collusion will also be high. But in the case where frictions are many, endogenous uncertainty will be low and the static negative aspects of collusion are then likely to dominate.

Frictions and rule-following behavior emerging from tacit or explicit collusion are substitute ways of overcoming the decision paralysis of endogenous uncertainty. Frictions imply that rivals, for a variety of reasons, do not find it possible or profitable to pursue a certain course of action such as the expansion of capacity. Collusive arrangements mean that rivals adhere to rules that prevent simultaneous attempts by all parties to exploit an opportunity. Impossible knowledge requirements are reduced to manageable ones.

Common law rules

The second important feature of genuine uncertainty is the perceived unlistability of all possible outcomes. As we have seen, this implies that maximization is impossible for the purely technical reason that the agent's problem is not well defined. It also suggests that an evolved system of rules may be quite effective in enabling the agent to attain his goals. Rules avoid the problem of attempting to fine tune a course of action when the requisite information is not available.

In this section we briefly discuss the relationship of the common law's rule orientation to the unlistability features of genuine uncertainty. In a world without genuine uncertainty it might be possible for the law to settle disputes in a way that is "optimal" in the circumstances. In such a world the judge might be able, for example, to trace the incentive effects of a given decision in various possible future states of the world. In other words, he might be able to make a fairly comprehensive list of the long-run consequences of each possible decision and then to determine which is optimal. When the judge is unable to determine all of the possible outcomes, however, he cannot choose the optimal course.[30] His decisions must be rule oriented, not based on a conscious cost-benefit calculation.[31] In fact, the legal rule must be followed regardless of its specific consequences in the particular case precisely because they cannot be known beforehand. This leads, as we have seen from our earlier discussion of rules, to an apparent rigidity in decisionmaking which accounts for what has been called the "static conception of the common law."[32]

Paradoxically, the same factor that is responsible for the static or rigid nature of the classical common law is also responsible for its dynamic tendency. To see this, consider that a judge cannot fully trace the future consequences of a decision in part because all of the future contexts in which that decision will be applied as the controlling precedent cannot be predicted. This implies that the rule itself is not fully formed or determinate ex ante. It is formed only in the process of its application. Suppose, for example, there is a rule that reads "no vehicles are permitted in the park."[33] The rule's meaning is not apparent until the judge is faced with a specific set of circumstances. Is a small motorized toy car driven by a child permitted or not? It might appear patently unjust in view of the purposes of public parks to forbid the toy car. Thus, the rule may be clarified to read "no vehicles beyond a certain size and which have a capacity for speeds beyond a certain level are permitted in the park." Because the circumstances of its application cannot be predicted the judge must wait until the rule is confronted with an actual context before he can decide how it should be formed, developed or modified. Although the current context thus affects the evolution of rules, the uncertainty of future contexts requires that judges confine any changes in the law to marginal increments. Since we cannot be sure of the future effects, we make only small changes and then wait to see what happens.

Unlistability is responsible for two opposite tendencies in the law: one static and the other dynamic. The common law is more rigid than it would be if judges could estimate the full future consequences of a decision. At the same time, it is dynamic in an unpredictable and marginal sense because the meaning of a legal rule emerges only in the process of its application.

Conclusion

In this essay, we have sketched the basic features of Austrian subjectivism. We have shown that the dynamic form of subjectivism involves the notion of time as a flow ("real time") and the extension of uncertainty to include endogeneity and unlistability. In a world characterized by real time and genuine uncertainty, continuous maximization fails to capture essential features of individual decision making. In this world entrepreneurial alertness and rule-following behavior both assume enormous analytical and practical importance. Without denying the need for further work on entrepreneurship, we chose here to concentrate on rules. The interrelation between uncertainty and rules was explored on a general and then on a specific level. We saw that rules have a crucial role in bargaining situations, in the coordination of competitive investment decisions, and in the common law process.

NOTES

* The views expressed in this paper do not represent official positions of either the Federal Reserve Bank of Dallas or New York University. A fuller treatment of the topics in part I can be found in O'Driscoll and Rizzo, *The Economics of Time and Ignorance* (Oxford and New York: Basil Blackwell, 1985), pp. 1–91.

1. Gerald P. O'Driscoll, Jr., "Carl Menger and Modern Economics," unpublished manuscript (Dallas, 1985).
2. James M. Buchanan, "The Domain of Subjective Economics: Between Predictive Science and Moral Philosophy," in *Method, Process and Austrian Economics: Essays in Honor of Ludwig von Mises*, ed. I. M. Kirzner (Lexington, Mass.: Lexington Books, 1982).
3. Compare Marshall's definition of economics as the "study of men as they live and think in the ordinary business of life." Alfred Marshall, *Principles of Economics*, 9th ed. (London: Macmillan, 1961), vol. I, p. 14.
4. F. A. Hayek, "Degrees of Explanation," in *Studies in Philosophy, Politics, and Economics* (Chicago: University of Chicago Press, 1967), pp. 3–21.
5. Ronald A. Heiner, "The Origin of Predictable Behavior," *American Economic Review*, 73 (September 1983), pp. 560–95.
6. For an analysis, see Gerald P. O'Driscoll, Jr., "Knowing, Expecting and

Theorizing," C. V. Starr Center for Applied Economics Working Paper no. 81–82 (New York: New York University, 1981).

7. This assumption characterizes much of rational expectations theory. See O'Driscoll and Rizzo, *The Economics of Time and Ignorance*, pp. 213–26; Gerald P. O'Driscoll, Jr., "Expectations and Monetary Regimes," Federal Reserve Bank of Dallas *Economic Review* (September 1984), pp. 5–9.
8. See, especially, Henri Bergson, *Time and Free Will*, trans. F. L. Pogson (New York: Humanities Press, 1971); *Creative Evolution* trans. Arthur Mitchell (New York: Henry Holt & Co., 1923).
9. "As soon as we permit time to elapse we must permit knowledge to change. . . ." L. M. Lachmann, "Professor Shackle on the Economic Significance of Time," *Metroeconomica*, XI (1973).
10. For an analysis, see O'Driscoll and Rizzo, *Economics of Time and Ignorance*, op. cit., pp. 22–7.
11. Nicholas Kaldor, "A Classificatory Note on the Determinateness of Equilibrium," *Review of Economic Studies*, I (1934), p. 147.
12. Contrast the maintained hypothesis of the Chicago school that "in the absence of sufficient evidence to the contrary, one may treat observed prices and quantities as good approximations to their long-run competitive equilibrium values." Melvin Reder, "Chicago Economics: Permanence and Change," *Journal of Economic Literature*, 20 (March 1982), p. 12.
13. See Israel M. Kirzner, *Competition and Entrepreneurship* (Chicago: University of Chicago Press, 1973).
14. Joseph A. Schumpeter, *The Theory of Economic Development* trans. R. Opie (Cambridge: Harvard University Press, 1934).
15. Murray N. Rothbard, *Man, Economy, and State* (Princeton: Van Nostrand, 1962), vol. II, pp. 464–9.
16. F. A. Hayek, "The Use of Knowledge in Society," *American Economic Review* (September 1945), p. 526.
17. J. M. Keynes, *The General Theory of Employment, Interest and Money* (New York: Harcourt, Brace & World, 1964 [1936]), p. 156.
18. Oskar Morgenstern, "Vollkommene Voraussicht und wirtschaftliches Gleichgewicht," *Zeitschrift für Nationalökonomie* 6 (part 3), in trans. Frank H. Knight, ed. A. Schotter, *Selected Writings of Oskar Morgenstern* (New York: New York University Press, 1976).
19. Brian Loasby, *Choice, Complexity, and Ignorance* (Cambridge: Cambridge University Press, 1976), p. 217.
20. See Heiner, "The Origin of Predictable Behavior," op. cit., pp. 562–3.
21. Ibid., pp. 564–5.
22. Robert Cooter, "The Cost of Coase," *Journal of Legal Studies*, 11 (1982), pp. 1–33.
23. O'Driscoll and Rizzo, *Economics of Time and Ignorance*, op. cit., pp. 213–26.
24. It is possible, of course to postulate in ad hoc fashion some type of convergence mechanism. This would, however, beg the question rather than resolve the problem.
25. The role of conventions will also be greater the larger the difference between the buyer's maximum purchase price and the seller's minimum sale price. This is well known.

26. G. B. Richardson, *Information and Investment* (Oxford: Oxford University Press, 1960).
27. If expectations are rational then each firm can optimize with respect to those expectations. Industrywide capacity expansion will then be right on average.
28. Richardson, op. cit., pp. 49–71.
29. For an exception see Donald Dewey, "Information, Entry, and Welfare: The Case for Collusion," *American Economic Review*, 69 (September 1979), pp. 587–94.
30. F. A. Hayek, *Law, Legislation and Liberty: The Mirage of Social Justice* (Chicago: University of Chicago Press, 1976), pp. 19–20.
31. Mario J. Rizzo, "Rules versus Cost-Benefit Analysis in the Common Law," *Cato Journal*, 5 (Spring 1985), pp. 865–84.
32. Richard A. Epstein, "The Static Conception of the Common Law," *Journal of Legal Studies*, 9 (1980), pp. 253–89.
33. H. L. A. Hart, *The Concept of Law* (Oxford: Clarendon Press, 1961), pp. 125–6.

19 Subjectivism and American Institutionalism

MARK PERLMAN

Subjectivism, the lodestone of Viennese thinking towards the end of the last century, has frequently been identified as one of the principal Austrian contributions to modern orthodox economics. This essay is an effort to perceive the impact of that element on several of the pioneer writers in the tradition of American institutionalism. There is a timely significance to a consideration of this topic because not only has there been a long-time continuous American recognition of the role of these seemingly heterodox writers, but more recently a new interest has appeared in several areas originally developed by them. These include contract theory, business cycle analysis, and even the psychology of interpersonal bargaining (now called game theory). Each of these areas is now emerging at the forefront of professional economics journal discussion.

Beside this aspect of timeliness, there is also the point that as others and I read some of Professor Hayek's more recent writings [Hayek, 1973, pp. 44–5], a good case can be made for noting the increasing role that the American institutionalist legacy has even come to play in his work, that is, in contemporary Austrian economic thinking, itself.[1]

For the record's sake let me start by noting that *subjectivism* was neither invented by the Austrians nor was its alleged alternative, Benthamite or Millian utilitarianism ("the greatest good for the greatest number"), without its own subjective aspects. The OED defines subjectivism as a doctrine suggesting that knowledge is within the mind of the individual and that there is no external test of truth. Insofar as I grasp that definition, it does not suggest that all life is lived in the mind of the individual, nor does it suggest that individuals really cannot communicate because each individual's thought is so personal in its perceptions that intercourse is impossible. It merely says that in the end one person cannot prove the truth of something to another by reference to cognitive perception. Proof, such as it may exist, thus seemingly depends upon *wertfrei* specification of assumptions and reliance upon the syllogism. Proof, however, is of subtle stuff, and most of what we consider professionally falls far short of proof (or of truth, for that matter).

The amazing point, however, about the American institutionalists is not that they built their own systems on the centrality of subjectivism (which in two of the three individuals discussed below was admittedly taken from the works of the original Austrian trio, Carl Menger, Boehm Bawerk, and Wieser), but that the three institutionalists I consider (Mitchell, Veblen, and Commons) were explicitly critical of the original Austrian "trio" for not incorporating into their theoretical contributions the full measure of subjectivism available to them.

The doctrine of individualism, a companion principal aspect of the Austrian economics legacy, has an even more complex history. In its usual form it stresses a social theory favoring free choice and action of individuals. But, it does not, and this is the important point, claim that all values are individually derived, even if a case can be made for the view that individuals may wish to make their own choices from a spectrum of socially influenced values. At the end of this essay, I shall return to an expansion of this point.

Given the vicissitudes of permitted length, this essay can undertake to consider, and even that superficially, only three somewhat separate aspects of the title. The first is simply to note that there was great variety of view about disciplinary objectives in each of the three of the original principal American institutionalist camps, Veblen's, Commons', and Mitchell's. The second is to identify and to assess, again admittedly only superficially, the role of Austrian (Viennese?) subjectivism in each of them. And, the third is to speculate a bit about the reasons why Commons' variant of institutionalism is becoming significantly a pattern for Professor Hayek's recent work in such form as to be, in truth, an unacknowledged precursor.

I

American institutional economics had several origins as well as several purposes. Of the former, one was an interest in the ways that markets, free and "semi-free," actually operate, as seen from some kinds of empirical standpoints. This approach clearly dominates the work of Commons and is also an essential element in Mitchell's perception of the roles of intermediate and final markets in the transmission of specific cycles in the process of forming business cycles.

A second was a desire to incorporate into then contemporary economic theory "discoveries" purportedly originating in the fields of clinical and social psychology and general anthropology. This emphasis seems to me to underlie the positive side of most of the work of Thorstein Veblen, a writer whose major contribution was correctly self-perceived as being on the negative side, albeit as a form of what Schumpeter later was to call "creative destruction."

A third was methodological in the purest sense and reflects an unusually strong professional desire to get away from abstractions (formal models) as well as any ideological preconditional commitments to free market price determination.[2] Instead, it reflected a behaviorist attitude towards market relationships, both because of an occasionally perceived need for social controls to aid those who from ethical and/or political standpoints should have greater market power, but also because virtually all (antimonopolist) efforts to reform the market (either in the simple name of more competition or greater social responsibility) seemed doomed to failure. I specifically eschew discussion in this essay of any of those institutionalist writers who were advocating various forms of socialism—ethical, efficiency, or scientific.

Because of the timing of the development of these three institutional writers, it became common for many mainstream economists to lump their views about institutionalism. Doing so was an error; differences between the institutionalists were greater than their similarities. Nor was any a simple offshoot of either German historical school. Quite the contrary, each reflected principally the impact of other influences, a point I share with Schumpeter (Schumpeter, 1954, p. 820). Mitchell was taken with statistical specification and an early form of index number analysis; Veblen, whatever his actual performance, was taken with Darwinism and the emerging disciplines of anthropology and psychology. And Commons was taken with legal history as a mirror of changing societies.

But it was in their purposes that they had significant similarities, one of which was to distinguish their work from the orthodoxy of their day. Characteristic of that orthodoxy was the Austrian contributions, built not only upon subjectivism but also upon a presumption of individualism. As important (or possibly even more so) was the Austrian preference for Descartian (i.e., Cartesian) abstraction and model building, a preference which none of the three Americans shared or even considered desirable. Thus, my point that the three Americans shared an interest in subjectivism with their Austrian "rivals," should not be stretched to assume that the differences were less than the similarities. This introductory remark would not be complete if I were to neglect to acknowledge that at least two of the writers, Veblen and Mitchell, were sufficiently stimulated by mainline or orthodox economists' criticism to respond to it; and, since much of that mainline thinking was inspired by Carl Menger, their replies suggested basic agreement with yet surviving differences anent his views. But I think that a case can be made that often the differences, particularly with regard to the making of decisions, were more apparent than real. And that is what this essay is about.

II

Wesley Clair Mitchell's path to his form of institutionalism started with a problem posed to him by J. Laurence Laughlin, his dissertational supervisor at the University of Chicago. It was to assess (and, if possible, to discredit as *simplistic*) Irving Fisher's quantity theory of money as the explanation for price fluctuations, specifically, and for business fluctuations, generally. Mitchell's method was to study the fluctuations of American gold prices before and after the 1879 resumption of specie payments. He found insufficient relationship between the quantity of gold traded and general business conditions to accept the Fisherian assertions (as he understood them).

This finding sufficed to satisfy Laughlin, and Mitchell was awarded his doctorate (Mitchell, 1903). Nonetheless, the finding did not satisfy Mitchell, who proceeded to ask a very Austrian-type question, "If not that, then what?" (Mitchell, 1908). He found *his* answer cognitively in the pressure of increasing cost prices on selling prices, with the businessman/entrepreneur feeling (and then acting on that feeling) caught in the squeeze (Mitchell, 1913). I italicize *feeling* because that is pure subjectivism; one cannot know what went on in the individual's mind, but judging from his actions, it seems probable that the feeling was strong. It was a feeling associated *ex ante* with a policy having profound social *ex post* consequences. In brief, I do not see that there was anything up to this point in Mitchell's analysis which was totally unacceptable to the Austrians, as surely the establishment of the

Austrian Institute for Business Cycle Research must have indicated. Indeed, Oskar Morgenstern's seminal role in its development (he was the director) suggests that one could be Mitchellian and Austrian at the same time.

As for Mitchell's individualism, what one can certainly say is that he expressed the profoundest of doubts about Bentham's assertion that individuals could actually cope with very many data in order to make considered, rational decisions. It is against rational individualism in action, not subjectivism, that Mitchell actually wrote. Nonetheless, since individualism was one of his targets, it can possibly be understood why the mainline economists, particularly those who were influenced by Carl Menger, believed Mitchell fundamentally hostile to all of their influences.

Mitchell's book of collected essays *The Backward Art of Spending Money* [1937], offers the fullest treatment on subjectivism, which one can find in his writings. The book is one which scholars truly overlook at the peril of their sophistication. Mitchell's key thought was that individuals might aspire to systematic decision making, but the effort did not guarantee anything except the likely findings that each effort was sui generis in conception and in consequence, situations to be regretted but unfortunately not likely to be changed.

In sum, if Mitchell's principal concern was to make measurements, like all sophisticated scholars he was acutely alert to the qualitative (perhaps subjective) bases in any measuring process. Mitchell was, it is true, strongly critical of the way subjectivism was handled in the Carl Menger-Austrian tradition, because it was Menger's methodological dictum that the psyche resists probing. One must take it as "there," but do no more about it. Actually, Mitchell's examination of Friedrich von Wieser's *Social Economics* (1941), is lengthy, and considering Mitchell's detailed assessment, respectful. It was even (as I see it) favorable (Mitchell, 1937, pp. 225–257). Mitchell urges the study of the translation of the book to which he wrote a Preface largely because the Wieser version of subjectivism is "agreeably realistic," the all but ultimate praise (p. 253).

Yet, in the end Mitchell also parts company with Wieser, largely along the Veblenian lines. It is not with subjectivism, as such, that Mitchell has doubts; it is with Wieser's limited psychologism including a refusal to go into subjectivism with enough enthusiastic penetration, which is the source of the difficulty. Specifically, Mitchell objects to Wieser's eschewing the insights into motivation and data-processing provided by modern psychology, especially of the groups interested in cognition. My point is best made by quoting Mitchell (1937, as noted).

> Yet if he had been willing to utilize psychology, Wieser might have made out a better case for his own theory (p. 255). . . . It is an old and valid criticism that the Austrian theory of value throws little light on the process of valuation. It supposes men to come to the market with their minds definitely made up regarding the prices they will pay. The demand schedules it presents are purely imaginary and are used only as illustrations. Everything that happens in the market . . . is supposed to be predetermined in an almost mechanical way by such schedules. Nevertheless, a serious study of them has been no part of orthodox theory. . . . We all know that our wants are standardized by certain social habits, that these habits present remarkable uniformities, and that they have a long recorded history (p. 257).

As seen by Mitchell, Wieser's fault was that, because Wieser was leery of the uses of observation, he rejected much of what subjectivism really can offer. In brief, Mitchell, far from rejecting subjectivism, argued that the Austrians (of whom Wieser was the most flexible on the topic) did not go far enough. On this point, at least, Mitchell was far more royalist than the king.

And even in his assessment of his own teacher, Thorstein Veblen (whose attacks on Austrian theory dominated much of his time), Mitchell took pains to show that Veblen misstated his criticisms about the origins of economic analysis. The target of Mitchell's arrows was the impact on the economics discipline of a Bentham-espoused "irrational passion for rationality" (John Maurice Clark's phrase), not the Austrian contribution of subjectivism. Fetter, the American mainline economic theorist Mitchell professed most to admire, was admired clearly because he was the linkage to the Austrian contributions (Mitchell, 1939, pp. 155–60).

Thorstein Veblen's passion was to recast economics into an entity he called "evolutionary science." His attack on the discipline started with an assertion that, unlike anthropologists, orthodox economists assumed that individuals were Benthamite calculators, using efficiency rules of maximization and minimization to reach their decisions. If Bentham was the principal target of his attacks, very few others were completely spared. Cairnes, whom he regarded as the most competent of the classical expositors, was a taxonomist whose work was variously described in 1898 as "a monocotyledonous wage doctrine and a cryptogamic theory of interest, with involute, loculicidal, tomentous and moniliform variants," and "if we ... tire [of it] what is the cytoplasm, centrosome, or karyokinetic process to which we may turn?" Even Carl Menger, whose leadership he almost admires, seems unable to break with a taxonomic preference because he does not realize that subjectivism is not a state of mind at rest (identifying states of satisfaction), but rather a description of a mind in action (where satisfaction comes from the becoming rather than the being) [Veblen, 1919, p. 70].

Given a certain perverse attractiveness to Veblen's choice of an outrageous vocabulary and to the obvious point that adjectives seem more interesting than nouns, the crucial fact is that his criticisms, however valid, are not easy to implement. In the end he, himself, sets as his goal a description of the impact of certain instinct upon the choosing of relevant experiences. The choice of these instincts seem to me to rely upon authority albeit not economic authority. Like Mitchell, he is against sophomoric reliance upon the Benthamite pleasure-pain calculus. His target is more obvious than any path proposed by him.

John R. Commons' goal seems to have been more concrete. He wanted to know whether one could discover what externally influenced internal individual decision making. Institutions he decided were the key; they were collective choice in charge of individual choice. Whence came, however, precise institutions? He, himself, admits that he started with Boehm-Bawerk's answer (Commons, 1924, p. vi). But he found that an individualistic hedonism (which he associated with the Austrians) did not explain observable life, as he observed it.

The question of where one can find the "records of life" became central to his investigations and speculation. In the end, Commons turned not to anthropologists' findings nor even to sociologists' measures (the kind of things which attracted Veblen) but to written court records (see Holmes' concluding *dictum*, "the Common Law [as recorded] is the life of the people") which Commons came to treat as the kind of hard evidence one needs to discover the process of socially controlled decision making at one kind of an individual's margin.

Thus, relying overtly on Frederick Maitland's method (and less overtly on Otto von Gierke's), Commons came to argue that it was in the formal relationships between conflicted individuals that one could most easily discover the subjective valuation process in being. Discovering how that process actually operated was the precise point which he had wanted to and had failed to get from the works of Menger and Boehm-Bawerk (he did not treat von Wieser's contributions).

The conflicts could be highly stylized as in court cases, or they could be lower key as in simple contractual negotiations. What characterized both (he preferred the generic term *transaction*) was a method (1) for discovering what individuals seemed to want, (2) for seeing how the price of getting what they wanted affected the total value of their seeming wants, and in time, (3) for creating a ceremony or administrative method to achieve the desired ends in some efficient but also in some Paretian manner, which, itself, became part of the satisfaction. If in Commons' world the goal was to understand the individual, Commons' individual was all but invariably part of a going community, where the community provided institutions which were one and at the same time constraints upon and mechanisms for the realization of certain of most individuals' presumably independent preference schedules. In his words,

> This [transaction] process has three attributes which gives us three meanings of value, each of which was separately emphasized by different schools of economists. Value has that subjective or volitional meaning of *anticipation* which may be named *psychological value* and which is the moving force . . . (Commons, 1924, p. 8).

The others, less important to this point, involved objective *commodities* (or services) which were actually traded and had a real value aspect, and *prices* which offered only nominal value.

More could be made of Commons' appreciation of the subjectivism of the valuation process, particularly his fascinations with the idea of the market role (and valuation) of *goodwill*, but space does not permit that discussion here (however, see Commons, 1919).

We come now to the more recent absorption of the Commons legacy. Again, it is worth stressing that I am not claiming anything more than the point that in Professor Hayek's recent work his approach to the way that the mind operates as well as the way that the market operates is strangely consistent with Commons' thinking of a good many decades earlier. One could cite several sources; I shall mention only two.

In volume I of *Law, Legislation and Liberty: Rules and Order* (Hayek 1973, pp. 35–54), Hayek lays out in explicit terms his view that institutions are social rules which govern individual behavior.[3] Two of the younger "Austrians," O'Driscoll and Rizzo, make a great deal of this point:

> Rules provide, as it were, safe bounds for behavior in a relatively unbounded world. *Institutions are the social crystallization of rule-following behavior or, in other words, the overall pattern of many individuals following a similar rule*. Thus, the circle is closed. Time and genuine uncertainty promote the following of rules and development of institutions. The latter, in turn, serve to reduce, but not eliminate, the unboundedness of the economic system by providing the stable pattern of interaction (emphasis added).

In his 1974 Nobel Award Lecture Professor Hayek concluded his general argument with the words

> We are only beginning to understand on how subtle a communication system the functioning of an advanced industrial society is based—a communications system which we call the market and which turns out to be a more efficient mechanism for digesting dispersed information than any that man has deliberately designed (Hayek, 1978, p. 34).

If this is pure Hayek, it is also amazingly resemblant of vintage Commons, who some half century earlier wrote in what I presume is among the best of his studies

> The system of prices is like the system of words or the system of numbers. They are signs and symbols needed for the effective means by which human beings can deal with each other securely and accurately with regard to things that are real. But each may be insecure and inaccurate. Words are deceptive if they do not convey the meaning intended; number are liars if they do not indicated the actual quantities; prices are inflated or deflated if they do not reflect the course of real value (Commons, 1924, p. 9).

Subjectivism underlies the decision, but the decision, itself, has to depend upon concrete language.

The meaning of the convergence of the two quite different schools of economic thought is not only that they are now trying to deal with the same problem, the problem which Commons and Mitchell had tried to define earlier, but also that there was within the Austrian tradition an all but dormant conceptual element, which both Commons and Mitchell perceived as crucial to the "actual" (meaning *nominalist*) operation of markets. That conceptual element was "ignorance," or as I prefer to phrase it *unknowledge*.

This element can be seen in Thuenen's writing; it is noted by Frank Knight in his own doctoral dissertation [Knight, 1921 p. 26n,n. 4], where he undertakes to make a strong point of it. In our time, the preeminent theorist dealing with this idea is George L. S. Shackle, whose work integrates the essence of subjectivism[4] of the Austrians with the peculiarly significance contribution of John Maynard Keynes to probability analysis [Keynes, 1921, 1973]. This was reflected strongly in Chapter 12, "Long-term Expectations" (in contrast to Chapter 11, "The Marginal Efficiency of Capital," in *The General Theory* ... [Keynes, 1936]) and even more strongly in his article, "The General Theory of Employment" [Keynes, 1937], which was a reply to two of his principal critics (Viner and Robertson).

Obviously, I am not implying that the Austrians of the original order or of the modern Hayekian period are converging with Commons, much less Mitchell. The Austrian faith in perfect competition remains strong; Commons (and probably Mitchell) never had much faith in such a concept. Commons actually thought that little could be done to stem the tide of bigness except to encourage countervailing power. (This is not Commons' but John Maurice Clark's and John Kenneth Galbraith's perception.) While Commons often and Hayek almost always had frequently voiced and certainly well-founded doubts about the efficacy of governmental (national, state, and local) intervention into the market or what Commons called "transactions," Commons was far less reluctant than Hayek to accept such intervention when there seemed no easy and obvious alternative, but even here Hayek's record is far from alien to the idea of social security.[5]

What were Commons' principal concerns, particularly after he came to the University of Wisconsin in 1903, included an understanding of how group values that permeated individual decision making (how the *Genossenchaft*, to use von Gierke's phrase) were defined and enforced, and what effect that definition had on transaction performance. As I see Professor Hayek's recent work he has come to the same set of concerns, except that his terminology is not only different but more typical of what the economics profession has always used. In brief, the reason why there is a similarity of conclusion, due allowance being made both for semantic differences and for over 75 years having passed, is that the current question Hayek considers is the same as the one Commons pondered and because Commons' system always incorporated the Austrian contribution of subjectivism. Unlike Veblen and Mitchell Commons did not feel any need to apply cognitive psychology and certainly not modern psychiatric analysis to individual decisions. In this sense, Commons, clearly even more than Veblen and Mitchell, is the obvious linkage to the Austrians.

NOTES

1. This position is put well in a recent manuscript by O'Driscoll and Rizzo (1985, chap. 1), who cite Hayek (1973).
2. Karl Pribram identifies as one of the current, and even dominant, strands of economics an empirico-hypothetical method. He credits it to Roger Bacon. I would consider Francis Bacon's "Great Insaturation" (Baconian *Scientific Method*) as the better example. Mitchell and Commons, however, were even somewhat more explicitly nominalist (empiricism oriented) than Francis Bacon. I am somewhat less persuaded than was the late Tjalling C. Koopmans (see "Measurement without Theory" [Koopmans, 1947]) that they really followed their own precepts as closely as they claimed, since each depended upon conceptualizations, which must be in their development abstractions as well as generalizations.
3. To quote Hayek (1973, p. 45): "The question which is of central importance as much for social theory as for social policy is thus what properties the rules must possess so that the separate actions of the individuals will produce an overall order. Some such rule all individuals of a society will obey because they will be part of their common cultural tradition. But there will be still others which they may have to be made to obey since, although it would be in the interest of each to disregard them, the overall order on which the success of their actions depends will arise only if these rules are generally followed.

   In a modern society based on exchange, one of the chief regularities in individual behavior will result from the similarity of situation in which most individuals find themselves in working to earn an income; which means that they will normally prefer a larger return from their efforts to a smaller one, and often that they will increase their efforts in a particular direction if the prospects of return improve. This is a rule that will be followed at least with sufficient frequency to impress upon such a society an order of a certain kind. But the fact that most people will follow this rule will still leave the character of the resulting order very indeterminate, and by itself certainly would not be sufficient to give it a beneficial character. For the resulting order to be beneficial people must also observe some conventional rules, that is, rules which do not simply follow from their desires and their insight into relations of cause and effect, but which are normative and tell them what they ought to or ought not to do."
4. What could be more subjective than "Does it take two people to make an exchange? Not when one and the same person has before him a choice of this or that. If takes *this*, he will in effect be giving *that* in exchange for it" (Shackle, 1973, p. 1).

5. In 1944 when Hayek wrote *The Road to Serfdom* his endorsement in principle of social insurance (social security) did not go unnoticed or uncriticized by some of the leaders of the Austrian school (Hayek, 1944. pp. 120–121). Here, again, there is a parallel with Commons. Commons' student, Paul Rauschenbush, designed the first enacted unemployment insurance act (Wisconsin, 1931); another Commons student, Edwin E. Witte, chaired the national committee which drew up the federal Old Age and Survivors' Insurance Bill (1935). And it was a "next-generation" Wisconsin student, Wilbur Cohen, who drew up the Medicare legislation.

REFERENCES

Commons, John R. (1924), *Legal Foundations of Capitalism* (New York: Macmillan).

Hayek, Friedrich A. (1973), *Law, Legislation and Liberty: Rules and Order*, (Chicago: University of Chicago Press), vol. 1.

—— (1944), *The Road to Serfdom* (Chicago: University of Chicago Press).

Keynes, John Maynard (1973), *A Treatise on Probability* (London: Macmillan, 1919).

—— (1973), *The General Theory of Employment, Interest and Money*. (London: Macmillan).

—— (1977), "The General Theory of Employment," *Quarterly Journal of Economics*, 51, pp. 209–223.

Knight, Frank H. (1921), *Risk, Uncertainty, and Profit* (New York: Houghton Mifflin).

Koopmans, Tjalling Charles (Aug. 1947), "Measurement without Theory," *Review of Economic Statistics*, 29, pp. 161–72.

Mitchell, Wesley Clair (1903), *A History of the Greenbacks, With Special Reference to the Economic Consequences of Their Issue: 1862–1865* (Chicago: University of Chicago Press).

—— (1908), *Gold, Prices, and Wages Under the Greenback Standard*. University of California Publications in Economics (Berkeley: University of California Press), vol. 1.

—— (1913), *Business Cycles* (Berkeley: University of California Press).

—— (1950), *The Backward Art of Spending Money* (New York: McGraw-Hill).

O'Driscoll, Gerald P., and Mario J. Rizzo (1985), *The Economics of Time and Ignorance* (Oxford: Basil Blackwell).

Pribram, Karl (Feb. 1951), "Prolegomena to the History of Economics Reasoning," *Quarterly Journal of Economics*, pp. 1–37.

—— (May 1953), "Patterns of Economic Reasoning," *American Economic Review*, 43, pp. 358–369.

—— (1983), *A History of Economic Reasoning* (Baltimore: Johns Hopkins University Press). See particularly Part II, 4.

Schumpeter, Joseph A. (1954), *The History of Economic Analysis* (New York: Oxford University Press).

Shackle, George L. S. (1973), *An Economic "Querist"* (Cambridge: Cambridge University Press).

Veblen, Thorstein (1919), *The Place of Science in Modern Civilization* (New York: B. W. Heubsch). (The 1898 reference is to the essay, "Why Economics is Not an Evolutionary Science," *Quarterly Journal of Economics* 12 [July 1898].

von Wieser, Friedrich (1927), *Social Economics*, trans. A. Ford Heinrichs (New York: Adelphi).

20 The Origination of Choice

GEORGE L. S. SHACKLE

THOUGHT AND TIME

With Cantillon, economic theory came suddenly to full flower in one great work, as a description of business. Business depends on numerical comparisons, and thus economic theory took on at the outset the air of a quantitative science. Many of the notions involved were measurements of natural or technical processes to the relations of which the principles of nature gave repetitive constancy. But Cantillon incisively made plain that these relations provided only the rules of the game, within which the play and its results were the work of thought, of knowledge, and irremediable lack of knowledge, and of the powers of mind which exploit that lack. Business appears as technics, but behind this lies psychics. Imagination, the power of conceiving the unprecedented, the alchemy of thought, are liberated and ignited by mankind's elemental predicament, human imprisonment in *present time*.

Present time is the transience of thought. Each moment of thought exists by its passage into another. It is succeeded by another. This succession is experienced, but it can also be imagined. The imagined unceasing succession of moments is time-to-come. Imagined time must itself be filled by work of imagination drawing suggestions from the present. The chooser among rival actions open to him, rival deployments of his resources, asks himself; What will the sequel be, if I do this, or if I do this? What can be the form of his answer?

Can the answer describe a singular, unequivocal path which, given his commitment to some specific action, the chooser supposes his affairs will follow? This would imply that he can know, when he makes his decision, just how the course of his affairs will be affected by choices of action made by others in time-to-come. Such knowledge of choices-to-come could only exist in the present, if each such choice was entirely determined by present circumstances and takings-place. To suppose that choices-to-come are thus predetermined destroys the meaning of choice, robbing human choices of all power of their own. The notion of choice would be empty and the act of choice sterile. A nondeterminist view of history requires us to suppose that a choice can be in some respects exempt from governance by antecedent thought or contemporary circumstances, that a choice can be in some respects an *uncaused cause*. If so, the question that the chooser can validly ask himself, concerning a particular envisaged action, is: What, at best and at worst, can the sequel be? If, as my theme assumes, there is an essential, irreducible, pervasive nondeterminacy in human affairs, no single supposed sequel can be deemed certain to prove true, no *list* of such hypotheses can be deemed certain to contain amongst its members the one that will prove true. The valid concept is a skein of imagined, invented sequels, a list *endlessly variant and augmentable*, subject only to the constraint of adjudged *possibleness*.

THE SKEIN OF POSSIBLES EPITOMIZED BY BEST AND WORST

What the chooser should seek, for each of the rival actions he envisages, is a conception of the best and of the worst outcome he can deem possible for it. Then, how must he interpret "best" and "worst," and how must he interpret "possible"? How, among rival envisaged actions, must he conceive the degree to which, in each, the best outcome deemed possible outweighs the worst for his purpose of choice? "Best" and "worst" refer, of course, to the desiredness or counter-desiredness of the outcomes according to his own psychics and circumstances and to the character of the imagined outcomes in any degree of their complexity. It seems evident that such a business of weighing good and bad and comparing the results of such weighing cannot in general be explicitly dissected. What splendor resides for the individual in some formal result, and what exposure to possible crippling misfortune he will accept for its sake, are matters surely unsearchable. There is little to be gained, I think, by searching for a scalar proxy for desiredness and counter-desiredness when these judgments apply to a complex or a vague result. It is only when they apply to an imagined sequel which is itself inherently numerical that the chooser between two available actions can make explicit the grounds of his choice. But in business it is just such cases that are pervasively typical. They arise momentously in the investment decision, where large resources committed to an enterprise will bring their return only in the course of many years. All these suggestions, however, refer to sequels imagined for specific courses of action, and deemed *possible*. How is *possible* to be understood?

POSSIBLENESS

In order to bear upon choices of action, a hypothesis of the outcome must be deemed possible, that is to say, it must seem, after critical scrutiny, to be compatible with the chooser's entire body of suppositions about the nature of things and their existing posture, and about their orientation, the place assigned to them in the plans of others. I shall call this body of suppositions the chooser's subjective knowledge. We can suppose the chooser to ask himself, concerning each hypothesis he forms of the sequel of some action, whether it is entirely compatible with his body of knowledge, and if it is not, to dismiss it. This is to treat possibleness as a category. This view would simplify my theme, for it reduces the rivalry amongst imagined sequels of some action to the matter of their desiredness or counter-desiredness. Their possibleness is a matter of yes or no, not of degree. When, in this rivalry of content, the sequels which, up to the deadline moment for decision, the chooser has had time to conceive are arranged in order from most desired to most counter-desired, it is evident, I think, that all others will be *eclipsed* by one or other of these two extremes. It is these two extremes amongst the sequels all equally deemed possible which will constitute for the chooser the power of his action to benefit or harm him. He cannot know what his action *will* do for him. The two extremes are what, at best and worst, he supposes that it *can* do.

The conception and procedure of the business of choice amongst actions, to which my suggestions lead, on the one hand, and those derived from the calculus of probabilities, on the other, stand in absolute contrast. Probabilities can be assigned only to the members of a list of kinds (a list of classes of result) taken to be exhaustive and therefore certain to include the true kind or class. The probability table is a sharing of certainty and thus consists, in meaning if not in realizable practice, of proper fractions summing to unity. Probabilities in such a table are additive, and, when multiplied respectively into the utilities of the items of the list, are, in fact used additively, even when each choosable action will be, if adopted, a one-time, singular, crucial, and self-destructive experiment. When the table of probabilities refers to a one-time experiment, it implies the meaningless adding together of mutual exclusives. Its irrelevance in such a case is made explicit when it is called a "frequency table." By contrast with these contradictions, possibleness is adjudged to a hypothesis or imagined sequel of specific action in its own right, regardless of the number of its rivals.

When the grounds of desiredness and counter-desiredness are themselves numerical, and when possibleness is for the chooser a yes-or-no category and not a matter of degree, the business of choice between two courses of action can be formalized explicitly. I shall refer to the best and the worst sequel deemed possible for some actions respectively as its focus-gain and focus-loss. We may suppose the chooser to compare the numerical excess of the focus-gain of course *Z* over that of course *Y*, with the numerical excess of the focus-loss of course *Z* over that of course *Y*. According to his tastes and circumstances, the former of these differences may outweigh the latter. If so, his choice will fall on course *Z*. Let it be noticed that the ultimate comparison is not a numerical one. It is subjective, and its decision could be different for a different individual, or for the same individual in different circumstances. It will be evident also that we have here a decision problem simplified in two respects. Desiredness is scalar, and possibleness is a category.

THE EPISTEMIC INTERVAL

Possibleness need not be a category. Sometimes the chooser will feel, as his decision date approaches, that he has not had time to examine fully the congruity of some hypothesis with his subjective knowledge. Sometimes that knowledge will seem plainly insufficient in relevant respects. For his business of choice amongst actions he still needs to decide what is the best and what is the worst that a specified course would expose him to, but now the location of those extremes may depend on the degree of doubt he feels about the possibility of this or that hypothesis. If so, he is treating possibleness as a variable. Its range of definition will lie between entire possibility and nonpossibility, and these two are the natural bounds of what we may call the "epistemic interval." His judgments of possibleness, as of desiredness, will be the product of grounds and intuitions peculiar to himself and his experience. If, from that experience, he can select instances where typical assemblages of evidence led him to adjudge degrees of possibleness roughly or vaguely fixable in memory, some approach to a stable graduation of the epistemic interval may be within reach. At best, however, this would be a matter of private thought scarcely communicable to others. Even in private thought the fixing of degrees of possibleness raises a further question. Possibleness is not objective. It is, in itself, an abstraction. In order to make it in any sense fixable or graduable, it needs to find reflection in some emotion whose intensities lend themselves to comparison. Such an emotion, responding directly to epistemic circumstances, is to hand in the feeling of *surprise*.

To envisage a specific sequel of some course of action and to find this thought engendering the thought that such a sequel would be surprising is a direct reflection of doubt concerning its possibility. The intensity of that potential surprise will surely reflect the impressiveness of the doubt. Degrees of potential surprise may provide the chooser with a means of expressing to himself his judgments of comparative possibleness. However, such a frame of thought need not be supposed to provide a permanent scale. The act of decision is a fusing of judgments of different kinds, and these judgments in effect are made all at once in that moment and have their mutually relevant existence in that moment. The chooser of action wishes to fix upon the best and the worst imagined outcome of each action that are *possible enough*: the best that is possible enough to be worth hoping for, and the worst that is too possible to be dismissed.

REFINEMENTS

There is a temptation to think in terms of continuous functions. Their manipulations are elegantly incisive and lend to any argument which can be forced into their mould an air of conclusive truth. But decision is an act not only of deliberative thought but of moral commitment. It is an action taken in face of unknowledge of its sequel. The decision maker's knowledge allows him to imagine that sequel in many widely variant forms. His choice of one action rather than another is not a matter of small exact differences but of a quantum shift. Decision is discrete. Yet these admissions need not deny us the suggestiveness of continuity. If the epistemic interval can be vaguely graduated, let us suppose it to be precisely graduable. Then we shall be able to say that for some specified action, the desiredness of outcomes imagined for it, and the degrees of potential surprise respectively assigned to them will, over some ranges, be functions of each other. Let us allow ourselves a third variable, that of ascendancy or the attention-arresting power of some degree of desiredness or counter-desiredness, and its assigned degree of potential surprise. Ascendancy will assuredly be an increasing function of desiredness, and a decreasing function of potential surprise. There will be, within some range of greater or less desiredness, a constrained maximum of ascendancy; and again within some range of greater or less counter-desiredness, another such constrained maximum. When we treat possibleness as a variable, and represent it by potential surprise, the two constrained maxima of ascendancy can serve as the focus-gain and focus-loss of the action. One further refinement will exploit continuity to the utmost in aid of formal elegance. The constrained maxima of ascendancy can be thought of as maxima of a "twisted curve" (in American, a "space curve") that is to say, a path traced on an implicit surface in which every point will correspond to some pair of values of desiredness and potential surprise conceived in abstraction from any specific action. On this surface, equal-ascendancy lines will enable us to find the "entirely possible" equivalent of any particular pair of associated values of desiredness and potential surprise.

EPISTEMIC STANDING: THE INVERTED MEASURE

In the foregoing I have defined the epistemic interval as the range from entire adjudged possibility through entangled possibility to eliminated possibility. However, it is better to relate the term epistemic interval to the notion of epistemic standing, that is to say, the seriousness with which the chooser of action treats a hypothesis of the sequel, regardless of its desiredness or the opposite. Epistemic standing is traditionally represented by probability, somehow defined, somehow determined or adjudged. I have argued that probability, as a sharing of certainty, is illicit in the case of an essentially ever-extensible list of hypotheses, since this can at no stage be treated as necessarily including what will prove to be the truth. *Disbelief*, in any particular degree that may be fixable, can be accorded to mutually *rival* hypotheses without limit of number. It can be so accorded in zero degree and will then correspond to adjudged entire possibility. Disbelief, or potential surprise, is thus an inverted expression of epistemic standing. By this inversion of measurement we rid ourselves of the crippling additive character of probability, inherited from its origin in games of chance.

At the root of my theme lies the supposition that thought can be an uncaused cause, what I would call a beginning. This notion involves a leap of thought that many will find senseless. Yet how else can we claim to be (as plenipotentiaries, if you will) the authors of our history? Certainly the scrambled writing of many hands in the book reads differently from what any individual intended. But if we can suppose that not all of these writings were dictated, that gives meaning to the idea of originative choice. My theme repudiates the possibility of a calculable dynamics of history. In seeking to express it I am handicapped by the lack of a word for *ex nihilo* origination. It is this meaning that I intend in calling this brief paper the "Origination of Choice."

21 The Economics of Information: a Subjectivist View

P. D. F. STRYDOM

Although the importance of information in the economic process will not be disputed by economists, Stigler maintained that it occupies a "slum dwelling in the town of economics."[1] Since this assertion was made in 1961, the economics of information has attracted the attention of several authors who followed Stigler in analyzing information in terms of probability theory.[2] It could be claimed that this approach to the economics of information is closely linked with equilibrium economics.[3] Similarly, a recent attempt by Stonier who considered information as a factor of production could also be classified as an equilibrium approach since information is analyzed within the static neoclassical framework of perfect foresight.[4] Machlup has followed a different approach by associating the economics of information with the so-called "knowledge industries" while the dissemination of knowledge became the focal point of the analysis.[5]

It is claimed here that there is no meaningful link between equilibrium economics and the economics of information since such an analysis is dependent on the static paradigm of perfect foresight. Information should primarily be associated with a changing and dynamic environment. Although the dissemination of knowledge is an important aspect of the economics of information the subject should be encouraged to develop beyond the mere dissemination of knowledge, while taking cognizance of the value added of the Machlupian knowledge industries. The problem of information can only be analyzed meaningfully in a dynamic context. We maintain that the subjectivist approach, as for instance proposed by Lachmann, constitutes an intellectual framework which could place the analysis of information within the orbit of dynamic economics.[6]

I INFORMATION AND EQUILIBRIUM ECONOMICS[7]

The term "equilibrium economics" is used here to describe that particular intellectual framework in economic analysis which dispenses with time.[8] In equilibrium economics the future and the past are combined into a single dimension of logical time where what has happened in the past will also happen in future. In such a world the suggestion by Hicks is appropriate, viz., we can "go straight ahead, setting our mathematical engines to work on it, churning it out."[9] This analytical framework is primarily static, characterized by the hypothesis that the equilibrating forces overrule the forces that induce change. Equilibrium economics has had substantial support in the literature. In the Walrasian mathematical framework the static assumptions of the model imply instantaneous adjustments which, in the terminology of Lachmann means that the correct information about equilibrium prices and quantities should be readily available to all market participants.[10] Market participants also have perfect foresight in this framework, and consequently we are addressing a world with no uncertainty. As indicated by Walsh and Gram such a static framework means that there can be no speculative gains or losses owing to uncertainty.[11] More importantly, with no uncertainty there is no entrepreneur in the sense employed by Schumpeter or Knight. The instantaneous adjustments in equilibrium economics are only possible because of the perfect foresight with which market participants are endowed. Because of the static framework of these models, they can only address equilibrium situations, and, as indicated by Torr, equilibrium economics has nothing to say about nonequilibrium situations since no trading is allowed at nonequilibrium prices.[12] From this exposition it is evident that equilibrium economics is characterized by a framework in which perfect foresight is attributed to market participants while instantaneous adjustment prevails. Within such a framework there is no uncertainty, and information dissemination through the market process has no meaning. As soon as we enter the orbit of uncertainty we no longer have perfect information and in the terminology of Baumol and Quandt decision making is optimally imperfect.[13] We address the problem of optimal solution as opposed to a maximal solution, the maximal solution being attainable within the framework of perfect foresight. In the absence of perfect foresight the plans of market participants do not match instantaneously. In fact they diverge, and their divergence creates opportunities that could be exploited advantageously by those with superior information.[14] We can thus, address the problem of information economics meaningfully only if we depart from the intellectual framework of equilibrium economics. Information only has meaning in a world of uncertainty.

II THE SUBJECTIVIST APPROACH AS AN ALTERNATIVE TO EQUILIBRIUM ECONOMICS

As has already been indicated, the economics of information can only be studied meaningfully within a dynamic framework, and the subjectivist approach offers interesting and helpful building blocks in this regard. A dynamic framework is attained by introducing a time dimension which means that we dispense with the static framework of equilibrium economics where the past and the future are the same. This statement is in line with that of Hicks, who maintained that the essence of dynamic analysis is that the present and the future are not identical.[15] The importance of formulating a time dimension with this distinction in mind has the advantage that one explicitly introduces the concept of change as one goes from one period to the next. It is the concept of change within a time dimension which signals the importance of the subjectivist approach since it is uniquely related to the actions of human beings, and as we start analyzing these actions the subjectivist approach enters the exposition. Kirzner maintained that "The core of the concept of human action is to be found in the unique property possessed by human beings of engaging in operations designed to attain a state of affairs that is preferred to that which has hitherto prevailed."[16] The essence of the subjectivist approach is that human beings apply their reason to prevailing and known circumstances to attain a preferred state of affairs, and in doing so they become active within a time dimension, going from the present to the future.[17] From the point of view of information economics there are a number of interesting aspects in this dynamic process. First, it is important to note that the only systematic knowledge is that of the past, and it is composed of a stock of knowledge together with experience and understanding of the environment. Second, we can apply this knowledge to come to an understanding of the present. In order to bring the future into the analysis we have to consider a third aspect, viz., expectations.[18] The importance of introducing expectations into the analysis is that it enables us to invoke the time dimension explicitly. Expectations about the future can be derived by applying our imagination to conceive certain states of affairs which are different from the past. These states are, of course, different from each other in a dynamic framework, while, by definition, in a static framework, they never change. The future cannot be the subject of scientific analysis, but we can conceive it by applying our imagination. It is this subjectivist view of expectations and of the future which is important in dynamic processes. By applying our imagination to the future we are able to plan and the divergence of human plans is the basis for dynamics. If the plans of different individuals match there is no need for change, and we may signal the existence of equilibrium in terms of Hayek.[19] By applying one's imagination the human mind conceives a state of affairs in the future which is preferred to that of the past. The attainment of this state of affairs is achieved by means of a systematic plan, setting out a program of action to attain the goal. By implementing these actions one goes from the past into the future, and we are then addressing a dynamic framework. Within this framework we are not only concerned with the plans of the individual in isolation. The actions taken by others are also important, but probably more important are the most likely actions to be taken by them. The plans of a particular person will therefore not only relate to his actions but it will also be based on his expectations regarding the likely actions of other persons.[20]

Furthermore, there must be some degree of compatibility between different plans if they are to be carried out.[21] Information is now of crucial importance since changing circumstances are identified through information. As soon as new information becomes available expectations regarding the future change and new plans are formulated to guide the actions of market participants. In the dynamic framework it becomes important to be informed, to know the latest information. More importantly, one could ensure a competitive advantage by becoming informed ahead of other market participants, enabling the amendment of plans in accordance with the new perceptions of the future, and the likely actions to be taken by other market participants.

The exposition has now progressed beyond the limits of equilibrium economics where expectations are only important because they reflect "beliefs concerning states of nature,"[22] such as the future condition of the weather. We are now addressing the subject matter of decentralized competitive markets in the terminology of Frydman, where decisions are taken individually by market participants in terms of their private information.[23] The subject of private information requires further elaboration since it is a very important aspect of the subjectivist approach to the economics of information. The significance of private information has been recognized explicitly by Lachmann. While referring to the importance of the interpretation of information, he maintained that "It follows that any experience made conveys knowledge to us only insofar as it fits, or fails to fit, into a pre-existent frame of knowledge. But the frame of knowledge in terms of which we interpret a new experience is always 'private and subjective'. Knowledge always belongs to an individual mind."[24] This is a further dimension of the dynamic process, namely, the interpretation of information. We claim that, although the distribution and transmission of information by Machlupian knowledge industries is interesting in itself, the economics of information is primarily concerned with the interpretation of information. By this is meant that after the information has been disseminated by the market, the handling and application of information is characterized by diversity since the interpretation of information involves the activities of different minds, or to put it in the terminology of Lachmann: "Knowledge always belongs to an individual mind," which means that information is interpreted differently by different market participants since individual minds are different.[25] We are now in a position to extend our dynamic exposition. In a dynamic world where the future and the past are different markets disseminate information. As the information becomes available, market participants start interpreting the information, and while doing so they shape their expectations of the future of which as yet they have no knowledge. Then they start making plans in terms of which they could reach a particular future state of affairs. New evidence in support of the existing plan is of the utmost importance and the plan will only be revised if warranted by the interpretation of the new information. The interpretation of information could therefore be of greater importance than the information itself. In terms of the subjectivist approach it is not the dissemination of information which is the focal point of analysis in the economics of information, but the interpretation thereof.

III CONCLUSION

Several attempts have been made in the literature to analyze the economics of information within the framework of equilibrium economics, but it is maintained here that the typical problems associated with the economics of information cannot be analyzed meaningfully within the paradigm of equilibrium economics. The economics of information can only be analyzed meaningfully in a dynamic framework, and, since equilibrium economics dispenses with time, it is of little help in analyzing these problems. The subjectivist approach constitutes a meaningful dynamic framework by taking cognizance of a time dimension. Furthermore, the time dimension is applied explicitly by considering the actions taken by market participants to attain a particular preferred state of affairs in future. This state of affairs is attained in terms of a plan which is based on the existing stock of knowledge, expectations regarding the future, and the likely action by other market participants. Within this dynamic framework the economics of information is primarily concerned with the interpretation of information, which means that it is associated with the actions of the human mind. When new information becomes available the plans regarding the actions by market participants are revised, provided that revision is warranted by the interpretation of the information. Since human minds operate uniquely, it stands to reason that there will be different interpretations of the information disseminated by markets. This, of course, is in line with the characteristics of a dynamic system since plans only match perfectly when market participants have perfect foresight. The subjectivist approach claims that the focal point of interest in economics of information is the interpretation of information.

NOTES

1. G. J. Stigler, "The Economics of Information," *Journal of Political Economy*, 69 (1961), p. 213.
2. For a survey of the literature, see J. Hirshleifer, "Where are We in the Theory of Information?" *American Economic Review*, 63 (1973), pp. 31–9; J. Hirshleifer, and J. G. Riley, "The Analytics of Uncertainty and Information an Expository Survey," *Journal of Economic Literature*, 17 (1979), pp. 1375–421. For applications and extensions of Stigler's analysis, see M. Rothschild, "Models of Market Organisation with Imperfect Information: A Survey," *Journal of Political Economy*, 81 (1973), pp. 1283–308.
3. G. J. Stigler, "Nobel Lecture: The Process and Progress of Economics," *Journal of Political Economy*, 91 (1983), pp. 529–45.
4. T. Stonier, *The Wealth of Information: A Profile of the Post-Industrial Economy* (London: Methuen, 1983).
5. F. Machlup, *The Production and Distribution of Knowledge in the United States* (Princeton: Princeton University Press, 1962).
6. L. M. Lachmann, *Capital Expectations, and the Market Process: Essays on*

the Theory of the Market Economy (Kansas City: Sheed Andrews & McMeel, 1977).

7. This section is based on P. D. F. Strydom, "The Economics of Information," *Investment Analyst Journal*, 24 (1984), p. 11.
8. J. R. Hicks, "Is Interest the Price of a Factor of Production?" in *Time, Uncertainty, and Disequilibrium: Exploration of Austrian Themes*, ed. M. J. Rizzo (Lexington: Heath, 1979), chap. 3.
9. J. R. Hicks, op. cit., p. 53.
10. L. M. Lachmann, op. cit., p. 140.
11. V. Walsh and H. Gram, *Classical and Neoclassical Theories of General Equilibrium: Historical Origins and Mathematical Structure* (New York: Oxford University Press, 1980).
12. C. S. W. Torr, *Equilibrium, Expectations and Information: A study of the General Theory, the Neo-classical Synthesis and Modern Classical Macroeconomics* (unpublished doctoral dissertation, Rhodes University, 1983). See also C. S. W. Torr, "The Role of Information in Economic Analysis," *South African Journal of Economics*, 48 (1980), pp. 115–31.
13. W. J. Baumol, and R. E. Quandt, "Rules of Thumb and Optimally Imperfect Decisions," *American Economic Review*, 54 (1964), pp. 23–46.
14. M. J. Rizzo, "Disequilibrium and All That: An Introductory Essay," in *Time, Uncertainty, and Disequilibrium: Exploration of Austrian Themes*, ed. M. J. Rizzo (Lexington: Heath, 1979), chap. 1.
15. J. R. Hicks, *Capital and Growth* (London: Oxford University Press, 1965), p. 32.
16. I. M. Kirzner, *The Economic Point of View: An Essay in the History of Economic Thought* (Princeton: Van Nostrand, 1960), p. 148.
17. G. L. S. Shackle, *Expectation, Enterprise and Profit: The Theory of the Firm* (London: Allen & Unwin, 1970), p. 154; Kirzner, op. cit., p. 151.
18. G. L. S. Shackle, *Expectation, Investment, and Income* (London: Oxford University Press, 1968), p. 1; Hicks, *Capital and Growth*, p. 24.
19. Hayek, "Economics and Knowledge," *Economica*, 4 (1937), pp. 33–54.
20. Hayek, op. cit., p. 38.
21. Hayek, op. cit., pp. 37–8.
22. F. Hahn, *Money and Inflation* (Oxford: Basil Blackwell, 1982), pp. 2–3.
23. R. Frydman, "Towards an Understanding of Market Processes: Individual Expectations, Learning and Convergence to Rational Expectations Equilibrium," *American Economic Review*, 72 (1982), pp. 652–68.
24. Lachmann, op. cit., p. 91.
25. Lachmann, op. cit., p. 91.

22 Convergent and Divergent Expectations

CHRISTOPHER TORR

Recent years have witnessed a renewed interest in the field of expectations, an obvious example being the rational expectations approach. A curious feature of the latter is the following. On the one hand, the reader is informed that expectations play a vital role in economic activity.[1] On the other hand, one often gains the impression from the rational expectations literature that expectations are rather unimportant.[2] The reader's confusion would be compounded were he to venture into the fields of modern Ricardian economics. Modern Ricardians argue that expectations are not particularly important and should be left out of analysis as far as possible. Their treatment of expectations does not, however, differ markedly from the rational expectations approach.

What is one expected to make of this? How can two schools of thought differ so widely on whether expectations are important and yet treat expectations in much the same way? Professor Lachmann's writings on expectations (which began to appear over 40 years ago) provide a key to resolving the problem.

The key lies in the fact that word expectations can be used in two different contexts. It is to Professor Lachmann's credit that he introduced the terms *divergent* and *convergent* expectations in order to distinguish the two. If the future is largely unknown, different individuals are bound to entertain different expectations, i.e., divergent expectations will be present. Conversely, if the future course of events is reasonably certain, different people will have rather similar expectations, in which case we may refer to the presence of convergent expectations.

In a stationary world it is possible to appeal to the constancy of the

> "data" and the continuous recurrence of events to justify the belief that all members of such a society will sooner or later become familiar with them and their expectations will converge on the recurrent pattern of events. In an uncertain world this is impossible. Experience shows that different people will entertain widely divergent expectations.[3]

The reader is often left in the dark as to whether a writer is talking about convergent or divergent expectations. An obvious test is to ask the following question. In the situation envisaged, will different people entertain different views of the future? If the answer is yes, the writer must obviously have divergent expectations in mind, and, if the answer is no, convergent expectations are under discussion. The reader can try out this test by comparing the expectations of astronomers about the appearance of an eclipse (say five years hence) with the expectations of economists about the price of gold in 1990.

At first sight, the presence of divergent expectations appears to herald the appearance of market chaos. If everybody has a different idea on the future gold price, it might appear that the market can never reach a state of rest. Do we not require expectations to be convergent in equilibrium? The answer to this question is no, not necessarily. Convergent expectations can exert an equilibrating force, but they may also be disequilibrating. In the case of a speculative market such as the gold market, convergent expectations play a dis-equilibrating role, and divergent expectations an equilibrating one.[4]

If some people think that the price of gold is going to go up, while others think that it is going to fall, the market can come to a state of rest if the views of the bulls are counterbalanced by those of the bears. This is the route employed by Keynes in explaining equilibrium in the money (bond) market.[5] In such a market, convergent expectations constitute a disequilibrating force. For if everybody thinks (convergent expectations) that the future course of gold is upward, the price of gold will increase, and it will continue increasing until some bulls start changing into bears (divergent expectations), and halt the upward movement. Such a speculative market is therefore brought to a state of rest by the opposing views of the bulls and bears. Shackle notes that

> The price can *come to rest*. But it will only do so by convincing enough members of the market that the prospects are now for a rise. The necessary condition for its coming to rest is a suitable *division* of opinion concerning the movement of the price in the coming days or months.[6]

The reader will note at once that Shackle is talking about divergent expectations. In fact, whenever Lachmann or Shackle write about expectations, they are inevitably referring to divergent expectations. The reason is not hard to find, for in a sense, convergent expectations are not expectations at all, if by expectations we mean anticipations about a fundamentally unknown future. As we now hope to show, writers employing the rational expectations approach are limited to the field of convergent expectations. The attempt on the part of such practitioners to introduce divergent expectations leads to the introduction of irrational behavior (in terms of the rational expectations approach).

Muth introduced the rational expectations approach by arguing that market participants form expectations of an endogenous variable (price) by making forecasts about exogenous elements (the state of nature).[7] Of more immediate concern is another version of the rational expectations approach introduced by Lucas. Lucas argues that if market participants know the relationship between endogenous components, they can form expectations about the latter by observing prices. To understand this approach, it should be remembered that in the rational expectations literature, the terms "model" and "expectations" are used interchangeably. The model builder entertains certain expectations of how prices are formed. Such expectations are enshrined in a model—normally a supply-and-demand one. The essence of the rational expectations approach is to specify that the market participants form their expectations about prices with the aid of the same model as the model builder. In equilibrium the expectations (model) of the market participants will conform to the model (expectations) of the model builder.

In Lucas' approach, therefore, the model builder furnishes the market participants with a model specifying the link between the endogenous and exogenous elements. Agents who employ this model are acting rationally and those who do not are acting irrationally. If all the market participants are employing the same model (forming the same expectations), the expectations in question are ipso facto convergent. The model builder could no doubt introduce divergent expectations by providing different agents with different models and there have, in fact, been such attempts.[9] The difficulty with such an approach is that it involves the introduction of irrational behavior.[10] The problem can be viewed from a slightly different angle. The rational expectations approach requires that the market participants employ the same model as the model builder. The introduction of divergent expectations accordingly leads to a contradiction. For if some agents are employing a model different from the model builder, they are not acting rationally. Alternatively we may say that if the model builder equips the market participants with different models (expectations) of the link between endogenous and exogenous elements, the model builder himself must be in at least two minds as to how prices are formed. The application of rational expectations accordingly requires expectations to be convergent if ad hoc assumptions (the most heinous crime in the rational expectations calendar) are to be avoided.

The modern Ricardian attitude towards expectations is that they should be disregarded as far as possible since they introduce indeterminacy into analysis. Insofar as expectations are to be included at all, they should be related "uniquely to objective phenomena, so as to bypass them and relate the facts explaining the expectations directly to the actions of the individuals."[11] Such expectations can be regarded as "inescapable." The reader will note that if expectations are introduced in this manner, they will be of the convergent variety. The Ricardians argue that in the long run the system converges upon a center of gravity dictated by a uniform rate of profit. Expectations not in line with this objective phenomenon should be ignored.

We see therefore that both the rational expectations approach of Lucas and the modern Ricardian approach of Garegnani require expectations to be convergent. Modern classical economists link expectations to the relevant economic theory and call such expectations "rational." Modern Ricardians link expectations to an underlying center of gravity and call them "inescapable." Whether termed "rational" or "inescapable," the expectations are of the convergent variety.

The distinction between convergent and divergent expectations makes it easier to understand why modern Ricardians and modern classical economists can adopt seemingly different positions on the importance of expectations and yet employ largely similar approaches. When modern classical economists link expectations to the relevant economic theory, they are taking convergent expectations into account and ignoring divergent expectations. When modern Ricardians say that expectations should be avoided as far as possible, they are referring to divergent expectations, since their approach has no difficulty in incorporating convergent expectations. Both approaches are critical of Keynes' treatment of expectations, which is not surprising, since Keynes was implicitly referring to divergent expectations when he stressed the importance of expectations.

> By "uncertain" knowledge, let me explain, I do not mean merely to distinguish what is known for certain from what is only probable. The game of roulette is not subject, in this sense, to uncertainty; nor is the prospect of a Victory bond being drawn. Or, again, the expectation of life is only slightly uncertain. Even the weather is only moderately uncertain.[12]

In the examples above, individuals are likely to entertain convergent expectations. Keynes goes on to explain, however, what he means by uncertainty, and in the process provides examples of divergent expectations:

> The sense in which I am using the term is that in which the prospect of a European war is uncertain, or the price of copper and the rate of interest twenty years hence, or the obsolescence of a new invention, or the position of private wealth owners in the social system in 1970. About these matters there is no scientific basis on which to form any calculable probability whatever. We simply do not know.

When we come across a writer remarking that expectations are important, we should establish, first of all, whether he has convergent or divergent expectations in mind. In a sense, convergent expectations are not expectations at all, but rather part of existing knowledge. (I may certainly say that I expect the sun to rise at, say, 5.30 in the morning, one year from today, but there is a world of difference between such expectations and expectations about the price of gold.) We should therefore be wary of arguments that expectations are important if the expectations in question are convergent. Rational expectations models require expectations to be convergent if ad hoc assumptions are to be avoided. This is why a reader of the rational expectations literature may well come away with the feeling that expectations are rather unimportant.

No rational expectations practitioner would deny that divergent expectations are part and parcel of everyday life. If such divergent expectations are introduced into a rational expectations model, however, the model builder exposes himself to the charge that he has introduced irrational behavior, for in equilibrium the expectations of the market participants and the model builder must be the same. We have here an example of the fact that the *verbal* content of a model may not be in conformity with its *formal* properties.[13]

Professor Lachmann's distinction between convergent and divergent expectations thus provides us with a key to unlock some of the mysteries in the literature on the role of expectations.

NOTES

1. B. Kantor, "Rational Expectations and Economic Thought," *Journal of Economic Literature*, 17 (1979), p. 1437.
2. C. S. W. Torr, "Expectations and the New Classical Economics," *Australian Economics Papers*, 23 (1984), p. 197.
3. L. M. Lachmann, *Capital, Expectations, and the Market Process* (Kansas City: Sheed Andrews & McMeel, 1977), p. 187.
4. L. M. Lachmann, *Information, Knowledge and the Human Mind* (forthcoming).
5. J. M. Keynes, *The General Theory of Employment, Interest and Money* (London: Macmillan, 1936).
6. G. L. S. Shackle, *Epistemics and Economics. A Critique of Economic Doctrines* (Cambridge: Cambridge University Press, 1972), p. 199.
7. J. F. Muth, "Rational Expectations and the Theory of Price Movements," *Econometrica*, 29 (1960), pp. 315–35.
8. R. E. Lucas, "Expectations and the Neutrality of Money," *Journal of Economic Theory*, 4 (1972), pp. 103–24.
9. S. J. Grossman and J. E. Stiglitz, "On the Impossibility of Informationally Efficient Markets," *American Economic Review*, 70 (1980), pp. 393–408.
10. J. Tirole, "On the Possibility of Speculation under Rational Expectations," *Econometrica*, 50 (1982), pp. 1163–81.
11. P. Garegnani, "On a Change in the Notion of Equilibrium in Recent Work on Value and Distribution," in *Essays in Modern Capital Theory*, eds. M. Brown, K. Sato, and P. Zarembka (Amsterdam: North-Holland, 1976), p. 39.
12. J. M. Keynes, *The General Theory and After, Part II: Defence and Development* in *Collected Writings* (London: Macmillan, 1973), vol. XIV, p. 113.
13. R. W. Clower (ed.), *Monetary Theory: Selected Readings* (Harmondsworth: Penguin), p. 16.

23 A Subjectivist Perspective on the Definition and Identification of Money

LAWRENCE H. WHITE

In a clear statement of the subjectivist research program in economics, Professor Ludwig M. Lachmann instructed us that there are dual aspects to economic inquiry:

> Economics has two tasks. The first is to make the world around us intelligible in terms of human action and the pursuit of plans. The second is to trace the unintended consequences of such action.[1]

The present paper attempts to take these tasks seriously in discussing two very basic questions in the economics of money. The first question asks: What is the proper definition of money? The second question asks: What actual items in the modern economies of the nineteenth and twentieth centuries meet this definition?[2]

DEFINING MONEY

The question of the proper definition of money is really a question of the attributes essential to an item's being properly considered to be money. This question has been widely debated among economists. Dale K. Osborne has recently identified no fewer than ten approaches to the definition of money, each emphasizing a particular attribute.[3] From a subjectivist perspective, it is clear that the defining set of attributes of money is to be sought in the role that money plays (and alone plays) in the plans of individual economic agents. This immediately rules out approaches that focus on the statistical behavior of an aggregate as the essential criterion for deciding whether components of that aggregate ought to be considered money. Moneyness is a property conferred on an item by individuals' plans, not by the econometric performance of an aggregate containing that item relative to an aggregate omitting it.

It should not be surprising or objectionable to many students of money that the definition of money must invoke subjective purposes. After all, it is a commonplace observation that money has taken widely varying physical forms, from shells to metal disks to imprinted slips of paper, in various historical economies. At least since the early medieval period in Europe there have been non-tangible assets (transferable deposits at commercial or central banks) which most economists would identify as a form of money. Thus it should not be controversial to recognize that money cannot be defined by its physical attributes. It must instead be defined by its role in purposive human activity. In this respect money is like capital. The definition of each necessarily refers to the plans of its respective owners.[4] Because these plans are not directly observable, there may be some practical difficulty in identifying or counting up the units of money (or capital) in an economy. But this does not bear on the proper choice of a definition of money (or capital).

Several potential definitions of money can pass through this subjectivist filter. Obviously a supplemental criterion for choosing among definitions is needed. It seems natural to suggest choosing the definition of money that best captures what monetary economists have generally meant in using the term "money," though the consensus may be less than complete.[5] Rather than take the space necessary for an exhaustive comparative study ranking the major candidate definitions on this score, I will simply propose that the following definition is both compatible with subjectivism and represents the most standard usage among experts: The money of an economy consists of its *generally accepted media of exchange*.[6] In what follows I will refer to this as the GAMOE definition of money. The terms making up this acronym clearly require further definition themselves.

A *medium of exchange*, following what I take to be standard economics usage, is an item acquired through exchange with the intention of later disposal in exchange for some further good, i.e., acquired in order to be spent.[7] In still other words, a medium of exchange is an item acquired as an intermediate link in a planned chain of exchanges. Normally this chain is intended to transform an agent's initial endowment into the goods he ultimately desires to consume. In a premonetary economy there may be many media of exchange. One trader may exchange his wares for salt with the intention of exchanging the salt for the food and clothing he wants; another may trade his produce for nails which he plans to trade for whatever he may want subsequently. Though his plans may be more or less successful, a single agent's plan to use a good as a medium of exchange is sufficient to make that good a medium of exchange for that agent.

Money, by contrast, is a social institution. It is not the case that whatever any individual in an economy plans to use as money is properly considered part of the economy's stock of money. A Rip van Winkle awakening today with a pocketful of gold coins (from a slumber that began in 1920) would not, despite his natural beliefs and plans for disposal, have a pocketful of money. Moneyness depends not merely on one person's plans, but on an interwoven net of many individuals' plans. This is the import of the modifiers "generally accepted" in the definition of money. A generally accepted medium of exchange is a good which not only plays an intermediate role in one agent's plans, but which other agents are routinely ready to accept in trade. This definition of money reflects its intersubjective and not merely subjective character.[8]

Once it is granted that the essential or defining function of money is its function as a generally accepted medium of exchange, it is easy to show that the other functions of money commonly mentioned in old and new textbooks are implied by, or subsidiary to, the essential function.[9] Any item that serves as money must also serve as a "store of value," i.e., must be an asset held for positive lengths of time. A unit of money is naturally used as the "unit of account" because buyers and sellers naturally find it convenient to denominate their prices in terms of the media of exchange they are routinely ready to accept. Profit-and-loss accounts are in turn most conveniently kept in the same units as buying and selling prices and cash balances.[10] The use of money as a "standard of deferred payments," or denominator for long-term contracts, is in turn subsidiary to its general use as the unit of account. Finally, the function of money as a "means of payment" or "means of *final* payment" is nothing other than its function as a generally accepted medium of exchange in the context of transactions where one party's (the "buyer's") receipt of the (nonmoney) good for which he has traded is separated from the other party's (the "seller's") receipt of the (money) good for which he has bargained.

A proper definition of money is important principally because the definition necessarily guides the identification of items as part of the stock of money or not. (A secondary function of the definition is that it allows critical scrutiny of how closely what is called "money" in an abstract economic model really resembles money as we think of it.) The proper identification of the components of the money stock is in turn vitally important for the application of monetary theory to historical experience. Statistical and other historical work in monetary economics needs to know to what items the propositions of theory are supposed to apply. This is true both for research into the evolution of payments systems and for the more common sorts of work on the relationship of changes in money stock to change in price indices, interest rates, measures of nominal and real income, and other aggregates.

IDENTIFYING MONEY

In identifying the assets that serve as money in today's economy it is natural to consider the easiest case first. Clearly hand-to-hand fiat currency (in the United States, Federal Reserve notes and token coins) is generally accepted and serves as a medium of exchange. Currency is not *universally* accepted, as some sellers (e.g., mail-order outlets) require other payment media, but it is nearly so. There is no controversy over including fiat currency as part of the stock of money.

In considering the commodity-based monetary systems of the past, the case for including coins in the money stock is equally compelling. Gold coins clearly were acquired as a media of exchange and were near-universally accepted in exchange. The case for banknote currency is somewhat less straightforward in that the notes of a particular issuer were not always generally accepted outside the vicinity of the bank's offices.[11] If we define the sphere of acceptance for a type of assets as the set of markets within which transactors are routinely ready to accept those assets in exchange for what they are selling, it seems proper to say that banknotes were money within their sphere of acceptance. Recall that our definition of money began: "The money *of an economy* is. . . ." The notion of a sphere of acceptance is simply a subjectivist way of delimiting "an economy" within which a set of items is to be identified as money.

The boundaries of a sphere of acceptance need not be purely geographical. There would be no semantic impropriety in saying (though it may or may not be a fact) that Bank of Ireland notes in 1800 were money among the merchants, manufacturers, and landed gentry of County Cork, but they were not money among the wage laborers and small farmers of the same area who insisted on payment in gold. The notion of a sphere of acceptance can be applied to demand deposits as readily as to banknotes. Today, for instance, the sphere of acceptance for ordinary bank checks does not encompass capital markets, where securities dealers insist on payment in Immediately Available Funds.[12] We consider other questions regarding the moneyness of demand deposits below.

The inclusion of raw gold and ingots of gold bullion in the stock of money under a gold standard confronts the fact (almost a logically necessary feature of any commodity money system) that some of the metal commodity was acquired and held not for the purpose of using it as a medium of exchange, but for the purpose of using it as an input in a noncoinage production process (e.g., filling molars) or as a consumption good (e.g., jewelry). It may not always be easy to distinguish cleanly in practice between gold bullion holdings intended as a medium of exchange and gold inventories that were not to be exchanged. (Indeed, some plans may have been intentionally flexible enough to allow for either possible use, depending on the realization of certain contingencies.) But to the extent that such a distinction can be made, an uncoined monetary gold stock can be identified, a subset of the total gold stock and a component of the stock of money within its sphere of circulation. In historical practice its sphere was largely limited to international trade.

The inclusion of traveler's checks in today's money stock has been a subject of controversy. Examining this question at some length—a length disproportionate to its relative magnitude as a potential component of the money stock, to be sure—may therefore prove instructive. Certainly traveler's checks serve as a medium of exchange. People purchase the checks with the intention of later spending them. Within their sphere of acceptance (retail transactions, at least), it seems clear that they ought to be considered money. In a classic article Leland B. Yeager has argued the contrary on two grounds. The first ground is that traveler's checks do not *circulate*, i.e., they are not routinely "accepted with the intention of passing them along to others and without anyone's asking the issuer to redeem them."[13] This raises intricate issues. It is certainly neither antisubjectivist (note Yeager's reference to intentions) nor logically unsound to take repeated circulation rather than merely general acceptance to be a defining characteristic of money. This definition is, however, narrower than the GAMOE definition. It requires of money not only that it be used as a medium of exchange, but that it be generally intended to be used as a medium of exchange by those who accept it. For instance, it would rule out any gold bullion being considered money, even if gold bullion is generally accepted in trade and some fraction is intended to be reexchanged, if a sizable enough fraction of those accepting it intended to use it for industrial purposes. Or, it would rule out considering any subway (or pay-telephone) tokens to be money, even if some individuals do acquire them purely for re-exchange and find them generally accepted in exchange at their par value, if the preponderance of their acceptors intend to redeem them for rides (or calls). The GAMOE definitions would allow that some fraction of the stock of gold bullion, or of subway tokens, should be considered money if generally accepted in trade, namely, that fraction acquired with the intention of use as a medium of exchange. The task of measuring the stock of money will be naturally more difficult in the case that something like gold or subway tokens has both a monetary and a non-monetary use, but that may be the way the economy is. The purpose of a definition of money is not to make the statistician's measurements as easy as possible, but to help them be as meaningful as possible.

Another way of highlighting the comparative narrowness of Yeager's definition is by pointing out his unusual (nonstandard) construal of the term "medium of exchange." He writes that only if traveler's checks were passed from party to party without encashment would they constitute "an actual medium of exchange."[14] This builds routine circulation into the definition of a medium of exchange. But in standard usage a medium of exchange is anything acquired with the intention of later disposal in exchange for something new, regardless of how the eventual acceptor of the thing disposes of it. In a nonmonetary economy, corn serves as a medium of exchange for Smith if he trades his wool for corn in order to trade corn for fish with Jones (who has no interest in wool), even if Jones intends to eat the corn rather than pass it along. It is surely a defect of Yeager's usage that we must come up with some new term to describe the role of corn in this situation. It is convenient, for example, to summarize Carl Menger's theory of the origin of money as an explanation of why traders in a barter setting would individually (like Smith) begin to use commodities as media of exchange and would then eventually converge socially on a few commodities or a single commodity as the generally accepted media or medium of exchange. When routine circulation is taken to be a defining characteristic of any medium of exchange, however, no distinction can be made between *a* medium of exchange and a generally accepted medium of exchange.

A strict insistence on routine circulation without redemption as a defining characteristic of a medium of exchange, or of money, limits the identification of money to those items acquired repeatedly with the intention of direct disposal in trade. No one-use-only means of payment may be considered money. Under a preferably broader interpretation, by contrast, an item counts as a medium of exchange provided that any one party acquires it with the intention of spending it for some further good.

Strictly applied, Yeager's criterion would have the surprising implication that checkable demand deposits in a multibank system are not money, contrary to Yeager's own readiness to include them.[15] Demand deposit claims on Bank A are not accepted by customers of other banks with the intention of passing them along without redemption. When a customer of Bank B accepts a check written against an account balance in Bank A, he accepts it only because he can readily convert it via deposit into an account balance at Bank B. When he deposits the check into his Bank B account, he thereby initiates a collection process which does result in the issuer Bank A being asked to redeem the check. Bank A must transfer reserves through the clearinghouse to Bank B in the amount of the check.

On average, of course, most deposit outflows of the sort just described are paired off at the clearinghouse against deposit inflows, and net adverse or positive clearings on any day are a small fraction of total funds cleared. But at the economically relevant margin, the adverse clearing takes place just as indicated.

Elsewhere in his discussion Yeager recognizes general acceptability as the defining characteristic of money. He quite rightly notes that "an asset cannot be a generally acceptable means of payment if some inducement is required not merely to persuade people to hold it for some time but even to persuade them to accept payment in that particular form in the first place." He now argues that a traveler's check is not money on the second ground that merchants who may accept it "have to be persuaded to take it . . . by the prospect of losing a sale if the seller did not thus accommodate the customer." It is difficult to distinguish this from the sense in which merchants "have to be persuaded" to take a regular bank check. More to the point, given that these statements occur in the context of a discussion of transactions costs, it is not at all apparent why taking (and subsequently depositing to one's bank account) a traveler's check is generally any more troublesome or costly than taking a regular bank check. Physical handling procedures would appear to be identical. So would the process of depositing the check to one's own bank account and receiving a positive clearing. Casual empiricism suggests that the transactions costs associated with accepting traveler's checks may in fact be lower: many establishments accept traveler's checks while refusing regular bank checks.[16] The reason is presumably that there is less risk of having a traveler's check "bounce" due to insufficient funds.

If the foregoing argument is correct, it is clearly invalid to exclude traveler's checks from the category of money while including checkable demand deposits (transactions balances). On the GAMOE definition of money advanced here, the case for acknowledging checkable bank balances (as well as traveler's checks) to be money is straightforward. Checkable balances (including NOW accounts, Super NOW accounts, and money market deposit accounts) are acquired with the intention of later exchange; hence they are media of exchange.[17] If checks written against balances at a particular bank are generally accepted in most exchanges conducted within an economic sphere (the vicinity of the bank, say), then they are money within that sphere.

The inclusion of checkable demand deposits is not uncontroversial, however. It has been challenged by Dale K. Osborne on the "simultaneity" criterion, which he attributes to G. L. S. Shackle, that the actual stock of means of payment existing at any moment is equal to the total of payments that could be made simultaneously under any conceivable pattern of payments. Osborne argues that checkable transactions balances (in excess of bank reserves) in a multibank system fail to meet this criterion applied strictly because a bank could not execute outflowing payments beyond the quantity of its reserves in the event that it received no inflowing deposits.[18] It would be a fallacy of composition, however, to suppose that since any *single* bank could thus be depleted, all banks together could thus be depleted by check-writing, and therefore that the volume of simultaneous payments always possible is no greater than the volume of bank reserves. In fact the volume of payments always possible through simultaneous check-writing is equal to the volume of reserves in other banks plus the volume of demand deposits in the smallest bank. This is because the worst-case scenario (generating the maximum of adverse clearings against banks) is one in which customers of every other bank attempt to transfer their entire balances to customers of the smallest bank. Only transfers equal to the volume of those banks reserves can actually be executed for their customers in this case. But customers of the smallest bank can at the same time spend their entire balances without hindrance. (In a single-bank system, the monopoly bank would be the smallest bank, because it was the only bank, and hence the entire volume of demand deposits would always be simultaneously spendable.)[19] Surely the identification of the stock of money as the sum of the monetary base plus the smallest bank's demand deposits (minus its reserves) is unappealing.

Osborne notes that if cash redemption of demand deposits for the sake of their holders is considered a form of payment, the worst-case scenario is one in which redemption of all checking balances is simultaneously demanded. In that case only a volume of payments equal to the monetary base is possible. If redemption is considered a payment, then under the simultaneity criterion the money stock equals the monetary base.[20] We could also reach this conclusion under the GAMOE definition by stipulating that an item is not to be considered "generally accepted" in exchange unless it is accepted in "exchanges" where banks deposits are being redeemed. But this is an unduly restrictive way of defining acceptance and therefore of defining money in general.

With redemptions included, what the simultaneity criterion really helps to identify is not the stock of money as such, but the stock of *outside money*. Outside money is a subset of money, namely, money that is nonredeemable. Under a gold-coin standard the stock of outside money equals the stock of monetary gold. Under the present American fiat money system it equals the stock of currency plus bank reserves held at the Federal Reserve.[21] The concept of outside money is crucial for monetary theory in at least two ways. (1) The number of units of outside money must be considered the basic nominal scalar for an economy using a fiat monetary unit as its unit of accounts. (2) As Osborne indicates, monetary disequilibria are most consistently analyzed in terms of positive or negative excess demand for outside money.[22] Outside money plays these theoretical roles better than the total of outside plus inside money simply because its composition is more uniform in terms of the plans of economic agents. Changes in the desired composition of total money balances as between outside and inside (redeemable) money can cause changes in the size of the stock of money (by changing the "money multiplier"), but changes in the desired composition of outside money balances cannot change the size of the stock of outside money. Despite these differences, however, both outside and inside money share the property of being generally accepted media of exchange, and therefore both are properly called money. It would be not only inappropriate but awkward to introduce another phrase to cover the sum of (outside) money plus redeemable claims that serve as generally accepted media of exchange.[23]

Having now identified outside currency, inside currency, and checkable demand deposits as money, the next candidate to consider is the checkable money market mutual fund (MMMF). Its inclusion may be plausible because it functions for its owner very much like a checking account.[24] MMMF shares are acquired with the intention of later being spent, so that they do function as media of exchange. The sticky question, however, is whether MMMF shares are generally accepted in exchange *as such*. When a check is written on an MMMF, the recipient does not acquire a claim on the fund's portfolio; rather, he acquires an inside-money claim against the bank which the fund uses to hold its transactions balances and to clear its checks. The check travels through the clearing mechanisms in the usual fashion, with the fund's bank redeeming it by transferring reserves to the recipient's bank, and debiting the fund's deposit balance. The fund in turn replenishes its deposit account (at the margin) by selling securities out of its portfolio (or rather, when a day's net daily clearings are less than the value of its maturing assets, by reinvesting less than all of its maturing funds).[25] In this way the item that the check-writing MMMF customer relinquishes (ownership of shares in a portfolio of assets) is not what the payee accepts (ownership of an inside-money claim to bank reserves). Because the actual MMMF shares are not what the second party accepts (or intends to accept), MMMF shares cannot be considered a generally accepted medium of exchange; hence, they are not money.

By a similar argument it can be seen that time deposits such as certificates of deposit, passbook savings accounts, and other noncheckable claims on banks, should not be identified as money. Because these claims are not directly transferable, they do not serve as media of exchange, let alone as generally accepted media.[26] If they were transferable, the situation might conceivably be different,[27] though there are fairly obvious reasons why a ready claim should be more generally accepted than a future-dated claim.[28]

Finally, credit cards present an interesting case. The credit card itself never changes hands, of course. But it might be argued that the merchant does acquire the signed charge slip as a medium of exchange since he uses it as a link in a planned chain of transactions leading him to exchange for other goods. Within the retail sphere where an individual's debt instruments in the form of signed charge slips are generally acceptable, then, they should qualify as a form of money. The flaw in this argument cannot be quite as simple as conflating debt items with money since demand deposits are both money and a liability (debt) of the issuing bank. The flaw is rather that the debt instrument in this case is not *acquired through trade in order to be spent* by anyone. The card holder exchanges or "spends" the debt instrument, if you like, but he does not acquire it through trade. The merchant acquires the instrument (the charge slip) in trade, but does not intend to spend it. The merchant must redeem the instrument, receiving guaranteed reimbursement from the credit card issuer which in turn seeks reimbursement from the card holder. Redemption does not count as spending. It is a transaction, perhaps, but not a link in a chain of exchanges. In general, a debt instrument can satisfy the medium-of-exchange aspect of the GAMOE definition of money only if it is spent, and therefore acquired in order to be spent, by someone other than the debtor.

CONCLUSION

This essay proposes defining money in a way (though certainly not the only way) consistent with the methodological subjectivism espoused by Ludwig M. Lachmann. In particular, it defines money as the generally accepted media of exchange in an economy. Together with supplemental subjectivist-oriented definitions of "medium of exchange" and "generally accepted in an economy," this definition of money allows identification of the components of the stock of money in present and past economies. In the present United States economy, considered as the union of various economic spheres, the stock of money consists of currency, traveler's checks, and checkable claims on banks. Noncheckable bank liabilities, and money market mutual fund shares, are not money because they are not directly spendable and hence not generally accepted in exchange. The stock of money thus identified, it turns out, corresponds to the official monetary aggregate M1 (as defined in 1985), plus money market deposit accounts. (The inclusion of MMDA's is perhaps debatable, but only because their checkability is artificially limited by legislated restrictions on the number of transfers per month from any account.) If this identification of the stock of money, and the definition of money underlying it, are intelligible in terms of human action and the pursuit of plans, this essay will have accomplished its task.

NOTES

1. Ludwig M. Lachmann, "Sir John Hicks as a Neo-Austrian," in *Capital,*

Expectations, and the Market Process, ed. Walter E. Grinder (Kansas City: Sheed Andrews & McMeel, 1977, pp. 261–2.

2. The distinction between *defining* money (the first question) and *identifying* money (the second question) is cogently made by Dale K. Osborne, "Ten Approaches to the Definition of Money," Federal Reserve Bank of Dallas *Economic Review* (March 1984), p. 2. The title of the article by Murray N. Rothbard, "Austrian Definitions of the Supply of Money," in *New Directions in Austrian Economics*, ed. Louis M. Spadaro (Kansas City: Sheed Andrews & McMeel, 1978), pp. 143–56, actually refers to identifications of money.
3. Osborne, op. cit., pp. 1–23. The ten candidates are (1) tangible media of exchange, (2) liquid assets, (3) *any* routine means of payment, (4) means of *potentially simultaneous* payment, (5) means of *final* payment, (6) the set of liquid assets most highly correlated with national income, (7) a set of liquid assets exhibiting a stable demand function, (8) routinely circulating exchange media, (9) temporary abodes of purchasing power, and (10) nondebt assets with legally fixed interest yield.
4. On the definition of capital see Ludwig M. Lachmann, *Capital and Its Structure* (Kansas City: Sheed Andrews & McMeel, 1978), pp. 11–12.
5. We do not want a definition that tries to capture whatever the man in the street may mean in using the term, for he is likely to use "money" when he means income, wealth, profits, or cash. In deferring to monetary economists on the meaning of "money" one respects the linguistic division of labor in society. On this division, and on the value of making sense of past endeavors in a discipline, see Hilary Putnam, *Meaning and the Moral Sciences* (London: Routledge, 1978), pp. 114 and 22–5.
6. This definition seems to be implicit in the discussion of Ludwig von Mises, *The Theory of Money and Credit* [1912] (Irvington-on-Hudson, N.Y. Foundation for Economic Education, 1971), pp. 29–37. It also seems consistent with the entry "Money, functions of" in G. Bannock, R. E. Baxter, and R. Rees, *A Dictionary of Economics* (Harmondsworth, Penguin, 1972), p. 287.
7. A lot is packed into these words. "Some *further* good" is meant to exclude an asset which is bought with money (or good X) and later sold for money (or X) from being considered a medium of exchange since it is not used as a vehicle for carrying forward the exchange process. (This raises difficulties in interpreting formal economic models containing only two goods, one of them labelled "money." A charitable interpretation, since typically there is no rationale for holding the money unless it can be carried between periods more cheaply than the other consumption good, is that the consumption good in period t and the consumption good in period $t + 1$ are two different goods, economically speaking.) "Disposal *in* exchange for" something else does not include disposal via redemption. But an item "acquired *through* exchange" may have been acquired by redeeming a claim itself acquired *in* exchange.
8. In its intersubjectivity, money is unlike capital. It is perfectly sensible to speak of an autarkic Robinson Crusoe's using certain items as capital goods but not of his using money.
9. This point is made by Carl Menger, *Principles of Economics* (New York:

New York University Press, 1981), pp. 272–80, and by Mises, op. cit., pp. 34–7.

10. Menger, op. cit., pp. 276–7; see also Lawrence H. White, "Competitive Payments Systems and the Unit of Account," *American Economic Review*, 74 (September 1984), p. 704. Jurg Niehans, *The Theory of Money* (Baltimore: Johns Hopkins University Press, 1978), p. 118, makes the point that money per se is not a unit of account because money is not a unit; money is rather "the good whose unit is used as the unit of account." Niehans calls money itself the "medium of account."
11. The Scottish banking system as it developed in the nineteenth century eventually eliminated this problem, principally by branch banking and a systemwide arrangement among banks for reciprocal par acceptance of notes. In the United States and England, the problem persisted because branch banking and nationwide clearing arrangements were artificially stunted by legislated restrictions.
12. Dale K. Osborne, "What is Money Today?" Federal Reserve Bank of Dallas *Economic Review* (January 1985), p. 3.
13. Leland B. Yeager, "Essential Properties of the Medium of Exchange," *Kyklos*, 21 (1968), p. 57. Osborne, "Ten Approaches to the Definition of Money," op. cit., p. 19, cites this passage and elaborates upon Yeager's argument.
14. Yeager, op. cit., p. 66.
15. Osborne, "Ten Approaches to the Definition of Money," op. cit., accepts without argument the idea that demand deposits circulate. But the simple fact of the matter is that the deposits of any particular bank do not circulate in Yeager's sense.
16. Yeager, op. cit., p. 67, n. 28, notes: "Currency has the lowest transactions costs—loosely speaking, it is the most convenient medium of exchange—in some types of transactions, and demand deposits have the lowest costs in others. But no other asset has lower transactions costs than currency and demand deposits, respectively, in the types of transactions in which each predominates." Yes, and traveler's checks have the lowest costs in still other types of transactions, namely, the ones in which *they* predominate.
17. Money market deposit accounts (MMDAs) are restricted (by the Garn-St. Germain Act) from being drawn upon by check more than three times a month. Some holders of MMDAs may, especially if automated teller machines make it easy to transfer balances between MMDAs and regular checking accounts, never write checks against them or even have checks printed. In principle one would like to exclude at least the MMDAs for which checks are never ordered, because they are not immediately checkable, from a measure of the stock of money.
18. Osborne, "What is Money Today?" op. cit., p. 3.
19. Osborne, ibid., p. 5, considers the case of the monopoly bank.
20. As Osborne, ibid., concludes.
21. These reserve balances may be converted into fiat currency, and vice versa, but they are not *redeemable* for any asset not also a figment of the Federal Reserve's balance sheet. (I assume that coins are issued by the Treasury acting passively as an agent of the Federal Reserve.)
22. Ibid., pp. 8–9.

23. Mises, op. cit., pp. 133, 482–3, for example, refers to "money in the narrower sense" (*Geld in engeren Sinne*) plus "money-substitutes" (*Geld-surrogaten*) equalling the sum of "money in the broader sense" (*Geld in weiteren Sinne*). This is confusing because the term "money-substitutes" suggests nonmoneyness, yet these items are counted as part of "money in the broader sense." It is much easier to speak simply of outside money and inside money together constituting money.
24. Its weekly yield is known only after the week is over, rather than before the week begins (as with MMDAs), but that feature is not relevant to the present question.
25. See Gerald P. O'Driscoll, Jr., "Financial Deregulation and Monetary Control," forthcoming in Federal Reserve Bank of Dallas *Economic Review*, ms. p. 13.
26. Rothbard, op. cit., pp. 146–8, argues that passbook accounts should be considered money because they can be redeemed on demand for cash. But this feature is irrelevant when they fail to satisfy the medium of exchange criterion for money, which Rothbard himself (p. 144) enunciates.
27. It is thus conceivable (it may or may not be a fact) that bills of exchange, short-maturity IOUs issued by merchants and manufacturers, transferable by consecutive endorsement, served as money within a limited sphere of nineteenth-century Britain. Mises, op. cit., pp. 284–6, argues that in fact they naturally did *not* serve as money because they could not be *routinely* accepted even in that sphere.
28. First, the acceptor of a certificate of deposit must remain a creditor of the bank that issued it until he can trade it away; he cannot cash or deposit it in order to realize funds in another form. Secondly, there are inconveniences associated with recalculating the present value of the claim with each passing day and with every change in interest rates.

Index